D0791591

JavaScript® & AJAX

FOR

DUMMIES®

by Andy Harris

WILEY

Wiley Publishing, Inc.

JavaScript® & AJAX For Dummies®

Published by
Wiley Publishing, Inc.
111 River Street
Hoboken, NJ 07030-5774

www.wiley.com

WILEY

About the Author

Andy Harris began his teaching life as a special education teacher. As he was teaching young adults with severe disabilities, he taught himself enough computer programming to support his teaching habit with freelance programming. Those were the exciting days when computers started to have hard drives, and some computers began communicating with each other over an arcane mechanism some were calling the Internet.

All this time Andy was teaching computer science part time. He joined the faculty of the Indiana University-Purdue University Indianapolis Computer Science department in 1995. He serves as a Senior Lecturer, teaching the introductory course to freshmen as well as numerous courses on Web development, general programming, and game programming. As manager of the Streaming Media Laboratory, he developed a number of online video-based courses, and worked on a number of international distance education projects including helping to start a computer science program in Tetevo, Macedonia FYR.

Andy is the author of several other computing books including *HTML, XHTML, and CSS All-in-One Desktop Reference For Dummies*, *Flash Game Programming For Dummies*, and *Game Programming: the L Line*. He invites your comments and questions at andy@aharrisbooks.net, You can visit his main site and find a blog, forum, and links to other books at http://www.aharrisbooks.net.

Dedication

I dedicate this book to Jesus Christ, my personal savior, and to Heather, the joy in my life. I also dedicate this project to Elizabeth, Matthew, Jacob, and Benjamin. I love each of you.

Author's Acknowledgments

Thank you first to Heather. Even though I type all the words, this book is a real partnership, like the rest of our life. Thanks for being my best friend and companion. Thanks also for doing all the work it takes for us to sustain a family when I'm in writing mode.

Thank you to Mark Enochs. It's great to have an editor who gets me, and who's willing to get excited about a project. I really enjoy working with you.

Thanks a lot to Steve Hayes. It's been a lot of fun to dream up this idea with you, and to see it evolve from something a little messy to a project we can all be proud of. I'm looking forward to working with you more.

Thank you to the copy editors: Barry Childs-Helton, Virginia Sanders, and Rebecca Whitney. I appreciate your efforts to make my geeky mush turn into something readable. Thanks for improving my writing.

A special thanks to Jeff Noble for his technical editing. I appreciate your vigilance. You have helped to make this book as technically accurate as possible.

Thank you to the many people at Wiley who contribute to a project like this. The author only gets to meet a few people, but so many more are involved in the process. Thank you very much for all you've done to help make this project a reality.

A big thank you to the open source community which has created so many incredible tools and made them available to all. I'd especially like to thank the creators of Firefox, Firebug, Aptana, HTML Validator, the Web Developer toolbar, Notepad++, PHP, Apache, jQuery, and the various jQuery plugins. This is an amazing and generous community effort.

I'd finally like to thank the IUPUI computer science family for years of support on various projects. Thank you especially to all my students, current and past. I've learned far more from you than the small amount I've taught. Thank you for letting me be a part of your education.

Publisher's Acknowledgments

We're proud of this book; please send us your comments through our online registration form located at http://dummies.custhelp.com. For other comments, please contact our Customer Care Department within the U.S. at 877-762-2974, outside the U.S. at 317-572-3993, or fax 317-572-4002.

Some of the people who helped bring this book to market include the following:

Acquisitions, Editorial, and Media Development

Senior Project Editor: Mark Enochs

Executive Editor: Steve Hayes

Copy Editors: Barry Childs-Helton, Virginia Sanders, Rebecca Whitney

Technical Editor: Jeff Noble

Editorial Manager: Leah Cameron

Media Development Project Manager: Laura Moss-Hollister

Media Development Assistant Project Manager: Jenny Swisher

Media Development Assistant Producers: Josh Frank, Shawn Patrick

Editorial Assistant: Amanda Graham

Sr. Editorial Assistant: Cherie Case

Cartoons: Rich Tennant (www.the5thwave.com)

Composition Services

Project Coordinator: Kristie Rees

Layout and Graphics: Carl Byers, Melissa K. Jester, Christine Williams

Proofreaders: John Greenough, Content Editorial Services

Indexer: Sharon Shock

Publishing and Editorial for Technology Dummies

    Richard Swadley, Vice President and Executive Group Publisher

    Andy Cummings, Vice President and Publisher

    Mary Bednarek, Executive Acquisitions Director

    Mary C. Corder, Editorial Director

Publishing for Consumer Dummies

    Diane Graves Steele, Vice President and Publisher

Composition Services

    Debbie Stailey, Director of Composition Services

Contents at a Glance

Introduction 1

Part I: Programming with JavaScript 7

Chapter 1: Taking the Web to the Next Level 9
Chapter 2: Writing Your First Program 31
Chapter 3: Changing Program Behavior with Conditions 55
Chapter 4: Loops and Debugging 71
Chapter 5: Functions, Arrays, and Objects 97

Part II: Using JavaScript to Enhance Your Pages 129

Chapter 6: Talking to the Page 131
Chapter 7: Getting Valid Input 157
Chapter 8: Moving and Grooving 181

Part III: Moving Up to AJAX 221

Chapter 9: AJAX Essentials 223
Chapter 10: Improving JavaScript and AJAX with jQuery 239
Chapter 11: Animating jQuery 265
Chapter 12: Using the jQuery User Interface Toolkit 293
Chapter 13: Improving Usability with jQuery 317
Chapter 14: Working with AJAX Data 339

Part IV: The Part of Tens 367

Chapter 15: Ten Amazing jQuery Plugins 369
Chapter 16: Ten Great Resources 397

Index 401

Table of Contents

Introduction *1*

What You Will Need 2
How This Book Is Organized 3
  Part I: Programming with JavaScript............................ 3
  Part II: Using JavaScript to Enhance Your Pages 3
  Part III: Moving Up to AJAX 4
  Part IV: The Part of Tens.. 4
It's Even on the Internet!... 4
Icons Used in This Book 5
Where to Go from Here... 5
A Final Word... 6

Part 1: Programming with JavaScript *7*

Chapter 1: Taking the Web to the Next Level 9

Building Something Cool 9
Getting Started... 14
  Overview of the Core Technologies 14
  Choosing your computer 15
Picking an Editor.. 16
  Avoiding the problem tools...................................... 16
  Using a WYSIWYG editor 17
  Introducing programmer's editors 18
  Getting familiar with some important editors................. 19
  Introducing Aptana 23
Creating Your Browser Collection.................................. 24
  Setting the standard 24
  Picking a browser or two 25
Turning Firefox into a Development Machine 26
  Web Developer Toolbar 27
  HTML Validator extension....................................... 27
  Firebug 28

Chapter 2: Writing Your First Program .... .31

Becoming a Programmer 31
  Choosing a JavaScript editor.................................... 32
  Picking your test browser....................................... 33
  Adding a script to your page.................................... 34

Embedding your JavaScript code 35
Creating comments... 36
Using the alert() method for output... 36
Adding the semicolon... 37
Introducing Variables... 37
Creating a variable for data storage.. 38
Asking the user for information 39
Responding to the user 39
Using Concatenation to Build Better Greetings 40
Comparing literals and variables... 41
Including spaces in concatenated phrases 41
Understanding the string Object 42
Introducing object-oriented programming (and cows)................... 42
Investigating the length of a string.. 43
Using string methods to manipulate text 44
Understanding Variable Types 47
Adding numbers.. 47
Adding the user's numbers 48
The trouble with dynamic data... 49
The pesky plus sign 50
Changing Variables to the Desired Type.. 51
Using variable conversion tools 51
Fixing the addInput code 52

Chapter 3: Changing Program Behavior with Conditions 55

Working with Random Numbers 55
Creating a die to die for... 56
Rolling the dice 56
Using if to Control Flow 58
If and only if... 59
Using conditions 60
Comparison operators 60
Do What I Say or Else 61
Using else-if for more complex interaction 62
The mystery of the unnecessary else.. 64
It's Time to Switch Your Thinking... 64
Creating an expression.. 65
Switching with style... 67
Nesting if Statements 67
Building the nested conditions 69
Making sense of nested ifs 69

Chapter 4: Loops and Debugging. 71

Building Counting Loops with for.. 71
Building a standard for loop.. 72
Making a backwards loop 73
Counting five at a time 74

Looping for a while..75
    Creating a basic while loop 75
    Avoiding loop mistakes 77
Introducing Some Bad Loops 77
    Managing the reluctant loop 77
    Managing the compulsive loop 78
Debugging Your Code 79
    Letting Aptana help 79
    Debugging JavaScript on IE 81
    Finding errors in Firefox 82
    Catching syntax errors with Firebug 82
Catching Logic Errors 84
    Logging to the console with Firebug 84
    Looking at console output 86
Using an Interactive Debugger..86
    Adding a breakpoint 88
    Running the debugger 88
    Using the Debug perspective 89
    Examining Debug mode with a paused program 91
    Walking through your program 92
    Viewing expression data..93
    Using the Firebug debugger..94

Chapter 5: Functions, Arrays, and Objects.......................97
Breaking Code into Functions..97
    Inviting ants to the picnic 98
    Thinking about song (and program) structure............................98
    Building the antsFunction.html program....................................99
Passing Data into and out of Functions 100
    Examining the main code..102
    Looking at the chorus line 102
    Handling the verses 103
Managing Scope 105
    Introducing local and global variables......................................106
    Examining variable scope 106
Building a Basic Array..109
    Storing a list of data in an array..109
    Accessing array data 110
    Using arrays with for loops 111
    Visiting the ants one more time..112
Working with Two-Dimensional Arrays 114
    Setting up the arrays 115
    Getting a city 116
    Creating a main() function..117

Creating Your Own Objects...118
    Building a basic object...118
    Adding methods to an object..................................120
    Building a re-usable object.....................................121
    Using your shiny new objects.................................123
Introducing JSON...124
    Storing data in JSON format...................................124
    Building a more complex JSON structure.................125

Part II: Using JavaScript to Enhance Your Pages 129

Chapter 6: Talking to the Page.................................131

Understanding the Document Object Model......................131
    Navigating the DOM..132
    Changing DOM properties with Firebug...................132
    Examining the document object..............................134
Harnessing the DOM through JavaScript.........................135
    Getting the blues, JavaScript-style.........................135
    Writing JavaScript code to change colors................137
Managing Button Events...137
    Setting up the playground......................................139
    Embedding quotes within quotes............................141
    Writing the changeColor function...........................141
Interacting with Text Input and Output...........................142
    Introducing event-driven programming....................142
    Creating the XHTML form.......................................143
    Using getElementById() to get access to the page.....144
    Manipulating the text fields...................................145
Writing to the Document...146
    Preparing the HTML framework...............................147
    Writing the JavaScript...147
    Finding your innerHTML...148
Working with Other Text Elements.................................148
    Building the form..150
    Writing the function..151
    Understanding generated source code......................153

Chapter 7: Getting Valid Input.................................157

Getting Input from a Drop-Down List..............................157
    Building the form..158
    Reading the list box..159
Managing Multiple Selections.......................................160
    Coding a multiple-selection select object................161
    Writing the JavaScript code...................................162

Check, Please — Reading Check Boxes 164
    Building the checkbox page 165
    Responding to the check boxes 166
Working with Radio Buttons 167
    Interpreting radio buttons 169
Working with Regular Expressions 170
    Introducing regular expressions 174
    Characters in regular expressions 176
    Marking the beginning and end of the line 176
Working with Special Characters 177
    Matching a character with the period 177
    Using a character class 177
    Specifying digits 178
    Marking punctuation characters 178
    Finding word boundaries 178
Repetition Operations 178
    Finding one or more elements 179
    Matching zero or more elements 179
    Specifying the number of matches 179
Working with Pattern Memory 179
    Recalling your memories 180
    Using patterns stored in memory 180

Chapter 8: Moving and Grooving **181**
Making Things Move 181
    Looking over the HTML 183
    Getting an overview of the JavaScript 185
    Creating global variables 185
    Initializing 186
    Moving the sprite 187
    Checking the boundaries 189
Reading Input from the Keyboard 191
    Building the keyboard page 191
    Looking over the keyboard.js script 193
    Overwriting the init() function 193
    Setting up an event handler 193
    Responding to keystrokes 194
    Deciphering the mystery of keycodes 196
Following the Mouse 197
    Looking over the HTML 197
    Setting up the HTML 199
    Initializing the code 199
    Building the mouse listener 199
Automatic Motion 200

Image-Swapping Animation 203
Preparing the images.. 203
Building the page 204
Building the global variables.. 206
Setting up the interval 206
Animating the sprite 207
Improving the animation with preloading............................... 207
Working with Compound Images 209
Preparing the image 211
Setting up the HTML and CSS.. 211
Writing the JavaScript 212
Setting up global variables 212
Building an init() function 213
Animating the sprite 213
Movement and Swapping 214
Building the HTML framework 214
Building the code 216
Defining global variables... 217
Initializing your data 218
Animating the image.. 218
Updating the image.. 218
Moving the sprite... 218

Part III: Moving Up to AJAX 221

Chapter 9: AJAX Essentials 223
AJAX: Return to Troy 223
AJAX Spelled Out... 225
A is for asynchronous 225
J is for JavaScript 226
A is for . . . and? 226
And X is for . . . data?.. 226
Making a Basic AJAX Connection 227
Building the HTML form... 230
Creating an XMLHttpRequest object.. 230
Opening a connection to the server 232
Sending the request and parameters 232
Checking the status 233
All Together Now: Making the Connection Asynchronous 234
Setting up the program 236
Building the getAJAX() function 236
Reading the response... 237

Chapter 10: Improving JavaScript and AJAX with jQuery **239**

Introducing JavaScript Libraries 239
Getting to Know jQuery 241
    Installing jQuery.. 242
    Importing jQuery from Google 242
    Using jQuery with Aptana 243
Writing Your First jQuery App.. 245
    Setting up the page... 246
    Meet the jQuery node object... 247
Creating an Initialization Function 248
    Using $(document).ready() 248
    Discovering alternatives to document.ready 250
Investigating the jQuery Object... 250
    Changing the style of an element...................................... 251
    Selecting jQuery objects 252
    Modifying the style 253
Adding Events to Objects 253
    Adding a hover event 254
    Changing classes on the fly 256
Making an AJAX Request with jQuery... 258
    Including a text file with AJAX... 258
    Building a poor man's CMS with AJAX................................. 260

Chapter 11: Animating jQuery **265**

Getting Prepared for Animation 265
    Writing the HTML and CSS foundation 269
    Initializing the page... 270
    Working with callback functions 271
Hiding and Showing the Content.. 271
    Toggling visibility... 272
    Sliding an element... 272
    Fading an element in and out 273
Changing an Element's Position with jQuery.................................. 273
    Creating the HTML framework... 276
    Setting up the events.. 277
    Don't go chaining 277
    Building the move() function with chaining.......................... 278
    Building time-based animation with animate()....................... 279
    Move a little bit: Relative motion...................................... 280
Modifying Elements on the Fly.. 280
    Building the basic page... 286
    Initializing the code 287
    Adding text 287
    Attack of the clones... 288

It's a wrap..289
Alternating styles..290
Resetting the page..290
More fun with selectors and filters.................................291

Chapter 12: Using the jQuery User Interface Toolkit.............293

Looking Over the ThemeRoller..294
Visiting the Theme Park...296
Wanna Drag? Dragging and Dropping Elements..........................297
Downloading the Library...300
Resizing on a Theme...301
    Examining the HTML and standard CSS.............................304
    Importing files...304
    Making a resizable element......................................305
    Adding themes to your elements..................................305
    Adding an icon..308
Dragging, Dropping, and Calling Back................................309
    Building the basic page...312
    Initializing the page...312
    Handling the drop...314
    Dropping out can be fun...315
    Cloning the elements..315

Chapter 13: Improving Usability with jQuery....................317

Multi-Element Designs...317
    Using the Accordion widget......................................318
    Building a tabbed interface.....................................322
    Using tabs with AJAX..325
Improving Usability...327
    The dating game...329
    Picking numbers with the slider.................................331
    Selectable elements...333
    Building a sortable list..335
    Creating a custom dialog box....................................336

Chapter 14: Working with AJAX Data.............................339

Getting an Overview of Server-Side Programming......................339
    Introducing PHP...340
    Writing a form for PHP processing...............................341
    Responding to the request.......................................344
Sending Requests AJAX-Style...345
    Sending the data..346
    Responding to the results.......................................348
Building a More Interactive Form....................................349
    Creating an AJAX form...350
    Writing the JavaScript code.....................................352
    Processing the result...353
    Simplifying PHP for AJAX..353

Working with XML Data 354
    Review of XML 354
    Manipulating XML with jQuery 356
    Creating the HTML 358
    Retrieving the data 358
    Processing the results 358
    Printing out the pet name 359
Working with JSON Data 360
    Understanding JSON 360
    Reading JSON data with jQuery 362
    Managing the framework 364
    Retrieving the JSON data 364
    Processing the results 365

Part IV: The Part of Tens.............................. 367

Chapter 15: Ten Amazing jQuery Plugins 369
Using the Plugins 369
ipwEditor 370
    Adding a basic editor with editable 370
    Incorporating more advanced editing with FCKedit 373
jQuery Cookies 376
flot 378
Tag Cloud 380
Tablesorter 383
Jquery-translate 385
Droppy 388
galleria 390
Jmp3 393

Chapter 16: Ten Great Resources 397
jQuery PHP library 397
JSAN — JavaScript Archive Network 397
W3Schools tutorials and examples 398
Google AJAX APIs 398
Aflax 398
MochiKit 398
Dojo 399
Ext JS 399
YUI 399
DZone 399

Index.. 401

Introduction

The World Wide Web officially celebrated its 20th birthday as I began writing this book. In one sense, it's hard to believe that the technology has been around this long already. At another level, it's amazing how much has happened in that short time. When I started teaching and writing about the Internet (long before the Web was practical), none of us had any idea what it was going to turn into one day.

If you're reading this book, I don't have to tell you that the Web is a big deal. It's come a long way, and it's doing very interesting things. What I want to show in this book is where the Web is going. Web technology is changing faster than ever, and people who don't understand these changes are going to have a hard time staying on top of things.

In the early days of the Web, we talked about Web pages, as if the Internet were a set of ordinary documents connected by links. This was true (and still is largely), but I don't think that's the best way to think of the Web any more. Today's Web is not about documents, but about applications. Users and developers expect their pages to do things, not just be glorified documents.

This book describes two critical and inter-related technologies: JavaScript and AJAX. JavaScript has been a part of the Web since the relatively early days. It is a simple but powerful programming language that was designed from the beginning to work within the context of a Web document. While JavaScript has been with us for a long time, it has recently seen a resurgence of interest in the form of AJAX. This new technology promises a lot of cool things, but it's still rooted in the heritage of JavaScript and HTML.

The great thing about JavaScript and AJAX is the amount of power they give you. If you already know HTML or XHTML, you know how to create Web documents, but those documents are relatively lifeless and static.

JavaScript is a real programming language, and it allows you to add real programming capabilities to your pages. If you've never programmed before, this is a great place to start. JavaScript is a pleasant and relatively easy language for beginners. It uses the familiar Web page as a user interface, which makes it an easy way to develop forms and user interfaces. If you're already a programmer, you'll find that your previous knowledge extends easily to JavaScript, and you'll be fluent in this skill in no time.

AJAX extends the capabilities of JavaScript in new ways that are still being explored. In one sense, the AJAX libraries assist in creating great user experiences with new interface elements like menus and sliders. In another sense, AJAX allows some very important features like the ability to perform client-side includes (a very handy tool for making your pages more efficient) and direct control of server-side scripts.

If you read this entire book, you'll be able to do amazing things with your Web pages. You'll be able to get input from users, test the validity of user input, animate your pages, and interact with Web servers.

What You Will Need

One of the great things about JavaScript is how easy it is to get into. You don't need a whole lot to get started:

- **Any computer will do.** If your computer is relatively recent (it can run Firefox or Safari, for example), you have enough horsepower for Web development. Netbooks are fine, too. Theoretically you could do Web development on a cell phone, but I wouldn't want to do it for long.

- **Any operating system is fine.** I wrote this book on a combination of Windows XP and Fedora Core Linux machines. Most of the programs I recommend have versions for Windows, Mac, and Linux.

- **All the best tools are free.** Don't bother purchasing any expensive software for Web development. All the tools you need are free. You don't need a fancy editor like DreamWeaver or expressionWeb. While these tools have their place, they aren't necessary. Everything I show in this book uses entirely free tools.

- **No programming experience is necessary.** If you already know computer programming in some other language, you'll have no trouble with JavaScript and AJAX. But if you have never programmed at all before, this is a great place to start. If you're already a programmer, JavaScript is a pretty easy language to pick up. If not, it's a great place to start. I'm expecting you have some familiarity with XHTML and CSS, and you know how to get your Web pages to a server. (See my book *HTML, XHTML, and CSS All-in-One Desk Reference For Dummies* if you want more information on these topics.) I've also added two bonus chapters to the Web site: one on HTML and XHTML, and another on CSS. See them at www. aharrisbooks.net/jad and www.dummies.com/go/javascript andajaxfd if you need a refresher.

So what *do* you need? Imagination, perseverance, and a little bit of time.

How This Book Is Organized

I organized this book by renting time on a supercomputer and applying a multilinear Bayesian artificial intelligence algorithm. No, I didn't. I don't even know what that means. I really just sketched it out during a meeting when I was supposed to be paying attention. In any case, the book is organized into a number of sections that describe various aspects of Web development with JavaScript and AJAX.

Like the other books in the *For Dummies* series, you can use this reference in many ways, depending on what you already know and what you want to learn. Each chapter of this book describes a particular facet of JavaScript or AJAX programming. You can read the chapters in any order you wish, especially if you already have some knowledge and you're looking for a particular skill. However, the chapters do build in complexity from beginning to end, so if you find you don't understand something in a later chapter, you might want to review some earlier chapters. (I'll point out exactly where you can find things you might need as we go.) If you're just starting out, it's probably easiest to go from beginning to end, but the main thing is to dig in and have some fun.

Part I: Programming with JavaScript

If you've never written a computer program before, consider this your boot camp. (But it's kind of a fun boot camp, with a little more silliness than most — and no pushups in the rain.) Begin by building your toolkit of powerful but free tools and applications. Here you learn what programming is all about — with JavaScript as the language of choice. You'll be introduced to new friends like variables, conditions, loops, arrays, and objects.

Part II: Using JavaScript to Enhance Your Pages

The main reason people use JavaScript is to trick out Web pages. In this section you learn how to write programs that talk to the Web page they live in. Your programs will be able to read user input, validate that input, and dance around on the screen. It's pretty fun.

Part III: Moving Up to AJAX

If you've been hanging around with Web geeks, you've probably heard of AJAX. It's kind of a big deal, and it has the potential to change the way Web development works. Learn what this thing is really about. Create some AJAX requests by hand, and then use the incredible jQuery library to do more powerful programming. Learn how jQuery introduces new ways to think about programming, and how to use the jQuery User Interface extension to build snappy user experiences. You'll also learn how to work with various kinds of data, from PHP programs to XML and JSON. Yummy.

Part IV: The Part of Tens

No *Dummies* book would be complete without a Part of Tens. I'm really excited about these chapters. In one, you explore ten of my favorite jQuery plugins. These amazing tools make it easy to add amazing features to your sites. You'll see plugins for automatically sorting tables, translating text into foreign languages, building graphs, showing image galleries, playing mp3 files, and much more. Another chapter points you toward some amazing resources on the Web to learn even more.

It's Even on the Internet!

This book has a couple of companion Web sites that are critical to understanding the book. Web programming is about making Web pages *do* things, and you just won't be able to see all of that in a book. As you're going through this book, I strongly advise you to visit either www.dummies.com/go/javascriptandajaxfd or my Web site: www.aharrisbooks.net/jad. A running version of every program in the book is available on both of these sites. You'll also be able to view the source code of each program in its natural habitat — running on the Web.

The www.aharrisbooks.net/jad site is also a great place to start when you're collecting your tools and libraries. Every tool or library that I describe in this book is linked from the Web page, so you'll definitely want to check it out. I also have a forum where I'm happy to answer your questions and share projects with you. I'm looking forward to seeing you there.

Icons Used in This Book

Every once in a while, a concept is important enough to warrant special attention. This book uses a few margin icons to point out certain special information.

These are tidbits of additional information you ought to think about or at least keep in mind.

Occasionally I feel the need to indulge my "self-important computer science instructor" nature, and I give some technical background on things. These things are interesting but not critical, so you can skip them if you want. You might want to memorize a couple of them before you go to your next computer science cocktail party. You'll be the hit of the party.

Tips are suggestions to make things easier.

Be sure to read anything marked with this icon. Failure to do so might result in a plague of frogs, puffs of black smoke, or your program not working like you expect.

Where to Go from Here

Before you start banging out some code, let's take stock of your needs. If you've never dealt with JavaScript or AJAX, you might want to start off in Part I. If you know JavaScript but not AJAX, skip ahead to Part IV. If you want to brush up on your JavaScript, go to Parts II and III.

Well, just dig in and have some fun!

- **Skim the book.** Get an overview, look at the figures, and get a sense of the fun to be had.

- **Visit the Web sites.** You can't taste the recipes in a cookbook, and you can't get a real sense of Web programs in a computing book. Go to either of the companion Web sites at `www.aharrisbooks.net/jad` or `www.dummies.com/go/javascriptandajaxfd` and play around with the sample programs. Note that you will also find two bonus chapters on HTML and CSS programming on these companion sites, as well as all the code from the programs used throughout the book.

- **Check out the Cheat Sheet.** The Cheat Sheet at `www.dummies.com/ cheatsheet/javascriptandajax` is a handy reference of common programming variables and coding miscellany.

- **Pick a spot and dig in.** If you're already comfortable with JavaScript programming, take a look at Part III on AJAX. If not, you might need to back up a little bit and find the more appropriate spot. If in doubt, you could always go from beginning to end (but what's the fun in that?)

- **Have fun.** Programming is a serious business. You can actually make a living doing this stuff. But it's also a lot of fun. Have a good time, relax, and enjoy making your Web pages do things you never thought they could do.

A Final Word

Thank you for buying this book. I truly hope you find it fun and useful. I had a great time writing this book, and I think you'll have a good time using it. I'm looking forward to hearing from you and seeing what you can do with the skills you pick up here. Drop me a line at `andy@aharrisbooks.net` and let me know how it's going!

Part I
Programming with JavaScript

The 5th Wave   By Rich Tennant

"Look into my Web site, Ms. Carruthers.
Look deep into its rotating spiral,
spinning, spinning, pulling you deeper
into its vortex, deeper...deeper..."

In this part . . .

You enter the world of JavaScript programming. The kind of programming you learn in this part is suitable for any kind of language. You'll be able to translate these ideas to any major language without difficulty. Of course, the examples and emphasis are in JavaScript.

Chapter 1 helps you gather your tools. Most of the tools you need for professional JavaScript program are completely free. Learn what you need in terms of editors, browsers, and plugins.

Chapter 2 gets you started in JavaScript. You'll store data in variables, work with text data, and do some basic input and output.

Chapter 3 takes you into the wonderful world of decision making. You'll learn how to generate random numbers and then use them to experiment with several decision-making mechanisms. Your programs will make decisions like the best of them.

Chapter 4 introduces the powerful idea of loops. Your programs will be able to repeat as many times as you want, and will stop on a dime. Loops can also cause difficult-to-spot logic problems, so this chapter also describes a number of debugging techniques.

Chapter 5 helps you build more powerful programs by combining elements. You can combine variables to make arrays, and you can combine statements to make functions. You also learn how to combine both instructions and data to make objects, including the powerful JSON object.

Chapter 1

Taking the Web to the Next Level

In This Chapter

▶ Reviewing HTML, XHTML, and CSS

▶ Examining the role of JavaScript and AJAX

▶ Exploring what JavaScript and AJAX can add to Web pages

▶ Choosing an editor

▶ Building your browser toolkit

The Web is a pretty big deal. It's a lot of fun to build Web pages, and just about every business needs them. As the Web has grown and changed, the expectations of what a Web page is and does have also changed. If you already know HTML or XHTML, you know how to create Web documents — if you need a refresher, check out Bonus Chapter 1 on either the companion Web site at www.dummies.com/go/javascriptandajaxfd or my own site at www.aharrisbooks.net/jad.

As the Web has evolved so have the tools that are used to create Web pages and documents. JavaScript and AJAX are two powerful tools for creating dynamic Web documents. This chapter gets you started with a look at some of the primary technologies out there for building Web pages.

Building Something Cool

This book is about adding features to Web pages that you cannot do with simple HTML and CSS.

Make no mistake; we're talking about programming here — and programming is a little bit harder than plain old Web development. However, it's really worth it, as the example page in Figure 1-1 illustrates.

To keep this example simple, I'm using some external libraries. They are explained in Part IV of this book, but for now just appreciate that something exciting is happening here.

The text in this box changes.

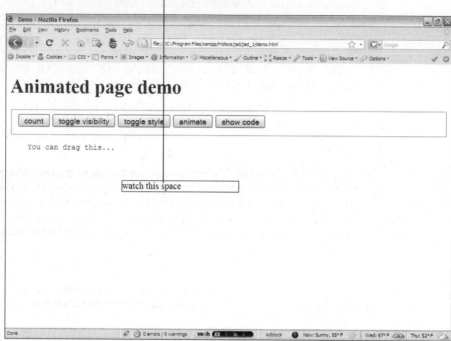

Figure 1-1:
This page
has some
interesting
features
that would
not be pos-
sible in
basic HTML.

This program requires you to have an active Internet connection to work correctly. Check Chapter 10 to see some alternatives for connecting to external
libraries.

If you want to see this page in action (and you really should), please go to the
companion Web sites for this book: `www.aharrisbooks.net/jad` or `www.
dummies.com/go/javascriptandajaxfd`. This program and every other
program and example in the book are available at that site.

At first, the Web page looks pretty simple, but when you open it in your own
browser (as you should) and begin playing with it, you'll soon discover that it
packs a lot of surprises. This very simple page illustrates a lot of the reasons
why you should learn JavaScript and AJAX.

✔ **The buttons do something.** You might already have a handle on creating form elements (such as buttons and text fields) in plain HTML, but
HTML can't do anything with the buttons and text fields; that's why you
need a programming language.

If you want something interesting to happen, you need a programming
language. Each of these buttons uses JavaScript to do some interesting

work, but the fact that the page is now interactive is a huge change. With JavaScript, you can build *applications*, not just pages.

✔ **The Count button dynamically changes the page.** When you click the Count button, new content is added to the page automatically. A program counts how many times the Count button is pressed and adds text to the "watch this space" section. As the user interacts with the page, the page has material that wasn't originally on the server.

Of course, this example is simple, but you will be able to add any kind of text to any Web element dynamically. That's a very powerful capability. Figure 1-2 shows how the page looks after I click the Count button a few times.

✔ **The Toggle Visibility button makes things appear and disappear.** You can't really modify whether things appear or go away in HTML. You can do so in CSS to some level, but JavaScript gives you a much more powerful set of tools for changing what parts of the page are visible to the user at any time. Look at Figure 1-3 to see the page with the output segment hidden.

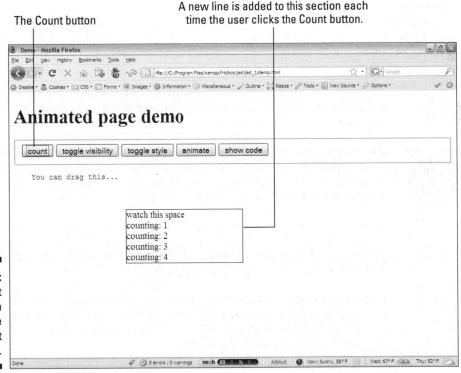

The Count button

A new line is added to this section each time the user clicks the Count button.

Figure 1-2: The Count button changes the text in part of the page.

I clicked the Toggle Visibility button, and the output disappeared.

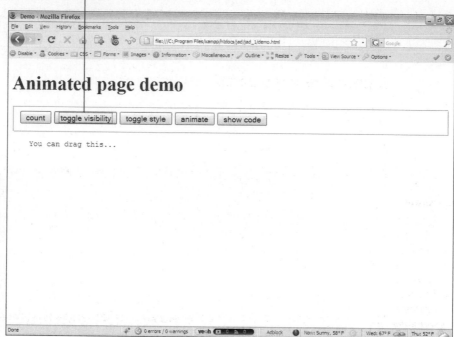

Figure 1-3:
Click the Toggle Visibility button to make the panel with the output reappear.

✔ **The Toggle Style button instantly changes the appearance of part of the page.** You can use JavaScript to change the contents of any part of the page (that is, the HTML) — but you can *also* use JavaScript to modify the appearance (the CSS) in real time. In this example, I've created a special CSS class called `funky` that is added to or removed from the output box every time the user clicks the button. This approach works with any CSS class. (Amazing, huh?) Figure 1-4 shows the page with the `funky` class applied.

If you need a refresher on CSS or XHTML, please look over the bonus chapters on the Web site: www.dummies.com/go/javascriptand ajaxfd or www.aharrisbooks.net/jad.

I've added callouts to some of the figures in this chapter to describe what's happening. The images in this book are not sufficient to understand what the page does. Find the program at www.dummies.com/go/ javascriptandajaxfd or www.aharrisbooks.net/jad and look at it yourself.

✔ **The Animate button is even more fun.** The Animate button makes a series of gradual changes to the output box, changing its size, shape, and appearance over time. (You've really got to try it; a screen shot won't do it justice.)

The Toggle Style button

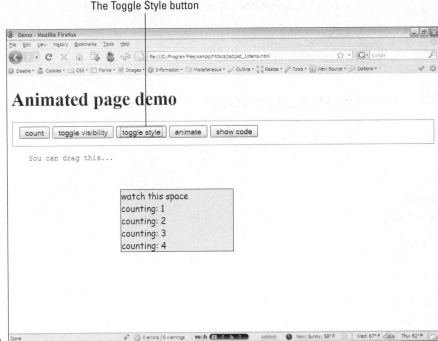

✔ **The Show Code button brings in text from an external file.** This button uses a simple form of AJAX to load an external file into the page in real time. This is an easy way to build modular pages. In this case, I'm actually pulling in a copy of the JavaScript code so you can see how it works. Don't worry if you don't understand it yet. That's what this book is for! Figure 1-5 shows this operation in action.

✔ **Let the user drag the code.** The user can pick up the code and move it wherever she wants. This is another kind of functionality unheard of in ordinary Web pages.

No, you wouldn't normally display your code to users. I'm just illustrating that it's pretty easy to pull in an arbitrary text file from a server. Since you are a programmer now, I chose to show you a preview of the code as the text file I brought in.

These capabilities are profound, and they're just the beginning. Learning to program transforms your Web pages from static documents to living applications that can interact with your users in new and exciting ways.

Feel free to look over the code for this project. It's actually in three files: `demo.html`, `demo.css`, and `demo.js`. All can be found in the Chapter 1 folder of the book's companion Web site. Use View Source when the page is displayed in your browser to see the source code of the HTML file.

Click to see the code from another file.

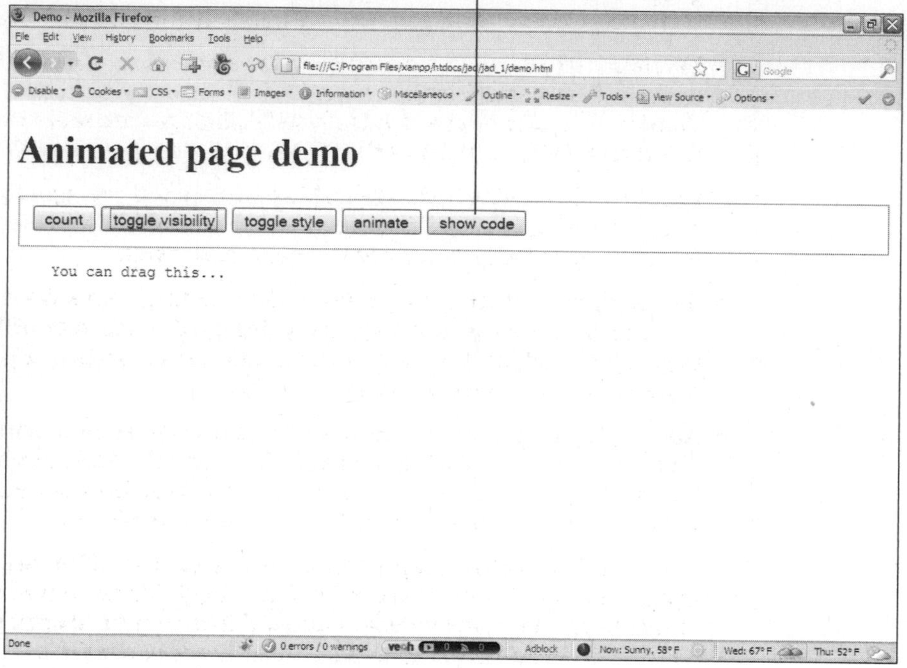

Figure 1-5:
The Show
Code but-
ton pulls
code from
another file
and shows it
on-screen.

I've added plenty of comments in the code to help you see what's going on, but it's okay if you don't have all the intricacies nailed down yet. Think of this as a preview of things you'll get to do in this book.

Getting Started

Making your pages do all this stuff looks like fun, and it is. There's a lot to get under your belt, but don't panic; I take you through everything. The first step is to review the core technologies that JavaScript and AJAX are based on, and see how they're related to some other (more advanced) technologies you'll eventually need.

Overview of the Core Technologies

Powerful as they are, JavaScript and AJAX do not stand on their own. They only have meaning in the context of Web pages, so they rely on various Web technologies. If you want to build a JavaScript application, you'll need several other technologies, too:

- ✔ **HTML:** HTML (HyperText Markup Language) is the basic markup language that describes Web pages. It's a relatively simple technique for building Web sites that requires nothing but a plain text editor.

- ✔ **XHTML:** XHTML is often considered the successor to HTML. Because it doesn't allow certain kinds of tags, XHTML is actually a smaller language that's a bit easier to use. Typically XHTML pages are more dependent on CSS than HTML, as many of the HTML tags are replaced with CSS tools.

- ✔ **CSS:** CSS (Cascading Style Sheets) is a way to add specific style information to an HTML or XHTML page. HTML and XHTML provide the general framework, and CSS describes the color and layout.

- ✔ **JavaScript:** JavaScript is a programming language embedded in all modern Web browsers. It's specially designed to interact with Web pages; you can use it to extract information from parts of a page, and to manipulate the page in real time.

- ✔ **AJAX:** (Asynchronous JavaScript And XML) is a technique that allows JavaScript to communicate more directly with the Web server. It creates an interesting new relationship between the Web browser and the Web server. About half of this book is dedicated to AJAX.

- ✔ **PHP:** (PHP Hypertext Preprocessor) is one of several important languages for working on a Web server. Although it's not a primary focus of this book, the PHP language can do things that JavaScript cannot do. AJAX is frequently used to connect JavaScript applications to PHP programs. You get a brief introduction to PHP in Chapter 14.

- ✔ **Java:** Java is a language that's entirely different from JavaScript (despite the similar names). Although Java is useful on both the client and server sides of the client-server relationship, it's not a primary focus of this book.

When you're looking for online help about JavaScript, be sure that you talk to Java*Script* experts and not *Java* programmers. Although the languages have similar names, they're entirely different languages. Java programmers love to act superior, and they'll give you grief if you ask a JavaScript question in a Java forum. If in doubt, ask on my Web site (www.aharrisbooks.net). I can help you with either language, and I won't mind (or bug you about it) if you're a little confused.

Choosing your computer

Of course, you'll need a computer. Fortunately, it doesn't have to be anything special. Any computer you can use to view Web pages can also be used to create them. Any of the major operating systems (Windows, Mac, and Linux) is perfectly fine. I do most of my work on a combination of Linux (Fedora Core) and Windows XP, but all the programs in the book will work exactly the same on any reasonably modern computer.

At some point you'll want your Web pages to be available on the Internet. Although you can install a server on your home computer, it's usually better to use an online hosting service. You can often get very good online hosting very cheaply or even free. If you want to have a specific name attached to your Web site (such as www.mySite.com), then you'll need to pay about $10 a year to register the domain. Hosting services frequently use Linux, but you'll probably use an online interface that hides all the details from you.

The right tools make any job easier, but for Web development, many of the really great software tools are available entirely free of charge. Because these tools are open source (available with a license that encourages distribution), they are entirely legal to use without paying for them, unlike commercial programs obtained using illicit methods.

You can do basic Web development on any computer with a text editor and browser. As your Web-tweaking skills get more sophisticated, you might want more powerful tools. Read on to see some great tools that cost absolutely nothing.

Picking an Editor

Web pages, JavaScript, HTML, and CSS are all ultimately forms of text. You don't really need any particular program to write them. Still, having exactly the right tool can make your life a lot easier. Since you're going to spend a lot of time with your Web tools, you should be aware of your options.

Avoiding the problem tools

Using the wrong tool for the job can really make your life difficult. Here are a few tools that don't really stand up to the job of Web development:

- ✔ **Microsoft Word:** Word processors are great (I'm using one to write this book), but they aren't really designed for creating Web pages. Word (and all other word processors) store lots of information in their files besides plain text. All the formatting stuff is great for non-Web documents, but HTML and CSS have their own ways of managing this data, and the other stuff gets in the way. Even the Save as HTML command is problematic. Although it stores the page in a form of HTML, Word's formatting is extremely clunky and difficult to work with. The resulting pages will not be suitable for adapting to JavaScript.

- ✔ **Notepad:** This is the classic tool built into most versions of Windows. It saves pages in plain text, so it's better than Word for Web development, but Notepad is too simplistic for any sort of serious work. It lacks such basic features as line numbers — and it can't handle multiple documents at once. You'll quickly outgrow Notepad as a Web-development tool.

✔ **TextEdit:** The default text editor on the Mac is a very powerful tool, but it's more like a word processor than what I'd call a true text editor. When you save an HTML file in TextEdit, it's usually not stored the way you need it to: Rather than seeing the results of the code, you'll see the code itself. If you want to use TextEdit for HTML or JavaScript, make sure you choose Format⇨Make Plain Text before saving your file.

✔ **Graphics editors:** Some high-end graphics editors like Adobe Photoshop, Adobe Fireworks, and Gimp also have the ability to export to HTML, but the code they produce is not easy to work with. It's really better to use these programs to edit your graphics and use a dedicated text editor to handle your code.

Using a WYSIWYG editor

The promise of WYSIWYG ("what you see is what you get") editing is very alluring. Word-processing programs have had this capability for years. As you edit a document on-screen, you can see in real time exactly how it will look on paper. A number of tools promise this kind of functionality for Web pages: Adobe Dreamweaver is the most popular, followed by Microsoft FrontPage and its replacement ExpressionWeb. Although these tools are popular for traditional Web development, they have some drawbacks when it comes to the kind of interactive work we do in this book:

✔ **WYSIWYG is a lie.** The whole assumption of WYSIWYG works fine when the output is *a paper document printed on a printer*. You can predict how the output will work. Web pages are different, because the output shows up on a display that belongs to somebody else. You don't know what size it will be, what colors it will support, or what fonts are installed. You also don't know which browser the user will be viewing pages with, which can make a major difference in the output of the page.

✔ **The editor hides details you need.** A visual editor tries to protect you from some of the details of Web development. That's fine at first, but at some point you'll need that level of control. Most professionals who use Dreamweaver spend most of their time in Code view, ignoring the advantages of a visual editor. Why pay for features you're going to ignore?

✔ **Visual editors assume static documents.** A visual editor is based on the idea that a Web page is an ordinary document. The kinds of pages we build in this book are much more than that. You will (for example) be writing code that creates and modifies Web documents on the fly. You need to know how to build Web documents by hand so you can write code that builds them and changes them dynamically.

Introducing programmer's editors

A number of specialty editors have propped up which seek to fill the gap between plain-text editors and the WYSIWYG tools. These editors write in plain text, but they have additional features for programmers, including:

- ✔ **Awareness of languages:** Programmer's editors often know what language you're writing in and can adapt, helping you whether you're writing HTML, JavaScript, or CSS code. Most general-purpose programmer's editors can handle all these languages natively, and often can help with many more languages.

- ✔ **Syntax highlighting:** Various elements are colored in different ways so you can see what is in plain text, what is part of an HTML tag, and so on. This simple feature can make it much easier to find problems like missing quotes, and to see the general structure of your page quickly.

- ✔ **Syntax support:** Programmer's editors often provide some sort of help for remembering the syntax of your language. This boost can be in the form of buttons and macros for handling common code, pre-written templates for standard layouts and patterns, and syntax completion (which looks at what you're typing and suggests completions based on the current language you're using).

- ✔ **Multiple document support:** Advanced Web applications often involve editing several different documents at once. You might have a dozen Web pages with a few CSS style sheets and an external JavaScript file or two. A programmer's editor allows you to view and edit all these files simultaneously. Many also allow you to generate a *project file* so you can save all the related files automatically and load them in one batch.

- ✔ **Macro tools:** Programming often requires repetitive typing tasks. Having a feature that records and plays back sequences of keystrokes as *macros* (short automated operations) can be incredibly helpful.

- ✔ **Debugging and preview support:** Most programmer's editors have a tool for previewing your code in a browser (or sometimes directly in the editor). The editors also often have tools for predicting certain errors, or responding to errors when they occur. At a minimum, you need the capability to jump directly to a particular line or section of your code.

- ✔ **Indentation support:** Most programmers use indentation as a powerful tool to help them understand the structure of the Web documents they're building. A good editor can assist you with this indentation and also help you recognize when you've made mistakes in the structure of your document.

Getting familiar with some important editors

A couple of multi-purpose programmer's editors immediately come to mind. You should consider investigating one or more of these free programs:

✔ **vi and emacs:** These are the granddaddies of all text editors. Both are very common on Unix/Linux environments. They are also available for Windows and Mac. Though extremely capable editors, vi and emacs were developed at a time when modern ideas about usability weren't practical. If you already know how to use one of these tools, by all means investigate a modern variant. (Frankly, I still use emacs as my primary text editor, though I don't know if I'd learn it today with all the easier options out there.) Figure 1-6 shows a Web page being edited with emacs.

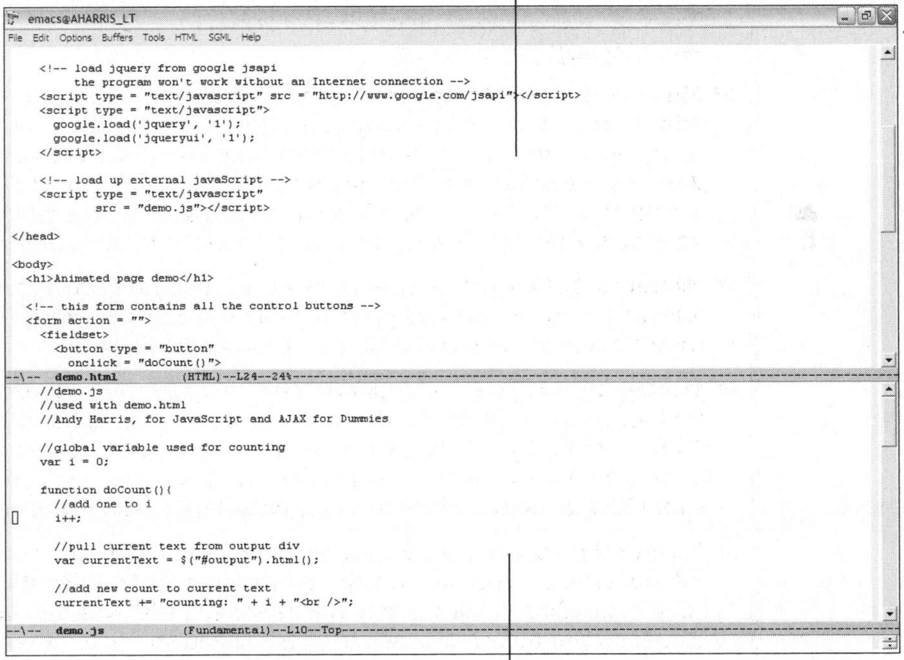

Clean interface without buttons or gadgets

Figure 1-6: Emacs isn't pretty, but it's very powerful. Use it for extra geek points.

You can have many files open at once or look at two spots in the same file.

- ✔ **notepad++:** This is what Notepad for Windows should be. It starts with the speed and simplicity of Windows Notepad, but adds tons of features for programmers. I especially like the built-in support for page validation. This is one of the few programs to earn a permanent shortcut on my desktop. Unfortunately, it's only for Windows. Figure 1-7 shows the same page being edited in notepad++.

- ✔ **Bluefish:** The Bluefish text editor is rapidly becoming a favorite tool for Web developers. It's quick and powerful, and it has plenty of great features for Web developers. One especially powerful tool is the CSS generator, which helps you develop style sheets with a menu system so you don't have to memorize any syntax. It also has a great generator for default templates, which makes XHTML-strict Web pages much easier to build. Bluefish is available for all major platforms (for the Windows version, you'll also need to install the free GTK library). You can see Bluefish running in Figure 1-8.

Extensive set of commands and tools for text editing

Support for multiple documents

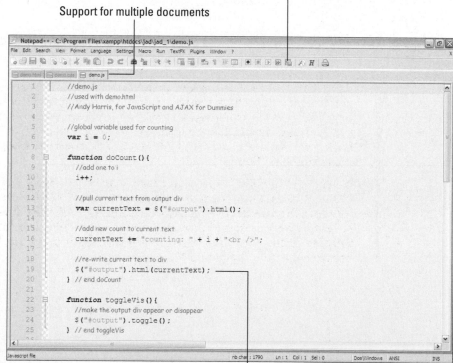

Figure 1-7:
You'll find
notepad++
a very
powerful
alternative
to Notepad.

Automatic syntax highlighting in dozen of languages

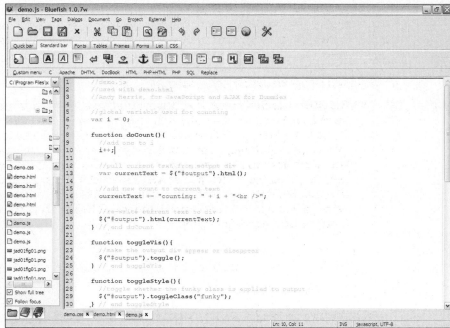

Figure 1-8:
Bluefish is
a very nice
editor for
XHTML and
JavaScript.

✔ **jEdit:** This powerful editor is written in Java, so it is available on virtu-
ally every platform. It is a very powerful editor in its basic format, but its
best feature is the extensive plugin library that allows you to customize
it to your own needs. If you install the free XML library, jEdit has incredible support for HTML and XHTML. Figure 1-9 shows the sample program
being edited in jEdit.

✔ **codetch:** This editor is unique because rather than being a standalone
editor, it is actually an extension for the popular Firefox browser. It has
most of the same features as the other editors, with the convenience
of being already a part of your browser. It is not quite as configurable
as some of the other tools, but it's still extremely handy. You can see
codetch in action in Figure 1-10.

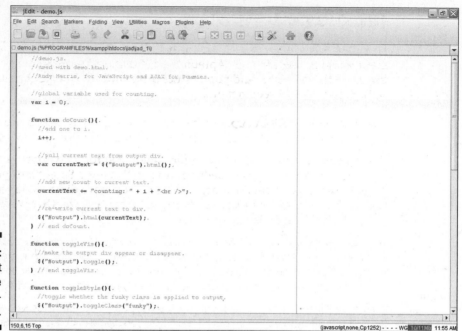

Figure 1-9:
jEdit is a fast
and capable
editor writ-
ten in Java.

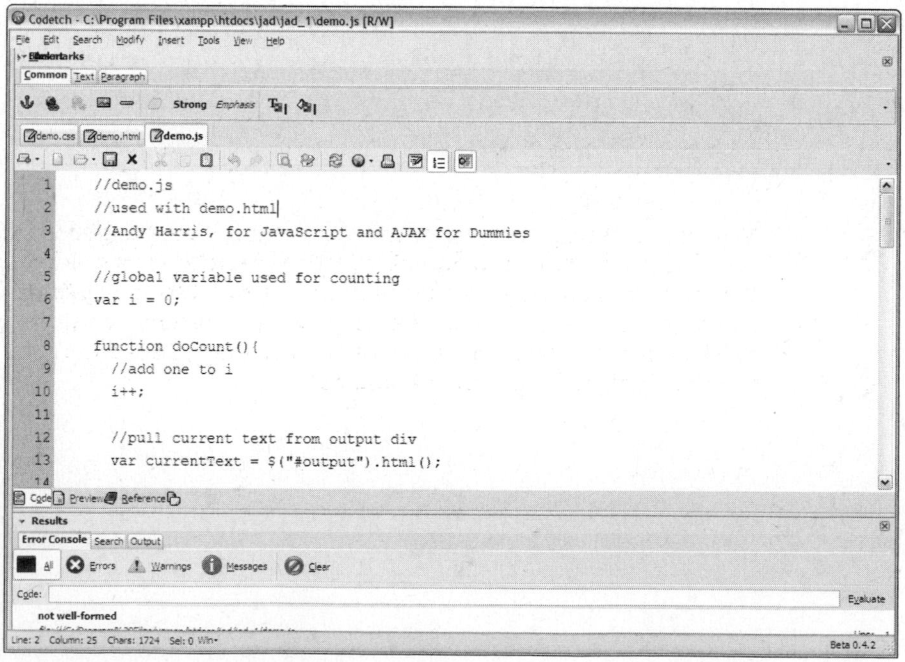

Figure 1-10:
The codetch
plugin for
Firefox is a
complete
Web editor.

Introducing Aptana

One particular programmer's editor has really taken over the Web development world in recent years. Aptana is a full-featured programmer's editor based on the powerful and popular Eclipse editor for Java programming. Aptana has a lot to recommend:

- **Extensive built-in support for Web languages:** Aptana comes out of the box with support for HTML/XHTML, CSS, JavaScript, and AJAX.

- **Syntax highlighting:** Most programmer's editors have syntax highlighting, but Aptana is especially capable in this area. Sometimes you'll have the same physical document with three or more different languages active, and Aptana can usually sense by context whether you're writing CSS, XHTML, or JavaScript code.

- **Code completion:** This is one of Aptana's most impressive features. When you start writing a line of code, Aptana will pop up a menu of suggestions. This helps you avoid mistakes, so you don't have to memorize all the various CSS attributes and JavaScript commands exactly.

- **Error detection:** Aptana can look over your document as you create it and highlight some areas in real time. This feature can help you write better code, and can also help hone your skills at writing code.

- **AJAX support:** AJAX is a relatively new technology, and most editors do not directly support it. Aptana has a number of features that help you with AJAX, including built-in support of all the major AJAX libraries.

Aptana is completely free. I've placed a link to Aptana (and indeed all the tools mentioned here) on the Web site for this book. You can see Aptana in action in Figure 1-11.

My personal setup varies from machine to machine, but generally I use Aptana for my heavy programming, with notepad++ as a quick editor on Windows, and emacs as my primary basic text editor on Linux or Mac machines. Of course, you'll develop your own preferences as you go. All these editors are free and available at `www.aharrisbooks.net/jad`, so they're worthy of some experimentation.

Automatic syntax highlighting and code completion

Multiple document support

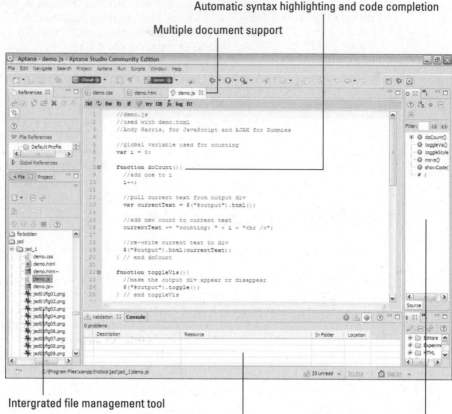

Figure 1-11:
Aptana
might be the
best Web
editor avail-
able at any
price.

Intergrated file management tool

Console area for debugging and error messages

Automatically generated map showing the main sections of a page or program

Creating Your Browser Collection

Web pages live within the context of Web browsers. Each browser interprets HTML and CSS a bit differently, and the differences are magnified when you start talking about JavaScript and AJAX. Subtle (and sometimes not-so-subtle) differences in the way browsers support your code can be very important.

Setting the standard

Every Web browser has its own particular way of displaying Web pages. Although those ways are pretty similar, the differences can sometimes be a problem. Worse, as you begin to write JavaScript code, you'll find that each browser has its own interpretation of the code. That can be a real mess.

Fortunately, there's been a big push toward standardization in recent years. The various browser developers have been getting together and agreeing to various standards set forth by a centralized team called the *World Wide Web Consortium* (W3C). When a browser implements JavaScript, it now agrees (theoretically, at least) to adhere to a set of standards for behavior. As long as your code follows the same standards, you can expect everything to work pretty well. (Most of the time, anyway.)

In this book, I adhere to accepted JavaScript standards as practiced by most developers. All the code in this book is tested on IE7 for Windows, Firefox 3 for Windows, and Firefox 3 for Linux. Any time the code is likely to cause particular browser problems, I try to point out the specific issues.

Picking a browser or two

Here are a few browsers you should be aware of:

✔ **Legacy browsers:** You'll find a lot of older browsers still being used on the Internet. Some people have continued to stick with whatever browser was on their machine when they got it, and haven't upgraded in years. The browsers earlier than IE6 or Firefox are a particular problem, because support for Web standards *and* for JavaScript was very uneven in the early days of the Web. For the most part, this book assumes that your users will be using at least a somewhat modern browser.

AJAX in particular won't work on really old browsers.

✔ **Microsoft Internet Explorer 6:** This is a very common browser, still in popular use. At one point it was the dominant browser on the Internet, but it has fallen from favor in recent years, being replaced by newer offerings from Microsoft as well as competitors like Firefox and Opera. This browser is well-known for a number of "features" that don't comply with community standards. Its use is declining, but as of this writing, you still have to consider supporting it; a lot of users still have it.

✔ **Firefox:** The Firefox Web browser from Mozilla reopened the so-called "browser wars" by providing the first significant competition to Microsoft in many years. Firefox really opened eyes with its impressive features: tabbed browsing, improved security, and integrated searching. For developers, Firefox was among the first browsers to truly support Web standards in a serious way. Firefox is especially important to developers because of its extension architecture, which allows a programmer to turn Firefox into a high-powered development tool. Look at the next section of this chapter for suggestions on some great extensions to add to Firefox.

- ✔ **Microsoft Internet Explorer 7 and 8:** IE7 could be considered a tribute to Firefox, as it incorporates many of the same features. While this book was being written, IE8 came out, and added a few more improvements. Although the support for standards is not as complete in IE7 and IE8 as it is in some of the other current fleet of browsers, they are much better than in any earlier versions of IE.

- ✔ **Opera:** Opera is an important browser because it was one of the earliest browsers to actively support Web standards. It's very popular in certain circles, but has never gained widespread popularity. Since it supports Web standards, it will typically run any code written for a standards-compliant browser.

- ✔ **Safari:** Safari is the Web browser packaged with Mac OS. It is a very capable standards-compliant browser. There is now a Windows version available. The Web browser built into iPhones uses the same engine as Safari, so this is an important consideration if you're building applications for mobile devices.

- ✔ **Chrome:** This newer browser was created by Google. It is highly standards-compliant, and it's especially powerful at handling Java Script and AJAX. This is not surprising, considering Google is one of the companies that pioneered the use of AJAX and is actively promoting its use. Chrome has one of the fastest JavaScript interpreters in common use.

- ✔ **Other browsers:** There are many other browsers in use today, including specialty browsers on various forms of Linux, cell phones, and PDAs. It is nearly impossible to support them all, but many browsers now at least try to support Web standards.

I prefer to do most of my testing with Firefox 3, because it has very good standards support and an excellent set of tools for improving and debugging your code. I then check my pages on other browsers including IE6, IE7, and Chrome.

Turning Firefox into a Development Machine

Firefox is an especially important browser for Web developers. It has a number of attractive features including its excellent standards support in HTML and JavaScript. However, the most important advantage of Firefox as a developer's tool might be its support for extensions. Many commercial browsers keep their code a closely guarded secret, and are very difficult to extend. Firefox was designed from the beginning to have its capabilities extended — and a number of very clever programmers have added incredible extensions to the tool. A few of these extensions have become "must haves" for Web developers:

Web Developer Toolbar

The Web Developer Toolbar by Chris Pederick is an incredible tool. It adds a new toolbar to Firefox with a number of extremely useful capabilities:

- ✔ **Edit CSS:** You can pop up a small window and type in CSS code. The CSS will take effect immediately in real time, so you can see exactly what effect your CSS has on the view of the page.

- ✔ **Display Ruler:** This incredibly handy tool allows you to draw a ruler on your page to see exactly how large various elements are. This is really useful for debugging Web layouts.

- ✔ **Outline tables:** This tool helps you make sense of table-based layouts. It's a good way to see how a complex table-based design is created.

  It's best to avoid table-based layout, but sometimes you have to look at somebody else's pages.

- ✔ **Resize menu:** The Resize menu lets you see how your page looks in a number of other standard sizes. This can be very useful when you're designing a layout.

- ✔ **Validation tools:** Web Developer includes a number of really handy tools for validating your Web pages. It includes links for validating HTML and CSS, as well as the primary accessibility standards.

HTML Validator extension

This incredible extension brings the same validation engine used by the W3C to your browser. It gives quick feedback on the validity of any page you view. It also adds much more information to Firefox's View Source page, including feedback on exactly which validation errors you have. (Validation information is not provided by the normal View Source page.) The hints for fixing the errors are actually helpful, and there's also a tool for automatically repairing the code with the excellent HTML Tidy program. HTML is the foundation for your JavaScript code, and invalid HTML provides a faulty framework. With the HTML Validator, there's no reason to have invalid pages. Figure 1-12 shows the improved View Source window with the warnings tab and the buttons for fixing the code with HTML Tidy.

View Source window

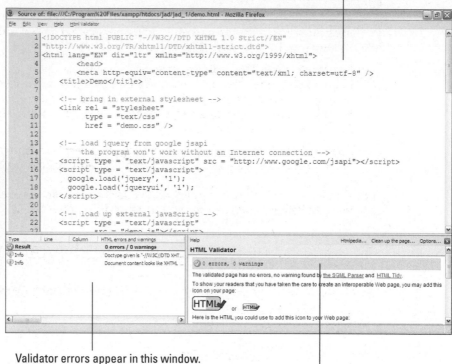

View Source window

Figure 1-12:
The HTML
Validator
extension
adds very
useful
features to
the View
Source tool.

Validator errors appear in this window.

The Validor extension provides helpful error messages.

Firebug

The Firebug extension is one of the most important tools in Web development. It turns Firefox into a complete debugging tool. Firebug has several especially useful features:

- ✔ **Inspect Window:** This incredible tool allows you to move your mouse over any element in your page and instantly see the code that created that section in another panel. This is a very easy way to analyze and debug pages. You can also see instantly what CSS applies to a particular snippet of code, and highlight code to see the corresponding output.

- ✔ **CSS View and Edit:** You can look over the CSS of your page in a panel, see previews of any colors, and edit the values. You'll see the results in real time on the page.

- ✔ **JavaScript Debugging:** Even pros make mistakes — and up to now, few debugger tools have been available for JavaScript programmers. Firebug has better mechanisms for error-trapping than the browsers do, and it also incorporates a very nice debugger that can really help you find your errors as your program runs.

- ✔ **AJAX monitoring:** AJAX programming is based on a series of requests back and forth from the server. Firebug helps you to keep track of these requests and watch your data move.

- ✔ **Live code view:** The ordinary view source menu of most browsers helps you see the code as it originally comes from the browser. In JavaScript programming, you're often changing the page code on the fly. Firebug shows you the page as it really is, even if it's being changed by JavaScript. This is a very useful facility.

- ✔ **Firebug lite:** This is a variation of firebug that works in IE and other browsers. This adds most of the power of firebug to any browser.

Figure 1-13 shows Firebug in inspect mode. As the user moves over a piece of the page, the related code segment appears in the code window.

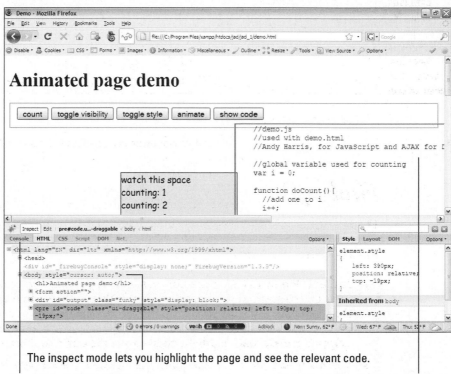

Figure 1-13:
Firebug being used to inspect a Web page.

The inspect mode lets you highlight the page and see the relevant code.

View and edit HTML, CSS, or JavaScript

View the CSS or DOM info for the currently selected window.

Chapter 2

Writing Your First Program

In This Chapter

▶ Adding JavaScript code to your pages

▶ Setting up your environment for JavaScript

▶ Creating variables

▶ Input and output with modal dialog boxes

▶ Using concatenation to build text data

▶ Understanding basic data types

▶ Using string methods and properties

▶ Using conversion functions

*W*eb pages begin with XHTML code. This basic code provides the framework. CSS adds decoration to the basic structure, but to make your pages literally sing and dance, you'll need to learn a programming language.

The JavaScript language is a very popular first language, because it's designed to interact with Web pages, and it's already built into most Web browsers. It's reasonably easy to learn, and it's very powerful.

The whole idea of learning a programming language might seem intimidating, but don't worry. Programming isn't really that hard. I show you exactly how to get started in this chapter. You'll be coding like a pro in a very short time.

Becoming a Programmer

JavaScript is a programming language first developed by Netscape communications. It is now standard on nearly every browser. There are a few things you should know about JavaScript right away:

✔ **It's a real programming language.** Sometimes people who program in other languages such as C++ and VB.NET scoff at JavaScript and claim it's not a "real" programming language because it lacks some features. These features (particularly the ability to communicate with the local file system) were left out on purpose to keep JavaScript safe. (You're introduced to some AJAX alternatives that provide access to these features in the last half of this book.) JavaScript is a real language, and it's a very good place to start programming.

✔ **It's not Java.** There is another popular programming language called Java (without the script part), which is also used for Web programming. JavaScript and Java are *completely* different languages (despite the similar names). Make sure you don't go onto a Java forum and start asking JavaScript questions. Those Java programmers can be kind of snooty and superior. (They shouldn't be; I program in Java, too. It's just a language.)

✔ **It's a scripting language.** JavaScript is a pretty easy language to get to know. It isn't nearly as strict as certain other languages (I'm looking at you, Java), and it has a relatively relaxed view of things (for one, it's less demanding about exactly what sort of data goes where). This lets you concentrate more on trying to solve your problem than worrying about exactly how your code is written. It's still a programming language, so there are a few rules you must obey, but scripting languages such as JavaScript tend to be much more forgiving to beginners than the big monster languages.

Choosing a JavaScript editor

JavaScript (like XHTML and CSS) is really just text. You can modify your JavaScript code in the same editor you use for XHTML and CSS. If you used Aptana before (mentioned in Chapter 1) and liked it, you're going to love the editor now. Of course, you can continue to use another editor if you prefer.

JavaScript is an entirely different language and uses a different syntax than HTML and CSS. It isn't hard to learn, but there's a lot to learn in any true programming language. Aptana has a number of really great features that help you tremendously when writing JavaScript code:

✔ **Syntax highlighting:** Just like HTML and CSS, Aptana automatically adjusts code colors to help you see what's going on in your program. As you see later in this chapter, this can be a big benefit when things get complicated.

✔ **Code completion:** When you type in the name of an object, Aptana provides you with a list of possible completions. This can be really helpful, so you don't have to memorize all the details of the various functions and commands.

- ✔ **Help files:** The My Aptana page (available from the File menu if you've dismissed it) has links to really great help pages for HTML, CSS, and JavaScript. The documentation is actually easier to read than some of what you'll find on the Web.

- ✔ **Integrated help:** Hover the mouse pointer over a JavaScript command or method and a nifty little text box pops up, explaining exactly how it works. Often the box includes an example or two.

- ✔ **Error warnings:** When Aptana can tell something is going wrong, it tries to give you an error message and places a red squiggly line (like the ones spellcheckers use) under the suspect code.

I'm unaware of a better JavaScript editor at any price, and Aptana is free, so there's just not a good reason to use anything else. Of course, you can use any text editor you like if you don't want or need these features.

There's one strange characteristic I've noticed in Aptana: The Preview tab isn't as reliable a technique for checking JavaScript code as it is for XHTML and CSS. I find it better to run the code directly in my browser or use the Run button to have Aptana run it in the external browser for me.

Picking your test browser

In addition to your editor, you should carefully choose your browser based on how it works when you're testing JavaScript code.

All the major browsers support JavaScript, and it works relatively similarly across the browsers (at least until things get a bit more advanced). However, all browsers are not equal when it comes to testing your code.

Things will go wrong when you write JavaScript code, and the browser is responsible for telling you what went wrong. Firefox is way ahead of IE when it comes to reporting errors. Firefox errors are much easier to read and understand, and Firefox supports a feature called the _JavaScript console_ (described in Chapter 4) that makes it much easier to see what's going on. If at all possible, use Firefox to test your code, and then check for discrepancies in IE.

Chapter 4 gives you more about finding and fixing errors — and some great tools in Firefox and Aptana to make this important job easier.

That's enough preliminaries. Pull out your editor, and start writing a real program. It's simple enough to get started. The foundation of any JavaScript program is a standard Web page.

Adding a script to your page

The context of JavaScript programs is Web pages, so begin your JavaScript journey by adding some content to a basic Web page. If you aren't familiar with XHTML or CSS (the languages used for basic Web development), please review the bonus chapters available on either of the two Web sites dedicated to this book (www.dummies.com/go/javascriptandajaxfd or www.aharrisbooks.net/jad), or look into a more complete reference like *HTML, XHTML, and CSS All-in-One Desk Reference For Dummies* (Wiley).

It's pretty easy to add JavaScript code to your pages. Figure 2-1 shows the classic first program in any computer language.

This page has a very simple JavaScript program in it that pops up the phrase "Hello, World!" in a special element called a *dialog box*. It's pretty cool.

Here's an overview of the code, and then I'll explain all the details step by step.

```
<!DOCTYPE html PUBLIC "-//W3C//DTD XHTML 1.0 Strict//EN"
"http://www.w3.org/TR/xhtml1/DTD/xhtml1-strict.dtd">
<html lang="EN" dir="ltr" xmlns="http://www.w3.org/1999/
          xhtml">
  <head>
    <meta http-equiv=»content-type» content=»text/xml;
          charset=utf-8» />
    <title>HelloWorld.html</title>
    <script type = «text/javascript»>
      //<![CDATA[
        // Hello, world!
        alert(«Hello, World!»);
      //]]>
    </script>
  </head>

  <body>

  </body>
</html>
```

As you can see, there's nothing in the HTML body in this page at all. You can (and will) incorporate JavaScript with XHTML content later. For now, though, you can simply place JavaScript code in the head area of your Web page in a special tag and make it work.

Hello, World?

There's a long tradition in programming languages that your first program in any language should simply say "Hello, World!" and do nothing else. There's actually a very good practical reason for this habit. Hello World is the simplest possible program you can write that you can prove works. Hello World programs are used to help you figure out the mechanics of the programming environment — how the program is written, what special steps you have to do to make the code run, and how it works. There's no point in making a more complicated program until you know you can get code to pop up and say hi.

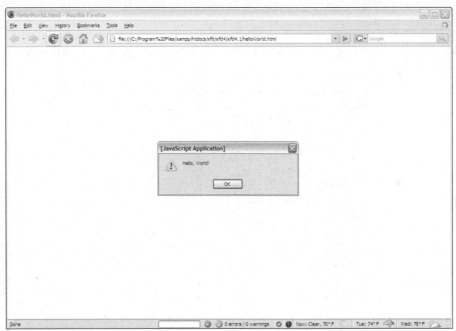

Figure 2-1:
A
JavaScript
program
caused
this little
dialog box
to pop up!

Embedding your JavaScript code

JavaScript code is placed in your Web page via the `<script>` tag. JavaScript code is placed inside the `<script></script>` pair. The `<script>` tag has one required attribute, `type`, which will usually be `text/javascript`. (Other types are possible, but they are rarely used.)

The other funny thing in the code in the previous section is that crazy CDATA stuff. Immediately inside the `<script>` tag, the next line is

```
//<![CDATA[
```

This bizarre line is a special marker explaining that the following code is character information, and shouldn't be interpreted as XHTML. The end of the script finishes off the character data marker with this code:

```
//]]>
```

In modern browsers, it's a good idea to mark off your JavaScript code as character data. If you don't, the XHTML validator will sometimes get confused and claim you have errors when you don't.

That CDATA business is bizarre. It's hard to memorize, I know, but just type it a few times, and you'll own it.

 A lot of older books and Web sites do not include the character data trick, but it's well worth mastering. You've invested too much effort into building standards-compliant pages to have undeserved error messages pop up because the browser mistakes your JavaScript for badly-formatted XHTML.

Creating comments

As with XHTML and CSS, JavaScript comments are important to include. Because programming code can be more difficult to decipher than XHTML or CSS, it's even more important to comment your code in JavaScript than it is in those other two environments. The comment character in JavaScript is two slashes (//). The browser ignores everything from the two slashes to the end of the line. You can also use a multi-line comment (/* */) just like the one in CSS.

Using the alert() method for output

There are a number of ways to output data in JavaScript. In this example, I use the alert() method. This technique pops up a small dialog box containing text for the user to read. The alert box is an example of a *modal dialog box*. Modal dialog boxes interrupt the flow of the program until the user pays attention to them. Nothing else will happen in the program until the user acknowledges the dialog box by clicking the OK button. The user can't interact with the page until after clicking the button.

Modal dialog boxes might seem a bit rude. In fact, you probably won't use them much once you learn some other input and output techniques. The fact that the dialog box demands attention makes it a very easy tool to use when you start programming. When you've got the basic programming ideas under your belt, I show you more elegant ways to communicate with the Web page.

Adding the semicolon

Each command in JavaScript ends with a semicolon (;) character. The semicolon in most computer languages acts like the period in English: It indicates the end of a logical thought. Usually each line of code is also one line in the text editor.

To tell the truth, JavaScript usually works fine if you leave out the semicolons, but you should add them anyway because they can clarify your meaning. Besides, most other languages (such as PHP, introduced in Chapter 14) require semicolons. You might as well start a good habit now.

Introducing Variables

Computer programs get their power by working with information. Figure 2-2 shows a program that gets data from the user and uses it in a customized greeting.

Figure 2-2:
The program asks for the user's name.

This program introduces a new kind of dialog box that allows the user to enter some data. The information is stored in the program for later use. Figure 2-3 shows the first part of the response at the top. The user must click OK to get the rest of the greeting in a second alert dialog box, as shown at the bottom of Figure 2-3.

Figure 2-3:
A two-dialog box response to user input.

The output might not seem that incredible, but take a look at the source code to see what's happening:

```
<!DOCTYPE html PUBLIC "-//W3C//DTD XHTML 1.0 Strict//EN"
"http://www.w3.org/TR/xhtml1/DTD/xhtml1-strict.dtd">
<html lang="EN" dir="ltr" xmlns="http://www.w3.org/1999/
          xhtml">
  <head>
    <meta http-equiv=»content-type» content=»text/xml;
          charset=utf-8» />
    <title>prompt.html</title>
    <script type = «text/javascript»>
      //<![CDATA[

      var person = «»;
      person = prompt(«What is your name?»);
      alert(«Hi»);
      alert(person);

      //]]>
    </script>
  </head>

  <body>

  </body>
</html>
```

Creating a variable for data storage

This program is interesting because it allows user interaction. The user can enter a name that is stored in the computer and then returned in a greeting. The key to this program is a special element called a *variable*. Variables are simply places in memory for holding data. Any time you want a computer program to "remember" something, you can create a variable and store your information in it.

Variables typically have the following characteristics:

- **The** var **statement.** Indicates you are creating a variable with the var command.

- **A name.** When you create a variable, you are required to give it a name.

- **An initial value.** It's useful to give each variable a value immediately

- **A data type.** JavaScript automatically determines the type of data in a variable (more on this later), but you should still be clear in your mind about what type of data you expect a particular variable to contain.

Asking the user for information

Variables are more interesting when they contain information. JavaScript has a simple tool called the *prompt*, which allows you to easily ask a question and store the answer in a variable. Here's the relevant line from `prompt.html`:

```
person = prompt("What is your name?");
```

The `prompt` statement does several interesting things:

- ✔ **It pops up a dialog box.** The `prompt()` method creates a modal dialog box much like the `alert` technique discussed earlier.

- ✔ **It asks a question.** The `prompt` command expects you to ask the user a question.

- ✔ **It provides space for a response.** There is a space in the dialog box for the user to type a response of some kind, and buttons to indicate that the user is finished or wants to cancel the operation.

- ✔ **It passes the information to a variable.** The purpose of a `prompt` command is to get data from the user, so prompts are nearly always connected to a variable. When the code is finished, the variable will contain the indicated value.

Responding to the user

This program uses the `alert()` method to begin a greeting to the user. The first alert works just like the one from the `helloWorld` program:

```
alert("Hi");
```

The content of the parentheses is the text you want the user to see. In this case, you want the user to see the literal value `"Hi"`.

The second `alert` statement is a little bit different:

```
alert(person);
```

This `alert` statement has a parameter with no quotes. Since there are no quotes, JavaScript understands you don't really want to say the text `"person"`. Instead, it looks for a variable named `person`, and returns the value of that variable.

So the variable can take any name, store it, and return a customized greeting.

Using Concatenation to Build Better Greetings

It seems a little awkward to have the greeting and the person's name on two different lines. Figure 2-4 shows a better solution. The program asks for a name again, and stores it in a variable. This time, the greeting is combined into one alert dialog box, and it looks a lot better:

Figure 2-4:
Now there's just one dialog box response to the user's input.

The secret to Figure 2-4 is one of those wonderful gems of the computing world: a really simple idea with a really complicated name. Take a look at the code and you'll see that combining variables with text is not all that complicated:

```
<script type = "text/javascript">
  //<![CDATA[
  // from concat.html

  var person = "";
  person = prompt("What is your name?");
  alert("Hi there, " + person + "!");

  //]]>
</script>
```

For the sake of brevity, I've only included the `<script>` tag and its contents; the rest of this page is a standard blank XHTML page. (As always, see the complete document on the Web site: www.aharrisbooks.net/jad). I use this approach throughout this chapter, but I also include a comment in each JavaScript snippet to indicate where you can get the entire file on the Web site.

Concatenation and your editor

The hard part about concatenation is figuring out which part of your text is a literal value and which part is a string. It won't take long before you start going cross-eyed trying to understand where the quotes go.

Modern text editors (like Aptana) have a wonderful feature that can help you here. They color different kinds of text in different colors. By default, Aptana colors variable names black, and literal text dark green (at least when you're in JavaScript — in HTML, literal text is in blue).

Personally, I find it hard to differentiate the dark green from black, so I changed the Aptana color scheme: I have it make string literals blue whether I'm in JavaScript or HTML. With this setting in place, I can easily see what part of the statement is literal text and what's being read as a variable name. That makes concatenation a lot easier.

To change the color scheme in Aptana, click Window⇨Preferences. You'll see an expandable outline in the resulting dialog box. Click Aptana⇨Editors⇨JavaScript Editor⇨Colors. You can then scroll down and find color settings for any type of data. I found "string" (another term for text) under "literals" and changed the color of my text strings from dark green to blue.

If you make a mistake, there's a button to revert back to the default values.

Most editors that have syntax highlighting allow you to change settings to fit your needs. Don't be afraid to use these tools to help you program better.

Comparing literals and variables

In this program there are really two different kinds of text. The whole expression `"Hi there, "` is a *literal* text value. That is, you really mean to say "Hi there." On the other hand, `person` is a variable; you can put any person's name in it. You can combine literal values and variables in one phrase if you want:

```
alert("Hi there, " + person + "!");
```

The secret to this code is to follow the quotes. `"Hi there, "` is a literal value, because it is in quotes. In this line, `person` is a variable name (because it is *not* in quotes) and `"!"` is a literal value. You can combine any number of text snippets together with the plus sign as shown in the preceding code.

Using the plus sign to combine text is called *concatenation*. (I told you it was a complicated word for a simple idea.)

Including spaces in concatenated phrases

You might be curious about the extra space between the comma and the quote in the output line:

```
alert("Hi there, " + person + "!");
```

This is important because you want the output to look like a normal sentence. If you don't have the space, the computer won't add one, and the output would look like:

```
Hi there,Benjamin!
```

Be sure to construct the output as it should look on-screen, including spaces and punctuation.

Understanding the string Object

The `person` variable used in the previous program is designed to hold text. Programmers (being programmers) devised their own mysterious term to refer to text. In programming, text is referred to as *string* data.

The term *string* comes from the way text is stored in computer memory. Each character is stored in its own cell in memory, and all the characters in a word or phrase reminded the early programmers of beads on a string. (Surprisingly poetic for a bunch of geeks, huh?)

Introducing object-oriented programming (and cows)

JavaScript (and many other modern programming languages) use a powerful model called *object-oriented programming (OOP)*. This style of programming has a number of advantages. Most important for beginners, it allows you access to some very powerful objects that do interesting things out of the box.

Objects are used to describe complicated things that can have a lot of characteristics — for instance, a cow. You can't really put an adequate description of a cow in an integer variable.

In many object-oriented environments, objects can have these characteristics (imagine a `cow` object for the examples):

- **Properties:** Characteristics about the object, such as `breed` and `age`.
- **Methods:** Things the objects can do, such as `moo()` and `giveMilk()`.
- **Events:** Stimuli the object responds to, such as `onTip()`.

Each of these ideas will be described as they are needed, as not all objects support all these characteristics.

If you have a variable of type `cow`, it describes a pretty complicated thing. This thing might have properties, methods, and events. All could be used together to build a good representation of a cow. (Believe it or not, I've built cow programming constructs more than once in my life — and you thought programming was dull.)

Most variable types in JavaScript are actually objects — and most JavaScript objects have a full complement of properties and methods (many even have event handlers). When you get a handle on how all these things work, you've got a powerful and compelling programming environment.

Okay, before somebody sends me some angry e-mails, I know there is some debate about whether JavaScript is a *truly* object-oriented language. I'm not going to get into the (frankly boring and not terribly important) details in this book. We're going to call it object-oriented for now, because it's close enough for beginners. If that bothers you, you can refer to JavaScript as an object-*based* language. Nearly everyone agrees with that. More information on this topic is throughout the book as you learn how to build your own objects in Chapter 5 and how to use HTML elements as objects in Chapter 6.

Investigating the length of a string

When you assign text to a variable, JavaScript automatically treats the variable as a string object. The object instantly takes on the characteristics of a string object. Strings have a couple of properties, and a bunch of methods. The one interesting property (at least for beginners) is `length`. Look at the example in Figure 2-5 to see the `length` property in action:

Figure 2-5:
This
program
reports the
length of
any text.

That's kind of cool. The cooler part is the way it works. As soon as you assign a text value to a variable, JavaScript treats that variable as a string, and since it's a string, it now has a `length` property. This property returns the length of the string in characters. Here's how it's done in the code:

```
<script type = "text/javascript">
//<![CDATA[
//from nameLength.html

  var person = prompt("Please enter your name.");
  var length = person.length;

  alert("Hi, " + person + "!");
  alert("The name " + person + " is " + length + "
      characters long.");

  //]]>
</script>
```

This code uses the `length` property as if it were a special subvariable. For example, `person` is a variable in the previous example — and `person`.`length` is the `length` property of the `person` variable. In JavaScript, an object and a variable are connected by a period (with no spaces).

The string object in JavaScript has only two other properties (`constructor` and `prototype`). Both of these properties are only needed for advanced programming, so I skip them for now.

Using string methods to manipulate text

The `length` property is kind of cool, but the string object has a lot more up its sleeve. Objects also have *methods* (things the object can do). Strings in JavaScript have all kinds of methods. Here's a few of my favorites:

- `toUpperCase()`: Makes an entirely uppercase copy of the string.
- `toLowerCase()`: Makes an entirely lowercase copy of the string.
- `substring()`: Returns a specific part of the string.
- `indexOf()`: Determines if one string occurs within another.

The string object has many other methods, but I'm highlighting these because they're useful for beginners. Many of the string methods — such as `big()` and `fontColor()` — simply add HTML code to text. They aren't used very often, because they produce HTML code that won't validate, and they don't really save a lot of effort anyway. Some of the other methods — such as `search()`, `replace()`, and `slice()` — use advanced constructs like arrays and regular expressions that aren't necessary for beginners. (To learn more about working with arrays, see Chapter 5. You learn more about regular expressions in Chapter 7.)

Why are the first three characters (0, 3)?

The character locations for JavaScript (and most programming languages) will probably seem somewhat strange to you until you know the secret. You might expect `text.substring(1,3)` to return the first three characters of the variable `text`, yet I used `text.substring(0,3)` to do that job. Here's why: The indices don't correspond to character numbers; instead, they are the indices *between* characters.

```
|a|b|c|d|
0 1 2 3 4
```

So if I want the first three characters of the string `"abcd"`, I use `substring(0,3)`. If I want the `"cd"` part, it's `substring(2,4)`.

TIP

Don't take my word for it. Look up the JavaScript string object in the Aptana online help (or one of the many other online JavaScript references) and see what properties and methods it has.

Like properties, methods are attached to an object by using a period. Methods are distinguished by a pair of parentheses, which sometimes contains special information called *parameters*. Parameters are information that will be passed to the method so it can do its job. Some methods require parameters, and some do not. It all makes sense once you start using methods.

The best way to see how methods work is to check out some in action. Look at the code for `stringMethods.html`:

```html
<script type = "text/javascript">
//<![CDATA[
//from stringMethods.html

var text = prompt("Please enter some text.");

alert("I'll shout it out:");
alert(text.toUpperCase());

alert("Now in lowercase...");
alert(text.toLowerCase());

alert("The first 'a' is at letter...");
alert(text.indexOf("a"));

alert("The first three letters are ...");
alert(text.substring(0, 3));

//]]>
</script>
```

The output produced by this program is shown in Figure 2-6.

Here's yet another cool thing about Aptana: When you type the term `text.` (complete with period), Aptana understands that you're talking about a string variable and automatically pops up a list of all the possible properties and methods. (I wish I'd had that when I started doing this stuff.)

You can see from this code that methods are pretty easy to use. When you have a string variable in place, you can invoke the variable's name, followed by a period and the method's name. Some of the methods require more information to do their job. Here's a look at the specifics:

- `toUpperCase()` and `toLowerCase()`: Takes the value of the variable and converts it entirely to the given case. This is often used when you aren't concerned about the capitalization of a variable.

- `indexOf(substring)`: Returns the character position of the substring within the variable. If the variable doesn't contain the substring, return the value -1.

- `substring(begin, end)`: Returns the substring of the variable from the beginning character value to the end.

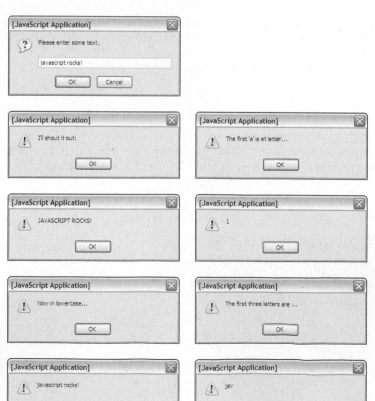

Figure 2-6:
String methods can be fun. . . .

Understanding Variable Types

JavaScript isn't too fussy about whether a variable contains text or a number, but the distinction is still important, because there *is* a difference in the way these things are stored in memory, and this difference can cause some surprising problems.

Adding numbers

To see what can go wrong when JavaScript misunderstands data types, try a little experiment. First, take a look at the following program (as usual for this chapter, I'm only showing the script part because the rest of the page is blank):

```
<script type = "text/javascript">
  //<![CDATA
  //from addNumbers.html

  var x = 5;
  var y = 3;
  var sum = x + y;

  alert(x + « plus « + y + « equals « + sum);

  //]]>
</script>
```

This program features three variables. I've assigned the value 5 to x, and 3 to y. I then add x + y and assign the result to a third variable, sum. The last line prints out the results, which are also shown in Figure 2-7.

Figure 2-7:
This program (correctly) adds two numbers together.

Note a few important things from this example:

✔ **You can assign values to variables.** It's best to read the equals sign as "gets" so the first assignment should be read as "variable x gets the value 5."

```
var x = 5;
```

✔ **Numeric values are not enclosed in quotes.** When you refer to a text literal value, it is always enclosed in quotes. Numeric data (like the value 5) are not placed in quotes.

✔ **You can add numeric values.** Since x and y both contain numeric values, you can add them together.

✔ **The results of an operation can be placed in a variable.** The result of the calculation x + y is placed in a variable called sum.

✔ **Everything works as expected.** The program behaves in the way you intended it to. That's important because it's not always true as you'll see in the next example — I *love* writing code that blows up on purpose!

Adding the user's numbers

The natural extension of the addNumbers.html program would be a feature that allows the user to input two values and then return the sum. This could be the basis for a simple adding machine. Here's the JavaScript code:

```
<script type = "text/javascript">
//<![CDATA[
//from addInputWrong.html

var x = prompt("first number:");
var y = prompt("second number:");
var sum = x + y;

alert(x + " plus " + y + " equals " + sum);

//]]>
</script>
```

This code seems reasonable enough. It asks for each value and stores them in variables. It then adds the variables up and returns the results, right? Well, look at Figure 2-8 and you'll see a surprise.

Something's obviously not right here. To understand the problem, you need to see how JavaScript makes guesses about data types.

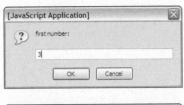

Figure 2-8:
Wait a
minute . . .
3 + 5 = 35?

The trouble with dynamic data

Ultimately, all the information stored in a computer, from music videos to e-mails, is stored as a bunch of ones and zeroes. The same value 01000001 could mean all kinds of things: it might mean the number 65 or the character A. (In fact, it *does* mean both of those things in the right context.) The same binary value might mean something entirely different if it's interpreted as a real number, a color, or a part of a sound file.

The theory isn't critical here, but one point is really important: Somehow the computer has to know what kind of data is stored in a specific variable. Many languages (like C and Java) have all kinds of rules about this. If you create a variable in one of these languages, you have to define exactly what kind of data will go in the variable — and you can't change it.

JavaScript is much more easygoing about variable types. When you make a variable, you can put any kind of data in it that you want. In fact, the data type can change. A variable can contain an integer at one point and the same variable might contain text in another part of the program.

JavaScript uses the context to determine how to interpret the data in a particular variable. When you assign a value to a variable, JavaScript puts the data in one of the following categories:

- ✔ **Integer:** Integers are whole numbers (no decimal part). They can be positive or negative values.

- ✔ **Floating-point number:** A floating-point number has a decimal point like 3.14. Floating-point values can also be expressed in scientific notation like 6.02e23 (Avagadro's number: 6.02 times 10 to the 23rd). Floating-point numbers can also be negative.

- ✔ **Boolean:** A Boolean value can only be true or false.

- ✔ **String:** Text is usually referred to as "string" data in programming languages. String values are usually enclosed in quotes.

- ✔ **Arrays and objects:** These are more complex data types you can ignore for now. They are covered in depth in Chapter 5.

These different data types are necessary because the computer uses different techniques to store different types of data into the binary format that all computer memory ultimately uses. Most of the time, when you make a variable, JavaScript guesses right and you have no problems. But sometimes JavaScript makes some faulty assumptions and things go wrong.

The pesky plus sign

I've used the plus sign in two different ways throughout this chapter. The following code uses the plus sign in one way:

```
var x = "Hi, ";
var y = "there!";

result = x + y;
alert(result);
```

In this code, x and y are text variables. The `result = x + y` line is interpreted as "concatenate x and y," and the result will be `"Hi, there!"`.

Here's the strange thing: The following code is almost identical:

```
var x = 3;
var y = 5;

result = x + y;
alert(result);
```

The behavior of the plus sign is different here, even though the statement `result = x + y` is identical!

In this second case, x and y are numbers. The plus operator has two entirely different jobs. If it's surrounded by numbers, it adds. If it's surrounded by text, it concatenates! Automatically. (Hoo boy.)

That's what happens to the first adding-machine program (the one that blows up): When the user enters data in prompt dialog boxes, JavaScript assumes the data is text. So when I try to add x and y, it "helpfully" concatenates instead.

There's a fancy computer-science word for this phenomenon (an operator doing different things in different circumstances). Those Who Care About Such Things call this an *overloaded operator*. Smart people sometimes have bitter arguments about whether overloaded operators are a good idea or not, because they can cause problems like the program concatenating when you think it will add. Overloaded operators can also make things easier in other contexts. I'm not going to enter into that debate here. It's not a big deal, as long as you can see the problem and fix it when it occurs.

Changing Variables to the Desired Type

If JavaScript is having a hard time figuring out what type of data is in a variable, you can give it a friendly push in the right direction with some handy conversion functions as shown in Table 2-1.

Table 2-1	Variable Conversion Functions			
Function	*From*	*To*	*Example*	*Result*
parseInt()	String	Integer	parseInt("23")	23
parseFloat()	String	Floating-point	parseFloat ("21.5")	21.5
toString()	Any variable	String	myVar.toString()	varies
eval()	Expression	Result	eval("5 + 3")	8
Math.ceil()	Floating-point	Integer	Math.ceil(5.2)	6
Math.floor()			Math.floor(5.2)	5
Math.round()			Math.round(5.2)	5

Using variable conversion tools

The conversion functions are incredibly powerful, but you only need them if the automatic conversion causes you problems. Here's how they work:

✔ parseInt(): Used to convert text to an integer. If you put a text value inside the parentheses, the function returns an integer value. If the string has a floating-point representation ("4.3" for example), an integer value (4) will be returned.

✔ `parseFloat()`: Converts text to a floating-point value.

✔ `toString()`: Takes any variable type and creates a string representation. Note that it isn't usually necessary to use this function, because it's usually invoked automatically when needed.

✔ `eval()`: This is a special method that accepts a string as input. It then attempts to evaluate the string as JavaScript code and return the output. You can use this for variable conversion or as a simple calculator — `eval("5 + 3")` will return the integer 8.

✔ `Math.ceil()`: One of several methods of converting a floating-point number to an integer. This technique always rounds upward, so `Math.ceil(1.2)` will be 2, and `Math.ceil(1.8)` will also be 2.

✔ `Math.floor()`: Similar to `Math.ceil`, except it always rounds downward, so `Math.floor(1.2)` and `Math.floor(1.8)` will both evaluate to 1.

✔ `Math.round()`: Works like the standard rounding technique used in grade school. Any fractional value less than .5 will round down, and greater than or equal to .5 will round up, so `Math.round(1.2)` is 1, and `Math.round(1.8)` is 2.

Fixing the addInput code

With all this conversion knowledge in place, it's pretty easy to fix up the `addInput` program so it works correctly. Just use `parseFloat()` to force both inputs into floating-point values before adding them. Note that you don't have to convert the result explicitly to a string. That's done automatically when you invoke the `alert()` method:

```
//<![CDATA[
// from addInput.html

var x = prompt("first number:");
var y = prompt("second number:");
var sum = parseFloat(x) + parseFloat(y);

alert(x + " plus " + y + " equals " + sum);

//]]>
```

You can see the program works correctly in Figure 2-9.

Conversion methods allow you to ensure the data is in exactly the format you want.

Figure 2-9:
Now the program asks for input and correctly returns the sum.

Chapter 3

Changing Program Behavior with Conditions

In This Chapter

▶ Generating random numbers and converting them to integers

▶ Understanding conditions

▶ Using the if-else structure

▶ Managing multiple conditions

▶ Using the switch structure

▶ Handling unusual conditions

*O*ne of the most important aspects of computers is their apparent ability to make decisions. Computers can change their behavior based on circumstances. In this chapter you learn how to create random numbers in JavaScript, and several ways to have your program make decisions based on the roll of a digital die.

Working with Random Numbers

Random numbers are a big part of computing. They add uncertainty to games, but they're also used for serious applications like simulations, security, and logic. In this chapter, you generate random numbers to simulate dice and then explore various ways to modify the computer's behavior based on the value of the roll.

Most languages have a feature for creating random numbers, and JavaScript is no exception. The `Math.random()` function returns a random floating-point value between 0 and 1.

Technically, computers can't create *truly* random numbers. Instead, they use a complex formula that starts with one value and creates a second semi-predictable value. In JavaScript, the first value (called the random *seed*) is taken from the system clock in milliseconds, so the results of a random number call seem truly random.

Creating a die to die for

It's very easy to create a random floating-point number between 0 and 1, because that's what the Math.random() function does. What if you want an integer within a specific range? For example, you might want to simulate rolling a six-sided die. How do you get from the 0-to-1 floating-point value to a 1-to-6 integer?

Here's the standard approach:

1. **Get a random floating-point value.**

   Use the Math.random() function to get a floating-point value between 0 and 1.

2. **Multiply the zero-to-one value by 6.**

   This gives you a floating-point value between 0 and 5.999 (but never 6).

3. **Use** Math.ceil() **to round up.**

   Here's where you need to convert the number to an integer. In Chapter 2 I mention three functions to convert from a float to an integer. Math. ceil() always rounds up, which means you'll always get an integer between 1 and 6.

Rolling the dice

Take a look at the RollDie.html code that rolls your digital dice:

```
<!DOCTYPE html PUBLIC "-//W3C//DTD XHTML 1.0 Strict//EN"
"http://www.w3.org/TR/xhtml1/DTD/xhtml1-strict.dtd">
<html lang="EN" dir="ltr" xmlns="http://www.w3.org/1999/
          xhtml">
  <head>
    <meta http-equiv=»content-type» content=»text/xml;
          charset=utf-8» />
    <title>rollDie.html</title>
    <script type = «text/javascript»>
      //<![CDATA[
      // from rollDie.html
```

```
        var number = Math.random();
        alert(number);

        var biggerNumber = number * 6;
        alert(biggerNumber);

        var die = Math.ceil(biggerNumber);
        alert(die);

        //]]>

    </script>
  </head>

  <body>
    <div id = «output»>

    </div>
  </body>
</html>
```

As you can see, I converted the strategy from the previous section directly into JavaScript code:

1. **Create a random floating-point value.**

   The `Math.random()` function creates a random floating-point number and stores it in the variable `number`.

2. **Multiply the number by 6.**

   To move the number into the appropriate range (6 values), I multiplied by 6, and stored the result in `biggerNumber`.

3. **Round up.**

   I used the `Math.ceil()` function to round the number up to the next highest integer.

Figure 3-1 shows the program running.

You might need to run the `rollDice.html` page a few times to confirm that it works as suspected.

If you want to re-run a program you've already loaded into the browser, just hit the Refresh button on the browser toolbar.

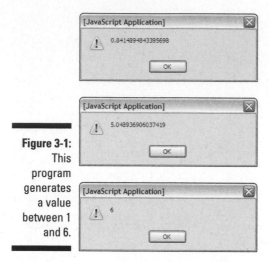

Figure 3-1:
This program generates a value between 1 and 6.

Using if to Control Flow

If you can roll a die, you'll eventually want different things to happen in different circumstances. Figure 3-2 shows two different runs of a simple game called deuce.html.

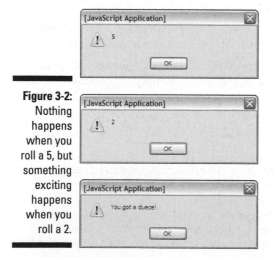

Figure 3-2:
Nothing happens when you roll a 5, but something exciting happens when you roll a 2.

Okay, it's not *that* exciting. I promise to add dancing hippos in a later version. In any case, the "You got a deuce" message only happens when you roll a 2. The code is simple but profound:

```
<script type = "text/javascript">
  //<![CDATA[
  // from deuce.html
  // get a random number
  // If it's a two, you win

    var die = Math.ceil(Math.random() * 6);
    alert(die);
    if (die == 2){
      alert («You got a Deuce!»);
    } // end if

  //]]>
</script>
```

As usual, I'm only showing the `<script>` tag and its contents here, because the rest of the page is blank.

If and only if

The key to this program is the humble `if` statement. This powerful command does a number of important things:

- ✔ **It sets up a condition.** More on conditions in a moment, but the main idea is this: A condition is a true or false question. `if` statements always include some type of condition in parentheses.

- ✔ **It begins a block of code.** `if` statements set up a chunk of code that won't always execute. The end of the `if` line includes a left brace (`{`).

- ✔ **It usually has indented code under it.** The line or lines immediately after the `if` statement are part of the block, so they are indented to indicate they are special.

- ✔ **It ends several lines later.** The end of the `if` statement is actually the right brace (`}`) several lines down in the code. In essence, an `if` statement *contains* other code.

- ✔ **It's indented.** The convention is to indent all the code between the `if` statement and its ending brace.

While not required, it's common to put a comment indicating that the right brace ends an `if` statement. In the C-like languages, the same symbol (`}`) is used to end a bunch of things, so it's nice to remind yourself what you think you're ending here.

Using conditions

A condition is the central part of `if` statements and several other important structures. Conditions deserve a little respect of their own. A condition is *an expression that can be evaluated to be true or false.* Conditions come in three main flavors:

- ✔ **A comparison:** This is by far the most common kind of condition. Typically you compare a variable to a value, or two variables to each other. A number of different types of comparisons are described in Table 3-1.

- ✔ **A Boolean variable:** Boolean variables are variables that only contain `true` or `false` values. In JavaScript, any variable can be a Boolean, if you assign it a `true` or `false` value. It's unnecessary to compare a Boolean to anything else, because it's already true or false.

- ✔ **A Boolean function:** Sometimes you'll have a function that returns a `true` or `false` value. This type of function can also be used as a condition.

Incidentally, Boolean variables are the only variable type capitalized in most languages. This is because they were named after a person, George Boole. He was a nineteenth-century mathematician who developed a form of binary arithmetic. He died thinking his logic research a failure. His work eventually became the foundation of modern computing. Drop a mention of George at your next computer-science function to earn muchos geek points.

Comparison operators

JavaScript supports a number of different types of comparisons, summarized in Table 3-1:

Table 3-1	JavaScript Comparison Operators		
Name	*Operator*	*Example*	*Notes*
Equal	`==`	`(x==3)`	Works with all variable types, including strings
Not equal	`!=`	`(x != 3)`	True if values are not equal
Less than	`<`	`(x < 3)`	Numeric or alphabetical comparison
Greater than	`>`	`(x > 3)`	Numeric or alphabetical comparison
Less than or equal to	`<=`	`(x <= 3)`	Numeric or alphabetical comparison
Greater than or equal to	`>=`	`(x >= 3)`	Numeric or alphabetical comparison

You should consider a few things when working with conditions:

- ✔ **Make sure the variable types are compatible.** You'll get unpredictable results if you compare a floating-point value to a string.

- ✔ **You can compare string values.** In JavaScript, the inequality operators can be used to determine the alphabetical order of two values, and you can use the same equality symbol (==) with strings that you use with other variables. (This is not true in all programming languages.)

- ✔ **Equality uses a double equals sign.** The single equals sign (=) is used to indicate *assignment*. When you're comparing variables, use a double equals sign (==) instead.

Don't confuse assignment with comparison! If you accidentally say (x = 3) instead of (x == 3), your code won't crash, but it won't work properly. The first statement simply assigns the value 3 to the variable x. It returns the value `true` if the assignment was successful (which it will be). You'll think you're comparing x to 3, but you're assigning x to 3, and the condition will always be true. It's a nightmare. I still do it once in a while.

Do What I Say or Else

The Deuce game is pretty exciting and all, but it would be even better if you had one comment when the roll is a 2 and another comment when it's something else. The `else-if` structure is designed to let you specify one behavior when a condition is true, and another behavior if the condition is false. Figure 3-3 shows a program with exactly this behavior.

Figure 3-3:
You get one
message
for deuces
and another
message for
everything
else.

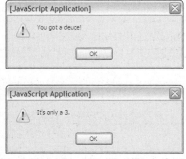

This program uses the same type of condition, but it adds an important section:

```
<script type = "text/javascript">
  //<![CDATA[
  // from deuceOrNot.html

  var die = Math.ceil(Math.random() * 6);
  if (die == 2){
    alert(«You got a deuce!»);
  } else {
    alert(«It's only a « + die + «.»);
  } // end if

  //]]>
</script>
```

The if statement is unchanged, but now there's an else clause. Here's how it works:

- **The if statement sets up a condition:** The if indicates the beginning of a code branch, and it prepares the way for a condition.

- **The condition establishes a test:** Conditions are true or false expressions, so the condition will indicate something that can be true or false.

- **If the condition is** true: The code between the condition and the else clause runs. After this code is finished, program control moves past the end of the if structure. (That is, the computer skips the else clause and executes then next line of code outside the if structure.)

- **If the condition is** false: The code between else and the end of the if runs instead.

The else clause acts like a fork in the road. The code will go along one path or another (depending on the condition), but never both at once.

You can put as much code as you want inside an if or else clause, including more if statements!

You can only use else in the context of an if statement. You can't use else by itself.

Using else-if for more complex interaction

The if-else structure is pretty useful when you have only two branches, but what if you want to have several different options? Imagine for example that you want to output a different value for every single possible die value. You'll need a variation of the if structure to make this work. I show such a tool next, but first, look at a program which uses this technique. Figure 3-4 shows a die only a geek could love. All its values are output in binary notation.

Binary?

Binary notation is the underlying structure of all data in a computer. It uses 1s and 0s to store other numbers, which can be combined to form everything you see on the computer, from graphics to text to music videos and adventure games. Here's a quick conversion chart so you can read the dice:

001 = 1	011 = 3	101 = 5
010 = 2	100 = 4	110 = 6

You can survive just fine without knowing binary (unless you're a computer science major — then you're expected to *dream* in binary). Still, it's kind of cool to know how things really work.

Figure 3-4:
A die for the true geek gamer.

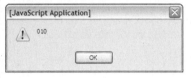

A simple `if-else` structure won't be sufficient here, because you have six different options, and `if-else` only gives you two choices. Here's some code that uses another variation of `if` and `else`:

```
<script type = "text/javascript">
  //<![CDATA[
  // from binaryDice.html

  var die = Math.ceil(Math.random() * 6);
  if (die == 1){
    alert(«001»);
  } else if (die == 2){
    alert(«010»);
  } else if (die == 3){
    alert(«011»);
  } else if (die == 4){
    alert(«100»);
  } else if (die == 5){
    alert(«101»);
  } else if (die == 6){
    alert(«110»);
  } else {
    alert(«something strange is happening...»);
  } // end if

  //]]>
</script>
```

This program begins with an ordinary `if` statement, but it has a number of `else` clauses. You can include as many `else` clauses as you want if each includes its own condition.

For example, imagine the computer generates the value 3. The process would look like this:

1. The first condition (`die == 1`) is false, so the program immediately jumps to the next `else`.

2. This sets up another condition (`die == 2`), which is also false, so program control goes to the next `else` clause.

3. This one has yet another condition (`die == 3`) — which is true! The code inside this clause is executed (alerting the value `"011"`).

4. A condition has finally been triggered — so the computer skips all the other `else` conditions and moves to the line after the `end if`.

5. This is the last line of code — so the program ends.

The mystery of the unnecessary else

When you use multiple conditions, you can (and should) still indicate an ordinary `else` clause without a condition as your last choice. This special condition sets up code that should happen if none of the other conditions is triggered. It's useful as a "garbage collection" function, in case you didn't anticipate a condition in the `else if` clauses.

If you think carefully about the binary dice program, the `else` clause seems superfluous. It isn't really necessary! You went through all that trouble to create a random number scheme that *guarantees* you'll have an integer between 1 and 6. If you checked for all six values, why have an `else` clause? It should never be needed.

There's a big difference between what *should* happen and what *does* happen. Even if you think you've covered every single case, you're going to be surprised every once in a while. If you use a multiple `if` structure, you should always incorporate an `else` clause to check for surprises. It doesn't need to do much but inform you that something has gone terribly wrong.

It's Time to Switch Your Thinking

The dice problem is a special type of branching, where you have one expression (the die) that could have multiple values (1 through 6). Many programming languages include a handy tool for exactly this type of situation. Take a look at Figure 3-5, where you'll see yet another variation of the die roller.

Figure 3-5:
Ancient
Roman dice,
useful if
we come
across any
ancient
Romans.

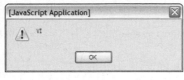

Once again I start with an ordinary 1 through 6 integer and assign a new value based on the original roll. This time I use another structure specialized for "one expression with lots of values" situations. Take a look at the code:

```
<script type = "text/javascript">
//<![CDATA[
// from RomanDice.html
var die = Math.ceil(Math.random() * 6);
var output = «»;
switch(die){
  case 1:
    output = «I»;
    break;
  case 2:
    output = «II»;
    break;
  case 3:
    output = «III»;
    break;
  case 4:
    output = «IV»;
    break;
  case 5:
    output = «V»;
    break;
  case 6:
    output = «VI»;
    break;
  default:
    output = «PROBLEM!!!»;
} // end switch
```

Creating an expression

The switch structure is organized a little bit differently than the if with a bunch of else ifs business.

The `switch` keyword is followed immediately by an expression in parentheses. The expression is usually a variable with several possible values. The `switch` structure then provides a series of test values and code to execute in each case.

Here's how to create a `switch` statement:

1. **Begin with the** `switch` **keyword.**

   This sets up the structure. You'll indent everything until the right brace (}) that ends the `switch` structure.

2. **Indicate the expression.**

   This is usually a variable you want to compare against several values. The variable goes inside parentheses and is followed by a left brace({).

3. **Identify the first case.**

   Indicate the first value you want to compare the variable against. Be sure the case is the same type as the variable.

4. **End the case description with a colon (:).**

   Be careful! Case lines end with a colon (indicating the beginning of a case) rather than the more typical semicolon. It's easy to forget this.

5. **Write code for the case.**

   You can write as many lines of code as you want. This code will only be executed if the expression is equal to the given case. Typically all the code in a case is indented.

6. **Indicate the end of the case with a** `break` **statement.**

   The `break` statement tells the computer to jump out of the `switch` structure as soon as this case has been evaluated (which is almost always what you want).

7. **Repeat with other cases.**

   Build similar code for all the other cases you want to test.

8. **Trap for surprises with the** `default` **clause.**

   The special case `default` works like the `else` in an `else if` structure. It manages any cases that haven't already been trapped. Even if you think you've got all the bases covered, you should put some default code in place just in case.

You don't need to put a `break` statement in the `default` clause, because it always happens at the end of the `switch` structure anyway.

Switching with style

The `switch` structure is powerful, but it can be a little tricky, because the format is a little strange. Here are a few handy tips to keep in mind:

- ✔ **You can compare any type of expression.** If you've used another language (like C or Java) you might have learned that switches only work on numeric values. JavaScript switches can be used on any data type.

- ✔ **It's up to you to get the type correct.** If you are working with a numeric variable and you compare it against string values, you might not get the results you're expecting.

- ✔ **Don't forget the colons.** At the end of most lines, the `switch` statement uses semicolons like most other JavaScript commands. The lines describing cases end with colons (`:`) instead. It's really easy to get confused.

- ✔ **Break each case.** Use the `break` statement to end each case, or you'll get weird results.

If you've got some programming experience, you might argue that another option involving something called *arrays* would be a better solution for this particular problem. I tend to agree, but for that, look ahead to Chapter 5. Switches and `if – else if` structures do have their place, too.

Nesting if Statements

It's possible to combine conditions in all kinds of crazy ways. One decision might include other decisions, which could incorporate other decisions. You can put `if` statements inside each other to manage this kind of (sometimes complicated) logic.

What's this L337 stuff?

Leet (L337) is a wacky social phenomenon primarily born of the online gaming community. Originally it began as people tried to create unique screen names for multiplayer games. If you wanted to call yourself "gamer," for example, you'd usually find the name already taken. Enterprising gamers started substituting similar-looking letters and numbers (and sometimes creative spelling) to make original names

that are still somewhat readable. The practice spread, and now it's combined with text messaging and online chat shortcuts as a sort of geek code. Get it? L337 94m3r is "Leet Gamer," or "Elite Gamer." Before you ask, I don't know why the referee is sometimes a surfer and sometimes a L337 94m3r. It must have been some sort of bizarre childhood circumstances.

Figure 3-6 shows a particularly bizarre example. Imagine you're watching the coin toss at your favorite sporting event. Of course, a coin can be heads or tails. Just for the sake of argument, the referee also has a complex personality. Sometimes he's a surfer and sometimes he's a L337 94m3r (translation: elite gamer). The figure shows a few tosses of the coin.

This is getting pretty strange, so you might as well look at some code:

```
<script type = "text/javascript">
  //<![CDATA[
  // from coinToss.html
  coin = Math.ceil(Math.random() * 2);
  character = Math.ceil(Math.random() * 2);
  if (character == 1){
    //It's a surfer referee
    if (coin == 1){
      alert("You got heads, Dude.");
    } else {
      alert("Dude! It's totally tails!");
    } // end coin if

  } else {
    //now it's a L337 Referee
    if (coin == 1){
      alert("h34D$ r0xx0r$");
    } else {
      alert("741L$ ruL3");
    } // end coin if
  } // end character if

  //]]>
</script>
```

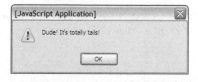

Figure 3-6: Heads or tails? Surfer or gamer?

Building the nested conditions

Once you understand how nested `if` structures work, you can see how this all fits together. The following refers to the example in the previous section:

1. **You flip a coin.**

   I just used a variation of the die-rolling technique. A coin can be only heads or tails, so I rolled a value that would be 1 or 2 for the `coin` variable.

2. **Flip another coin for the personality.**

   The referee's persona will be reflected in another random value between 1 and 2.

3. **Check for the surfer.**

   If the `character` roll is 1, we have a surfer, so set up an `if` statement to handle the surfer's output.

4. **If it's the surfer, check the coin toss.**

   Now that you know it's a surfer speaking, you'll need to check the coin for heads or tails. You'll need another `if` statement for this.

5. **Respond to the coin toss in surfer-speak.**

   Use `alert()` statements to output the result in the surfer dialect.

6. **Handle the L337 character.**

   The outer `if` structure determines which character is speaking. The `else` clause of this case will happen if `character` is not 1, so all the LEET stuff goes in the `else` clause.

7. **Check the coin again.**

   Now you know you're speaking in gamer code, determine what to say by consulting the coin in another `if` statement.

Making sense of nested ifs

As you can see, nested `if` structures aren't all that difficult, but they can be messy, especially as you get several layers deep (as you will, eventually). Here's a batch of tips to make sure everything makes sense:

✔ **Watch your indentation.** Indentation is a great way to tell what level of code you're on, but be vigilant on the indentation scheme you choose. An editor like Aptana, which automatically indents your code, is a big plus.

✔ **Use comments.** It's easy to get lost in the logic of a nested condition. Add comments liberally so you can remind yourself where you are in the logic. Note that in the examples in this chapter I specify which if statement is ending.

✔ **Test your code.** Just because you think it works doesn't mean it will. Surprises happen. Test thoroughly to make sure the code does what you think it should do.

Chapter 4

Loops and Debugging

● ●

In This Chapter

▶ Creating for loops

▶ Learning for loop variations

▶ Building flexible while loops

▶ Making well-behaved while loops

▶ Recognizing troublesome loops

▶ Catching crashes with debugging tools

▶ Catching logic errors

▶ Using the Aptana line-by-line debugger

▶ Using the Firebug debugger

▶ Watching variables and conditions

● ●

Computer programs can do repetitive tasks easily. This is accomplished through a series of constructs called *loops*. A loop is a structure that allows you to repeat a chunk of code. In this chapter you learn the two major techniques for managing loops.

Loops are powerful, but they can be dangerous. It's possible to create loops that act improperly, and these problems are very difficult to diagnose. But don't worry. I demonstrate a number of very powerful techniques for looking through your code to find out what's going on.

Building Counting Loops with for

One very standard type of loop is the for loop. You use these loops when you want to repeat code a certain number of times. Figure 4-1 shows a for loop in action:

It looks like ten different alert() statements, but there's only one. It just got repeated ten times.

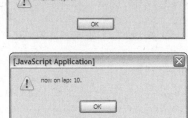

Figure 4-1:
This loop
repeats ten
times before
it stops.

In Figure 4-1, and some of the other looping demos in this chapter, I show the first few dialog boxes and the last. You should be able to get the idea. Be sure to look at the actual program on either of the companion Web sites (www. dummies.com/go/javascriptandajaxfd or www.aharrisbooks.net/ jad) to see how it really works.

Building a standard for loop

The structure of the for loop can be seen by studying the code:

```
<script type = "text/javascript">
//<![CDATA[
//from BasicFor.html
for (lap = 1; lap <= 10; lap++){
  alert("now on lap: " + lap + ".");
} // end for
//]]>
</script>
```

for loops are based on an integer (sometimes called a *sentry variable*). In this example, lap is serving as the sentry variable. The sentry variable is normally used to count the number of repetitions through the loop.

The for statement has three distinct parts:

- **Initialization:** This segment (lap = 1) sets up the initial value of the sentry.

- **Condition:** The condition (lap <= 10) is an ordinary condition (although it doesn't require parentheses in this context). As long as the condition is evaluated as true, the loop will repeat.

- **Modification:** The last part of the for structure (lap++) indicates the sentry will be modified in some way throughout the loop. In this case, I add one to the lap variable each time through the loop.

The `for` structure has a pair of braces containing the code that will be repeated. As usual, all code inside this structure is indented. You can have as much code inside a loop as you want.

The `lap++` operator is a special shortcut. It's very common to add one to a variable, so the `lap++` operation means "add one to lap." You could also write `lap = lap + 1`, but `lap++` sounds so much cooler.

When programmers decided to improve on the C language, they called the new language C++. Get it? It's one better than C! Those computer scientists are such a wacky bunch!

`for` loops are pretty useful when you know how many times something should happen.

Making a backwards loop

You can modify the basic `for` loop so it counts backward. Figure 4-2 shows an example of this behavior.

Figure 4-2:
This program counts backward by using a for loop.

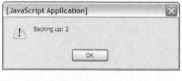
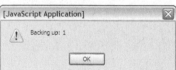

The backward version of the `for` loop uses the same general structure as the forward version, but with slightly different parameters:

```
<script type = "text/javascript">
//<![CDATA[
//from backwards.html

for (lap = 10; lap >= 1; lap--){
  alert("Backing up: " + lap);
} // end for

//]]>
</script>
```

If you want to count backward, just modify the three parts of the `for` statement:

- ✔ **Initialize the sentry to a large number:** If you're counting down, you need to start with a larger number than 0 or 1.

- ✔ **Keep going as long as the sentry is *larger* than some value:** The code inside the loop will execute as long as the condition is true. The number will continue to get smaller, so make sure you're doing a "greater than" or "greater than or equal to" comparison.

- ✔ **Decrement the sentry:** If you want the number to get smaller, you need to subtract something from it. The `--` operator is a quick way to do this. It subtracts 1 from the variable.

Counting five at a time

You can use the `for` loop to make other kinds of counting loops. If you want to count by fives, for example, you can use the following variation:

```
<script type = "text/javascript">
  //<![CDATA[

  //from byFive.html
  for (i = 5; i <= 25; i += 5){
    alert(i);
  } // end for

  //]]>
</script>
```

This code starts `i` as 5, repeats as long as `i` is less than or equal to 25, and adds 5 to `i` on each pass through the loop. Figure 4-3 illustrates this code in action.

If you want a `for` loop to skip numbers, you just make a few changes to the general pattern.

- ✔ **Initialize the sentry to 5:** I want the loop to start at 5, so that's the initial value.

- ✔ **Compare the sentry to 25:** It makes sense for a 5 loop to end at a multiple of 5. I want this loop to continue until we get to 25, so the loop will continue as long as `i` is less than or equal to 25.

- ✔ **Add 5 to `i` on each pass:** The statement `i += 5` adds 5 to i. (It's just like saying `i = i + 5`.)

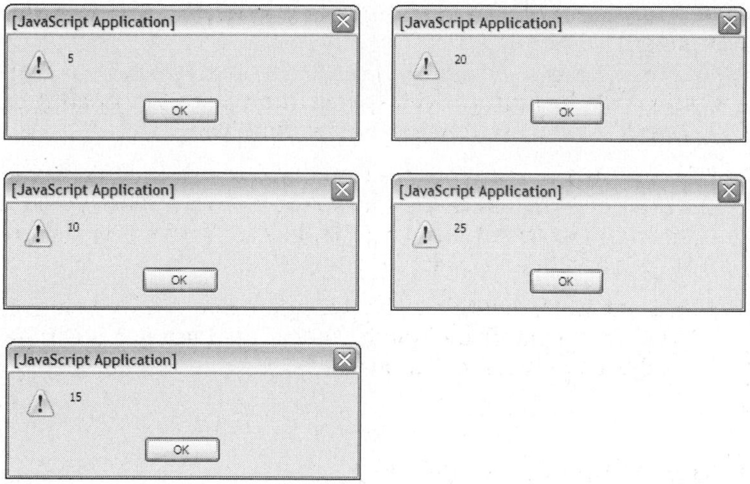

Figure 4-3:
A for loop
can also
skip values.

The key to building `for` loops is to remember these three elements and make sure they work together: Build a sentry variable, give it a sensible initial value, check against a condition, and modify the variable on each pass.

This is easy to do in a `for` loop, because all these elements are in the `for` loop structure. Still, if you find your loop isn't working as expected, you might need to look into the debugging tricks described later in this chapter.

Looping for a while

The `for` loop is useful, but it has a cousin that's even more handy, called the `while` loop. A `while` loop isn't committed to any particular number of repetitions. It simply repeats as long as its condition is true.

Creating a basic while loop

The basic `while` loop is deceptively simple to build. Here's an example:

```
<script type = "text/javascript">
  //<![CDATA[
  // from while.html
```

```
answer = "-99";
while (answer != "5"){
  answer = prompt("What is 3 + 2?");
  if (answer == "5"){
    alert("great!");
  } else {
    alert("try again...");
  } // end if
} // end while

//]]>
</script>
```

This script asks the user a simple math question — and keeps asking until the user responds correctly. You can see it in action in Figure 4-4.

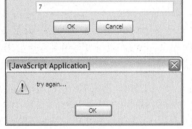

Figure 4-4:
This loop continues until the user enters the correct answer.

The operation of a `while` loop is pretty easy to understand. Here's how the math program works:

1. **Create a variable called** `answer`.

   This will act as a sentry variable for the loop.

2. **Initialize the variable.**

   The initial value of the variable is set to `"-99"`, which can't possibly be correct. Doing so guarantees that the loop will execute at least one time.

3. **Evaluate what's in the** `answer` **variable.**

   In this particular program the correct answer is 5. If the value of `answer` is anything but 5, the loop continues. I've preset the value of `answer` to `"-99"`, so you know it's going to happen at least once.

4. **Ask the user a challenging math question.**

   Well, a math question anyway. The important thing is to change the value of `answer` so it's possible to get 5 in `answer` and then exit the loop.

5. **Give the user some feedback.**

   It's probably good to let the user know how she did, so provide some sort of feedback.

Avoiding loop mistakes

A `while` loop seems simpler than a `for` loop, but `while` has exactly the same basic requirements:

✔ **There is usually a critical sentry variable.** `while` loops are usually (but not always) controlled by some key variable.

✔ **The sentry must be initialized.** If the loop is going to behave properly, the sentry variable must still be initialized properly. In most cases, you'll want to guarantee that the loop happens at least one time.

✔ **You must have a condition.** Like the `for` loop, the `while` loop is based on conditions. As long as the condition is true, the loop continues.

✔ **There must be a mechanism for changing the sentry.** Somewhere in the loop you need to have a line that changes the value of the sentry. Be sure that it's possible to make the condition logically false, or you'll be in the loop forever!

If you forget one of these steps, the `while` loop might not work correctly. It's easy to make mistakes with your `while` loops. Unfortunately, these mistakes don't usually result in a crash. Instead, the loop might either refuse to run altogether or continue indefinitely.

Introducing Some Bad Loops

Sometimes loops don't behave. Even if you've got the syntax correct, it's possible that your loop just doesn't do what you want. Two main kinds of loop errors are common: loops that never happen, and loops that never quit.

Managing the reluctant loop

You might write some code and find that the loop *never* seems to run. Here's some of a program that illustrates this woeful condition:

```
<script type = "text/javascript">
  //<![CDATA[

  //from never.html
  //Warning! this script has a deliberate error!

  i = 1;
  while (i > 10){
    i++;
  } // end while

  //]]>
</script>
```

This code looks innocent enough, but if you run it, you'll be mystified. It doesn't crash, but it also doesn't seem to do anything. If you follow the code step by step, you'll eventually see why. I initialize i to 1, and then repeat as long as i is greater than 10. See the problem? i is less than 10 at the very beginning, so the condition *starts out false*, and the loop never executes! I probably meant for the condition to be (i < 10). It's a sloppy mistake, but exactly the kind of bone-headed error I make all the time.

Managing the compulsive loop

The other kind of bad-natured loop is the opposite of the reluctant loop. This one starts up just fine, but never goes away!

The following code illustrates an endless loop:

```
<script type = "text/javascript">
  //<![CDATA[

  //from endless.html
  // Warning: this program has a deliberate
  // error! You will have to stop the browser
  // to end the loop.

  i = 0;
  j = 0;

  while (i < 10){
    j++;
    alert(j);
  } // end while

  //]]>
</script>
```

If you decide to run `endless.html`, be aware that it will not work properly. What's worse, the only way to stop it will be to kill your browser through the Task Manager program. I show you later in this chapter how to run such code in a "safe" environment so you can figure out what's wrong with it.

This code is just one example of the dreaded *endless loop*. Such a loop usually has perfectly valid syntax, but a logic error prevents it from running properly. The logical error is usually one of the following:

- ✔ **The variable was not initialized properly.** The initial value of the sentry is preventing the loop from beginning correctly.

- ✔ **The condition is checking for something that cannot happen.** Either the condition has a mistake in it, or something else is preventing it from triggering.

- ✔ **The sentry has not been updated inside the loop.** If you simply forget to modify the sentry variable, you'll get an endless loop. If you modify the variable, but do it *after* the loop has completed, you get an endless loop. If you ask for input in the wrong format, you might also get a difficult-to-diagnose endless loop.

Debugging Your Code

If you've been writing JavaScript code, you've also been encountering errors. It's part of a programmer's life. Loops are especially troublesome, because they can cause problems even if there are no syntax errors. Fortunately, there are some really great tricks you can use to help track down pesky bugs.

Letting Aptana help

If you're writing your code with Aptana, you already have some great help available. It gives you the same syntax-highlighting and code-completion features as you had when writing XHTML and CSS.

Also, Aptana can often spot JavaScript errors on the fly. Figure 4-5 shows a program with a deliberate error.

These markers indicate errors in the code.

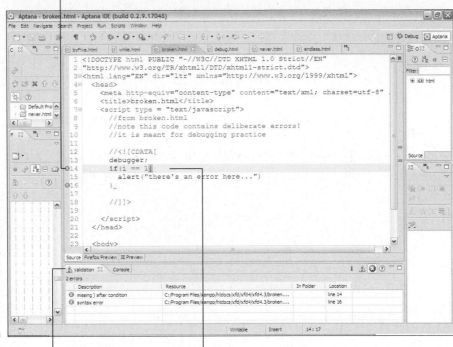

Figure 4-5:
Aptana
caught my
error and
provides
some help.

Click an error to be taken to that line in the editor.

The validation pane lists all known errors.

Aptana notifies you of errors in your code with a few mechanisms:

- ✔ **The suspect code has a red squiggle underneath.** It's just like what a word-processing spell-checker shows you for a suspect word.

- ✔ **A red circle indicates the troublesome line.** You can scan the margin and quickly see where the errors are.

- ✔ **All errors are summarized in the validation pane.** You can see the errors and the line number for each. Double-click an error to be taken to that spot in the code.

- ✔ **You can hover over an error to get more help.** Hover the mouse pointer over an error to get a summary of the error.

Aptana can catch some errors, but it's most useful for *preventing* errors with its automatic indentation and code-assist features. The browsers are where you'll usually discover logic and errors. Some browsers are more helpful than others when it comes to finding and fixing problems.

Debugging JavaScript on IE

Microsoft Internet Explorer has unpredictable behavior when it comes to JavaScript errors. IE6 will take you to some type of editor, but the editors have changed over the years, and are modified (without your knowledge or permission) when you installed new software. IE7 and IE8 (at least by default) simply do nothing. You won't see an error, or any indication there was an error. (Denial — my favorite coping mechanism.)

Here's how you can force IE to give you a little bit of help:

1. Choose Tools⇨Internet Options⇨Advanced.

You'll see a dialog box that looks like Figure 4-6.

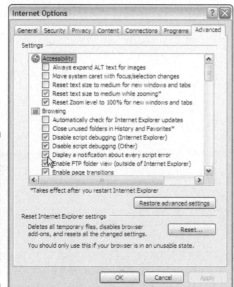

Figure 4-6:
The Internet Options dialog box allows you to get error warnings in Internet Explorer.

2. Choose "Display a Notification about Every Script Error."

Leave all the other settings alone for now. Yep, we're going to keep script debugging disabled, because it doesn't work very well. I'll show you a better technique later in this chapter (see the "Using the Firebug Debugger" section).

Now, when you reload broken.html in IE, you'll see something like Figure 4-7.

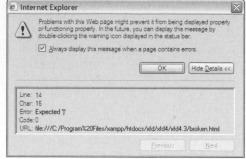

Figure 4-7:
I never
thought I'd
be happy to
see an error
message.

This is actually good news, because at least you know there's a problem, and you've got some kind of clue how to fix it. In this particular case, the error message is pretty useful. Sometimes that's the case, and sometimes the error messages seem to have been written by aliens.

Be sure to have the error notification turned on in IE so you know about errors right away. Of course, you'll also need to check your code in Firefox, which has tons of great tools for checking out your code.

Finding errors in Firefox

Firefox has somewhat better error-handling than IE by default, and you can use add-ons to turn it into a debugging animal. At its default setting, error notification is minimal. If you suspect JavaScript errors, open up the JavaScript Errors window. You can do this by choosing Error Console from the Tools menu, or by typing **javascript:** in the location bar. Figure 4-8 shows the error console after running `broken.html`.

I generally find the error messages in the Firefox console more helpful than the ones provided by IE.

The Error console doesn't automatically clear itself when you load a new page. When you open it up, there might be a bunch of old error messages in there. Be sure to clear the history (with the Error Console's Clear button) and refresh your page to see exactly what errors are happening on this page.

Catching syntax errors with Firebug

One of the best things about Firefox is the add-on architecture. Some really clever people have created very useful add-ons that add wonderful functionality. Firebug is one example. This add-on (available at `https://addons.mozilla.org/en-US/firefox/addon/1843`) tremendously expands your editing bag of tricks.

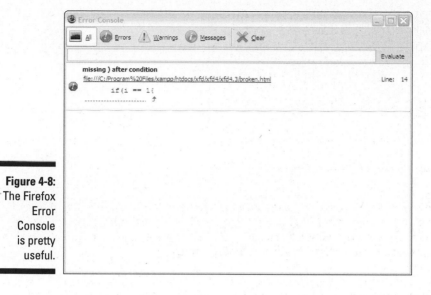

Figure 4-8:
The Firefox
Error
Console
is pretty
useful.

Firebug (first introduced in Chapter 1) is useful for HTML and CSS editing, but it really comes into its own when you're trying to debug JavaScript code.

When Firebug is active, it displays a little icon at the bottom of the browser window. If there are any JavaScript errors, a red error icon will appear. Click this icon, and the Firebug window appears, describing the problem. Figure 4-9 shows how it works.

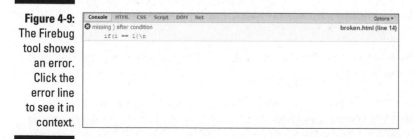

Figure 4-9:
The Firebug
tool shows
an error.
Click the
error line
to see it in
context.

If you click the offending code snippet, you can see it in context. This can be useful, because the error might not be on the indicated line. Generally, if I'm doing any tricky JavaScript, I'll have Firebug turned on to catch any problems.

TIP

The Firebug Lite version of Firebug can be used in other browsers (IE, Chrome, and Safari). This version is accessed as a *bookmarklet*, meaning you can put a link to the code in your bookmarks and use this program to get most of the features of Firebug in these other browsers. Check `http://getfirebug. com/lite.html` for details.

Catching Logic Errors

The dramatic kind of error you see in `broken.html` is actually pretty easy to fix. It crashes the browser at a particular part of the code, so you get a good idea what went wrong. Crashes usually result in error messages, which generally give some kind of clue about what went wrong. Most of the time, it's a problem with syntax. You spelled something wrong, forgot some punctuation, or something else pretty easy to fix once you know what's wrong.

Loops and branches often cause a more sinister kind of problem, called a *logical error* (as opposed to a *syntax error*). Logical errors happen when your code doesn't have any syntax problems, but it's still not doing what you want. These errors can be much harder to pin down, because you don't get as much information.

Of course, if you have the right tools, you can eventually track down even the trickiest bugs. The secret is to see exactly what's going on inside your variables — stuff the user usually doesn't see.

Logging to the console with Firebug

Firebug has another nifty trick: You can send quick messages to the Firebug console. Take a look at `log.html`:

```
<script type = "text/javascript">
  //<![CDATA[
  // from log.html
  // note this program requires firebug on firefox

  for (i = 1; i <= 5; i++){
    console.log(i);
  } // end for loop

  //another loop with a fancier output
  for (i = 1; i <= 5; i++){
    console.log("i is now %d.", i);
  }
```

```
        console.info("This is info");
        console.warn("This is a warning");
        console.error("This is an error");

    //]]>
    </script>
```

This code is special, because it contains several references to the `console` object. This object is only available to Firefox browsers with the Firebug extension installed. When you run the program with Firebug and look at the Console tab, you'll see something like Figure 4-10.

The `console` object allows you to write special messages that will only be seen by the programmer in the console. This is a great way to test your code and see what's going on, especially if things aren't working the way you want.

If you want to test your code in IE, there's a version of Firebug (called Firebug Lite) that works on other browsers. Check the Firebug main page to download and install this tool if you want to use console commands on these browsers. Note that the syntax for using the console might be a bit different when you're using Firebug Lite. Check the main site for details.

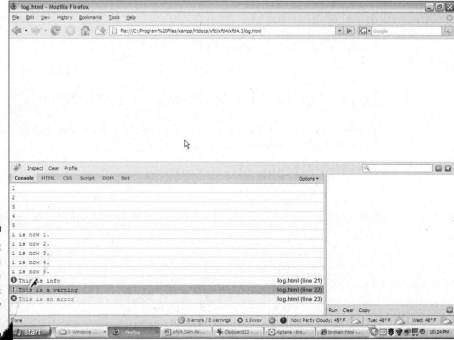

Figure 4-10:
The Firebug console shows lots of new information.

Looking at console output

Here's how it works:

- ✔ **The first loop prints the value of** i **to the console.** Each time through the first loop, the `console.log` function prints out the current value of i. This would be very useful information if (for example) the loop wasn't working correctly. You can use the `console.log()` method to print the value of any variable.

- ✔ **The second loop demonstrates a more elaborate kind of printing.** Sometimes you'll want to make clear exactly what value you're sending to the console. Firebug supports a special syntax called *formatted printing* to simplify this process.

  ```
  console.log("i is now %d.", i);
  ```

  The text string `"i is now %d"` indicates what you want written in the console. The special character `%d` specifies that you will be placing a numeric variable in this position. After the comma, you can indicate the variable you want inserted into the text.

  There are other formatting characters you can use as well. `%s` is for string, and `%o` is for object. If you're familiar with `printf` in C, you'll find this technique familiar.

- ✔ **You can specify more urgent kinds of logging.** If you want, you can use alternatives to the `console.log` if you want to impart more urgency in your messages. If you compare the code in `log.html` with the output of Figure 4-10 you'll see how info, warning, and error messages are formatted.

When your program isn't working properly, try using console commands to describe exactly what's going on with each of your variables. This will often help you see problems and correct them.

When you get your program working properly, don't forget to take the console commands out! Either remove them or render them ineffective with comment characters. The console commands will cause an error in any browser that does not have Firebug installed. Typically, your users will not have this extension (nor should they need it! You've debugged everything for them!).

Using an Interactive Debugger

Traditional programming languages often feature a special debugging tool for fixing especially troubling problems. A typical debugger has th   features:

✔ **The capability to pause a program as it's running:** Logic errors are hard to catch because the program keeps on going. With a debugger, you can set a particular line as a *breakpoint*. When the debugger encounters the breakpoint, the program is in a "pause" mode. It isn't completely running, and it isn't completely stopped.

✔ **A mechanism for moving through the code a line at a time:** You can normally step through code one line at a time checking to see what's going on.

✔ **A way to view the values of all variables and expressions:** It's usually important to know what's happening in your variables. (For example, is a particular variable changing when you think it should?) A debugger should let you look at the values of all its variables.

✔ **The capability to stop runaway processes:** As soon as you start creating loops, you'll find yourself accidentally creating endless loops. In a typical browser, the only way out of an endless loop is to kill the browser with the task manager (or process manager in some operating systems). That's a bit drastic. A debugger can let you stop a runaway loop without having to access the task manager.

Debuggers are extremely handy, and they've been very common in most programming languages. JavaScript programmers haven't had much access to debugging tools in the past, because the technical considerations of an embedded language made this difficult.

Fortunately, Firebug and Aptana both have interactive debuggers that provide all these features. Even better, they work together to provide you lots of useful help.

Aptana has a debugger built in. Originally, this involved a special Firefox plugin that sent information back to Aptana. The developers of Firebug and Aptana are now working together to give Firebug the ability to work directly with Aptana. When you use the Aptana debugger, it works automatically with Firebug.

To test the debuggers, I wrote a program with a deliberate error that would be hard to find without a debugger:

```
//<![CDATA[
//from debug.html
//has a deliberate error

var i = 0;
var j = 0;
while (i <= 10){
  console.log(i);
  j++;
} // end while

//]]>
</script>
```

This is another version of the `endless.html` program from earlier in this chapter. You might be able to see the problem right away. If not, stay tuned; you'll see it as you run the debugger. Even if you can tell what's wrong, follow along so you can learn how to use the debugger when you need it.

I used `console.log()` for output in this program just to avoid jumping back and forth from the browser to the editor to handle dialog boxes.

To step through a program using the Aptana debugger, begin by loading the file into the debugger.

Adding a breakpoint

So far your JavaScript programs have been pretty small, but they're going to get much larger. You usually won't want to start the line-by-line debugging from the beginning, so you need to specify a *breakpoint*. When you run a program in Debug mode, it runs at normal speed until it reaches a breakpoint — and then it pauses so you can control it more immediately.

To set a breakpoint, right-click a line number in the code editor.

Figure 4-11 shows me setting a breakpoint on line 12 of the `debug.html` code.

Running the debugger

The debugger requires you to run your program in a different way than you might be used to. Since your program is normally run by the browser (not Aptana), somehow you need a mechanism for passing information back from the browser to Aptana.

1. **Start the debugger by clicking the Debug icon.**

   It looks like a little bug.

2. **Install the Aptana Firefox plugin automatically.**

   When you debug a JavaScript program for the first time, Aptana asks permission to install an additional Firefox plugin. Click Yes to complete the installation. You will only need to do this once.

3. **Switch to the Debug perspective.**

   Aptana pops up a message box to ask whether you want to switch to the Debug perspective. Answer Yes to change Aptana (temporarily) to Debug configuration.

A breakpoint has been added to line 12.

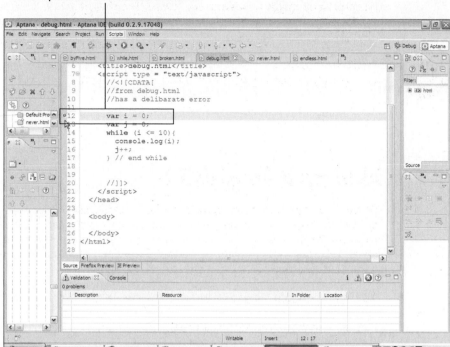

Figure 4-11:
Use a
breakpoint
to tell the
debugger
where to
pause.

Using the Debug perspective

When Aptana is used for debugging, it introduces a new layout (called a *perspective* in Aptana). This changes the way the screen looks, and optimizes the editor for debugging mode. Figure 4-12 shows the debug.html program in Debug perspective.

The Debug perspective changes the editor to emphasize debugging:

✔ **The code completion window is gone.** This feature isn't needed when you're debugging, so it's removed. You need the screen space for other goodies.

✔ **The file management window is also missing.** Likewise, you won't be doing a lot of file manipulation in Debug mode, so this window is gone too. (Don't worry; you'll get it back when you return to normal edit mode.)

The Debug panel   The variables panel

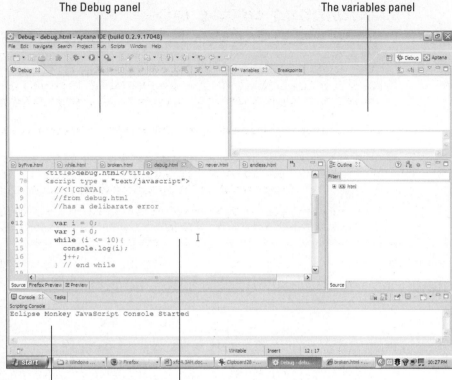

Figure 4-12:
Aptana
looks a little
different
in Debug
perspective.

Results of console commands

The ordinary code window where you can set waypoints.

✔ **You have a new debug window.** This window shows your active threads. The most important thing about it is the buttons along the top.

✔ **You also have a window showing breakpoints and variables.** This powerful new window describes the values of all your variables while the program is running.

✔ **Most of the other windows are the same.** You still have the code window, console, and outline window, but they are rearranged a little differently than normal. Of course you can adjust them if you wish.

Once you've got the debug mode running one time, you'll have a little Debug icon in the upper right of the Aptana interface. When this quick button is available, you can use it to switch into Debug mode. Use the Aptana button to move back to ordinary editing mode.

Examining Debug mode with a paused program

When you run your code through the debugger, Aptana fires up a new instance of Firefox, and loads your program into it. When your program is paused for debugging, you'll see a few new details, shown in Figure 4-13.

When your program is paused, you can see several important new indicators:

- ✔ **The Debug window shows which script is active.** Right now your programs have only one script, but later you'll have more. The thread window tells you which script currently has the processor's attention.

- ✔ **The buttons in the Debug window are active.** Mouse over each of the new buttons to see their tooltips. I explain these buttons in the upcoming section on stepping through your code.

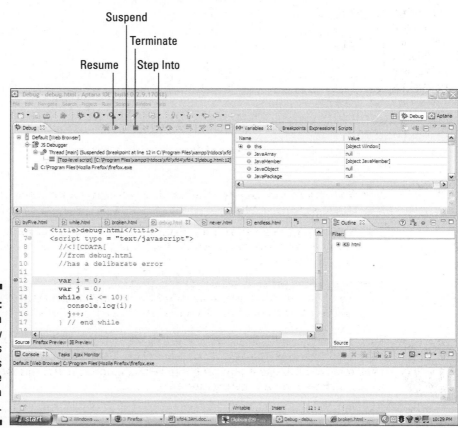

Figure 4-13: You get a few new buttons and tools when you're debugging a program.

✔ **The Breakpoints panel has more panes.** In addition to the breakpoints and variables panes, you'll see some new panes, expressions, and scripts.

✔ **The Variables panel lets you see all the variables the page knows about.** Even though this program contains only two explicitly defined variables, there seems to be a lot more than that. Every JavaScript program has a whole bunch of special variables built in. (I explain how to use this panel later in this chapter.)

✔ **The Breakpoints panel allows you to manage your breakpoints.** This is a good place for you to see all of the breakpoints in your project. You can enable or disable a breakpoint from this panel.

✔ **The Expressions panel allows you to follow particular variables or expressions.** It's an extremely powerful tool. I demonstrate its use later in this chapter.

✔ **The current line of code is highlighted.** If you set a breakpoint on line 12, you'll see that line highlighted. (It might be difficult to see in Figure 4-13.) As you move through the code, you'll see this highlight move. This will help you to follow the logic.

In some versions of Aptana, a message that starts `TypeError: request. loadGroup has no properties` appears sometimes when you are debugging a program. This is not an error in your code, and it doesn't seem to cause any problems. You can safely ignore this error. I've also run across a "socket connection" error once in a while. Normally you can restart Firefox to fix this problem.

Walking through your program

Here's the best part. You can run your program in super slow-mo, seeing every aspect of its behavior.

1. **Take a step.**

   Click on the Step Into button on the Debug panel. (It looks like a curved arrow pointing between two dots, or just use the F5 key.)

2. **Look at the code.**

   The highlighting has moved to the next line (line 13).

3. **Mouse over the variables.**

   Hover your mouse pointer over the two variables (i and j) in your code. You'll see a dialog box that describes the current value of each variable.

4. **Take a few more steps.**

   Use the Step Into button a few more times. Watch as the highlight moves through the program, looping.

5. **Check the variables again.**

   Take another look at the variables after a few times through the loop, and you'll begin to see what's wrong with this code: j is increasing, but i is still stuck at 0.

6. **Stop the debug session.**

   If you think you understand the problem, you can stop the debug session with the red square Terminate button. (You'll need to do that in this program, because it's an endless loop. It will never end on its own.) Aptana will close down the generated Firefox instance.

If the debugger isn't acting properly, be sure you've set a breakpoint. If you don't have a breakpoint, the program won't stop. Also, be sure you've used the Debug button to start the program. Using the Run program or viewing the page directly in the browser won't activate the debugger.

Viewing expression data

The whole point of debugging is to find difficult problems. Usually, these problems are variables that aren't doing what you expect. Aptana provides a Variables tab, which shows the value of all variables in a program, but it's surprisingly difficult to use. JavaScript programs come bundled with hundreds of variables. If you dig around, you can eventually find the i and j variables. (Scroll down in the variables panel to find them.) Every time you take another step, you have to scroll down again to see the values, or mouse over the variables in the code.

Fortunately, Aptana provides a much easier way. Select a variable with the mouse and right-click. In the resulting menu, choose Watch. Figure 4-14 shows the debugger after I've chosen to watch both variables and run through the loop a few times.

In this mode, you can see the exact values of the variables you've chosen to track. When the variable changes value, you can see it happen immediately.

The Expression window has one more cool trick: You can use it to watch complex expressions, not just variables. In this program, you want to know why the loop isn't exiting. Highlight the condition (i <= 10) and add it to the watch expressions just as you did the variables.

Now step through the program watching the variables and the condition. With all this information available to you, my coding mistake becomes obvious: I used the variable i in the condition, but I never changed it inside the loop. Instead, I changed the value of j, which has nothing at all to do with the loop!

Displays the value of any expression or variable

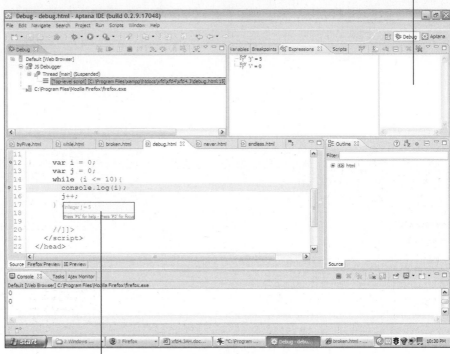

Figure 4-14:
The expressions window highlights the variables I'm interested in.

Hover the mouse over a variable name while the program is paused to see the current value of the variable.

Whenever you encounter a program that isn't doing what you want, fire up the debugger, watch the critical values, and step through the code a line at a time. This will often help you find even the most difficult errors.

Using the Firebug debugger

The Aptana debugger is very good, but I've found it to be a bit cranky. It complains if the version of Firebug isn't exactly right, and sometimes it gives you trouble with other extensions. Fortunately, Firebug has a debugger that's just as good as Aptana (except for one notable limitation). Figure 4-15 shows the Firebug debugger in action.

Add a breakpoint to Firebug's script panel.

Watch panel

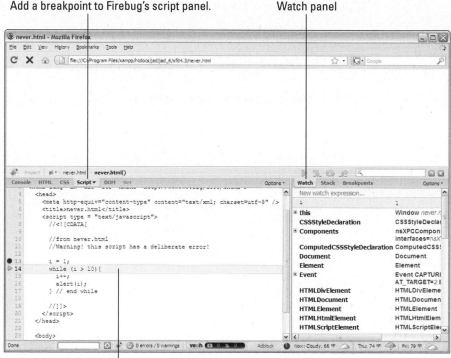

Figure 4-15:
The Firebug
debugger is
very similar
to the one in
Aptana.

The currently running line is highlighted.

Firebug's debugger works in the same general way as the Aptana debugger. Here's how to use it:

1. **Open up the suspect file in Firefox.**

   Of course, you'll need to load up the file before you do so.

2. **Open the Firebug** `<script>` **tag.**

   You might need to enable scripts for local files.

3. **Set a breakpoint.**

   Click the line number where you want the breakpoint to go. A red dot will appear, indicating the breakpoint.

4. **Reload the page.**

   Use the F5 key or reload button to reload the page in debug mode.

5. **Watch the page pause at the breakpoint.**

   As with the Aptana debugger, you're placed in a pause mode with the program resting at the breakpoint.

6. **Use the Step Into and Step Over buttons to move through the code.**

   The Firebug debugger has the same Step Into and Step Over buttons as the Aptana debugger. Use them to walk through your code one line at a time.

7. **Type in a variable name or condition in the watch expression menu.**

   This allows you to track any particular variables or conditions that are giving you trouble.

The Firebug debugger is very easy to use, but it has one significant flaw: It can only be used after a program has loaded into memory. If a program immediately goes into an endless loop (as endless.html in this chapter does), the program never stops executing and you never get access to the debug sessions.

Most JavaScript programs are written in a way that prevents this problem (look at Chapter 6 for information on how to pre-load JavaScript code). However, you might not be able to debug every program you encounter using the Firebug debugger.

Of course, you don't necessarily need a debugger at all. JavaScript debuggers are relatively new, and people have been writing JavaScript without them for years. You can always do it the old-fashioned way: good old alert() statements. If you're not sure what's going on in your code, alert every variable to see its value. Of course, don't forget to remove the alert() statements when you're done.

Chapter 5

Functions, Arrays, and Objects

- -

In This Chapter

▶ Making code manageable with functions

▶ Passing parameters into functions

▶ Returning values from functions

▶ Examining functions and variable scope

▶ Producing basic arrays

▶ Retrieving data from arrays

▶ Building a multi-dimensional array

▶ Creating custom objects with properties and methods

▶ Building object constructors

▶ Building JSON data structures

- -

*I*t doesn't take long for your code to become complex. Soon enough, you'll find yourself wanting to write more sophisticated programs. When things get larger, you need new kinds of organizational structures to handle the added complexity.

You can bundle several lines of code into one container and give this new chunk of code a name. That's called a *function*. You can also take a whole bunch of variables, put them into a container, and give it a name. That's called an *array*.

This chapter shows you how to work with more code and more data — in the form of functions and arrays — without going crazy.

Breaking Code into Functions

It doesn't take long for code to get complicated. It would be good to have some sort of tool for managing the complexity and making code easier to handle. That's exactly what a concept called *functions* does for you.

Inviting ants to the picnic

To explain functions better, think back to an old campfire song. Figure 5-1 re-creates this classic song for you in JavaScript format. (You might want to roast a marshmallow while you view this program.)

Figure 5-1:
Nothing reminds me of functions like a classic campfire song.

If you're unfamiliar with this song, it simply recounts the story of a bunch of ants. The littlest one apparently has some sort of attention issues (but we love him anyway). During each verse, the little one gets distracted by something that rhymes with the verse number. The real song typically has ten verses, but I'm just doing two for the demo.

Thinking about song (and program) structure

Before you look at the code, think about the structure of the song. Like many songs, it has two main parts. The *chorus* is a phrase repeated many times throughout the song. The song has several *verses*, which are similar to each other, but not quite identical.

Think about the song sheet passed around the campfire. (I'm getting hungry for a s'more.) The chorus is usually listed only one time, and each verse is listed. Sometimes you'll have a section somewhere on the song sheet that looks like this:

```
Verse 1
Chorus
Verse 2
Chorus
```

Musicians call this thing a "road map," and that's a great name for it. It's a higher-level view of how you progress through the song. In the road map, you don't worry about the details of the particular verse or chorus. The road map shows the big picture, and you can look at each verse or chorus for the details.

Building the antsFunction.html program

Take a look at the code for `antsFunction.html` and see how it resembles a song sheet:

```
<script type = "text/javascript">
//<![CDATA[
//from antsFunction.html

function chorus() {
  var text = "...and they all go marching down\n";
  text += "to the ground \n";
  text += "to get out \n";
  text += "of the rain. \n";
  text += " \n";
  text += "boom boom boom boom boom boom boom boom
    \n";
  alert(text);
} // end chorus

function verse1(){
  var text = "The ants go marching 1 by 1 hurrah,
    hurrah \n";
  text += "The ants go marching 1 by 1 hurrah,
    hurrah \n";
  text += "The ants go marching 1 by 1 \n";
  text += " The little one stops to suck his thumb
    \n";
  alert(text);
} // end verse1

function verse2(){
  var text = "The ants go marching 2 by 2 hurrah,
    hurrah \n";
  text += "The ants go marching 2 by 2 hurrah,
    hurrah \n";
  text += "The ants go marching 2 by 2 \n";
  text += " The little one stops to tie his shoe
    \n";
  alert(text);
} // end verse1
```

```
        //main code
        verse1();
        chorus();
        verse2();
        chorus();

        //]]>
    </script>
```

The program code breaks the parts of the song into the same pieces a song sheet does. Here are some interesting features of `antsFunction.html`:

- **I created a function called** `chorus()`**.** Functions are simply collections of code lines with a name.

- **All the code for the chorus goes into this function.** Anything I want to do as part of printing out the chorus goes into the `chorus()` function. Later, when I want to print the chorus, I can just call the `chorus()` function and it will execute all the code I stored there.

- **Each verse has a function, too.** I broke the code for each verse into its own function as well.

- **The main code is a road map.** After all the details are delegated to the functions, the main part of the code just controls the order in which the functions are called.

- **Details are hidden in the functions.** The main code handles the big picture. The details (how to print the chorus or verses) are hidden inside the functions.

Functions are a very useful tool for controlling complexity. You can take a large, complicated program and break it into several smaller pieces. Each piece stands alone and solves a specific part of the overall problem.

You can think of each function as a miniature program. You can define variables in functions, put loops and branches in there, and do anything else you can do with a program. A program using functions is basically a program full of subprograms.

When you have your functions defined, they're just like new JavaScript commands. In a sense, when you add functions, you're adding your own new commands to JavaScript.

Passing Data into and out of Functions

Functions are logically separated from the main program. This is a good thing, because this separation prevents certain kinds of errors. Sometimes, however, you want to send information into a function. You might also want a function to return some type of value. The `antsParam.html` page rewrites the "Ants" song in a way that takes advantage of function input and output:

```
<script type = "text/javascript">
//<![CDATA[
//from antsParam.html
```

I'm not providing a figure showing this program because it looks just like `antsFunction.py` to the user. That's one of the advantages of functions: You can improve the underlying behavior of a program without imposing a change in the user's experience. Here's what the code looks like now:

```
function chorus() {
  var text = "...and they all go marching down\n";
  text += "to the ground \n";
  text += "to get out \n";
  text += "of the rain. \n";
  text += " \n";
  text += "boom boom boom boom boom boom boom boom
    \n";
  return text;
} // end chorus

function verse(verseNum){
  var distraction = "";
  if (verseNum == 1){
    distraction = "suck his thumb.";
  } else if (verseNum == 2){
    distraction = "tie his shoe.";
  } else {
    distraction = "I have no idea.";
  }

  var text = "The ants go marching ";
  text += verseNum + " by " + verseNum + " hurrah,
    hurrah \n";
  text += "The ants go marching ";
  text += verseNum + " by " + verseNum + " hurrah,
    hurrah \n";
  text += "The ants go marching ";
  text += verseNum + " by " + verseNum;
  text += " the little one stops to ";
  text += distraction;
  return text;
} // end verse1

//main code
alert(verse(1));
alert(chorus());
alert(verse(2));
alert(chorus());

//]]>
</script>
```

There are a couple of important new ideas in this code (keep in mind that this is just the overview — specifics are coming in the next few sections):

- ✔ **These functions return a value.** The functions don't do their own alert statements any more. Instead, they create a value and return it to the main program.

- ✔ **There's only one verse function.** Because the verses are all pretty similar, it makes sense to have only one verse function. This improved function needs to know what verse it's working on to handle the differences.

Examining the main code

The main code has been changed in one significant way. In the last program, the main code called the functions, which did all the work. This time, the functions don't actually do the output themselves. Instead, they collect information and pass it back to the main program. Inside the main code, each function is treated like a variable.

You've seen this behavior before: The prompt() method returns a value. Now the chorus() and verse() methods also return values. You can do anything you want to this value, including printing it out or comparing it to some other value.

It's often considered a good idea to separate the creation of data from its use as I've done here. That way you have more flexibility. After a function creates some information, you can print it to the screen, store it on a Web page, put it in a database, or whatever.

Looking at the chorus line

The chorus has been changed to return a value. Take another look at the chorus() function to see what I mean:

```
function chorus() {
  var text_ = "...and they all go marching down\n";
  text += "to the ground \n";
  text += "to get out \n";
  text += "of the rain. \n";
  text += " \n";
  text += "boom boom boom boom boom boom boom boom
    \n";
  return text;
} // end chorus
```

Here's what changed:

- ✔ **The purpose of the function has changed.** The function is no longer designed simply to output some value to the screen. Instead, it now provides text to the main program, which can do whatever it wants with the results.

- ✔ **There's a variable called** `text`. This variable will contain all the text to be sent to the main program. (This was true before, but it's even more important now.)

- ✔ **The** `text` **variable is concatenated over several lines.** I used string concatenation to build a complex value. Note the use of newlines (`\n`) to force carriage returns.

- ✔ **The** `return` **statement sends** `text` **back to the main program.** When you want a function to return some value, simply use `return` followed by a value or variable. Note that `return` should be the last line of the function.

Handling the verses

The `verse()` function is quite interesting: To make the verse so versatile (get it? — VERSE-atile!), it must take input from the primary program and return output. It has these features:

- ✔ **It's more flexible than the previous functions.** The same function can be used to produce many different verses.

- ✔ **It takes input to determine which verse to print.** The road map sends a verse number to the function.

- ✔ **It modifies the verse based on the input.** The verse umber is used to determine how the rest of the verse should be created.

- ✔ **It returns a value, just as** `chorus()` **does.** The output of this function is passed back to the main program so it can do something with the newly minted verse.

Passing data to the verse () function

First, notice that the `verse()` function is always called with a value inside the parentheses. For example, the main program says `verse(1)` to call the first verse, and `verse(2)` to invoke the second. The value inside the parentheses is called an *argument*.

The `verse()` function must be designed to accept an argument. Look at the first line and you'll see how I did it:

```
function verse(verseNum){
```

I included a variable name, `verseNum`, in the function definition. Inside the function, this variable is known as a *parameter*. (Don't get hung up on the terminology. People often use the terms "parameter" and "argument" interchangeably.) The important idea is this: Whenever the `verse()` function is called, it automatically has a variable called `verseNum`. Whatever argument you send to the `verse()` function from the main program will become the value of the variable `verseNum` inside the function.

You can define a function with as many parameters as you want. Each parameter gives you the opportunity to send a piece of information to the function.

Determining the distraction

If you know the verse number, you can determine what distracts "the little one" in the song. There are a couple of ways to do this, but a simple `if / else if` structure is sufficient for this example:

```
var distraction = "";
if (verseNum == 1){
  distraction = "suck his thumb.";
} else if (verseNum == 2){
  distraction = "tie his shoe.";
} else {
  distraction = "I have no idea.";
}
```

Here I initialized the variable `distraction` to be empty. If `verseNum` is 1, set `distraction` to "suck his thumb." If `verseNum` is 2, `distraction` should be "tie his shoe". Any other value for `verseNum` is treated as an error by the `else` clause.

If you're an experienced coder, you might be yelling at the program. I know, it still isn't optimal. Later in this chapter, I show an even better solution for handling this particular situation with arrays.

By the time this code segment is complete, there is a legitimate value for both `verseNum` and `distraction`.

Creating the text

After you know these variables (`verseNum` and `distraction`), it's pretty easy to construct the output text:

```
var text = "The ants go marching ";
text += verseNum + " by " + verseNum + " hurrah,
    hurrah \n";
text += "The ants go marching ";
text += verseNum + " by " + verseNum + " hurrah,
    hurrah \n";
text += "The ants go marching ";
text += verseNum + " by " + verseNum;
text += " the little one stops to ";
text += distraction;
return text;
} // end verse1
```

There's a whole lotta concatenatin' going on, but it's essentially the same code as the original `verse()` function. This one's just a lot more flexible, because it can handle any verse. (Well, it can if the function has been pre-loaded to understand how to handle the particular verse number. More on that soon.)

Managing Scope

A function is much like an independent mini-program. Any variable you create inside a function only has meaning inside that function. When the function finishes executing, its variables disappear! This is actually a really good thing. A major program will have hundreds of variables. They can be very difficult to keep track of. It's possible to re-use a variable name without knowing it, or have a value changed inadvertently. When you break your code into functions, each function has its own independent set of variables. You don't have to worry about whether the variables will cause problems elsewhere.

Introducing local and global variables

You can also define variables at the main (script) level. These variables are considered *global* variables. A global variable is available at the main level and inside each function. A *local* variable (one defined inside a function) has meaning only inside the function. The concept of local-versus-global functions is sometimes referred to as *scope*.

Local variables are kind of like local police who have a limited geographical jurisdiction, but are very useful within that space. They know the neighborhood. Sometimes you'll encounter situations that cross local jurisdictions. This is the kind of situation that requires a state trooper or the FBI. Local variables are local cops, and global variables are the FBI.

In general, try to make as many of your variables local as possible. The only time you really need a global variable is when you want some information to be used in multiple functions.

Examining variable scope

To understand the implications of variable scope, take a look at scope. html:

```
<script type = "text/javascript">
//<![CDATA[
//from scope.html
var globalVar = "I'm global!";

function myFunction(){
  var localVar = "I'm local";
  console.log(localVar);
}

myFunction();

//]]>
</script>
```

This program defines two variables. globalVar is defined in the main code, and localVar is defined inside a function. If you run the program in Debug mode while watching the variables, you can see how they behave. Figure 5-2 shows what the program looks like early in the run.

Note that `localVar` doesn't have meaning until the function is called, so it remains undefined until the computer gets to that part of the code. Step ahead a few lines, and you'll see `localVar` has a value, as shown in Figure 5-3.

Be sure to use the Step Into technique for walking through a program rather than Step Over for this example. When Step Over encounters a function, it runs the entire function as one line. If you want to look into the function and see what's happening inside it (as you do here), use Step Into. Please look at Chapter 4 if you need a refresher on using debugging modes.

globalVar has a value, but localVar does not because the program has not yet reached the funtion containing localVar.

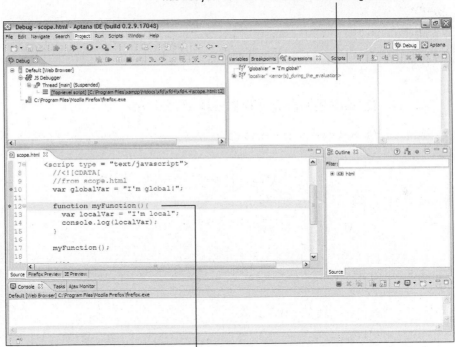

Figure 5-2:
Here globalVar is defined, but localVar is not.

Control has not been passed to the function yet.

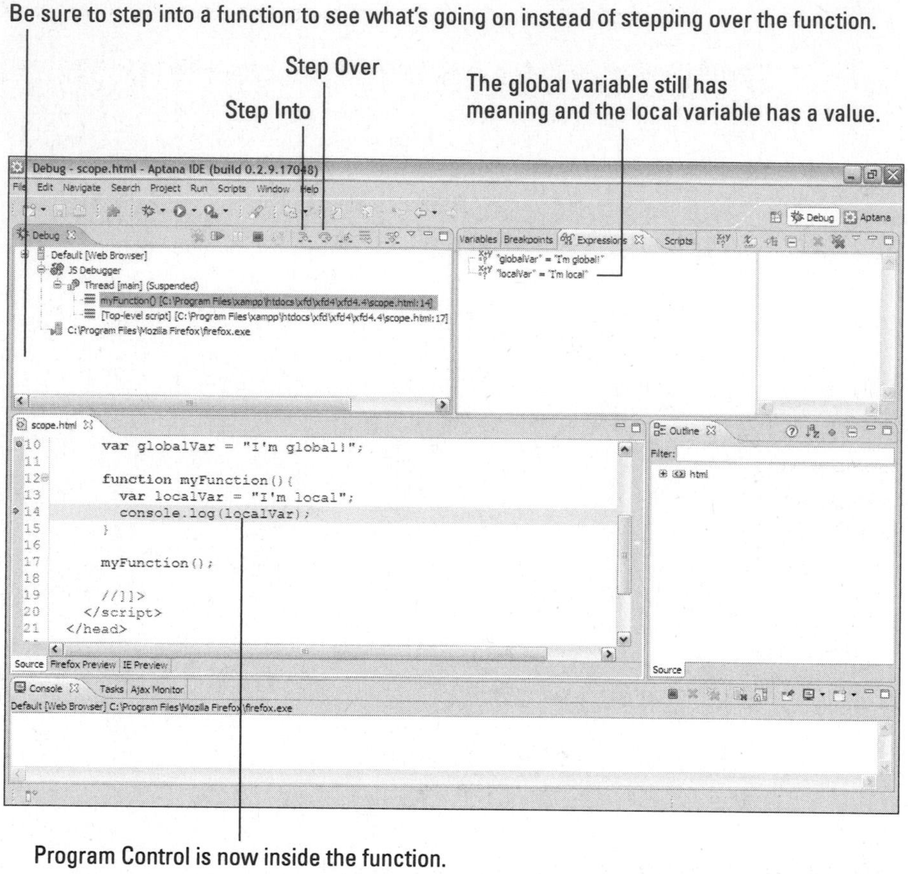

Be sure to step into a function to see what's going on instead of stepping over the function.

Step Over

Step Into

The global variable still has meaning and the local variable has a value.

Figure 5-3:
Behold!
localVar has
a value —
because I'm
inside the
function.

Program Control is now inside the function.

Note that `globalVar` still has a value — and so does `localVar`, because it's inside the function.

If you move down the code a few more steps, you'll find that `localVar` no longer has a value when the function ends. This is illustrated in Figure 5-4.

Variable scope is a good thing because it means you only have to keep track of global variables and the variables defined inside your current function. The other advantage of scope is that you can re-use a variable name. You can have ten different functions all using the same variable name and they won't interfere with each other, because each one is an entirely different variable.

Now the local variable has no meaning because its function is no longer in memory.

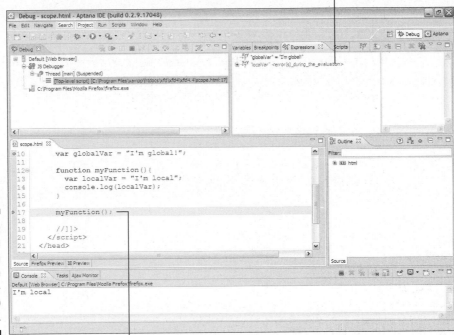

Figure 5-4:
When the function ends, once again local-Var has no meaning.

Control has moved again outside the function.

Building a Basic Array

If a function is a group of code lines with a name, an *array* is similar; it's a group of variables with a name. An array is actually a special kind of variable used to manage complexity. Use an array whenever you want to work with a list of similar data types.

Storing a list of data in an array

The following code shows a basic demonstration of arrays:

```
<script type = "text/javascript">
  //<![CDATA[
  //from genres.html

  //creating an empty array
  var genre = new Array(5);
```

```
        //storing data in the array
        genre[0] = "flight simulation";
        genre[1] = "first-person shooters";
        genre[2] = "driving";
        genre[3] = "action";
        genre[4] = "strategy";

        //returning data from the array
        alert ("I like " + genre[4] + " games.");

        //]]>
    </script>
```

The variable genre is a special variable, because it contains many different values. In essence, it is a list of game genres. The new Array(5) construct creates space in memory for five variables, all named genre.

Accessing array data

After you've specified an array, you can work with the individual elements using square brace syntax. Each element of the array is identified by an integer. The index usually begins with 0:

```
        genre[0] = "flight simulation";
```

This line means: Assign the text value "flight simulation" to the genre array variable at position 0.

Most languages require that all array elements be the same type. JavaScript is very forgiving about this. You can combine all kinds of stuff in a JavaScript array. This can sometimes be very useful, but be aware this trick won't work in all languages. In general, I try to keep all the members of an array the same type. Don't forget that array indices usually start with 0.

After you've got the data stored in the array, you can use the same square-bracket syntax to read the information.

The line

```
        alert ("I like " + genre[4] + " games.");
```

means "find element 4 of the genre array, and include it in an output message."

When genre.html is run, it shows what you see in Figure 5-5.

Figure 5-5:
This data
came from
an array.

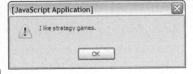

Using arrays with for loops

The main reason to use arrays is for convenience. When you have a lot of information in an array, you can write code to work with the data quickly. Whenever you have an array of data, you commonly want to do something with each element in the array. Take a look at `games.html` to see how this can be done:

```
<script type = "text/javascript">
  //<![CDATA[
  //from games.html

  //pre-loading an array
  var gameList = new Array("Flight Gear",
      "Sauerbraten",
      "Future Pinball", "Racer", "TORCS", "Orbiter",
      "Step Mania", "NetHack",
      "Marathon", "Crimson Fields");

  var text = "";
  for (i = 0; i < gameList.length; i++){
    text += "I love " + gameList[i] + "\n";
  } // end for loop
  alert(text);

  //]]>
</script>
```

This code has some noteworthy things about it:

- ✔ **It features an array called** `gameList`**.** This array contains the names of some of my favorite freeware games.

- ✔ **The array is pre-loaded with values.** If you provide a list of values when creating an array, JavaScript simply pre-loads the array with the values you indicated. It isn't necessary to specify the size of the array if you pre-load it.

- ✔ **A** `for` **loop steps through the array.** Arrays and for loops are natural companions. The `for` loop steps through each element of the array.

✔ **The array's length is used in the** `for` **loop condition.** Rather than specifying the value 10, I used the `length` property of the array in my `for` loop. This is good, because the loop will automatically adjust to the size of the array if I add or remove elements.

✔ **It does something with each element.** Because `i` goes from 0 to 9 (and these are they array indices), I can easily print out each value of the array. In this example, I simply add to an output string.

✔ **Note the newline characters.** The `\n` combination is a special character. It tells JavaScript to add a carriage return (which is like pressing the Enter key).

When `games.html` runs, it looks like Figure 5-6.

If you want to completely ruin your productivity, you might want to Google some of these game names shown in Figure 5-6. They are absolutely incredible, and every one of them is free. It's hard to beat that. (See, even if you don't learn how to program in this book, you get *something* good out of it!)

Figure 5-6:
Now I've
got a list
of games.
Arrays
and loops
are fun!

Visiting the ants one more time

Just when you got that ant song out of your head, take a look at one more variation. This one uses arrays and loops to simplify the code even more!

```
<script type = "text/javascript">
//<![CDATA[
//from antsArray.html

var distractionList = new Array("", "suck his
    thumb", "tie his shoe");

function chorus() {
  var text = "...and they all go marching down\n";
  text += "to the ground \n";
  text += "to get out \n";
  text += "of the rain. \n";
  text += " \n";
```

```
      text += "boom boom boom boom boom boom boom boom
        \n";
      return text;
    } // end chorus

    function verse(verseNum){
      //pull distraction from array
      var distraction = distractionList[verseNum];

      var text = "The ants go marching ";
      text += verseNum + " by " + verseNum + " hurrah,
        hurrah \n";
      text += "The ants go marching ";
      text += verseNum + " by " + verseNum + " hurrah,
        hurrah \n";
      text += "The ants go marching ";
      text += verseNum + " by " + verseNum;
      text += " the little one stops to ";
      text += distraction;
      return text;
    } // end verse1

    //main code is now a loop
    for (verseNum = 1; verseNum < distractionList.
        length; verseNum++){
      alert(verse(verseNum));
      alert(chorus());
    } // end for loop

  //]]>
  </script>
```

This code is just a little different from the `antsParam` program shown earlier.

- ✔ **It has an array called** `distractionList`. This array is (despite the misleading name) a list of distractions. I made the first one (element 0) blank so the verse numbers would line up properly

- ✔ **The** `verse()` **function looks up a distraction.** Because distractions are now in an array, the `verseNum` can be used as an index to loop up a particular distraction. Compare this function to the `verse()` function in `antsParam`. Although arrays require a little more planning than code structures, they can highly improve the readability of your code.

- ✔ **The main program is in a loop.** I step through each element of the `distractionList` array, printing out the appropriate verse and chorus.

- ✔ **The** `chorus()` **function remains unchanged.** There's no need to change `chorus()`.

Working with Two-Dimensional Arrays

Arrays are useful when working with lists of data. Sometimes you'll encounter data that's best imagined in a table. For example, consider if you wanted to build a distance calculator that determines the distance between two cities. The original data might look like Table 5-1.

Table 5-1	Distances between Major Cities			
	0) Indianapolis	*1) New York*	*2) Tokyo*	*3) London*
0) Indianapolis	0	648	6476	4000
1) New York	648	0	6760	3470
2) Tokyo	6476	6760	0	5956
3) London	4000	3470	5956	0

Think about how you would use this table to figure out a distance. If you wanted to travel from New York to London, for example, you'd pick out the New York row and the London column and figure out where they intersect. The data in that cell is the distance (3,470 miles).

When you look up information in any kind of a table you're actually working with a *two-dimensional data structure*. That's a fancy term, but it just means "table." If you want to look something up in a table, you need two indices, one to determine the row, and another to determine the column.

If this is difficult to grasp, think of the old game "Battleship." The playing field is a grid of squares. You announce "I-5" (meaning "column I, row 5") and your opponent looks in that grid to discover that you've sunk his battleship. In programming, typically you use integers for both indices, but otherwise it's exactly the same: Any time you have two-dimensional data, you access it with two indices.

Often we call these indices *row* and *column* to help you think of the structure as a table. Sometimes there are better names that more clearly describe how the behavior works. Take a look at Figure 5-7 and you'll see that the distance.html program asks for two cities and returns a distance according to the data table.

Yep, it's possible to have 3-, 4-, and *n*-dimension arrays in programming, but don't worry about that yet. (It might make your head explode.) Most of the time, 1 or 2 dimensions are all you need.

Figure 5-7:
It's a "Tale
of Two
Cities." You
even get the
distance
between
them!

This program is a touch longer than some of the others, so I break it into parts for easy digestion. Be sure to look at the program in its entirety on either of the companion Web sites: www.dummies.com/go/javascript andajaxfd or www.aharrisbooks.net/jad.

Setting up the arrays

The key to this program is the data organization. The first step is to set up two arrays, and it looks like this:

```
<script type = "text/javascript">
  //<![CDATA[
  //from distance.html

  //cityName has the names of the cities
  cityName = new Array("Indianapolis", "New York",
      "Tokyo", "London");

  //create a 2-dimension array of distances
  distance = new Array (
    new Array (0, 648, 6476, 4000),
    new Array (648, 0, 6760, 3470),
    new Array (6476, 6760, 0, 5956),
    new Array (4000, 3470, 5956, 0)
  );
```

The first array is an ordinary single-dimension array of city names. I've been careful to always keep the cities in the same order, so whenever I refer to city 0, I'm talking about Indianapolis (my home town.) New York is always going to be at position 1, and so on.

In your data design, take care that you always keep things in the same order. Be sure to organize your data on paper before you type it into the computer, so you'll understand what value goes where.

The `cityNames` array has two jobs. First, it reminds me what order all the cities will be in, and secondly, it gives me an easy way to get a city name when I know an index. For example, I know that `cityName[2]` will always be "Tokyo."

The `distance` array is very interesting. If you squint at it a little bit, it looks a lot like Table 5-1. That's because it *is* Table 5-1, just in a slightly different format.

Keep in mind that `distance` is an array. JavaScript arrays can hold just about everything, including other arrays! That's what `distance` does: It holds an array of rows. Each element of the `distance` array is another (unnamed) array holding all the data for that row. If you want to extract information from the array, you need two pieces of information. First you need the row. Then, because the row is an array, you need the column number within that array. So `distance[1][3]` means. "Go to row one (`New York`) of the array named `distance`. Within that row, go to element 3 (`London`) and return the resulting value (`3470`)." Cool, huh?

Getting a city

The program requires that you ask for two cities. You want the user to enter a city number, not a name, and you want to do this twice. This sounds like a good time for a function:

```javascript
function getCity(){
  // presents a list of cities and gets a number
    corresponding
  // to the city name
  var theCity = "";   //will hold the city number

  var cityMenu = "Please choose a city by typing a
    number: \n";
  cityMenu += "0) Indianapolis \n";
  cityMenu += "1) New York \n";
  cityMenu += "2) Tokyo \n";
  cityMenu += "3) London \n";

  theCity = prompt(cityMenu);
  return theCity;
} // end getCity
```

Here the `getCity()` function prints up a little menu of city choices, and asks for some input. It then returns that input.

There's all kinds of ways to improve `getCity()`. For one thing, maybe it should repeat until you get a valid number, so that users can't type in the city name or do something else crazy. I'll leave it simple for now. The next chapter shows you how to use the elements of a user interface to help the user submit only valid input.

Creating a main () function

The `main()` function handles most of the code for the program. Here's what that looks like:

```
function main(){
  var output = "";
  var from = getCity();
  var to = getCity();
  var result = distance[from][to];
  output = "The distance from " + cityName[from];
  output += " to " + cityName[to];
  output += " is " + result + " miles.";
  alert(output);
} // end main

main();
```

In this code, the `main()` function controls traffic. Here's how it works:

1. **Create an output variable.**

   The point of this function is to create some text output describing the distance. I begin by creating a variable called `output` and setting its initial value to empty.

2. **Get the city of origin.**

   Fortunately, you've got a really great function called `getCity()` that handles all the details of getting a city in the right format. Call this function and assign its value to the new variable `from`.

3. **Get the destination city.**

   That `getCity()` function sure is handy. Use it again to get the city number you'll call `to`.

4. **Get the distance.**

   Because you know two indices, and you know they're in the right format, you can simply look them up in the table. Look up `distance[from][to]` and store it in the variable `result`.

5. **Output the response.**

   Use concatenation to build a suitable response string and send it to the user.

6. **Get city names from the** `cityNames` **array.**

   The program uses numeric indices for the cities, but these don't mean anything to the user. Use the `cityNames` array to retrieve the two city names for the output.

7. **Run the** `main()` **function.**

   There's only one line of code that's not in a function. That line calls the `main()` function and starts the whole thing up.

I didn't actually write the program in the order in which I showed it to you. Sometimes it makes more sense to go "inside out" with your programming, and that was the case here: I actually created the data structure first (as an ordinary table on paper) and then constructed the `main()` function. This made it obvious that I needed a `getCity()` function, and gave me some clues about how `getCity` should work (that is, it should present a list of cities and then prompt for a numerical input).

Creating Your Own Objects

So far, you've used a lot of wonderful objects in JavaScript — but that's just the beginning. It turns out you can build your own objects too, and these objects can be very powerful and flexible. Objects typically have two important components: *properties* and *methods*. A *property* is like a variable associated with an object. It describes the object. A *method* is like a function associated with an object. It describes things the object can do.

Functions allow you to put code segments together; arrays allow you to put variables together; objects allow you to put both code segments and variables (and in fact functions and arrays) in the same large construct.

Building a basic object

JavaScript makes it trivially easy to build an object. Because a variable can contain any value, you can simply start treating a variable like an object and it becomes one.

Figure 5-8 shows a critter that has a property.

Figure 5-8:
This alert
box is actu-
ally using an
object.

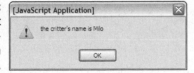

Take a look at the following code:

```
//from basicObject.html
//create the critter
var critter = new Object();

//add some properties
critter.name = "Milo";
critter.age = 5;

//view property values
alert("the critter's name is " + critter.name + ".");
```

The way it works is not difficult to follow:

1. **Create a new object.**

   JavaScript has a built-in object called `Object`. Make a variable with the `new Object()` syntax, and you'll build yourself a shiny new standard object.

2. **Add properties to the object.**

   A property is like a subvariable. It's nothing more than a variable attached to a specific object. When you assign a value to `critter.name`, for example, you're specifying that `critter` has a property called `name` and you're also giving it a starting value.

3. **An object can have any number of properties.**

   Just keep adding properties. This allows you to group a number of variables into one larger object.

4. **Each property can contain any type of data.**

   Unlike arrays — in which it's common for all the elements to contain exactly the same type of data — each property can have a different type.

5. **Use the dot syntax to view or change a property.**

   If the `critter` object has a name property, you can use `critter.name` as a variable. Like other variables, you can change the value by assigning a new value to `city.name` or you can read the content of the property.

If you're used to a stricter object-oriented language like Java, you'll find JavaScript's easy-going attitude quite strange and maybe a bit sloppy. Other languages do have a lot more rules about how objects are made and used, but JavaScript's approach does have its charms. Don't get too tied up in the differences. The way JavaScript handles objects is powerful and refreshing.

Adding methods to an object

Objects have other characteristics besides properties. They can also have *methods*. A method is simply a function attached to an object. To see what I'm talking about, take a look at this example:

```
//create the critter
//from addingMethods.html
var critter = new Object();

//add some properties
critter.name = "Milo";
critter.age = 5;

//create a method
critter.talk = function(){
  msg = "Hi! My name is " + this.name;
  msg += " and I'm " + this.age;
  alert(msg);
}; // end method

// call the talk method
critter.talk();
```

This example extends the `critter` object described in the last section. In addition to properties, the new `critter` has a `talk()` method. If a property describes a characteristic of an object, a method describes something the object can do. Figure 5-9 illustrates the `critter` showing off its `talk()` method.

Figure 5-9:
Now the critter can talk!

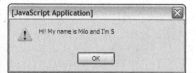

Here's how it works:

1. Build an object with whatever properties you need.

Begin by building an object and giving it some properties.

2. **Define a method much like a property.**

   In fact, methods are properties in JavaScript, but don't worry too much about that — it'll make your head explode.

3. **You can assign a pre-built function to a method.**

   If you've already created a function that you want to use as a method, you can simply assign it.

4. **You can also create an anonymous function.**

   More often, you'll want to create your method right away. You can create a function immediately with the `function(){` syntax.

5. **The `this` keyword refers to the current object.**

   Inside the function, you might want to access the properties of the object. `this.name` refers to the `name` property of the current object.

6. **You can then refer to the method directly.**

   After you've defined an object with a method, you can invoke it. For example, if the `critter` object has a `talk()` method, use `critter.talk()` to invoke this method.

Building a re-usable object

These objects are nice, but what if you want to build several objects with the same definition? JavaScript supports an idea called a *constructor*, which allows you to define an object pattern and re-use it.

Here's an example:

```
//building a constructor
//from constructor.html
function Critter(lName, lAge){
  this.name = lName;
  this.age = lAge;
  this.talk = function(){
    msg = "Hi! My name is " + this.name;
    msg += " and I'm " + this.age;
    alert(msg);
  } // end talk method
} // end Critter class def

function main(){
  //build two critters

  critterA = new Critter("Alpha", 1);
```

```
    critterB = new Critter("Beta", 2);
    critterB.name = "Charlie";
    critterB.age = 3;

    //have 'em talk
    critterA.talk();
    critterB.talk();

} // end main
main();
```

This example involves creating a *class* (a pattern for generating objects) and re-using that definition to build two different critters. First, look over how the class definition works:

1. **Build an ordinary function.**

   JavaScript classes are defined as extensions of a function. The function name will also be the class name. Note that the name of a class function normally begins with an uppercase letter. When a function is used in this way to describe an object, the function is called the object's constructor. The constructor can take parameters if you wish, but it normally does not return any values. In my particular example, I add parameters for name and age.

2. **Use** `this` **to define properties.**

   Add any properties you want, including default values. Note that you'll be able to change those values later if you like. Each property should begin with `this` and a period, so if you want your object to have a `color` property, you'd say something like `this.color = "blue";`. My example uses the local parameters to define the properties. This is a very common practice, because it's an easy way to pre-load important properties.

3. **Use** `this` **to define any methods you want.**

   If you want your object to have methods, define them using the `this` operator followed by the `function(){` keyword. You can add as many functions as you want.

The way JavaScript defines and uses objects is easy but a little nonstandard. Most other languages that support object-oriented programming do it in a different way than the technique described here. Some would argue that JavaScript is not a true OOP language, as it doesn't support a feature called *inheritance*, but instead uses a feature called *prototyping*. The difference isn't all that critical; most uses of OOP in JavaScript are very simple objects like the ones described here or JSON, described later in this chapter. Just appreciate that the introduction to object-oriented programming here is very cursory, but enough to get you started.

Using your shiny new objects

When you've defined a class, you can re-use it. Look again at the main function to see how I use my newly minted `Critter` class:

```
function main(){
  //build two critters

  critterA = new Critter("Alpha", 1);

  critterB = new Critter("Beta", 2);
  critterB.name = "Charlie";
  critterB.age = 3;

  //have 'em talk
  critterA.talk();
  critterB.talk();

} // end main
main();
```

After a class is defined, you can use it as a new data type. This is a very powerful capability. Here's how it works:

1. **Be sure you have access to the class.**

   A class isn't useful unless JavaScript already knows about it. In this example, the class is defined within the code.

2. **Create an instance of the class with the** `new` **keyword.**

   The `new` keyword means you want to make a particular `critter` based on the definition. Normally you'll assign this to a variable. My constructor expects the name and age to be supplied, so it automatically creates a `critter` with the given name and age.

3. **Modify the class properties as you want.**

   You can change the values of any of the class properties. In my example, I change the name and age of the second `critter` just to show how it's done.

4. **Call class methods.**

   Because the `Critter` class has a `talk()` method, you can use it whenever you want a particular `critter` to talk.

Introducing JSON

JavaScript objects and arrays are incredibly flexible. In fact, they are so well-known for their power and ease of use, that a special data format called JSON (JavaScript Object Notation) has now been adopted by many other languages.

JSON is mainly used as a way to store complex data (especially multi-dimension arrays) and pass the data from program to program. JSON is essentially another way of describing complex data in a JavaScript Object format. When you describe data in JSON, you generally do not need a constructor, because the data itself is used to determine the structure of the class.

JSON data is becoming a very important part of Web programming, because it allows an easy mechanism for transporting data between programs and programming languages. Throughout this book (especially in the sections on AJAX and the jQuery library), you'll see JSON used extensively to manage complex data easily.

Storing data in JSON format

To see how JSON works, begin by looking at this simple code fragment:

```
var critter = {
  "name": "George",
  "age": 10
};
```

This code describes a `critter` with two properties, a name and an age. The `critter` looks much like an array, but rather than using a numeric index (as most arrays do), the `critter` has string values to serve as indices. It is, in fact, an object.

You can refer to the individual elements with a variation of array syntax, like this:

```
alert(critter["name"]);
```

You can also use what's called *dot* notation (as used in objects,) like this:

```
alert(critter.age);
```

Both notations work in the same way. Most of the built-in JavaScript objects use the dot notation, but either is acceptable.

The reason JavaScript arrays are so useful is that they are in fact objects. When you create an array in JavaScript, you are building an object with numerical property names. This is why you can use either array or object syntax for managing JSON object properties.

Look at `jsonDistance.html` on my Web site (`www.aharrisbooks.net/jad`) to see the code from this section in action. I don't show a figure here, because all the interesting work happens in the code.

Here's how to store data in JSON notation:

1. **Create the variable.**

   You can use the `var` statement like you do any variable.

2. **Contain the content within braces({ }).**

   This is the same mechanism you use to create a pre-loaded array (as described earlier in this chapter).

3. **Designate a key.**

   For the `critter`, I want the properties to be named `"name"` and `"age"` — that is, with words rather than numeric indices. For each property, I begin with the property name. The key can be a string or an integer.

4. **Follow the key with a colon (`:`).**

   The key is followed by the colon character.

5. **Create the value associated with that key.**

   You can then associate any type of value you want with the key. In this case, I associate the value `"George"` with the key `"name"`.

6. **Separate each name/value pair with a comma (`,`).**

   You can add as many name/value pairs as you want.

If you're familiar with other programming languages, you might think of a JSON structure as being like a hash table or associative array. JavaScript does use JSON structures in the same way these other structures are used, but it isn't quite accurate to say JSON is either a hash *or* an associative array. It's simply an object. (But if you want to think of it as one of those things, I won't tell anybody.)

Building a more complex JSON structure

JSON is convenient because it can be used to handle quite complex data structures. For example, look at the following (oddly familiar) data structure written in JSON format:

```
var distance = {
  "Indianapolis" :
    { "Indianapolis": 0,
      "New York": 648,
      "Tokyo": 6476,
      "London": 4000 },

  "New York" :
    { "Indianapolis": 648,
      "New York": 0,
      "Tokyo": 6760,
      "London": 3470 },

  "Tokyo" :
    { "Indianapolis": 6476,
      "New York": 6760,
      "Tokyo": 0,
      "London": 5956 },

  "London" :
    { "Indianapolis": 4000,
      "New York": 3470,
      "Tokyo": 5956,
      "London": 0 },
};
```

This data structure is another way of representing the distance data used to describe two-dimension arrays. This is another two-dimension array, but it is a little different than the one previously described.

- distance **is a JSON object.** The entire data structure is stored in a single variable. This variable is a JSON object with name/value pairs.

- **The** distance **object has four keys.** These correspond to the four rows of the original chart.

- **The keys are actual city names.** The original 2D array used numeric indices, which are convenient but a bit artificial. In the JSON structure, the indices are the actual city names.

- **The value of each entry is another JSON object.** The value of a JSON element can be anything, including another JSON object. Very complex relationships can be summarized in a single variable.

- **Each row is summarized as a JSON object.** For example, the value associated with "Indianapolis" is a list of distances from Indianapolis to the various cities.

- **The entire declaration is one "line" of code.** Although placed on several lines in the editor (for clarity), the entire definition is really just one line of code.

Setting up the data in this way seems a bit tedious, but it's very easy to work with. The city names are used directly to extract data, so you can find the distance between two cities with array-like syntax:

```
alert(distance["Indianapolis"]["London"]);
```

If you prefer, you can use the dot syntax:

```
alert(distance.Indianapolis.Tokyo);
```

You can even go with some kind of hybrid:

```
alert(distance["London"].Tokyo);
```

JSON has a number of important advantages as a data format:

- ✔ **It is self-documenting.** Even if you see the data structure on its own without any code around it, you can tell what it means.

- ✔ **The use of strings as indices makes the code more readable.** It's much easier to understand `distance["Indianapolis"]["London"]` than to decipher `distance[0][3]`.

- ✔ **JSON data can be stored and transported as text.** This turns out to have profound implications for Web programming, especially in AJAX (the techniques described elsewhere in this book).

- ✔ **JSON can describe complex relationships.** The example shown here is a simple two-dimension array, but the JSON format can be used to describe much more complex relationships — including complete databases.

- ✔ **Many languages support JSON format.** Many Web languages now offer direct support for JSON. The most important of these is PHP, which is very frequently used with JavaScript in AJAX applications.

- ✔ **JSON is more compact than XML.** Another data format called XML is frequently used to transmit complex data. However, JSON is more compact and less "wordy" than XML.

- ✔ **JavaScript can read JSON natively**. Some kinds of must be translated before they can be used. As soon as your JavaScript program has access to JSON data, it can be used directly.

You might wonder whether you can embed methods in JSON objects. The answer is yes, but this isn't usually done when you're using JSON to transport information. In Part III of this book about AJAX, you'll see that methods are often added to JSON objects to serve as *callback functions*, but that usage won't make sense until you get more familiar with events. To get a start on that, flip to Chapter 14.

Part II
Using JavaScript to Enhance Your Pages

The 5th Wave   By Rich Tennant

"Evidently he died of natural causes following a marathon session animating everything on his personal Web site. And no, Morganstern — the irony isn't lost on me."

In this part . . .

JavaScript was developed as a language for manipulating Web pages. Use this part to learn how JavaScript interacts directly with the Web page.

Chapter 6 describes the powerful Document Object Model, and how this mechanism lets your JavaScript programs interact with the Web page. You'll learn how to listen for button events, and how to change parts of the page on the fly.

Chapter 7 describes ways to get more reliable input. First you learn how to use specialized user interface elements like list boxes and radio buttons. Secondly, you learn how to use regular expressions to ensure the value of text fields is in the correct format.

Chapter 8 teaches how to animate your page. You learn how to move page elements around on the page under user or program control. You learn how to animate elements and how to pre-load images for more efficient animation. You also learn how to read the keyboard and mouse.

Chapter 6

Talking to the Page

In This Chapter

▶ Introducing the Document Object Model

▶ Responding to form events

▶ Connecting a button to a function

▶ Retrieving data from text fields

▶ Changing text in text fields

▶ Sending data to the page

▶ Working with other text-related form elements

▶ Viewing the source of dynamically generated code

*J*avaScript is fun and all, but it lives in Web browsers for a reason: to let you change Web pages. The best thing about JavaScript is how it helps you control the page. You can use JavaScript to read useful information from the user and to change the page on the fly.

Understanding the Document Object Model

JavaScript programs usually live in the context of a Web page. The contents of the page are available to the JavaScript programs through a mechanism called the *Document Object Model (DOM)*.

The DOM is a special set of complex variables that encapsulate the entire contents of the Web page. You can use JavaScript to read from the DOM and determine the status of an element. You can also modify a DOM variable and change the page from within JavaScript code.

Navigating the DOM

The easiest way to get a feel for the DOM is to load up a page in Firefox and look at the Firebug window's DOM tab. I do just that in Figure 6-1. In order to see what's happening with the DOM, I'm using the Firebug extension. Check back to Chapter 1 if you need a refresher on using Firebug. Note also that some versions of Firebug (especially on the Mac) are slightly different, but the general idea is the same.

When you look over the DOM of a very simple page, it's easy to get overwhelmed. You'll see a lot of variables listed. Technically, these are all elements of a special object called `window`. The `window` object has a huge number of subobjects, all listed in the DOM view. Table 6-1 describes a few important `window` variables.

Table 6-1	Primary DOM Objects	
Variable	*Description*	*Notes*
`document`	Represents XHTML page	Most commonly scripted element.
`location`	Describes current URL	Change location.href to move to a new page.
`history`	A list of recently visited pages	Access this to view previous pages.
`status`	The browser status bar	Change this to set a message in the status bar.

Changing DOM properties with Firebug

To illustrate the power of the DOM, try this experiment in Firefox:

1. **Load any page.**

   It doesn't matter what page you work with. I'll use `simple.html`, a very basic page with only an `<h1>` header.

2. **Enable the Firebug extension.**

   You can play with the DOM in many ways, but the Firebug extension is one of the easiest and most powerful tools for experimentation.

3. **Enable the DOM tab.**

   This shows you a list of all the top-level variables.

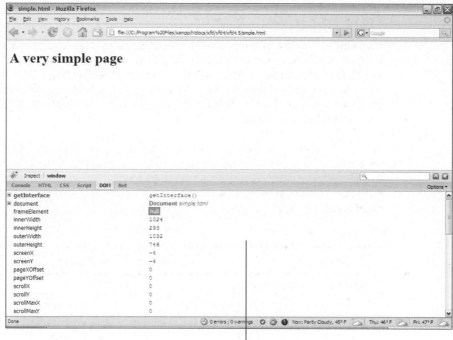

Figure 6-1:
Even a
simple page
has a com-
plex DOM.

You can view the DOM and interact with it in real time.

4. **Scroll down until you see the** `status` **element.**

   When you find the `status` element, double-click it.

5. **Type in a message to yourself.**

   In a dialog box that appears, type something in and press Enter.

6. **Look at the bottom of the browser.**

   The status bar at the bottom of the browser window should now contain your message!

7. **Experiment on your own.**

   Play around with the various elements in the DOM list. Many of them can be modified. Try changing `window.location.href` to any URL and watch what happens. (Don't worry — you can't permanently break anything here.)

This DOM experiment doesn't always work. You might have extensions that block the DOM, or it might not do exactly what you want. If this experiment does not work, just move on. You'll never really do it this way again. Once you learn how easy it is to manipulate the DOM through code, that's the only way you'll want to do it.

Examining the document object

If the window object is powerful, its offspring — the document object — is even more amazing.

Once again, the best way to get a feel for this thing is to do some exploring:

1. **Reload** simple.html **again.**

   If your previous experiments caused things to get really weird, you might have to restart Firefox. Be sure the Firebug extension is showing the DOM tab.

2. **Find the** document **object.**

   This is usually early in the window list. When you select document, it expands, showing a huge number of child elements.

3. **Look for the** document.body.

   Somewhere in the document you'll see the body. Select this to see what you discover.

4. **Find the** document.body.style.

   The document object has a body object, and the body object has a style subobject. Will it never end?

5. **Look through the style elements.**

   Some of the styles will be unfamiliar, but keep going and you'll see some old friends.

6. **Double-click** backgroundColor.

   Each CSS style attribute has a matching (but not quite identical) counterpart in the DOM. Wow. Type a new color (using a color name or hex color) and see what happens.

7. **Marvel at your cleverness.**

   You can navigate the DOM to make all kinds of changes in the page. If you can manipulate something here, you can write code to do it to.

If you're lost here, Figure 6-2 shows me modifying the backgroundColor of the style of the body of the document (on a wing on a bird on a branch on a tree in a hole in the ground). A figure can't really do this process justice, though. You have to experiment for yourself. But don't be overwhelmed. You don't really need to master the details of exactly how the Firebug DOM stuff works. Just know it's there, because it's the foundation of all the cool stuff you do next.

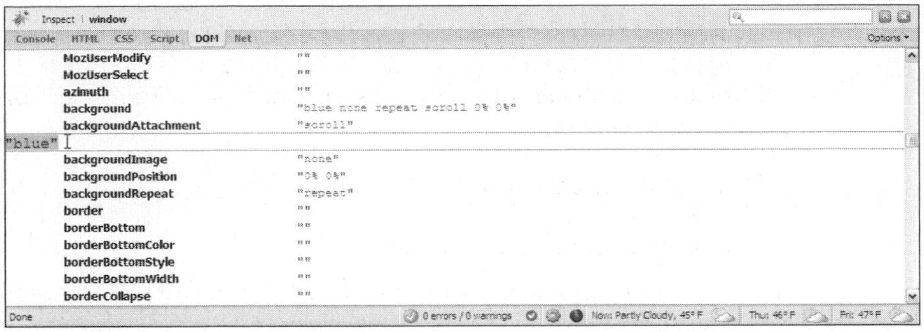

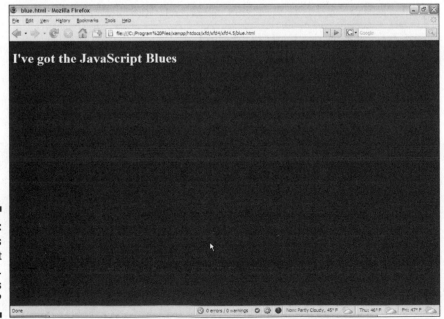

Figure 6-2:
Firebug lets
me modify
the DOM
of my page
directly.

Harnessing the DOM through JavaScript

Sure, using Firebug to trick out your Web page is geeky and all, but why
should you care? The whole purpose of the DOM is to provide JavaScript
magical access to all the inner workings of your page.

Getting the blues, JavaScript-style

It all gets to be fun when you start to write JavaScript code to access the
DOM. Take a look at `blue.html` in Figure 6-3.

Figure 6-3:
This page is
blue (trust
me, it is).
But where's
the CSS?

I've got the JavaScript Blues

Shouldn't it be "background-color?"

If you've dug through the DOM-style elements, you'll notice some interesting things. For openers, many of the element names are familiar but not quite identical: `background-color` becomes `backgroundColor` and `font-weight` becomes `fontWeight`. CSS uses dashes to indicate word breaks, and the DOM combines words and uses capitalization for clarity. You'll find all your old favorite CSS elements, but the names change according to this very predictable formula. Still, if you're ever confused, just use the Firebug DOM inspector to look over various style elements.

The page has white text on a blue background, but there's no CSS! Instead, it has a small script that changes the DOM directly, controlling the page colors through code. The script looks like this:

```
<!DOCTYPE html PUBLIC "-//W3C//DTD XHTML 1.0 Strict//EN"
"http://www.w3.org/TR/xhtml1/DTD/xhtml1-strict.dtd">
<html lang="EN" dir="ltr" xmlns="http://www.w3.org/1999/
          xhtml">
  <head>
    <meta http-equiv=»content-type» content=»text/xml;
          charset=utf-8» />
    <title>blue.html</title>

  </head>

  <body>
    <h1>I've got the JavaScript Blues</h1>
    <script type = «text/javascript»>
      //<![CDATA[

      // use javascript to set the colors
      document.body.style.color = «white»;
      document.body.style.backgroundColor = «blue»;

      //]]>
    </script>
  </body>
</html>
```

In the first few chapters of this book I concentrated on JavaScript without worrying at all about the HTML. The HTML code in those programs was unimportant, so I didn't include it in the code listings. This chapter is about how to integrate code with HTML, so now I incorporate the HTML as well as the

JavaScript segments. Sometimes I still print out code in separate blocks, so (as always) try to look at the code in its natural habitat, on either of the companion Web sites (www.aharrisbooks.net/jad or www.dummies.com/go/javascriptandajaxfd) through your browser.

Writing JavaScript code to change colors

The page is pretty simple, but it has a few new features:

- **It has no CSS.** A form of CSS will be dynamically created through the code.

- **The script is in the body.** I can't place this particular script in the header, because it refers to the body.

  When the browser first sees the script, there must be a body for the text to change. If I put the script in the head, there is no body yet when the browser reads the code, so it gets confused. If I place the script in the body, then there *is* a body, so the script can change it. (It's really okay if you don't get this nuance at first. This is probably the only time you'll see this particular trick, because I'll show a better way in the next example.)

- **Use a DOM reference to change the style colors.** That long "trail of breadcrumbs" syntax takes you all the way from the document through the body to the style and finally to the color. It's tedious but thorough.

- **Set the foreground color to white.** You can change the color property to any valid CSS color value (a color name or a hex value). It's just like CSS, because you *are* affecting the CSS.

- **Set the background color to blue.** Again, this is just like setting CSS.

Managing Button Events

Of course, there's no good reason to write code such as blue.html. It's just as easy to build CSS as it is to write JavaScript. The advantage comes when you use the DOM dynamically to change the page's behavior after it has finished loading.

Figure 6-4 shows a page called "backgroundColors.html".

The page is set up with the default white background color. It has two buttons on it, which should change the body's background color. Click the blue button, and you'll see that it works, as verified in Figure 6-5.

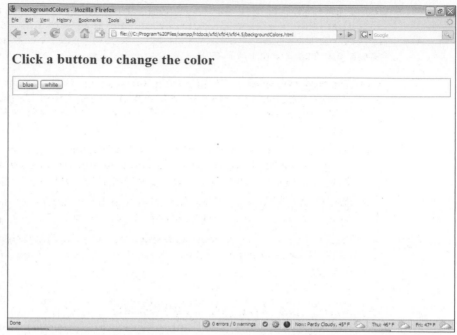

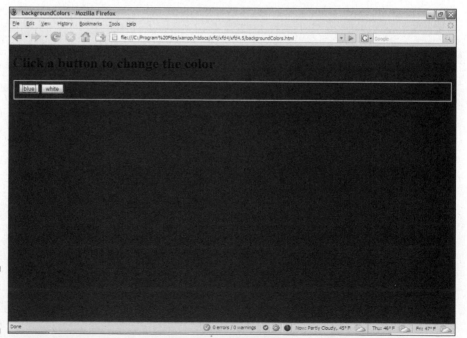

Again, the color change isn't very convincing in a black-and-white book. You should be able to tell from the figures that the color did indeed change, but look on the Web site for real color-changing action. Some really exciting things just happened:

- ✔ **The page has a form.** If you need a refresher on form elements, please check out Bonus Chapter 1 on either of the companion Web sites (www. dummies.com/go/javascriptandajaxfd or www.aharrisbooks. net/jad).

- ✔ **The button does something.** Plain old XHTML forms don't really do anything; you've got to write some kind of programming code to accomplish that. This program does something before your eyes.

- ✔ **There's a** setColor() **function.** The page has a function that takes a color name and applies it to the background style.

- ✔ **Both buttons pass information to the** setColor() **function.** The color name will be passed as a parameter to the setColor() function.

Setting up the playground

That's an overview. Take a closer look at the code:

```
<!DOCTYPE html PUBLIC "-//W3C//DTD XHTML 1.0 Strict//EN"
"http://www.w3.org/TR/xhtml1/DTD/xhtml1-strict.dtd">
<html lang=»EN» dir=»ltr» xmlns=»http://www.w3.org/1999/
        xhtml»>
  <head>
    <meta http-equiv="content-type" content="text/xml;
        charset=utf-8" />
    <title>backgroundColors</title>
    <script type = "text/javascript">
      //<![CDATA[
      // from backgroundColors

      function changeColor(color){
        document.body.style.backgroundColor = color;
      } // end changeColor

      //]]>
    </script>
  </head>
```

```
<body>
  <h1>Click a button to change the color</h1>
  <form action = "">
    <fieldset>
      <input type = "button"
             value = "blue"
             onclick = "changeColor('blue')"/>

      <input type = "button"
             value = "white"
             onclick = "changeColor('white')" />
    </fieldset>

  </form>
</body>
</html>
```

Most Web pages actually treat the XHTML page as the user interface and the JavaScript as the event-manipulation code that goes underneath. It makes sense, then, to look at the HTML code that acts as the playground first.

- ✔ **It contains a form.** Note that the form's `action` attribute is still empty. You won't mess with that until you work with the server in Chapter 14.

- ✔ **The form has a** `fieldset`. The input elements need to be inside something, and a `fieldset` seems like a pretty natural choice.

- ✔ **The page has two buttons.** The two buttons on the page are nothing new, but they've never done anything before.

- ✔ **The buttons both have** `onclick` **attributes.** This special attribute can accept one line of JavaScript code. Usually that line calls a function, as I have done in this program.

- ✔ **Each button calls the same function, but with a different parameter.** Both buttons call `changeColor()`, but one sends the value `"blue"` and the other `"white"`.

- ✔ **Presumably,** `changeColor` **will change a color.** That's exactly what it will do. In fact, it will change the background color.

Generally I write the XHTML code first before the script. As you can see, the form provides all kinds of useful information that will help me make the script. Specifically, it's clear that I need to write a function called `change-Color()`, this function should take a color name as a parameter, and should change the background to the indicated color. With that kind of information established, the function is half-written!

Embedding quotes within quotes

Take a careful look at the `onclick` lines. There's one important issue you might not have noticed: `onclick` is an XHTML parameter, and its value must be encased in quotes. The parameter happens to be a function call that sends a string value. String values must also be in quotes. This could be very confusing if you used double quotes everywhere, because the browser has no way to know the quotes are nested. If your code looks like this . . .

```
onclick = "changeColor("white")" />
```

. . . then XHTML will think the `onclick` parameter contains the value `"changeColor)"` and it will have no idea what `white")"` is.

Fortunately, JavaScript has an easy fix for this problem: If you want to embed a quote inside another quote, just switch to single quotes. The line is written with the parameter inside single quotes:

```
onclick = "changeColor('white')" />
```

Writing the changeColor function

The `changeColor()` function is pretty easy to write. Voilá . . .

```
<script type = «text/javascript»>
//<![CDATA[
// from backgroundColors

function changeColor(color){
  document.body.style.backgroundColor = color;
} // end changeColor

//]]>
</script>
```

It goes in the header area as normal. It's simply a function accepting one parameter called `color`. The body's `backgroundColor` property is set to `color`.

This time I can write JavaScript in the header that refers to the body because the header code is all in a function. The function is *read* before the body is in place, but it isn't *activated* until the user clicks the button. By this time, there's a body — and there's no problem.

Interacting with Text Input and Output

Perhaps the most intriguing application of the DOM is the ability to let the user communicate with the program through the Web page, without all those annoying dialog boxes. Figure 6-6 shows a page with a Web form containing two text boxes and a button.

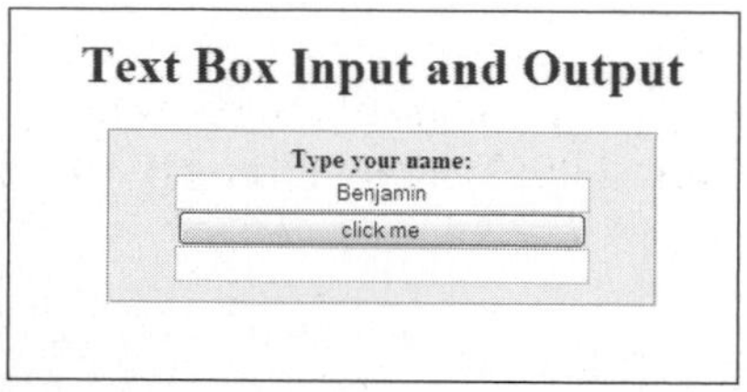

Figure 6-6:
I've typed a
name into
the top
text box.

Text Box Input and Output

Type your name:
Benjamin
click me

When you click the button, something exciting happens, as demonstrated by Figure 6-7.

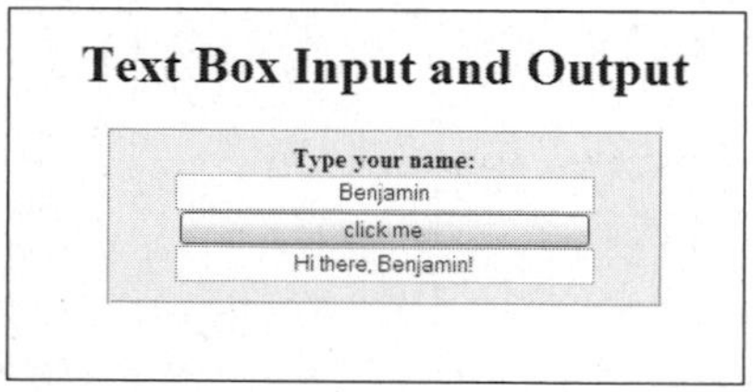

Figure 6-7:
I got a
greeting!
With no
alert box!

Text Box Input and Output

Type your name:
Benjamin
click me
Hi there, Benjamin!

Clearly, form-based input and output are preferable to the constant interruption of dialog boxes.

Introducing event-driven programming

Graphic user interfaces usually use a technique called *event-driven programming.* The idea is simple:

1. **Create a user interface.**

   In Web pages, the user interface is usually built of XHTML and CSS.

2. **Identify events the program should respond to.**

   If you have a button, users will click it. (If you want to guarantee they click it, put the text "launch the missiles" on the button. I don't know why, but it always works.) Buttons almost always have events. Some other elements do, too.

3. **Write a function to respond to each event.**

   For each event you want to test, write a function that does whatever needs to happen.

4. **Get information from form elements.**

   Now you are accessing the contents of form elements to get information from the user. You'll need a mechanism for getting information from a text field and other form elements.

5. **Use form elements for output.**

   For this simple example, I also use form elements for output. The output goes in a second text box, even though I don't intend for the user to type any text there.

Creating the XHTML form

The first step is to create the XHTML framework. Here's the XHTML code:

```
<title>textBoxes.html</title>

<link rel = "stylesheet"
      type = "text/css"
      href = "textBoxes.css" />

</head>

<body>
  <h1>Text Box Input and Output</h1>
  <form action = "">
    <fieldset>
      <label>Type your name: </label>
      <input type = "text"
             id = "txtName" />

      <input type = "button"
             value = "click me"
             onclick = "sayHi()"/>

      <input type = "text"
             id = "txtOutput" />
    </fieldset>
  </form>

</body>
</html>
```

As you look over the code, note a few important ideas:

✔ **The page uses external CSS.** The CSS style is nice, but it's not important in the discussion here. It stays safely encapsulated in its own file. Of course, you're welcome to look it over or change it.

✔ **Most of the page is a form.** All form elements must be inside a form.

✔ **A `fieldset` is used to contain form elements.** `input` elements need to be inside some sort of block-level element, and a `fieldset` is a natural choice.

✔ **There's a text field named** `txtName`. This text field will contain the name. I begin with the phrase `txt` to remind myself that this is a text box.

✔ **The second element is a button.** It isn't necessary to give the button an ID (as it won't be referred to in code), but it does have an `onclick()` event.

✔ **The button's** `onclick()` **event refers to a (yet undefined) function.** The `onclick()` event is named `"sayHi()"`.

✔ **A second text box will contain the greeting.** This second text box is called `txtOutput` because it's the text field meant for output.

After you've set up the HTML page, the function becomes pretty easy to write, because you've already identified all the major constructs. You know you'll need a function called `sayHi()`, and this function will read text from the `txtName` field and write to the `txtOutput` field.

Using getElementById() to get access to the page

XHTML is one thing, and JavaScript is another. You need some way to turn an HTML form element into something JavaScript can read. The magical `getElementById()` method does exactly that. First, look at the first two lines of the `sayHi()` function (defined in the header as usual):

```
function sayHi(){
  var txtName = document.getElementById("txtName");
  var txtOutput = document.
    getElementById("txtOutput");
```

Every element created in your Web page can be extracted by digging through the DOM. In the old days, this is how we used to access form elements. It was ugly and tedious. Modern browsers have the wonderful `getElementById()` function instead. This beauty searches through the DOM and returns a reference to an object with the requested ID.

A *reference* is simply an indicator where the specified object is in memory. You can store a reference in a variable. Manipulating this variable manipulates the object it represents. If you want, you can think of it as making the text box into a variable.

Note that I call the variable `txtName`, so its name is just like that of the original text box. This variable refers to the text field from the form, not the value of that text field. When I have a reference to the text field object, I can use its methods and properties to extract data from it and send new values to it.

Manipulating the text fields

When you have access to the text fields, you can manipulate the values of these fields with the `value` property:

```
var name = txtName.value;
txtOutput.value = "Hi there, " + name + "!"
```

Text fields (and in fact all input fields) have a `value` property. You can read this value as an ordinary string variable. You can also write to this property, and the text field will be updated on the fly.

This code, created by the following steps, handles the data input and output:

1. **Create a variable for the name.**

   This is an ordinary string variable.

2. **Copy the value of the text box into the variable.**

   Now that you have a variable representing the text box, you can access its `value` property to get the value typed in by the user.

3. **Create a message for the user using ordinary string concatenation.**

4. **Send the message to the output text box.**

   You can also write text to the `value` property, which will change the contents of the text field on the screen.

Text fields always return string values (just as prompts do). If you want to pull a numeric value from a text field, you might have to convert it with the `parseInt()` or `parseFloat()` functions.

Writing to the Document

Form elements are great for getting input from the user, but they are not ideal for output. It really doesn't make much sense for the output to be placed in an editable field. It would be much better to actually change the Web document.

The DOM supports exactly such a technique. Most XHTML elements feature an `innerHTML` property. This property describes the HTML code inside the element. In most cases, it can be read from and written to.

So what are the exceptions? Single-element tags (like `<img>` and `<input>`) don't contain any HTML, so obviously it doesn't make sense to read or change their inner HTML. Table elements can often be read from but not changed directly.

Figure 6-8 shows a program with a basic form.

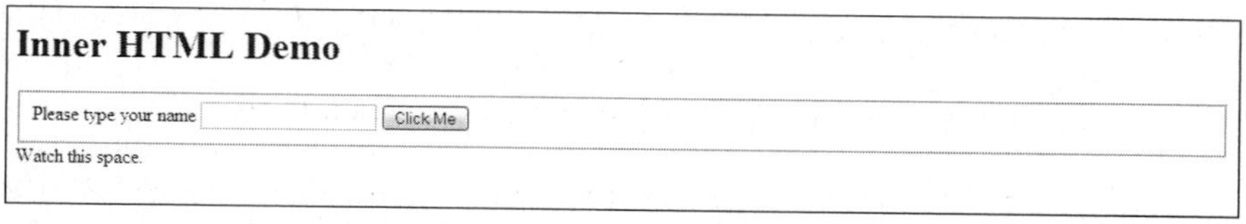

Figure 6-8:
Wait —
there's no
output text
field!

> **Inner HTML Demo**
>
> Please type your name [   ] [Click Me]
> Watch this space.

This form doesn't have a form element for the output. Enter a name and click the button, and you'll see the results in Figure 6-9.

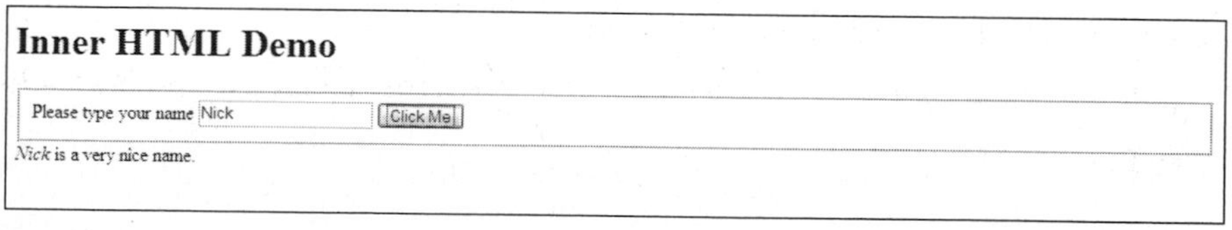

Figure 6-9:
The
page has
changed
itself.

> **Inner HTML Demo**
>
> Please type your name [Nick   ] [Click Me]
> *Nick* is a very nice name.

Amazingly enough, this page can make changes to itself dynamically. It isn't simply changing the values of form fields, but changing the HTML.

Preparing the HTML framework

To see how this is done, begin by looking at the XHTML body for
innerHTML.html:

```
<body>
  <h1>Inner HTML Demo</h1>
  <form action = "">
    <fieldset>
      <label>Please type your name</label>
      <input type = "text"
             id = "txtName" />
      <button type = "button"
              onclick = "sayHi()">
        Click Me
      </button>
    </fieldset>
  </form>

  <div id = "divOutput">
    Watch this space.
  </div>
</body>
```

The code body has a couple of interesting features:

- **The program has a form.** The form is pretty standard. It has a text field for input and a button, but no output elements.

- **The button will call a** sayHi() **function.** The page will require a function with this name. Presumably it will say hi somehow.

- **There's a** div **for output.** A div element in the main body is designated for output.

- **The** div **has an ID.** The id attribute is often used for CSS styling, but it can also be used by the DOM.

Any HTML elements that will be dynamically scripted should have an id field.

Writing the JavaScript

The JavaScript code for modifying inner HTML is pretty easy:

```
<script type = "text/javascript">
  //<![CDATA[
  //from innerHTML.html
```

```
function sayHi(){
  txtName = document.getElementById("txtName");
  divOutput = document.getElementById("divOutput");

  name = txtName.value;

  divOutput.innerHTML = "<em>" + name +  "<\/em>";
  divOutput.innerHTML += " is a very nice name.";
}
//]]>
</script>
```

The first step (as usual with Web forms) is to extract data from the input elements. Note that I can create a variable representation of any DOM element, not just form elements. The `divOutput` variable is a JavaScript representation of the DOM `div` element.

Finding your innerHTML

As with `form` elements, `div`s have other interesting properties you can modify. The `innerHTML` property allows you to change the HTML code displayed by the `div`. You can put any valid XHTML code you wish inside the `innerHTML` property, even HTML tags. Be sure that you still follow the XHTML rules so your code will be valid.

Even with the CDATA element in place, validators get confused by forward slashes (like the one in the `</em>` tag). Whenever you want to use a / character in JavaScript strings, precede it with a backslash (`<\/em>`). Doing so helps the validator understand that you intend to place a slash character at the next position.

Working with Other Text Elements

When you know how to work with text fields, you've mastered about half of the form elements. Several other form elements work exactly like text fields, including these:

- ✔ **Password fields:** Recall that a password field obscures the user's input with asterisks, but it preserves the text.

- ✔ **Hidden fields:** These allow you to store information in a page without revealing it to the user. (They're used a little bit in client-side coding, but almost never in JavaScript.)

- ✔ **Text areas:** These are multi-line text boxes. They can be sized to handle multiple lines of input.

Figure 6-10 is a page with all these elements available on the same form.

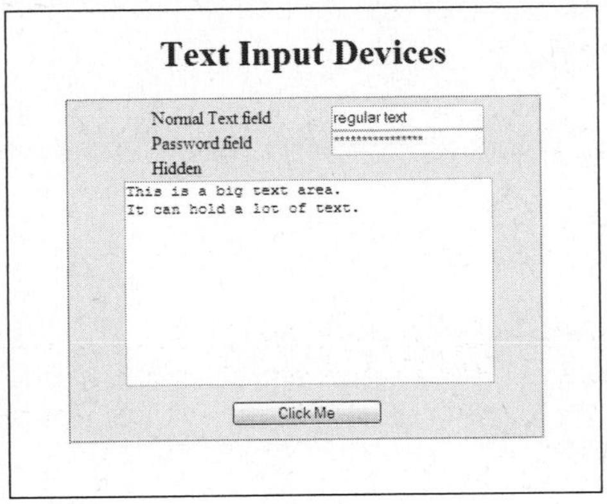

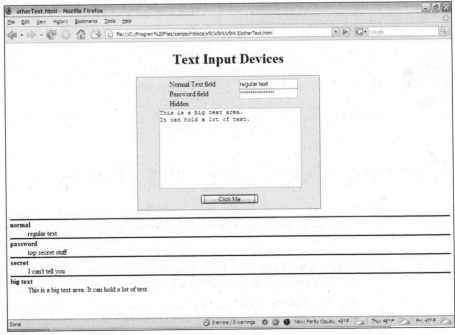

Figure 6-10:
Passwords,
hidden
fields, and
text areas
all look the
same to
JavaScript.

When the user clicks the button, the contents of all the fields (even the password and hidden field) are displayed on the bottom of the page, as illustrated in Figure 6-11.

Figure 6-11:
Now you
can see
what was in
everything.

Building the form

Here's the XHTML that generates the form:

```
<body>
  <h1>Text Input Devices</h1>
  <form action = "">
    <fieldset>
      <label>Normal Text field</label>
      <input type = "text"
             id = "txtNormal" />
      <label>Password field</label>
      <input type = "password"
             id = "pwd" />
      <label>Hidden</label>
      <input type = "hidden"
             id = "hidden"
             value = "I can't tell you" />
      <textarea id = "txtArea"
                rows = "10"
                cols = "40">
This is a big text area.
It can hold a lot of text.
      </textarea>
      <button type = "button"
              onclick = "processForm()">
        Click Me
      </button>
    </fieldset>
  </form>

  <div id = "output">

  </div>
</body>
```

The code should be familiar to you (look over Bonus Chapter 1 if you need more information on form elements). A few things are worth noting for this example:

✔ **There's an ordinary text field.** Just for comparison purposes. It has an id so it can be identified in the JavaScript.

✔ **The next field is a password field.** Passwords display asterisks, but store the actual text that was entered. This password has an id of pwd.

✔ **The hidden field is a bit strange.** Hidden fields can be used to store information on the page without displaying that information to the user. Unlike the other kinds of text fields, the user cannot modify a hidden field. (She usually doesn't even know it's there.) This hidden field has an id of secret and a value ("I can't tell you").

✔ **The text area has a different format.** The input elements are all single-tag elements, but the textarea element is designed to contain a large amount of text, so it has beginning and end tags. The text area's id is txtArea.

✔ **A button starts all the fun.** As usual, most of the elements just sit there gathering data, but the button has an onclick event associated with it, which calls a function.

✔ **External CSS gussies it all up.** The page has some minimal CSS to clean it up. (The CSS isn't central to this discussion, so I won't reproduce it.) Note that the page will potentially have a dl on it, so I have a CSS style for it, even though it doesn't appear by default.

The password and hidden fields seem secure, but they aren't. Anybody who views the page source will be able to read the value of a hidden field, and passwords transmit their information in the clear. You really shouldn't be using Web technology (especially this kind) to transport nuclear launch codes or the recipe of your secret sauce. (Hmmm — maybe the secret sauce recipe *is* the launch code — sounds like a bad spy movie.)

When I create a text field, I often suspend my rules on indentation, because the text field preserves everything inside it, including any indentation.

Writing the function

Now all you need is a function. Here's the good news: JavaScript treats all these elements in exactly the same way! The way you handle a password, hidden field, or text area is identical to the technique for a regular text field. Here's the code:

```
<script type = "text/javascript">
//<![CDATA[

// from otherText.html
function processForm(){
  //grab input from form
  var txtNormal = document.
    getElementById("txtNormal");
  var pwd = document.getElementById("pwd");
  var hidden = document.getElementById("hidden");
  var txtArea = document.getElementById("txtArea");

  var normal = txtNormal.value;
  var password = pwd.value;
  var secret = hidden.value;
  var bigText = txtArea.value;
```

```
      //create output
      var result = ""
      result += "<dl> \n";
      result += "  <dt>normal<\/dt> \n";
      result += "  <dd>" + normal + "<\/dd> \n";
      result += " \n";
      result += "  <dt>password<\/dt> \n";
      result += "  <dd>" + password + "<\/dd> \n";
      result += " \n";
      result += "  <dt>secret<\/dt> \n";
      result += "  <dd>" + secret + "<\/dt> \n";
      result += "    \n";
      result += "  <dt>big text<\/dt> \n";
      result += "  <dd>" + bigText + "<\/dt> \n";
      result += "<\/dl> \n";

      var output = document.getElementById("output");
      output.innerHTML = result;

  } // end function
```

The `processForm()` function is a bit longer than the others in this chapter, but it follows exactly the same pattern: It extracts data from the fields, constructs a string for output, and writes that output to the `innerHTML` attribute of a `div` in the page.

The code has nothing new, but it still has a few features you should consider:

✔ **Create a variable for each form element.** Use the `document.get ElementById` mechanism.

✔ **Create a string variable containing the contents of each element.** Don't forget: The `getElementById` trick returns an object. To see what's inside the object, you have to extract the `value` property.

✔ **Make a big string variable to manage the output.** When output gets long and messy like this, concatenate a big variable and then just output it in one swoop.

✔ **HTML is your friend.** This output is a bit complex, but `innerHTML` contains HTML, so you can use any HTML styles you want to format your code. The `return` string is actually a complete definition list. Whatever is inside the text box is (in this case) being reproduced as HTML text; if I want carriage returns or formatting, I'll have to add them with code.

✔ **Don't forget to escape the slashes.** The validator gets confused by ending tags, so add the backslash character to any ending tags occurring in JavaScript string variables (`</dl>` becomes `<\/dl>`).

✔ **Newline characters (\n) clean up the output.** If I were writing an ordinary definition list in HTML, I'd put each line on a new line. I try to make my programs write code just like I do, so I add newline characters everywhere I would add a carriage return in ordinary HTML.

Understanding generated source code

When you run the program, your JavaScript code actually changes the page it lives on. The code that doesn't come from your server but is created by your program is sometimes called `generated source`. The generated-code technique is powerful, but it can have a significant problem. Try the following experiment to see what I mean:

1. **Reload the page to view it without the form contents showing.**

   Now view the source.

2. **Note that everything is as expected.**

   The source code shows exactly what you wrote.

3. **Click the Click Me button.**

   Your function will run, and the page will change. You clearly added HTML to the `output div`, because you can see the output right on the screen.

4. **View the source again.**

   You'll be amazed. The `output div` will be empty, even though you'll be able to clearly see that it has changed.

5. **Validators won't check generated code.**

   Using the HTML validator extension or the `w3` validator won't check for errors in your generated code. You have to check it yourself, but it's hard to see the code!

Figure 6-12 illustrates this problem.

Here's what's going on: The `view source` command (on most browsers) doesn't *actually* view the source of the page as it currently stands. It goes back to the server and retrieves the page, but displays it as source rather than as rendered output. That means the `view source` command isn't useful for telling you how the page has changed dynamically. Likewise, the page validators check the page as it occurs on the server without taking into account things that could have happened dynamically.

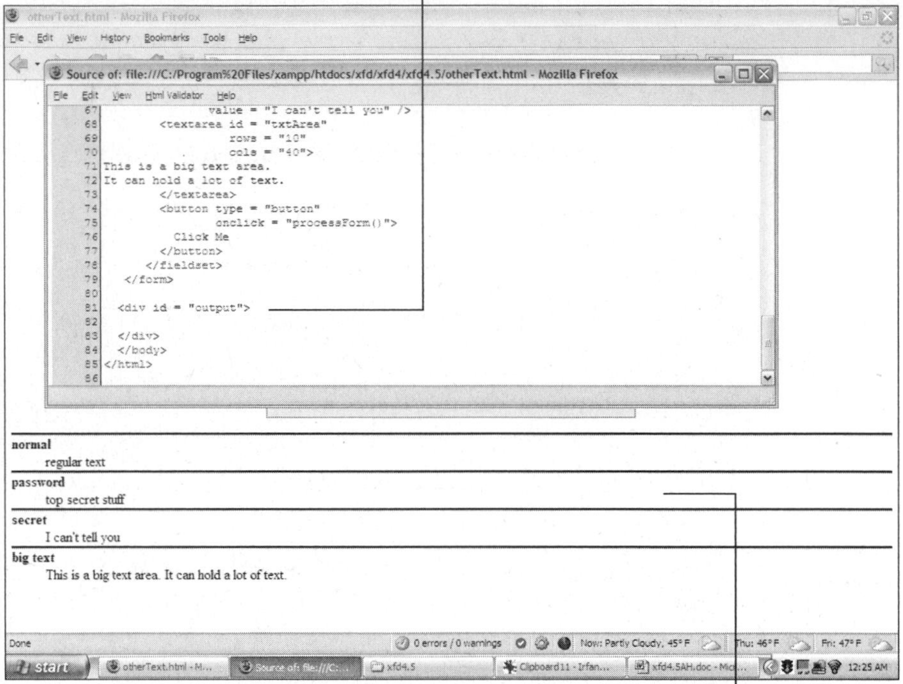

The output div in the source code is still empty.

Figure 6-12:
The ordinary
command
to view
source isn't
showing the
contents of
the div!

The div clearly has contents even though the source code shows it as empty!

When you were building regular Web pages, this wasn't a problem, because regular Web pages don't change. Dynamically generated pages can change on the fly, and the browser doesn't expect that. If you made a mistake in the HTML, you can't simply view the source to see what you did wrong in the code generated by your script. Fortunately, two easy solutions are available with Firefox plugins:

✔ **The Web developer toolbar.** This toolbar has a wonderful tool called `view generated source`, available on the `view source` menu. This allows you to view the source code of the current page in its current state, including any code dynamically generated by your JavaScript.

✔ **Firebug.** Open the Firebug window when a page is open and browse (with the HTML tab) around your page. Firebug gives you an accurate view of the page contents, even when they're changed dynamically. This can be extremely useful.

These tools will keep you sane when you're trying to figure out why your generated code isn't acting right. (I wish I'd had them years ago . . . .)

Figure 6-13 shows the Firebug toolbar — with the dynamically generated contents showing.

The contents of the div were dynamically changed by the code.

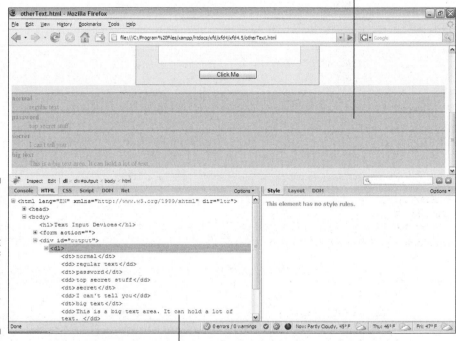

Figure 6-13:
Firebug shows the current status of the page, even if it's dynamically modified.

The Firebug inspector shows the code as it currently exists, even if it was modified by JavaScript code (as it was in this example).

Chapter 7

Getting Valid Input

In This Chapter

▶ Extracting data from drop-down lists

▶ Managing multiple-selection lists

▶ Getting data from check boxes

▶ Getting information from radio groups

▶ Validating input with regular expressions

▶ Using character, boundary, and repetition operators

▶ Working with pattern memory

*I*t's very nice to be able to get input from the user, but sometimes users make mistakes. It'd be great if some better ways existed to make the user's job easier and prevent certain kinds of mistakes.

Of course, there are tools for exactly that purpose. In this chapter, you get the lowdown on two main strategies for improving user input: specialized input elements and pattern-matching. Together, these tools can help you ensure that the data the user enters is useful and valid.

Getting Input from a Drop-Down List

The most obvious way to ensure that the user enters something valid is to *supply valid choices*. The *drop-down list* is an obvious and easy way to do this, as you can see from Figure 7-1.

The drop-down list box approach has a lot of advantages over text-field input:

- ✔ **The user can input with the mouse.** This is faster and easier than typing.

- ✔ **No spelling errors.** That's because the user doesn't have to type the response.

✔ **All answers are available.** The user knows which responses are available, because they're in a list.

✔ **You can be sure it's a valid answer.** That's because you supplied the possible responses.

✔ **User responses can be mapped to more complex values.** For example, you can show the user "red" and have the list box return the hex value "#FF0000".

Figure 7-1:
The user
selects
from a pre-
defined
list of valid
choices.

If you need a refresher on how to build a list box with the XHTML select object, please refer to Bonus Chapter 2 on either of the Web sites: www. aharrisbooks.net/jad or www.dummies.com/go/javascriptand ajaxfd.

Building the form

It's best to create the HTML form first, because it defines all the elements you'll need for the function. The code is a standard form:

```
<body>
  <form action = "">
    <h1>Please select a color</h1>
    <fieldset>
      <select id = "selColor">
        <option value = "#FFFFFF">White</option>
        <option value = "#FF0000">Red</option>
        <option value = "#FFCC00">Orange</option>
        <option value = "#FFFF00">Yellow</option>
        <option value = "#00FF00">Green</option>
        <option value = "#0000FF">Blue</option>
        <option value = "#663366">Indigo</option>
        <option value = "#FF00FF">Violet</option>
      </select>
```

```
        <input type = "button"
                value = "change color"
                onclick = "changeColor()" />
    </fieldset>
    </form>

  </body>
</html>
```

The `select` object's default behavior is to provide a drop-down list. The first element on the list is displayed, but when the user clicks the list, the other options appear.

A `select` object that will be referred to in code should have an `id` field.

In this and most examples in this chapter, I added external CSS styling to clean up each form. Be sure to look over the styles on the Web sites (`www.aharris books.net/jad` or `www.dummies.com/go/javascriptandajaxfd`) if you want to see how styling was accomplished.

The other element in the form is a button. When the button is clicked, the `changeColor()` function will be triggered.

Because the only element in this form is the `select` object, you might want to change the background color immediately without requiring a button press. You can do this by adding an event handler directly onto the `select` object, like this:

```
        <select id = "selColor"
                onchange = "changeColor()">
```

This will cause the `changeColor()` function to be triggered as soon as the user changes the `select` object's value. Typically you only do this if `select` is the only element in the form. If there are several elements, processing doesn't usually happen until the user signals she's ready by clicking a button.

Reading the list box

Fortunately, standard drop-down lists are quite easy to read. Here's the JavaScript code:

```
    <script type = "text/javascript">
      //<![CDATA[
      // from drop-downList.html
```

```
function changeColor(){
  var selColor = document.
    getElementById("selColor");
  var color = selColor.value;
  document.body.style.backgroundColor = color;
} // end function
//]]>
</script>
```

As you can see, the process for reading the `select` object is much like working with a text field:

1. **Create a variable to represent the** `select` **object.**

   The `document.getElementById()` **trick works here just like it does for text fields.**

2. **Extract the** `value` **property of the** `select` **object.**

   The `value` property of the `select` object will reflect the `value` property of the currently selected `option`. So, if the user has chosen `"yellow"`, the value of `selColor` will be `"#FFFF00"`

3. **Set the document's background color.**

   Use the DOM mechanism to set the body's background color to the chosen value.

Managing Multiple Selections

The `select` object can be used in a more powerful way: Figure 7-2 shows a page with a multiple-selection list box. To make multiple selection work, you have to make a few changes both to the HTML and the JavaScript code.

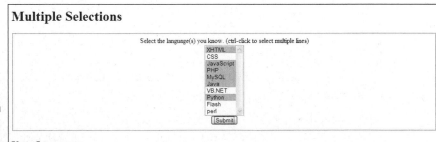

Figure 7-2:
You can pick multiple choices from this list.

Coding a multiple-selection select object

You'll have to modify the `select` code in two ways to make multiple selections:

- ✔ **Indicate multiple selections are allowed.** By default, `select` boxes have only one value. You'll need to set a switch to tell the browser to allow more than one item to be selected.

- ✔ **Make it a multi-line** `select`. The standard drop-down behavior doesn't make sense when you want multiple selections, because the user has to see all the options at once. Most browsers switch into a multi-line mode automatically — but you should control the process directly just to be sure.

The XHTML code for `multiSelect.html` is similar to the `drop-downList` page, but note a couple of changes:

```
<body>
  <h1>Multiple Selections</h1>
  <form action = "">
    <fieldset>
      <label>
        Select the language(s) you know.
        (ctrl-click to select multiple lines)
      </label>
      <select id = "selLanguage"
              multiple = "multiple"
              size = "10">
        <option value = "XHTML">XHTML</option>
        <option value = "CSS">CSS</option>
        <option value = "JavaScript">JavaScript</option>
        <option value = "PHP">PHP</option>
        <option value = "MySQL">MySQL</option>
        <option value = "Java">Java</option>
        <option value = "VB.NET">VB.NET</option>
        <option value = «Python»>Python</option>
        <option value = «Flash»>Flash</option>
        <option value = «Perl»>perl</option>
      </select>
      <button type = «button»
              onclick = «showChoices()»>
        Submit
      </button>
    </fieldset>
  </form>

  <div id = «output»>

  </div>
</body>
</html>
```

The code isn't shocking, but it does have some important features to recognize:

- ✔ **The** `select` **object is called** `selLanguage`**.** As usual, the form elements need an `id` attribute so you can read it in the JavaScript.

- ✔ **Add the** `multiple = "multiple"` **attribute to your** `select` **object.** This tells the browser to accept multiple inputs using Shift-click (for contiguous selections) or Control-click (for more precise selection).

- ✔ **Set the** `size` **to 10.** The size indicates the number of lines that will be displayed. I set the size to 10 because I have 10 options in the list.

- ✔ **Make a button.** With multiple selection, you probably won't want to trigger the action until the user has finished making selections. A separate button is the easiest way to do this.

- ✔ **Create an** `output div`**.** Something has to hold the response.

Writing the JavaScript code

The JavaScript code for reading a multiple-selection list box is a bit different than the standard selection code. The `value` property will only return one value, but a multiple-selection list box will often return more than one result.

The key is to recognize that a list of `option` objects inside a `select` object is really a kind of array. You can look more closely at the list of objects to see which ones are selected. That's essentially what the `showChoices()` function does:

```
<script type = "text/javascript">
  //<![CDATA[
  //from multi-select.html
  function showChoices(){
    //retrieve data
    var selLanguage = document.
      getElementById("selLanguage");

    //set up output string
    var result = "<h2>Your Languages<\/h2>";
    result += "<ul> \n";

    //step through options
    for (i = 0; i < selLanguage.length; i++){
      //examine current option
      currentOption = selLanguage[i];

      //print it if it has been selected
      if (currentOption.selected == true){
        result += "  <li>" + currentOption.value +
        "<\/li> \n";
```

```
      } // end if
    } // end for loop

    //finish off the list and print it out
    result += "<\/ul> \n";

    output = document.getElementById("output");
    output.innerHTML = result;
  } // end showChoices
 //]]>
</script>
```

At first the code seems intimidating, but if you break it down, it's not too tricky.

1. **Create a variable to represent the entire** `select` **object.**

   The standard `document.getElementById()` technique works fine:

   ```
   var selLanguage = document.getElementById("selLanguage");
   ```

2. **Create a string variable to hold the output.**

   When you're building complex HTML output, it's much easier to work with a string variable than to directly write code to the element:

   ```
   var result = "<h2>Your Languages<\/h2>";
   ```

3. **Build an unordered list to display the results.**

   An unordered list is a good way to spit out the results, so I create one in my `result` variable:

   ```
   result += "<ul> \n";
   ```

4. **Step through** `selLanguage` **as if it were an array.**

   Use a `for` loop to examine the list box line by line:

   ```
   for (i = 0; i < selLanguage.length; i++){
   ```

   Note that `selLanguage` has a `length` property like an array.

5. **Assign the current element to a temporary variable.**

   The `currentOption` variable will hold a reference to the each `option` element in the original `select` object as the loop progresses:

   ```
   currentOption = selLanguage[i];
   ```

6. **Check to see if the current element has been selected.**

   Here currentOption is an object, and it has a selected property. This property tells you if the object has been highlighted by the user. selected is a Boolean property, so the only possible values are true or false.

   ```
   if (currentOption.selected == true){
   ```

7. **If the element has been selected, add an entry to the output list.**

   If the user has highlighted this object, create an entry in the unordered list housed in the result variable:

   ```
   result += "  <li>" + currentOption.value + "<\/li> \n";
   ```

8. **Close up the list.**

   When the loop has finished cycling through all the objects, you can close up the unordered list you've been building:

   ```
   result += "<\/ul> \n";
   ```

9. **Print results to the** output div.

   The innerHTML property of the output div is a perfect place to print out the unordered list:

   ```
   output = document.getElementById("output");
   output.innerHTML = result;
   ```

There's something strange going on here. The options of a select box act like an array. An unordered list is a lot like an array, which is a lot like a select box. Bingo! They *are* arrays, just in different forms. Any listed data can be thought of as an array. Sometimes you organize it like a list (for display), sometimes like an array (for storage in memory,) and sometimes it's a select group (for user input). Now you're starting to think like a programmer!

Check, Please — Reading Check Boxes

Check boxes fulfill another useful data-input function: They're useful any time you have Boolean data. If some value can be true or false, a check box is a good tool. Figure 7-3 illustrates a page responding to check boxes.

It's important to understand that check boxes are independent of each other. Although they are often found in groups, any check box can be checked or unchecked regardless of the status of its neighbors.

Select as many boxes as you want.　　　Order Pizza button

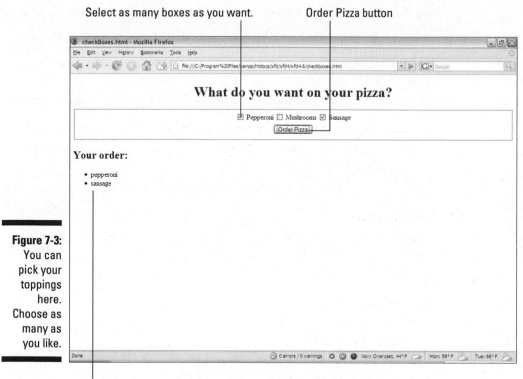

Figure 7-3:
You can
pick your
toppings
here.
Choose as
many as
you like.

When you click the Order Pizza button, the selected output displays here.

Building the checkbox page

As usual, start by looking at the HTML:

```
<body>
  <h1>What do you want on your pizza?</h1>
  <form action = "">
    <fieldset>
      <input type = "checkbox"
             id = "chkPepperoni"
             value = "pepperoni" />
      <label for = "chkPepperoni">Pepperoni</label>

      <input type = "checkbox"
             id = "chkMushroom"
             value = "mushrooms" />
      <label for = "chkMushroom">Mushrooms</label>
```

```
          <input type = "checkbox"
                 id = "chkSausage"
                 value = "sausage" />
          <label for = "chkSausage">Sausage</label>

          <button type = "button"
                  onclick = "order()">
            Order Pizza
          </button>
        </fieldset>
      </form>
      <h2>Your order:</h2>
      <div id = "output">

      </div>
    </body>
```

Each check box is an individual input element. Note that checkbox values are not displayed. Instead, a label (or similar text) is usually placed *after* the check box. A button calls an order() function.

Look at the labels. They each have the for attribute set to tie the label to the corresponding check box. Although this is not required, it's a nice touch, because then the user can click the entire label to activate the check box.

Responding to the check boxes

Check boxes don't require a lot of care and feeding. When you extract a checkbox object, it has two critical properties:

- ✔ **The** value **property:** Like other input elements, the value property can be used to store a value associated with the check box.

- ✔ **The** checked **property:** This property is a Boolean value, indicating whether the check box is currently checked.

The code for the order() function shows how it's done:

```
    <script type = "text/javascript">
      //<![CDATA[
      //from checkBoxes.html

      function order(){
        //get variables
        var chkPepperoni = document.
          getElementById("chkPepperoni");
        var chkMushroom = document.
          getElementById(«chkMushroom»);
        var chkSausage = document.
          getElementById("chkSausage");
```

```
        var output = document.getElementById(«output»);
        var result = «<ul> \n»

        if (chkPepperoni.checked){
          result += «<li>» + chkPepperoni.value + «<\/li>
          \n»;
        } // end if

        if (chkMushroom.checked){
          result += «<li>» + chkMushroom.value + «<\/li>
          \n»;
        } // end if

        if (chkSausage.checked){
          result += «<li>» + chkSausage.value + «<\/li>
          \n»;
        } // end if

        result += «<\/ul> \n»
        output.innerHTML = result;
      } // end function

    //]]>
  </script>
```

For each check box, make sure you use both of its properties:

1. **Determine whether the check box is checked.**

   Use the `checked` property as a condition.

2. **If the box is checked, return the `value` property associated with the check box.**

Often in practice the `value` property is left out. The important thing is whether the check box is checked. It's pretty obvious that if `chkMushroom` is checked, the user wants mushrooms, so you may not need to explicitly store that data in the `checkbox` itself.

Working with Radio Buttons

Radio-button groups appear to be pretty simple, but they are more complex than they seem. Figure 7-4 shows a page using radio-button selection.

The most important rule about radio buttons is that — like wildebeests and power-walkers — they must be in groups. Each group of radio buttons will have only one button active. The group should be set up so one button is active at the very beginning, so there is always exactly one active button in the group.

Figure 7-4:
One and
only one
member
of a radio
group can
be selected
at once.

With what weapon will you fight the dragon?

○ Spoon
○ Flower
◉ Wet Noodle
[fight the dragon]

You defeated the dragon with a wet noodle

You specify the radio button group in the XHTML code. Each element of the group can have an `id` attribute (although the IDs aren't really necessary in this application). What's more important here is the `name` attribute. Look over the code and you'll notice something interesting: All the radio buttons have the same name!

```
<body>
  <h1>With what weapon will you fight the dragon?</h1>
  <form action = "">
    <fieldset>
      <input type = "radio"
             name = "weapon"
             id = "radSpoon"
             value = "spoon"
             checked = "checked" />
      <label for = "radSpoon">Spoon</label>

      <input type = "radio"
             name = "weapon"
             id = "radFlower"
             value = "flower" />
      <label for = "radSpoon">Flower</label>

      <input type = "radio"
             name = "weapon"
             id = "radNoodle"
             value = "wet noodle" />
      <label for = "radNoodle">Wet Noodle</label>
      <button type = "button"
              onclick = "fight()">
        fight the dragon
      </button>
    </fieldset>
  </form>
  <div id = "output">

  </div>
</body>
```

It seems a little odd to have a name attribute when everything else has an id, but there's a good reason. The name attribute is used to indicate the *group* of radio buttons. Because all the buttons in this group have the same name . . .

- ✔ All these buttons are related, and only one of them will be selected.
- ✔ The browser recognizes this behavior, and automatically deselects the other buttons in the group whenever one is selected.
- ✔ I added a label to describe what each radio button means. (Very handy for human beings such as users and troubleshooters.) Labels also improve usability because now the user can click the label or the button to activate the button.

It's important to preset one of the radio buttons to true with the checked = "checked" attribute. If you fail to do so, you'll have to add code to account for the possibility that there is no answer at all.

Interpreting radio buttons

Getting information from a group of radio buttons requires a slightly different technique from what you'd use for most form elements. Unlike the select object, in this case there's no container object that can return a simple value. You also can't just go through every radio button on the page, because there could be more than one group. (Imagine, for example, a page with a multiple-choice test.)

This is where the name attribute comes in. Although ids must be unique, multiple elements on a page can have the same name. If they do, these elements can be treated as an array.

Look over the code and I show how it works:

```
<script type = "text/javascript">
//<![CDATA[
// from radioGroup.html
function fight(){

    var weapon = document.getElementsByName("weapon");

    for (i = 0; i < weapon.length; i++){
      currentWeapon = weapon[i];

      if (currentWeapon.checked){
        var selectedWeapon = currentWeapon.value;
      } // end if

    } // end for
```

```
      var output = document.getElementById("output");
      var response = "<h2>You defeated the dragon with a
         ";
      response += selectedWeapon + "<\/h2> \n";
      output.innerHTML = response;
  } // end function

  //]]>
</script>
```

This code looks much like other code in this chapter, but it has a sneaky difference that emerges in these steps:

1. **Use** `getElementsByName` **to retrieve an array of elements with this name.**

   Now that you're comfortable with `getElementById`, I throw a monkey wrench in the works. Note that it's plural =— `getElementsByName` (`Elements` with an *s*) — because this tool is used to extract an array of elements. It will return an array of elements (in this case, all the radio buttons in the `weapon` group).

2. **Treat the result as an array.**

   The resulting variable (`weapon` in this example) is an array. As usual, the most common thing to do with arrays is process them with loops. Use a `for` loop to step through each element in the array.

3. **Assign each element of the array to** `currentWeapon`**.**

   This variable holds a reference to the current radio button.

4. **Check to see whether the current weapon is checked.**

   The `checked` property indicates whether any radio button is currently checked.

5. **If the current weapon is checked, retain the value of the radio button.**

   If the current radio button is checked, its value will be the current value of the group, so store it in a variable for later use.

6. **Output the results.**

   You can now process the results as you would with data from any other resource.

Working with Regular Expressions

Having the right kinds of form elements can be very helpful, but things can still go wrong. Sometimes you *have* to let the user type things in, and that information must be in a particular format. As an example, take a look at Figure 7-5.

Figure 7-5:
This page
is a mess.
No user
name, and
it's not a
valid e-mail
or phone
number.

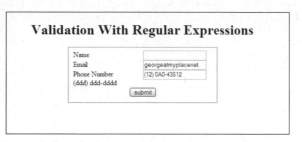

It would be great to have some mechanism for checking input from a form to see if it's in the right format. This can be done with string functions, but that can be really messy. Imagine how many `if` statements and string methods it would take to enforce the following rules on this page:

1. **There must be an entry in each field.**

   This one is reasonably easy: Just check for non-null values.

2. **The e-mail must be in a valid format.**

   That is, it must consist of a few characters, an ampersand (@), a few more characters, a period, and a domain name of two to four characters. That would be a real pain to check for.

3. **The phone number must also be in a valid format.**

   There are multiple formats, but assume you require an area code in parentheses, followed by an optional space, followed by three digits, a dash, and four digits. All digits must be entered as numeric characters (seems obvious, but you'd be surprised).

Although it's possible to enforce these rules, it would be extremely difficult to do so using ordinary string manipulation tools.

JavaScript strings have a `match` method, which helps find a substring inside a larger string. This is good, but we're not simply looking for specific text, but patterns of text. For example, we want to know if something's an e-mail address (text, an @, more text, a period, and two to four more characters).

Imagine how difficult that code would be to write . . . and then take a look at the code for the `validate.html` page:

```
<script type = "text/javascript">
  function validate(){
    // get inputs
    name = document.getElementById("txtName").value;
    email = document.getElementById("txtEmail").value;
    phone = document.getElementById("txtPhone").value;
```

```
                //create an empty error message
                errors = "";

                //check name - It simply needs to exist
                if (name == ""){
                  errors += "please supply a name \n";
                } // end if

                //check email
                emailRE = /^.+@.+\..{2,4}$/;
                if (email.match(emailRE)){
                  //console.log("email match");
                  //do nothing.
                } else {
                  //console.log("email not a match");
                  errors += "please check email address \n";
                } // end if

                //check phone number
                phoneRE = /^\(\d{3}\) *\d{3}-\d{4}/;
                if (phone.match(phoneRE)){
                  //console.log("phone matches");
                  //do nothing
                } else {
                  //console.log("phone problem");
                  errors += "please check phone #\n";
                } // end phone if

                //check for errors
                if (errors == ""){
                  alert ("now processing data");
                  //process the form
                } else {
                  alert(errors);
                } // end if

              } // end function


          </script>
```

I'm only showing the JavaScript code here, to save space. Look on the Web site to see how the HTML and CSS are written.

Surprise! The code isn't really all that difficult! Here's what's going on:

1. **Let the code extract data from the form in the usual way.**

2. **Create a variable to hold error messages.**

   The error variable begins empty (because there are no errors to begin with). As I check the code, I'll add any error text to this variable. If there are no errors, the error variable will remain empty.

3. **Do the name check.**

   That should be very simple; the only way this can go wrong is to have no name.

4. **If the name is wrong, add a helpful reminder to the error variable.**

   If the name isn't there, just add a message to the error variable. We'll report this problem (along with any others) to the user later on.

5. **Build a pattern.**

   All this seems pretty simple — until you look at the line that contains the `emailRE = /^.+@.+\..{2,4}$/;` business. It looks like a cursing cartoonist in there. It's a pattern that indicates whether it's a legal e-mail address or not. I explain in the next section how to build it, but for now just take it on faith so you can see the big picture.

6. **Notice we're trying to match the e-mail to emailRE.**

   Whatever emailRE is (and I promise I'll explain that soon), the next line makes it clear that we're trying to match the e-mail address to that thing. This turns out to be a Boolean operation. If it's true, the e-mail matches the pattern.

7. **Do nothing if the pattern is matched.**

   If the e-mail address is valid, go on with the other processing. (Note that I originally put a console log command for debugging purposes, but I commented that code out.)

8. **If the pattern match was unsuccessful, add another error message.**

   The error variable accumulates all the error messages. If the match was unsuccessful, that means the e-mail address is not in a valid format, so we'll add the appropriate hint to the error variable.

9. **Check the phone number.**

   When again, the phone number check is simple except the phoneRE business, which is just as mysterious: `/\(\d{3}\) *\d{3}-\d{4}/`. (Seriously, who makes this stuff up?) Again, if the match is successful, do nothing, but if there's a problem, add a report to the error variable.

10. **If everything worked, process the form.**

    The status of the error variable indicates whether there were any problems. If the error variable is still empty, all the input is valid, so it's time to process the form.

11. **Report any errors if necessary.**

    If you wrote anything to the error variable, the form should not be processed. Instead, display the contents of the error variable to the user.

Frequently you'll do validation in JavaScript before you pass information to a program on the server. This way your server program will already know the data is valid by the time it gets there, which reduces congestion on the server. JavaScript programs normally pass information to the server through the AJAX mechanism, which is the focus of part three of this book.

Introducing regular expressions

Of course, the secret is to decode the mystical expressions used in the match statements. They aren't really strings at all, but very powerful text manipulation techniques called *regular expression parsing*. Regular expressions have migrated from the Unix world into many programming languages, including JavaScript. A regular expression is a powerful mini-language for searching and replacing — text patterns in particular — even complex ones. It's a weird-looking language, but it has a certain charm after you get used to reading the arcane-looking expressions.

Regular expressions are normally used with the string match() method in JavaScript, but they can also be used with the replace() method and a few other places.

Table 7-1 summarizes the main operators in JavaScript regular expressions.

Table 7-1	JavaScript Main Operators			
Operator	**Description**	**Sample pattern**	**Matches**	**Doesn't match**
. (period)	Any single character except newline	.	E	\n
^	Beginning of string	^a	apple	banana
$	End of string	a$	banana	apple
[characters]	Any of a list of characters in braces	[abcABC]	A	D
[char range]	Any character in the range	[a-zA-Z]	F	9
\d	Any single numerical digit	\d\d\d-\d\d\d\d	123-4567	The-thing
\b	A word boundary	\bthe\b	the	theater

Operator	Description	Sample pattern	Matches	Doesn't match
`+`	One or more occurrences of the previous character	`\d+`	1234	text
`*`	Zero or more occurrences of the previous character	`[a-zA-Z]\d*`	B17, g	7
`{digit}`	Repeat preceding character *digit* times	`\d{3}-\d{4}`	123-4567	999-99-9999
`{min, max}`	Repeat preceding character at least *min* but not more than *max* times	`{2,4}`	ca, com, info	watermelon
`(pattern segment)`	Store results in pattern memory returned with code	`^(.).*\1$`	gig, wallow	Bobby

Don't memorize this table! I explain, in the rest of this chapter, exactly how it works. Just keep this page handy as a reference.

To see an example of how this works, take a look at `regex.html` in Figure 7-6.

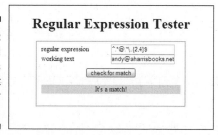

Figure 7-6:
This tool
allows
you to test
regular
expressions.

The top `textbox` element accepts a regular expression, and the second text field contains text you will examine. Practice the following examples to see how regular expressions work. They are really quite useful when you get the hang of them. As you walk through the examples, try them out in this tester. (I've included it on the Web page for you, but I don't reproduce the code here.)

Characters in regular expressions

The main thing you do with a regular expression is search for text. Say you work for the `bigCorp` company and you ask for employee e-mail addresses. You might make a form that only accepts e-mail addresses with the term `bigCorp` in them. You could do that with the following code:

```
if (email.match(/bigCorp/)){
   alert("match");
} else {
   alert("no match");
} // end if
```

This is the simplest type of match. I'm simply looking for the existence of the needle (bigCorp) in a haystack (the e-mail address stored in `email`) If the text `bigCorp` is found anywhere in the text, then the match is true and I can do what I want (usually I process the form on the server). More often, you'll want to trap for an error, and remind the user of what needs to be fixed.

Notice that the text inside the `match()` method is encased in forward slashes (/) rather than quotes. This is important, because the text "bigCorp" is not really meant to be a string value here. The slashes indicate that the text is to be treated as a regular expression, which requires extra processing by the interpreter.

If you accidentally enclose a regular expression in quotes instead of slashes, the expression will still work most of the time. JavaScript tries to quietly convert the text into a regular expression for you. However, this process does not always work as planned. Do not rely on the automatic conversion process, but instead enclose all regular expressions in slashes rather than quotes.

Marking the beginning and end of the line

You might want to improve the search, because what you really want is addresses that end with "bigCorp.com". You can put a special character inside the match string to indicate where the end of the line should be:

```
if (email.match(/bigCorp.com$/)){
   alert("match");
} else {
   alert("no match");
} // end if
```

The dollar sign at the end of the match string indicates that this part of the text should occur at the end of the search string, so andy@bigCorp.com would match, but not "bigCorp.com announces a new Web site".

If you're already an ace with regular expressions, you know this example has a minor problem, but it's pretty picky; I'll explain it in a moment. For now, just appreciate that you can include the end of the string as a search parameter.

Likewise, you can use the caret character (^) to indicate the beginning of a string.

If you want to ensure that a text field contains only the phrase oogie boogie (and why wouldn't you?), you can tack on the beginning and ending markers. /^oogie boogie$/ will only be a true match if there is nothing else in the phrase.

Working with Special Characters

In addition to ordinary text, you can use a bunch of special character symbols for more flexible matching.

Matching a character with the period

The most powerful character is the period (.), which represents a single character. Any single character except the newline (\n) will match against the period.

This may seem silly, but it's actually quite powerful. The expression /b.g/ will match big, bag, and bug. In fact, it will match any phrase that contains b followed by any single character then g, so bxg, b g, and b9g would also be matches.

Using a character class

You can specify a list of characters in square braces, and JavaScript will match if any one of those characters matches. This list of characters is sometimes called a *character class*. For example, b[aeiou]g will match on bag, beg, big, bog, or bug. This is a really quick way to check a lot of potential matches.

You can also specify a character class with a range. For example, the range [a-zA-Z] checks all the letters but no punctuation or numerals.

Specifying digits

One of the most common tricks is to look for numbers. The special character \d represents a number (an integer digit from 0 to 9). You can check for a U.S. phone number (without the area code — yet) using this pattern:

```
\d\d\d-\d\d\d\d
```

This looks for three digits, a dash, and four digits.

Marking punctuation characters

You can tell that regular expressions use a lot of funky characters, like periods and braces. What if you're searching for one of these characters? Just use a backslash (\) to indicate you're looking for the actual character, not using it as a modifier. For example, the e-mail address would be better searched with /bigCorp\.com/, because this specifies there must be a period. If you don't use the backslash, the regular expression tool interprets the period as "any character" and would allow something like bigCorpucom. Use the backslash trick for most punctuation, like parentheses, braces, periods, and slashes.

If you want to include an area code with parentheses, just use backslashes to indicate the parentheses: /\(\d\d\d\) \d\d\d-\d\d\d\d/.

Finding word boundaries

Sometimes you want to know if something is a word. Say you're searching for the word "the," but you don't want a false positive on "breathe" or "theater." The \b character means "the edge of a word," so /\bthe\b/ will match on "the" but not on words containing "the" inside them.

Repetition Operations

All the character modifiers refer to one particular character at a time. Sometimes you want to deal with several characters at a time. There are several operators that help you with this process.

Finding one or more elements

The plus sign (+) indicates "one or more" of the preceding character, so the pattern /ab+c/ will match on abc, abbbbbbc, or abbbbbbbc, but not on ac (there must be at least one b) or on afc (it's gotta be b).

Matching zero or more elements

The asterisk means "zero or more" of the preceding character. So /I'm .* happy/ will match on I'm happy (zero occurrences of any character between I'm and happy). It will also match on I'm not happy (because there are characters in between).

The .* combination is especially useful, because you can use it to improve matches like e-mail addresses: /^.*@bigCorp\.com$/ will do a pretty good job of matching e-mail addresses in our fictional company.

Specifying the number of matches

You can use braces ({}) to indicate the specific number of times the preceding character should be repeated. For example, you can re-write the phone number pattern like this: /\(\d{3}\) *\d{3}-\d{4}/. This means "three digits in parentheses, followed by any number of spaces (zero or more), then three digits, a dash, and four digits. Using this pattern, you'll be able to tell if the user has entered the phone number in a valid format.

You can also specify a minimum and maximum number of matches, so / [aeiou]{1, 3}/ means "at least one and no more than three vowels."

Now you can improve the e-mail pattern so it includes any number of characters, an @ sign, and ends with a period and two to four letters: /^.*@.*\.. {2,4}$/.

Working with Pattern Memory

Sometimes you'll want to "remember" a piece of your pattern and re-use it. The parentheses are used to group a chunk of the pattern and remember it. For example, /(foo){2}/ doesn't match on foo, but it does on foofoo. It's the entire segment that's repeated twice.

Recalling your memories

You can also refer to a stored pattern later in the expression. The pattern /^(.).*\1$/ matches any word that begins and ends with the same character. The \1 symbol represents the first pattern in the string, \2 represents the second, and so on.

Using patterns stored in memory

When you've finished a pattern match, the remembered patterns are still available in special variables. $1 is the first, $2 is the second, and so on. You can use this trick to look for HTML tags and report what tag was found: Match /^<(.*)>.*<\/\1>$/ and then print out $1 to see what the tag was.

There's much more to learn about regular expressions, but this basic overview should give you enough to write some powerful and useful patterns.

Chapter 8

Moving and Grooving

In This Chapter

▶ Moving an object onscreen

▶ Responding to keyboard input

▶ Reading mouse input

▶ Running code repeatedly

▶ Bouncing off the walls

▶ Using image-swapping and compound images

▶ Reusing code

▶ Using external script files

*J*avaScript has a serious side, but it can be a lot of fun, too. You can easily use JavaScript to make things move, animate, and wiggle. In this chapter, you get to make your pages dance. Even if you aren't interested in animation, you should look over this chapter to find out some important ideas about how to design your pages and your code more efficiently.

Making Things Move

You might think you need Flash or Java to put animation in your pages, but that's not true. You can use JavaScript to create some pretty interesting motion effects. Begin by taking a look at Figure 8-1.

Because this chapter is about animation, most of the pages feature motion. You really must see these pages in your browser to get the effect because a static screen shot can't really do any of these programs justice.

The general structure of this page provides a foundation for other kinds of animation:

> ✔ **The HTML is pretty simple.** As you'll see when you pop the hood, there really isn't much to the HTML code. It's a couple of divs and some buttons.

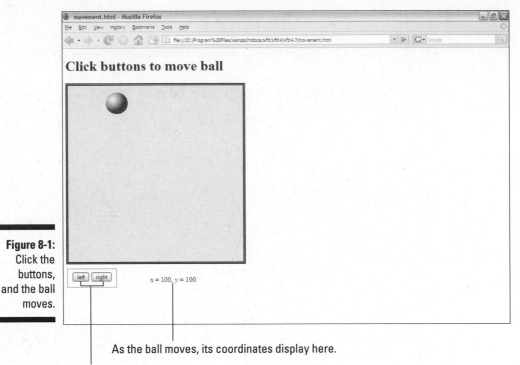

Figure 8-1:
Click the
buttons,
and the ball
moves.

As the ball moves, its coordinates display here.

Press to move the ball.

- ✔ **The ball is in a special** `div` **called** `sprite`. Game developers call the little images that move around on the screen *sprites,* so I use the same term.

- ✔ **The** `sprite` `div` **has a local style.** JavaScript animation requires a locally defined style.

- ✔ **The** `sprite` `div` **has absolute positioning.** Because I want to move this thing around on the screen, it makes sense that the `sprite` `div` is absolutely positioned.

- ✔ **The code and CSS are as modular as possible.** Things can get a little complicated when you start animating things, so I take care through this chapter to simplify as much as I can. The CSS styles are defined externally, and the JavaScript code is also imported.

- ✔ **Code is designed to be reused.** Many of the programs in this chapter are very similar to each other. To save effort, I've designed things so I don't have to rewrite code if possible.

Looking over the HTML

The following HTML code for the move.html program provides the basic foundation:

```
<!DOCTYPE html PUBLIC "-//W3C//DTD XHTML 1.0 Strict//EN"
"http://www.w3.org/TR/xhtml1/DTD/xhtml1-strict.dtd">
<html lang="EN" dir="ltr" xmlns="http://www.w3.org/1999/
          xhtml">
  <head>
    <meta http-equiv=»content-type» content=»text/xml;
          charset=utf-8» />
    <title>movement.html</title>
    <link rel = «stylesheet»
          type = «text/css»
          href = «movement.css» />

    <script type = «text/javascript»
            src = «movement.js»>
    </script>
  </head>
  <body onload = «init()»>
    <h1>Click buttons to move ball</h1>
    <div id = «surface»>
      <div id = «sprite»
            style = «position: absolute;
            top: 100px;
            left: 100px;
            height: 25px;
            width: 25px;» >
        <img src = «ball.gif»
             alt = «ball» />
      </div>
    </div>
    <form action = «»
          id = «controls»>
      <fieldset>
        <button type = «button»
                onclick = «moveSprite(-5, 0)»>
          left
        </button>
        <button type = «button»
                onclick = «moveSprite(5, 0)»>
          right
        </button>
      </fieldset>
    </form>
    <p id = «output»>
      x = 100, y = 100
    </p>
  </body>
</html>
```

You should notice a few interesting things about this code:

- ✔ **It has an external style sheet.** Most of the CSS (the stuff that defines the surface and the forms) is moved off-stage into an external style sheet. Some CSS has to be defined locally, but I have made as much of the CSS coding external as possible.

```
<link rel = "stylesheet"
      type = "text/css"
      href = "movement.css" />
```

- ✔ **The JavaScript is also outsourced.** The `<script>` tag has an `src` attribute, which you can use to load JavaScript code from an external file. The browser loads the specified file and reads it as though it were directly in the code. (Note that external scripts still require a `</script>` tag.) This program gets its scripts from a file called `movement.js`.

```
<script type = "text/javascript"
        src = "movement.js">
</script>
```

- ✔ **The `<body>` tag calls a method.** In animation (and other advanced JavaScript), you might have some code you want run right away. The body has an `onload` event. You can feed it the name of a function (just like you do with a button's `onclick` event). In this case, I want the function called `init()` to run as soon as the body finishes loading into the computer's memory.

```
<body onload = "init()">
```

- ✔ **The yellow box is a `div` called** `surface`. It isn't absolutely necessary, but when you have something moving around on the screen, it's nice to have some kind of boundary so the user knows where she can move the sprite.

- ✔ **There's a `sprite` div inside** `surface`. This sprite will be the thing that actually moves around.

```
<div id = "sprite"
     style = "position: absolute;
     top: 100px;
     left: 100px;
     height: 25px;
     width: 25px;" >
   <img src = "ball.gif"
        alt = "ball" />
</div>
```

- ✔ **The `sprite` div has a local style.** Your code can change only the styles that have been defined locally. The `sprite` div has a local style specifying absolute position, `top`, and `left` properties.

✔ **There's a form for buttons.** This particular program uses buttons to discern the user's intent. When you use buttons, you should place them in a form (even though in this case the form isn't absolutely necessary).

```
<button type = "button"
        onclick = "moveSprite(-5, 0)">
    left
</button>
```

✔ **Each button calls the** moveSprite() **method.** The moveSprite() method is defined in the movement.js file. It accepts two parameters: dx determines how much the sprite should move in the x (side to side) axis, and dy controls how much the sprite will move in the y (vertical) axis.

Getting an overview of the JavaScript

Because the JavaScript code is getting more complex, I recommend that you keep the following programming concepts in mind so that you can improve your programming efficiency:

✔ **Move code to an external file.** As with CSS code, when the JavaScript starts to get complex, it's a good idea to move it to its own file, so it's easier to manage and reuse.

✔ **Encapsulate code in functions.** Rather than writing a long, complicated function, try to break the code into smaller functions that solve individual problems. If you design these functions well, your code will be easier to write, understand, and recycle.

✔ **Create a few global variables.** A few key variables will be reused throughout your code. Create global variables for these key items, but don't make anything global that doesn't need to be.

✔ **Define constants for clarity.** Sometimes it's handy to have a few key values stored in special variables. In movement.html, I've created some constants to help me track the boundary of the visual surface.

Creating global variables

The first part of this document simply defines the global variables I use throughout the program:

```
//movement.js
//global variables
var sprite;
var x, y;    //position variables
```

```
//constants
var MIN_X = 15;
var MAX_X = 365;
var MIN_Y = 85;
var MAX_Y = 435;
```

The movement program has three main global variables:

- ✔ sprite: Represents the div that will move around on the screen.
- ✔ x: Is the x (horizontal) position of the sprite.
- ✔ y: Is the y (vertical) position of the sprite.

It isn't necessary to give values to global variables right away, but you should define them outside any functions so their values will be available to all functions. (Check Chapter 5 for more about functions and variable scope.)

Note that in computer graphics, the y axis works differently than it does in math. Zero is the top of the screen, and y values increase as you move down on the page. (This system is used because it models the top-to-bottom pattern of most display devices.)

This program also features some special *constants*. A constant is a variable (usually global) with a value that doesn't change as the program runs. Constants are almost always used to add clarity.

Through experimentation, I found that the ball's x value should never be smaller than 15 or larger than 365. By defining special constants with these values, I can make it clear what these values represent. (Look ahead to the boundary-checking code in the "Moving the sprite" section to see how this really works.)

Programmers traditionally put constants entirely in uppercase letters. Many languages have special modifiers for creating constants, but JavaScript doesn't. If you want something to be a constant, just make a variable with an uppercase name and *treat* it as a constant. (Don't change it during the run of the program.)

Initializing

The init() function is small but mighty:

```
function init(){
  sprite = document.getElementById("sprite");
} // end init
```

It does a simple but important job: It loads up the `sprite` div and stores it in a variable named `sprite`. Because `sprite` is a global variable, all other functions will have access to the `sprite` variable and will be able to manipulate it.

You'll often use the `init()` function to initialize key variables in your programs. You can also use this function to set up more advanced event handlers, as you see in the keyboard and mouse examples later in this chapter.

Moving the sprite

Of course, the most interesting function in the program is the one that moves sprites around the screen. Take a look at it and then look through my explanation for it.

```
function moveSprite(dx, dy){
  var surface = document.getElementById("surface");

  x = parseInt(sprite.style.left);
  y = parseInt(sprite.style.top);

  x += dx;
  y += dy;

  checkBounds();

  // move ball to new position
  sprite.style.left = x + «px»;
  sprite.style.top = y + "px";

  //describe position
  var output = document.getElementById(«output»);
  output.innerHTML = "x: " + x + ", y: " + y;
} // end MoveSprite
```

The function essentially works by first determining how much the sprite should be moved in x and y, and then manipulating the `left` and `top` properties of its style.

1. **Accept** dx **and** dy **as parameters.**

   The function expects two parameters: `dx` stands for *delta-x*, and `dy` is *delta-y*. (You can read them *difference in x, difference in y* if you prefer, but I like sounding like a NASA scientist.) These parameters tell how much the sprite should move in each dimension:

   ```
   function moveSprite(dx, dy){
   ```

   You might wonder why I'm working with `dx` *and* `dy` when this object moves only horizontally. See, I'm thinking ahead. I'm going to reuse this function in the next few programs. Even though I don't need to move vertically yet, I will soon, so I included the capability.

2. Get a reference to the surface.

Use the normal `document.getElementById` trick to extract the sprite from the page. Be sure the sprite you're animating has absolute position with `top` and `left` properties defined in a local style.

```
var surface = document.getElementById("surface");
```

3. Extract the sprite's x and y parameters.

The horizontal position is stored in the `left` property. CSS styles are stored as strings and include a measurement. For example, the original `left` value of the sprite is `100px`. For the program, we need only the numeric part. The `parseInt()` function pulls out only the numeric part of the `left` property and turns it into an integer, which is then stored in x. Do the same thing to get the y value.

```
x = parseInt(sprite.style.left);
y = parseInt(sprite.style.top);
```

4. Increment the x and y variables.

Now that you have the x and y values stored as integer variables, you can do math on them. It isn't complicated math. Just add dx to x and dy to y. This allows you to move the object as many pixels as the user wants in both x and y axes.

```
x += dx;
y += dy;
```

5. Check the boundaries.

If you have young children, you know this rule: When you have something that can move, it will get out of bounds. If you let your sprite move, it will leave the space you've designated. Checking the boundaries isn't difficult, but it's another task, so I'm just calling a function here. I describe `checkBounds()` in the next section, but basically it just checks to see whether the sprite is leaving the surface and adjusts its position to stay in bounds.

```
checkBounds();
```

6. Move the ball.

Changing the x and y properties doesn't really move the sprite. To do that, you need to convert the integers back into the CSS format. If x is `120`, you need to set `left` to `120px`. Just concatenate `"px"` to the end of each variable.

```
// move ball to new position
sprite.style.left = x + "px";
sprite.style.top = y + "px";
```

7. Print out the position.

For debugging purposes, I like to know exactly where the x and y positions are, so I just made a string and printed it to an output panel.

```
//describe position
var output = document.getElementById("output");
output.innerHTML = "x: " + x + ", y: " + y;
```

Checking the boundaries

You can respond in a number of ways when an object leaves the playing area. I'm going with *wrapping,* one of the simplest techniques. If something leaves the rightmost border, simply have it jump all the way to the left.

The code handles all four borders:

```
function checkBounds(){
  //wrap
  if (x > MAX_X){
    x = MIN_X;
  } // end if
  if (x < MIN_X){
    x = MAX_X;
  } // end if
  if (y > MAX_Y){
    y = MIN_Y;
  } // end if
  if (y < MIN_Y){
    y = MAX_Y;
  } // end if
} // end function
```

The checkBounds() function depends on the constants. This helps in a couple of ways. When you look at the code, it's really easy to see what's going on:

```
  if (x > MAX_X){
    x = MIN_X;
  } // end if
```

If x is larger than the maximum value for x, set it to the minimum value. You almost can't write it any more clearly than this. If the size of the playing surface changes, you simply change the values of the constants.

All this is very nice, but you probably wonder how I came up with the actual values for the constants. In some languages, you can come up with nice mathematical tricks to predict exactly what the largest and smallest values should be. In JavaScript, this technique is a little tricky because the environment just isn't that precise.

Shouldn't you just get size values from the surface?

In a perfect world, I would have extracted the position values from the playing surface itself. Unfortunately, JavaScript/DOM is not a perfect animation framework. HTML 5 supports a marvelous tag called the *canvas,* which serves as a perfect drawing and animating platform, but it isn't available on all browsers yet.

Because I'm using absolute positioning, the position of the sprite isn't attached to the surface (as it should be) but to the main screen. It's a little annoying, but some experimentation can help you find the right values. Remember, as soon as you start using absolute positioning on a page, you're pretty much committed to it. If you're using animation like this, you probably want to use absolute positioning everywhere or do some other tricks to make sure the sprite stays where you want it to go without overwriting other parts of the page. Regardless, using constants keeps the code easy to read and maintain even if you have to hack a little bit to find the specific values you need.

I chose a simple but effective technique. I temporarily took out the checkbounds() call and just took a look at the output to see what the values of x and y were. I looked to see how large x should be before the sprite wraps and wrote the value down on paper. Likewise, I found largest and smallest values for y.

When I knew these values, I simply placed them in constants. I don't really care that the maximum value for x is 365. I just want to know that when I'm messing around with x I don't want it to go past the MAX_X value.

If the size of my playing surface changes, I can just change the constants and everything will work out fine.

If you're interested, here are the other techniques you can use when a sprite is about to leave the visual area:

- **Bounce:** The object bounces off the wall. This is done by inverting the dx or dy value (depending on whether it's a vertical or horizontal wall).

- **Stop:** The object simply stops moving when it hits the wall. Set dx and dy to 0 to achieve this effect.

- **Continue:** The object keeps moving even though it is out of sight. This is sometimes used for air-traffic control simulations (where visualizing the location is part of the game) or orbital simulations (where presumably the object will return).

- **Combinations:** Sometimes you'll see combinations like the civilization games that simulate a cylindrical map by stopping on the top and bottom and scrolling on the sides.

Reading Input from the Keyboard

You can use JavaScript to read directly from the keyboard. Reading from the keyboard can be useful in a number of situations, but it's especially handy in animation and simple gaming applications.

Figure 8-2 shows a program with another moving ball.

Figure 8-2:
You can
move the
ball with the
arrow keys.

The `keyboard.html` page has no buttons because the arrow keys are used to manage all the input.

You know what I'm going to say. Look this thing over in your browser because it just doesn't have any charm unless you run it and mash on some arrow keys.

Building the keyboard page

The keyboard page is very much like the movement.html page shown earlier in this chapter.

```
<!DOCTYPE html PUBLIC "-//W3C//DTD XHTML 1.0 Strict//EN"
"http://www.w3.org/TR/xhtml1/DTD/xhtml1-strict.dtd">
<html lang="EN" dir="ltr" xmlns="http://www.w3.org/1999/
          xhtml">
  <head>
    <meta http-equiv=»content-type» content=»text/xml;
          charset=utf-8» />
    <title>keyboard.html</title>

    <link rel = «stylesheet»
          type = «text/css»
          href = «keyboard.css» />

    <script type = «text/javascript»
          src = «movement.js»>
    </script>
    <script type = «text/javascript»
          src = «keyboard.js»>
    </script>

  </head>

  <body onload = «init()»>
    <h1>Use arrow keys to move ball</h1>

    <div id = «surface»>
      <div id = «sprite»
          style = «position: absolute;
          top: 100px;
          left: 100px;
          height: 25px;
          width: 25px;» >
        <img src = «ball.gif»
            alt = «ball» />
      </div>
    </div>

    <p id = «output»>
      x = 100, y = 100
    </p>
  </body>
</html>
```

The `keyboard.html` page is very similar to the `movement.html` page described early in the chapter. This sort of situation is when it really pays off to build reusable code. I basically copied the `movement.html` page and made a couple of small but important changes:

✔ **Import the** `movement.js` **script.** This page uses the same functions as the `movement.html` page, so just import the script.

✔ **Add another script specific to reading the keyboard.** You need a couple of modifications, which are housed in a second script file called `keyboard.js`.

✔ **Keep the rest of the page similar.** You still call init() when the body loads, and you still want the same visual design, except for the buttons. The surface and sprite divs are identical to the movement.html design.

✔ **Take out the form.** This page responds to the keyboard, so you don't need a form any more.

Looking over the keyboard.js script

Remember that this program begins with the movement.js script. As far as the browser is concerned, that entire script file has been loaded before the keyboard.js script appears. The basic foundation is already in place from movement. The keyboard script just handles the modifications to make keyboard support work.

Overwriting the init() function

Working with a keyboard still requires some initialization. I need a little more work in the init() function, so I make a new version that replaces the version created in movement.js.

```
//assumes movement.js

function init(){
  sprite = document.getElementById("sprite");
  document.onkeydown = keyListener;
} // end init
```

The order in which you import scripts matters. If you duplicate a function, the browser interprets only the last one it reads.

Setting up an event handler

In my init() function, I still want to initialize the sprite (as I did in movement.js). When you want to read the keyboard, you need to tap into the browser's *event-handling* facility. Browsers provide basic support for page-based events (like body.onload and button.onclick), but they also provide a lower level of support for more fundamental input such as keyboard and mouse input.

If you want to read this lower-level input, you need to specify a function that will respond to the input.

```
document.onkeydown = keyListener;
```

This line specifies that a special function called `keyListener` will be called whenever the user presses a key. Keep the following things in mind when creating this type of event handler:

1. **The event handler should be called in** `init()`.

   You probably want keyboard handling to be available immediately, so you should set up event handlers in the `init()` function.

2. **The function is called as though it were a variable.**

   This is a slightly different syntax than you've seen before. When you create function handlers in HTML, you simply feed a string that represents the function name complete with parameters (`button onclick = "doSomething()"`). When you call a function within JavaScript (as opposed to calling the function in HTML), the function name is actually much like a variable, so it doesn't require quotes.

   If you want to know the truth, functions *are* variables in JavaScript. Next time somebody tells you JavaScript is a "toy language," mention that it supports automatic dereferencing of function pointers. Then run away before the person asks you what that means. (That's what I do.)

3. **You need to create a function with the specified name.**

   If you have this code in `init`, the browser calls a function called `keyListener()` whenever a key is pressed. (You could call the function something else, but `keyListener()` is a pretty good name for it because it listens for keystrokes.)

Responding to keystrokes

After you've set up an event handler, you need to write the function to respond to keystrokes, which is a pretty easy task. Here is the `keyListener` code (found in `keyboard.js`):

```
function keyListener(e){
  // if e doesn't already exist, we're in IE so make it

  if (!e){
    e = window.event;
  } // end IE-specific code

  //left
  if (e.keyCode == 37){
    moveSprite(-10, 0);
  } // end if
```

```
//up
if (e.keyCode == 38){
  moveSprite(0, -10);
} // end if

//right
if (e.keyCode == 39){
  moveSprite(10, 0);
} // end if

//down
if (e.keyCode == 40){
  moveSprite(0, 10);
} // end if

} // end keyListener
```

This code grabs an event object if needed, and then analyzes that object to figure out which key (if any) was pressed. It then calls the `moveSprite()` function to move the sprite. Here's the low-down:

1. **Event functions have event objects.**

   Just knowing that an event has occurred isn't enough. You need to know *which* key the user pressed. Fortunately, the browsers all have an *event* object available that tells you what has happened.

2. **Many browsers pass the event as a parameter.**

   When you create an event function, the browser automatically assigns a special parameter to the function. This parameter (normally called e) represents the event. Just make the function with a parameter called e, and most browsers create e automatically.

   ```
   function keyListener(e){
   ```

3. **Internet Explorer needs a little more help.**

   IE doesn't automatically create an event object for you, so you need to specifically create it.

   ```
   // if e doesn't already exist, we're in IE so make
        it

   if (!e){
     e = window.event;
   } // end IE-specific code
   ```

4. **You can use e to figure out which key the user pressed.**

   The e object has some nifty properties, including `keyCode`. This property returns a number that tells you which key the user pressed.

Do a quick search on *JavaScript event object* to find out other kinds of event tricks. I'm showing the most critical features here, but this is just an introduction to the many interesting things you can do with events.

5. **Compare the** `keycode` **property of the event object to the keycodes corresponding to keys you're interested in.**

   You can figure out the keycodes of any keys on your keyboard, and you can use basic `if` statements to respond appropriately. (I explain key-codes in the following section.)

```
//left
if (e.keyCode == 37){
  moveSprite(-10, 0);
} // end if
```

6. **Call appropriate variations of** `moveSprite`.

   If the user pressed the left-arrow key, move the sprite to the left. You can use the `moveSprite()` function defined in `movement.js` for this.

Deciphering the mystery of keycodes

When you look over the code in the `keyListener` function, you can see some odd numbers in there. For example, the code that looks for the left arrow key actually compares the `e.keyCode` to the value `37`. The big mystery is where all the numbers in the `keyListener` function (in the previous section) came from.

These numbers are called *keycodes*. They are numeric representations of the physical keys on the keyboard. Each physical key on the keyboard has a corresponding keycode. Keycodes are mapped to the physical key, which means the keycode corresponding to a key is the same even if the keyboard mapping is changed (to a foreign language or alternate input setting, for example).

How did I know that the left-arrow key corresponds to the keycode 37? It's pretty simple, really. I just wrote a program to tell me. Figure 8-3 shows `readKeys.html` in action.

Figure 8-3:
This pro-
gram reads
the key-
board and
reports the
key codes.

readKeys.html - Mozilla Firefox

File Edit View History Bookmarks Tools Help

file:///C:/Program%20Files/xampp/htdocs/xfd/xfd4/xfd4.7/readKeys.html

Press a key to see its code

keycode: 16

Run `readKeys` and press a few keys. You can then easily determine what keycode is related to which key. You might also want to look over the code in this format if you're a little confused; because all the code's in one place, you might it's easier to read than the movement examples.

If you use a notebook or an international keyboard, be aware that some of the keycodes can be nonstandard, especially numeric keypad keys. Try to stick to standard keys if you want to ensure that your program works on all keyboards.

Following the Mouse

You can create an event handler that reads the mouse. Figure 8-4 shows such a program.

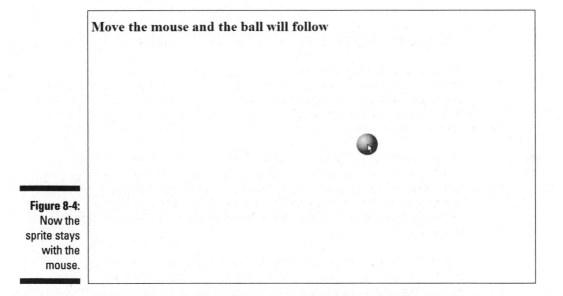

Move the mouse and the ball will follow

Figure 8-4: Now the sprite stays with the mouse.

Achieving this effect is actually quite easy when you know how to read the keyboard, because it works in almost exactly the same way.

Looking over the HTML

The code for `followMouse.html` is simple enough that I kept it in one file.

```
<!DOCTYPE html PUBLIC "-//W3C//DTD XHTML 1.0 Strict//EN"
"http://www.w3.org/TR/xhtml1/DTD/xhtml1-strict.dtd">
<html lang="EN" dir="ltr" xmlns="http://www.w3.org/1999/
          xhtml">
  <head>
    <meta http-equiv=»content-type» content=»text/xml;
          charset=utf-8» />
    <title>followMouse.html</title>
    <script type = «text/javascript»>
      var sprite;

      function init(){
        sprite = document.getElementById(«sprite»);
        document.onmousemove = mouseListener;
      } // end init

      function mouseListener(e){
        if (!e){
          e = window.event;
        } // end IE catch

        //get width and height
        height = parseInt(sprite.style.height);
        width = parseInt(sprite.style.width);

        //move center of sprite to mouse
        x = e.pageX - (width/2);
        y = e.pageY - (height/2);

        sprite.style.left = x + «px»;
        sprite.style.top = y + "px";
      } // end function
    </script>
  </head>

  <body onload = «init()»>
    <h1>Move the mouse and the ball will follow</h1>
    <div id = «sprite»
        style = «position: absolute;
                  left: 100px;
                  top: 100px;
                  width: 50px;
                  height: 50px;»>
      <img src = «ball.gif»
          alt = «ball» />
    </div>
  </body>
</html>
```

Setting up the HTML

The HTML page is simple. This time I'm letting the mouse take up the entire page. No borders are necessary, because the sprite won't be able to leave the page. (If the mouse leaves the page, it no longer sends event messages.)

Just create a sprite with an image as normal and be sure to call init() when the body loads.

Initializing the code

The initialization is pretty straightforward:

1. **Create a global variable for the sprite.**

   Define the sprite variable outside any functions so it will be available to all of them.

   ```
   var sprite;
   ```

2. **Build the sprite in** init().

   The init() function is a great place to create the sprite.

   ```
   function init(){
       sprite = document.getElementById("sprite");
       document.onmousemove = mouseListener;
   ```

3. **Set up an event handler for mouse motion.**

   Set up an event handler in init(). This time you're listening for mouse events, so call this one mouseListener.

   ```
   document.onmousemove = mouseListener;
   ```

Building the mouse listener

The mouse listener works much like a keyboard listener. The mouse listener is called whenever the mouse moves, and it examines the event object to determine the mouse's current position. It then uses that value to place the sprite:

1. **Get the event object.**

   Use the cross-platform technique to get the event object.

   ```
   function mouseListener(e){
     if (!e){
       e = window.event;
     } // end IE catch
   ```

2. **Determine the sprite's width and height.**

   The `top` and `left` properties will point to the sprite's top-left corner. It looks more natural to have the mouse in the center of the sprite. To calculate the center, you need the `height` and `width` values. Don't forget to add these values to the local style for the sprite.

   ```
   //get width and height
   height = parseInt(sprite.style.height);
   width = parseInt(sprite.style.width);
   ```

3. **Use** `e.pageX` **and** `e.pageY` **to get the mouse position.**

   These properties return the current position of the mouse on the page.

4. **Determine** `x` **and** `y` **under the mouse cursor.**

   Subtract half of the sprite's width from the mouse's `x` value (`e.pageX`) so the sprite's horizontal position is centered on the mouse. Repeat with the `y` position.

   ```
   //move center of sprite to mouse
   x = e.pageX - (width/2);
   y = e.pageY - (height/2);
   ```

5. **Move the mouse to the new x and y coordinates.**

   Use the conversion techniques to move the sprite to the new position.

   ```
   sprite.style.left = x + "px";
   sprite.style.top = y + "px";
   ```

 Another fun effect is to have the sprite *influenced* by the mouse. Don't make it follow the mouse directly but check to see where the mouse is in relationship with the sprite. Have the sprite move up if the mouse is above the sprite, for example.

Automatic Motion

You can make a sprite move automatically by attaching a special timer to the object. Figure 8-5 shows the ball moving autonomously across the page.

`Timer.html` is surprisingly simple, because it borrows almost everything from other code.

```
<!DOCTYPE html PUBLIC "-//W3C//DTD XHTML 1.0 Strict//EN"
"http://www.w3.org/TR/xhtml1/DTD/xhtml1-strict.dtd">
<html lang="EN" dir="ltr" xmlns="http://www.w3.org/1999/
        xhtml">
  <head>
    <meta http-equiv=»content-type» content=»text/xml;
        charset=utf-8» />
    <title>timer.html</title>
```

```
<link rel = «stylesheet»
      type = «text/css»
      href = «keyboard.css» />

<script type = «text/javascript»
        src = «movement.js»>
</script>

<script type = «text/javascript»>
  function init(){
    sprite = document.getElementById(«sprite»);
    setInterval(«moveSprite(5, 3)», 100);
  } // end init

</script>
</head>

<body onload = «init()»>
  <h1>Timer-based movement</h1>

  <div id = «surface»>
    <div id = «sprite»
         style = «position: absolute;
         top: 100px;
         left: 100px;
         height: 25px;
         width: 25px;» >
      <img src = «ball.gif»
           alt = «ball» />
    </div>
  </div>

  <p id = «output»>
    x = 100, y = 100
  </p>
</body>
</html>
```

The HTML and CSS are exactly the same as the button.html code. Most of the JavaScript comes from movement.js. The only thing that's really new is a tiny but critical change in the init() method.

JavaScript contains a very useful function called setInterval, which takes two parameters:

✔ **A function call:** Create a string containing a function call including any of its parameters.

✔ **A time interval in milliseconds:** You can specify an interval in 1,000ths of a second. If the interval is 500, the given function will be called twice per second; 50 milliseconds is 20 calls per second; and so on.

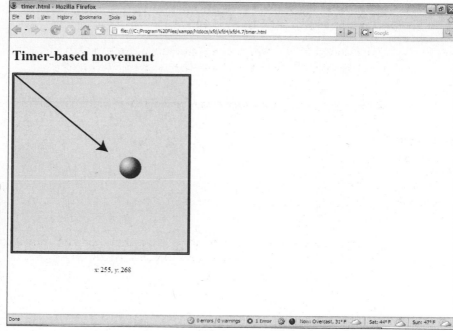

Figure 8-5:
This sprite
is moving
on its own.
(I added
the arrow
to show
motion.)

You can set the interval at whatever speed you want, but that doesn't guarantee things will work that fast. If you put complex code in a function and tell the browser to execute it 1,000 times per second, it probably won't be able to keep up (especially if the user has a slower machine than you do).

The browser calls the specified function at the specified interval. Put any code that you want repeated inside the given function.

Don't put anything in an interval function that doesn't have to go there. Because this code happens several times per second, it's called a *critical path*, and any wasteful processing here could severely slow down the entire program. Try to make the code in an interval function as clean as possible. (That's why I created the `sprite` as a global variable. I didn't want to recreate the sprite 20 times per second, making my program impossible for slower browsers to handle.)

By using automatically moving objects, you get a chance to play with other kinds of boundary detection. If you want to see how to make something bounce when it hits the edge, look at `bounce.html` and `bounce.js` on either of the companion Web sites (`www.aharrisbooks.net/jad` or `www.dummies.com/go/javascriptandajaxfd`) along with the other code featured in this chapter.

Image-Swapping Animation

The other kind of animation you can do involves rapidly changing an image. Look at Figure 8-6 to see one frame of an animated figure.

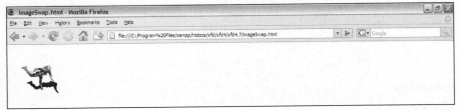

Figure 8-6:
This sprite is
kicking!

Animation is never that easy to show in a still screen shot, so Figure 8-7 shows the sequence of images used to build the kicking sprite.

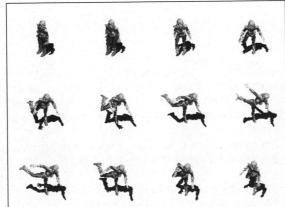

Figure 8-7:
I used this
series of
images to
build the
animation.

You can use any series of images you want. I got these images from a site called Reiner's Tilesets (http://reinerstileset.4players.de/englisch.html). It includes a huge number of sprites, each with several animations. These animations are called Freya.

Preparing the images

You can build your own images, or you can get them from a site like Reiner's Tilesets. In any case, there are a few things to keep in mind when building image animations:

✔ **Keep them small.** Larger images will take a long time to download and will not swap as smoothly as small ones. My images are 128 x 128 pixels, which is a good size.

✔ **Consider adding transparency.** The images from Reiner's Tilesets have a brown background. I made the background transparent by using my favorite graphics editor (GIMP).

✔ **Change the file format.** The images came in .bmp format, which is inefficient and doesn't support transparency. I saved them as .gif images to make them smaller and enable the background transparency.

✔ **Consider changing the names.** I renamed the images to make the names simpler and to eliminate spaces from the filenames. I called the images kick00.gif to kick12.gif.

✔ **Put animation images in a subdirectory.** With ordinary page images, I often find a subdirectory to be unhelpful. When you start building animations, you can easily have a *lot* of little images running around. This is a good place for a subdirectory.

✔ **Be sure you have the right to use the images.** Just because you can use an image doesn't mean you should. Try to get permission from the owner of the images, cite your source, and host the images on your own server. It's just good citizenship.

Building the page

The code for animation just uses variations of things you've already done: a setInterval function and some DOM coding.

```
<!DOCTYPE html PUBLIC "-//W3C//DTD XHTML 1.0 Strict//EN"
"http://www.w3.org/TR/xhtml1/DTD/xhtml1-strict.dtd">
<html lang="EN" dir="ltr" xmlns="http://www.w3.org/1999/
        xhtml">
  <head>
    <meta http-equiv=»content-type» content=»text/xml;
        charset=utf-8» />
    <title>imageSwap.html</title>
    <script type = «text/javascript»>
      //<![CDATA[
      var imgList = new Array (
        «freya/kick00.gif»,
        «freya/kick01.gif»,
        «freya/kick02.gif»,
        «freya/kick03.gif»,
        «freya/kick04.gif»,
        «freya/kick05.gif»,
        «freya/kick06.gif»,
```

```
      «freya/kick07.gif»,
      «freya/kick08.gif»,
      «freya/kick09.gif»,
      «freya/kick10.gif»,
      «freya/kick11.gif»,
      «freya/kick12.gif»
    );

    var frame = 0;
    var spriteImage

    function init(){
      setInterval(«animate()», 100);
      spriteImage = document.getElementById(«image»);
    } // end init

    function animate(){
      frame += 1;
      if (frame > imgList.length){
        frame = 0;
      } // end if
      spriteImage.src = imgList[frame];
    }
    //]]>
  </script>
</head>

<body onclick = «init()»>
  <div id = «sprite»>
    <img id = «image»
         src = «freya/kick00.gif»
         alt = «kicking sprite» />
  </div>
</body>
</html>
```

The HTML is incredibly simple:

1. **Set up the body with an** init() **method.**

   As usual, the body's onclick event calls an init() method to start things up.

2. **Create a** sprite div.

   Build a div named sprite. Because you won't be changing the position of this div (yet), you don't need to worry about the local style.

3. **Name the** img.

   In this program, you want to animate the img inside the div, so you need to give it an id.

Building the global variables

The JavaScript code isn't too difficult, but it requires a little bit of thought:

1. **Create an array of image names.**

   You have a list of images to work with. The easiest way to support this is with an array of image names. Each element of the array is the filename of an image. Put them in the order you want the animation frames to be shown.

   ```
   var imgList = new Array (
     "freya/kick00.gif",
     "freya/kick01.gif",
     "freya/kick02.gif",
     "freya/kick03.gif",
     "freya/kick04.gif",
     "freya/kick05.gif",
     "freya/kick06.gif",
     "freya/kick07.gif",
     "freya/kick08.gif",
     "freya/kick09.gif",
     "freya/kick10.gif",
     "freya/kick11.gif",
     "freya/kick12.gif"
   );
   ```

2. **Build a** `frame` **variable to hold the current frame number.**

   Because this animation has 12 frames, the `frame` variable will go from 0 to 11.

   ```
   var frame = 0;
   ```

3. **Set up** `spriteImage`.

   This variable will be a reference to the `img` tag inside the `sprite` tag.

   ```
   var spriteImage
   ```

Setting up the interval

The `init()` function attaches the `spriteImage` variable to the image object and sets up the `animate()` method to run ten times per second.

```
function init(){
  setInterval("animate()", 100);
  spriteImage = document.getElementById("image");
} // end init
```

Animating the sprite

The actual animation happens in the (you guessed it) `animate()` function.

The function is straightforward:

1. **Increment the frame counter.**

   Add one to the frame variable.

   ```
   frame += 1;
   ```

2. **Check for bounds.**

   Any time you change a variable, you should consider whether it could go out of bounds. I'm using `frame` as an index in the `imgList` array, so I check to see that `frame` is always less than the length of `imgList`.

   ```
   if (frame > imgList.length){
       frame = 0;
   } // end if
   ```

3. **Reset the frame if necessary.**

   If the frame counter gets too high, reset it to 0 and start the animation over.

4. **Copy the image filename from the array to the `src` property of the `spriteImage` object.**

   This step causes the given file to display.

   ```
   spriteImage.src = imgList[frame];
   ```

Improving the animation with preloading

When you run the image swap program, you will get some delays on the first pass as all the images load. (Making the images smaller and saving them in the `.gif` or `.png` format helps with the delays.) Most browsers store images locally, so the images will animate smoothly after the first pass.

If you want smoother animation, you can use a technique called preloading. This causes all the images to load before the animation begins. The `Preload.html` file makes a few changes to preload the image. (I don't show a figure because it looks just like `imageswap` to the user.)

There are no changes in the HTML code. The only changes are in the JavaScript code:

```
var imgFiles = new Array (
  "freya/kick00.gif",
  "freya/kick01.gif",
  "freya/kick02.gif",
  "freya/kick03.gif",
  "freya/kick04.gif",
  "freya/kick05.gif",
  "freya/kick06.gif",
  "freya/kick07.gif",
  "freya/kick08.gif",
  "freya/kick09.gif",
  "freya/kick10.gif",
  "freya/kick11.gif",
  "freya/kick12.gif"
);

var frame = 0;
var spriteImage
var images = new Array(12);

function init(){
  setInterval("animate()", 100);
  spriteImage = document.getElementById("image");
  loadImages();
} // end init

function animate(){
  frame += 1;
  if (frame >= images.length){
    frame = 0;
  } // end if
  spriteImage.src = images[frame].src;
} // end animate

function loadImages(){
  //preloads all the images for faster display.
  for (i=0; i < images.length; i++){
    images[i] = new Image();
    images[i].src = imgFiles[i];
  } // end for loop
} // end loadImages
```

Here's how the preloading works:

1. **Change the array name to** imgFiles.

   This distinction is subtle but important: The array doesn't represent actual images, but the filenames of the images. You need to create another array to hold the actual image data.

2. **Create an array of images.**

   JavaScript has a data type designed specifically for holding image data. The `images` array holds the actual image data (not just filenames, but the actual pictures). The `images` array should be global.

3. **Create a function to populate the `images` array.**

   The `loadImages()` function creates the array of image data. Call `loadImages()` from `init()`.

4. **Build a loop that steps through each element of the `imgFiles` array.**

   You build an image object to correspond to each filename, so the length of the two arrays needs to be the same.

5. **Build a new image object for each filename.**

   Use the `new Image()` construct to build an image object representing the image data associated with a particular file.

6. **Attach that image object to the `images()` array.**

   This array now contains all the image data.

7. **Modify `animate()` to read from the `images()` array.**

   The `animate()` function now reads from the `images()` array. Because the image data has been preloaded into the array, it should display more smoothly.

Preloading images doesn't make the animation faster. It just delays the animation until all the images are loaded into the cache, making it appear smoother. Some browsers still play the animation before the cache has finished loading, but the technique still has benefits.

Even if you don't like animation, these techniques can be useful. You can use the `setInterval()` technique for any kind of repetitive code you might want, including the dynamic display of menus or other page elements. In fact, before CSS became the preferred technique, most dynamic menus used JavaScript animation.

Working with Compound Images

Another common approach to image-swapping animation is to combine all images to a single graphic file and use CSS techniques to display only one part of that image. Figure 8-8 shows you what I mean.

Figure 8-8:
The chopper
compound
image.

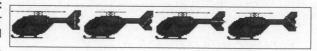

This image file contains several images of a helicopter. Each subimage shows a different position of main rotor and tail rotor. The `compound.html` page shows this image, but it shows only one segment of the image at a time. The part of the image that's displayed is changed rapidly to give the appearance of animation. This technique has some advantages:

- A single image loads more efficiently than a number of separate images.
- The entire image loads at once, eliminating the lag associated with multiple images
- You can combine very complex images with multiple animations in this way.

The completed HTML looks like Figure 8-9 (except, of course, you can see the helicopter's rotors spinning on the real page).

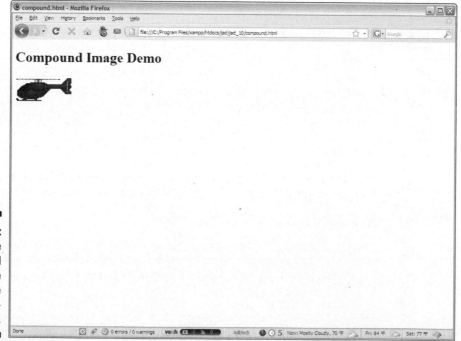

Figure 8-9:
The image
is moved
within the
div to give
the anima-
tion effect.

Preparing the image

Preparing an image to be used in this way does require some care. You must plan to ensure it's easy to animate the image:

- ✔ **Combine all images to a single file.** Use an image-editing tool, such as Gimp or Photoshop.

- ✔ **Make sure all subimages are the same size.** Your life will be easier if all the images are a consistent size. All the chopper images are 64 pixels tall and 132 pixels wide.

- ✔ **Make all subimages the same distance apart.** The images are all 132 pixels apart.

- ✔ **Arrange images in rows or columns.** If you have a single animation, place it in a row or column to simplify your math. You can combine more images for more complex animations (for example, a sequence of walk cycles in each direction.

The particular image used in this example is from Ari's SpriteLib (www. flyingyogi.com/fun/spritelib.html), an excellent resource of open-source game graphics. I modified the image slightly for use in this example.

Setting up the HTML and CSS

As with many animation examples, the HTML code is rather minimal. All that's necessary is a div with an id attribute:

```
<body onload = "init()">
  <h1>Compound Image Demo</h1>
    <div id = "chopper">
  </div>

</body>
```

As you can see, the div doesn't even have an image in it. The image is placed and manipulated through CSS with the background-image property.

The CSS is likewise quite simple:

```
<style type = "text/css">
  #chopper {
    background-image: url("heli.gif");
    height: 64px;
    width: 128px;
    background-position: 0px 0px;
  }
</style>
```

The CSS does a number of important tasks:

1. **Apply the image.**

   The entire image is applied as the background image of the `div`.

2. **Resize the `div`.**

   The `div` size is adjusted to reflect the size of a single subimage. If you look at the HTML at this point, the `div` looks like an ordinary image, showing only the first sub-image of the chopper.

3. **Set the initial background position.**

   Only the first chopper is showing, but the entire image (with four choppers) is attached to the `div`. I use CSS to move the image so different frames of the animation appear in the `div`'s visible space. The initial position is `0px  0px`, meaning that the upper-left corner of the image is aligned with the upper-left corner of the `div`.

This entire helicopter animation might seem like a lot of unnecessary grief. You might ask why I bother when I could just use an animated GIF image. The answer is control. I could use those alternatives, and sometimes they'd be a better choice. However, if you know how to control the animation directly through JavaScript, you can do things you can't do otherwise, like change the animation speed or freeze on a particular frame.

Writing the JavaScript

The general strategy is to run an ordinary animation loop but to change the background position of the `div` every frame so it displays a different frame of the animation. The second frame of the animation occurs at pixel 132, so if you move the background image to the left by 132px, you see the second frame. I stored the position necessary to display each frame in an array called offset. Much of this program looks like the previous image-swapping code.

Setting up global variables

Begin with some global variables that will be used throughout the application:

```
var offsetList = new Array(0, -132, -264, -396);
var frame = 0;
var chopper;
```

1. **Create an** `offsetList` **array.**

   This array holds the coordinates necessary to display each image in the list. Use an image editor to check the positions.

2. **Create a frame variable.**

   This integer describes which frame of the animation is currently show-ing. It will be used as an array index to display the various animation frames.

3. **Create a variable to hold the** div.

   The chopper variable will hold a reference to the div. Changing the style of the chopper variable will change the visible image.

Building an init() function

The initialization function sets up the animation:

```
function init(){
    chopper = document.getElementById("chopper");
    setInterval("animate()", 100);
} // end init
```

The init() function is called by the body onload event. It has two jobs:

1. **Create a reference to the** chopper div.

   Remember, the div doesn't exist until the body has finished loading, so you must populate the chopper variable in a function. The init() function is a perfect place for this kind of work.

2. **Use** setInterval() **to create an animation loop.**

   The program calls the animate() function every 100 milliseconds, or ten times per second.

Animating the sprite

The actual animation is easier than the preparation.

```
function animate(){
    frame++;
    if (frame >= offsetList.length){
        frame = 0;
    } // end if

    offset = offsetList[frame] + "px 0px";
    chopper.style.backgroundPosition = offset;
} // end animate
```

To make the animation finally work, follow these steps:

1. **Increment the frame counter.**

   This step indicates that you're going to a new frame.

2. **Check that the frame is within bounds.**

   The `frame` variable will be used as an index to the `offsetList` array, so you need to ensure that it's smaller than the length of the array. If it's too big, you can just reset it to 0.

3. **Create an `offset` value.**

   The `offset` value is generated from the `offsetList` array. Note that the array contains only the x value. Concatenate this with `"px 0px"` to create an offset in the legal format for CSS. (Look at the original CSS for background-position to see the format.)

4. **Apply the offset to the `chopper` variable.**

   Use the `backgroundPosition` attribute of the `style` attribute to dynamically change the background image's position.

Movement and Swapping

You can combine motion effects with image-swapping to have an image move around on the screen with animated motion. Figure 8-10 tries to show this effect, but you need to use a browser to really see it.

Making this program requires nothing at all new. It's just a combination of the techniques used throughout this chapter. Figure 8-11 shows the list of images used to make Freya run. (I added the arrow again just so you can see how the movement works.)

Building the HTML framework

The HTML is (as usual) pretty minimal here:

```
<!DOCTYPE html PUBLIC "-//W3C//DTD XHTML 1.0 Strict//EN"
"http://www.w3.org/TR/xhtml1/DTD/xhtml1-strict.dtd">
<html lang="EN" dir="ltr" xmlns="http://www.w3.org/1999/
          xhtml">
  <head>
    <meta http-equiv=»content-type» content=»text/xml;
          charset=utf-8» />
    <title>run.html</title>
    <script type = «text/javascript»
            src - «run.js»>
    </script>
  </head>
```

```
<body onload = «init()»>
   <div id = «sprite»
       style = «position: absolute;
                 top: 100px;
                 left: 100px;»>
     <img src = «freya/run0.gif»
          id = «image»
          alt = «running image» />
   </div>
 </body>
</html>
```

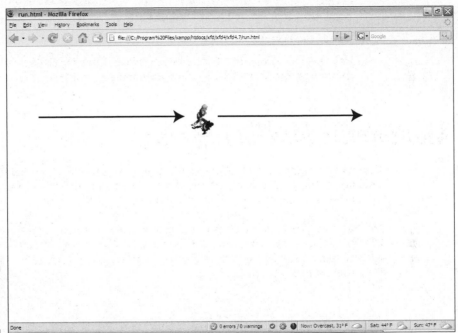

Figure 8-10:
Run, Freya,
Run!

Figure 8-11:
These are
the running
images from
Reiner's
Tilesets.

When you want to create a moving image-swap animation, follow these steps:

1. **Import the script.**

   You can build the script locally (as I did in the last example), but any time the script gets complex, it might be better in an external file.

2. **Call an** init() **method.**

   Most animation requires an init() method called from body. onload(), and this animation is no exception.

3. **Name the sprite.**

   The sprite is a div that will move, so it needs absolute position, top, and left properties all defined as local styles.

4. **Name the image.**

   You also want to animate the image inside the sprite. The only property you'll change here is the src, so no local styles are necessary here.

Building the code

The JavaScript code is familiar because all the elements can be borrowed from previous programs. Here's the code for run.js (used by run.html) in its entirety.

```
//run.js

var frame = 0;
var imgList = new Array(
  "freya/run0.gif",
  "freya/run1.gif",
  "freya/run2.gif",
  "freya/run3.gif",
  "freya/run4.gif",
  "freya/run5.gif",
  "freya/run6.gif",
  "freya/run7.gif"
);

var sprite;
var spriteImage;
var MAX_X = 500;

function init(){
  sprite = document.getElementById("sprite");
  spriteImage = document.getElementById("image");
```

```
    setInterval("animate()", 100);
} // end init

function animate(){
  updateImage();
  updatePosition();
} // end animate

function updateImage(){
  frame++;
  if (frame > imgList.length){
    frame = 0;
  } // end if
  spriteImage.src = imgList[frame];
} // end updateImage

function updatePosition(){
  sprite = document.getElementById("sprite");
  var x = parseInt(sprite.style.left);
  x += 10;
  if (x > MAX_X){
    x = 0;
  } // end if
  sprite.style.left = x + "px";
} // end function
```

Defining global variables

You have a few global variables in the code from the previous section:

✔ frame:The frame number. It is an integer from 0 to 11 that serves as the index for the imgList array.

✔ imgList: An array of filenames with the animation images.

✔ sprite: The div that will be moved around the screen.

✔ spriteImage: The img element of sprite. This is the image that will be swapped.

✔ MAX_X: A constant holding the maximum value of X. In this program, I'm moving only in one direction, so the only boundary I'm worried about is MAX_X. If the sprite moved in other directions, I'd add some other constants for the other boundary conditions.

Initializing your data

The init() function performs its normal tasks: setting up sprite variables and calling the animate() function on an interval.

```
function init(){
  sprite = document.getElementById("sprite");
  spriteImage = document.getElementById("image");

  setInterval("animate()", 100);
} // end init
```

When you move and swap images, sometimes you'll have to adjust the animation interval and the distance traveled each frame so the animation looks right. Otherwise the sprite might seem to skate rather than run.

Animating the image

I really have two kinds of animation happening at once, so in the grand tradition of encapsulation, the animate() function passes off its job to two other functions:

```
function animate(){
  updateImage();
  updatePosition();
} // end animate
```

Updating the image

The updateImage() function handles the image-swapping duties:

```
function updateImage(){
  frame++;
  if (frame > imgList.length){
    frame = 0;
  } // end if
  spriteImage.src = imgList[frame];
} // end updateImage
```

Moving the sprite

The sprite is moved in the updatePosition() function:

```
function updatePosition(){
  sprite = document.getElementById("sprite");
  var x = parseInt(sprite.style.left);
  x += 10;
  if (x > MAX_X){
    x = 0;
  } // end if
  sprite.style.left = x + "px";
} // end function
```

TIP

I know what you're thinking: You could use this stuff to make a really cool game. It's true. You can make games with JavaScript, but you'll eventually run into JavaScript's design limitations. I prefer Flash and Python as languages to do game development. Now that I mention it, I've written other Wiley books on exactly these topics: *Flash Game Programming For Dummies* and *Game Programming: The L Line*. See you there!

Part III

Moving Up to AJAX

The 5th Wave   By Rich Tennant

"Okay, I think I forgot to mention this, but we now have a Web management function that automatically alerts us when there's a broken link on The Aquarium's Web site."

In this part . . .

*E*very once in a while, a technology comes along that threatens to change everything. AJAX is one such technology. In this part, you learn what all the fuss is about and why AJAX is such a big deal. You learn how to make your own AJAX requests by hand, and then you do some real Web 2.0 work with the fun and powerful jQuery library.

Chapter 9 describes the nuts-and-bolts details of AJAX — how it works, how meaningless the acronym is, and everything. See how to build an AJAX connection by hand (but after you've seen it once, use a library like everyone else does).

Chapter 10 introduces the spiffy jQuery library. This free toolkit simplifies AJAX tremendously, and it adds amazing new capabilities to JavaScript. Learn how to incorporate jQuery into your pages and get started with this incredible toolkit.

Chapter 11 shows how to use jQuery's many cool animation features. You'll make various elements play hide-and-seek, slide around, fade, and animate. It's really fun.

Chapter 12 introduces the incredible jQuery user interface toolkit. This fun tool allows you to create and use beautiful CSS themes. You also learn how to add dragging, dropping, and resizing behavior to any element on the page.

Chapter 13 describes more of the jQuery user interface, especially elements that improve usability. You learn how to easily build accordions and tabbed interfaces, and you are introduced to automatic calendars, sortable lists, scrollers, and custom dialogs.

Chapter 14 explains how jQuery helps with more advanced AJAX functions, especially working with data. First you get an overview of traditional server-side programming with PHP. Then you learn how AJAX simplifies this process, and how to manage data in specialized formats like XML and JSON.

Chapter 9

AJAX Essentials

In This Chapter

▶ Understanding AJAX

▶ Using JavaScript to manage HTTP requests

▶ Creating an XMLHttpRequest object

▶ Building a synchronous AJAX request

▶ Retrieving data from an AJAX request

▶ Managing asynchronous AJAX requests

*I*f you've been following the Web trends, you've no doubt heard of AJAX. This technology has generated a lot of interest. Depending on who you listen to, it's either going to "change the Internet" or "it's a lot of overblown hype." In this book I show what AJAX really is, how to use it, and how to use a particular AJAX library to supercharge your Web pages.

AJAX: Return to Troy

Okay, AJAX has nothing to do with a sequel to the *Iliad* (though that would be pretty cool). But since I have your attention, let's discuss AJAX, the mighty and very real Web technology. The first thing to do is figure out exactly what AJAX is and what it isn't. It isn't . . . :

- ✔ **A programming language.** Nope. It isn't one more language to cram into your head (along with the many others you encounter).

- ✔ **New.** No. Most of the technology in AJAX isn't really all that new. It's the way it's being used that's different.

- ✔ **Remarkably different.** Not really. For the most part, AJAX is really the same kinds of things you see in the rest of this book. It's about building compliant Web pages that interact with the user.

So you've got to wonder why people are so excited about AJAX. It's a relatively simple thing, but it has the potential to change the way people think about Internet development. Here's what it really is, has, and does:

- **Direct control of client-server communication.** Rather than relying on the automatic communication between client and server that happens with Web sites and server-side programs, AJAX is about managing this relationship more directly.

- **Use of the** `XMLHttpRequest` **object.** This is a special object that's been built into the DOM of all major browsers for some time, but hasn't been used heavily. The real innovation of AJAX was finding creative (perhaps unintentional) uses for this heretofore-obscure utility.

- **A closer relationship between client-side and server-side programming.** Up to now, client-side programs (usually JavaScript) did their own thing, and server-side programs (PHP) operated without too much knowledge of each other. AJAX helps these two types of programming work together better.

- **A series of libraries that facilitate this communication.** AJAX isn't all that hard to use, but it does have a lot of details. Several great libraries have sprung up to simplify using AJAX technologies. You'll find AJAX libraries for both client-side languages (like JavaScript) and server-side languages (like PHP). As an added bonus, these libraries often include other great features that make JavaScript programming easier and more powerful.

Let's say you're making an online purchase with a shopping-cart mechanism.

In a typical (pre-AJAX) system, an entire Web page is downloaded to the user's computer. There might be a limited amount of JavaScript-based interactivity, but anything that requires a data request needs to be sent back to the server. For example, if you're on a shopping site and you want more information about that fur-lined fishbowl you've had your eye on, you might click the "More information" button. Doing so sends a request to the server, which builds an entire new Web page for you, containing your new request.

Every time you make a request, the system builds a whole new page on the fly. The client and server have a long-distance relationship.

In the old days when you wanted to manage your Web site's content, you had to refresh each Web page — time-consuming to say the least. But with AJAX, you can update the content without refreshing the page. Instead of the server sending an entire-page response just to update a few words, the server only sends the words you want to update and nothing else.

If you're using an AJAX-enabled shopping cart, you might still click the fish-bowl image. An AJAX request goes to the server and gets information about the fishbowl. And here's the good part: This information appears immediately on the current page, without having to completely refresh the page.

AJAX technology allows you to send a request to the server, which can then change just a small part of the page. With AJAX, you can have a whole bunch of smaller requests happening all the time, rather than a few big ones that rebuild the page in large, distracting flurries of activity.

To the user, this makes the Web page look more like a traditional application. That's the big appeal of AJAX: It allows Web applications to act more like desktop apps, even if the Web apps have complicated features (such as remote database access).

Google's Gmail was the first major application to use AJAX, and it blew people away because it felt so much like a regular application inside a Web browser.

AJAX Spelled Out

Technical people love snappy acronyms. There's nothing more intoxicating than inventing a term. *AJAX* is one term that has taken on a life of its own. As with many computing acronyms, it's a fun word, but it doesn't really mean much. AJAX stands for Asynchronous JavaScript And XML. I suspect these terms were chosen to make a pronounceable acronym rather than for their accuracy or relevance to how AJAX works. (But what do I know?)

A is for asynchronous

An asynchronous transaction (at least in AJAX terms) is one in which more than one thing can happen at once. For example you can have an AJAX call process a request while the rest of your form is being processed. AJAX requests do not absolutely *have* to be asynchronous, but they usually are. (It's really okay if you don't follow this completely. It's not an important part of understanding AJAX, but vowels are always nice in an acronym.)

When it comes to Web development, *asynchronous* means you can send and receive as many different requests as you want — independently. Data might start transmitting at any time without having any effect on other data transmissions. You could have a form that saves each field to the database as soon as it's filled out. Or perhaps a series of drop-down lists that generates another drop-down list based on the value you just selected.

In this chapter, I show you how to implement both synchronous and asynchronous versions of AJAX.

J is for JavaScript

If you want to make an AJAX call, you simply write some JavaScript code that simulates a form. You can then access a special object hidden in the DOM (the XMLHttpRequest object) and use its methods to send that request to the user. Your program acts like a form, even if there was no form there. In that sense, when you're writing AJAX code, you're really using JavaScript. Of course, you can also use any other client-side programming language that can speak with the DOM, including Flash and (to a lesser extent) Java. JavaScript is the dominant technology, so it's in the acronym.

A lot of times, you also use JavaScript to decode the response from the AJAX request.

A is for . . . and?

I think it's a stretch to use "and" in an acronym, but AJX just isn't as cool as AJAX. I guess they didn't ask me.

And X is for . . . data?

The X is actually for XML, which is one way to send the data back and forth from the server.

Because the object we're using is the XMLHttpRequest object, it makes sense that it requests XML. It can do that, yes, but it can also get *any* kind of text data. You can use AJAX to retrieve all kinds of things:

- ✔ **Plain old text:** Sometimes you just want to grab some text from the server. Maybe you have a text file with a daily quote in it or something.

- ✔ **Formatted HTML:** You can have text stored on the server as a snippet of HTML/XHTML code and use AJAX to load this page snippet into your browser. This gives you a powerful way to build a page from a series of smaller segments. You can use this to re-use parts of your page (say headings or menus) without duplicating them on the server.

✓ **XML data:** XML is a great way to pass data around (That's what it was invented for.) You might send a request to a program that goes to a database, makes a request, and returns the result as XML.

✓ **JSON data:** A new standard called JSON (JavaScript Object Notation, introduced in Chapter 5) is emerging as an alternative to XML for formatted data transfer. It has some interesting advantages.

In this chapter, I stick with plain old text and HTML. Chapter 14 describes mechanisms for working with XML and JSON data in AJAX.

Making a Basic AJAX Connection

AJAX uses some pretty technical parts of the Web in ways that might be unfamiliar to you. Read through the rest of this chapter so you know what AJAX is doing, but don't get bogged down in the details. Nobody does it by hand! (Except for people who write AJAX libraries or books about using AJAX.) In Chapter 10 I show a library that does all the work for you. If all these details are making you misty-eyed, just skip ahead to the next chapter and come back here when you're ready to see how all the magic works.

The `basicAJax.html` program shown in Figure 9-1 illustrates AJAX at work.

Figure 9-1:
Click the button and you'll see some AJAX magic.

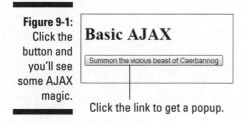

Click the link to get a popup.

When the user clicks on the link, a small pop-up shown in Figure 9-2 appears.

If you download this file to your own machine, it will probably not run correctly. That's because AJAX relies on a Web server for its magic. AJAX code will only work properly if it is on a Web server. If you want to test AJAX, you'll need to post it onto a Web host or install a server on your own machine. Chapter 14 outlines this process. The examples are working on my Web site, so you can always look there: `www.aharrisbooks.net/jad`.

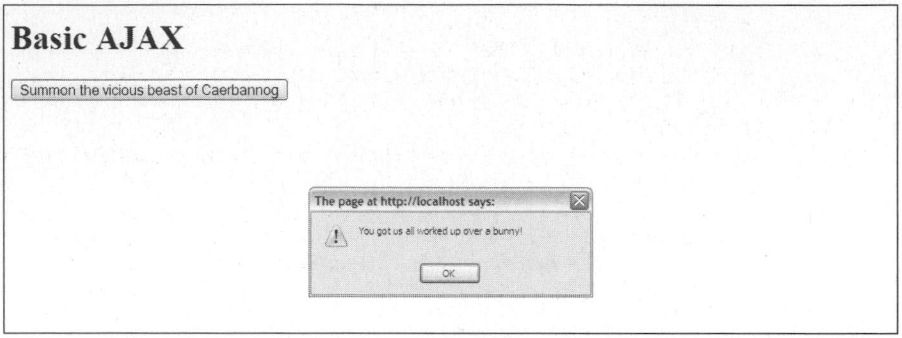

Basic AJAX

Summon the vicious beast of Caerbannog

Figure 9-2:
This text
came from
the server.

The page at http://localhost says:

⚠ You got us all worked up over a bunny!

OK

If you don't get the joke, you need to go rent *Monty Python and the Holy Grail*. It's part of geek culture. Trust me. In fact, you should really own a copy.

It's very easy to make JavaScript pop up a dialog box, but the interesting thing here is where that text came from: The data was stored on a text file on the server. Without AJAX, there's no easy way to get data from the server without reloading the entire page.

You might claim that HTML frames allow you to pull data from the server, but frames have been *deprecated* (labeled obsolete) in XHTML because they cause a lot of other problems. You can use a frame to load data from the server, but you can't do all the other cool things with frame-based data that you can with AJAX. Even if frames were allowed, AJAX is a much better solution most of the time.

This particular example uses a couple of shortcuts to make it easier to understand:

✔ **It isn't fully asynchronous.** The program will pause while it retrieves data. As a user, you won't even notice this, but as you'll see, this can have a serious drawback. It's a bit simpler, so I start with this example and then extend it to make the asynchronous version.

✔ **It isn't completely cross-browser.** The AJAX technique I use in this program works fine for IE 7 and 8 and all versions of Firefox (and most other standards-compliant browsers). It does not work correctly, however, in IE 6 and earlier. I recommend you use jQuery or another library (described in Chapter 10) for cross-browser compatibility.

Look over the code, and you'll find it reasonable enough:

```
<!DOCTYPE html PUBLIC
"-//W3C//DTD XHTML 1.0 Strict//EN"
"http://www.w3.org/TR/xhtml1/DTD/xhtml1-strict.dtd">
<html lang = "EN" xml:lang = "EN" dir = "ltr">
<head>
<meta http-equiv=»content-type» content=»text/xml;
            charset=utf-8» />

<title>Basic AJAX</title>
<script type = «text/javascript»>
//<![CDATA[

function getAJAX(){
  var request = new XMLHttpRequest();
  request.open(«GET», «beast.txt», false);
  request.send(null);

  if (request.status == 200){
    //we got a response
    alert(request.responseText);
  } else {
    //something went wrong
    alert(«Error- « + request.status + «: « + request.
          statusText);
  } // end if
} // end function
//]]>

</script>


</head>

<body>
<h1>Basic AJAX</h1>

<form action = «»>
  <p>
    <button type = «button»
            onclick = «getAJAX()»>
      Summon the vicious beast of Caerbannog
    </button>
  </p>
</form>


</body>
</html>
```

Building the HTML form

You don't absolutely *need* an HTML form for AJAX, but I have a simple one here, complete with a button. Note that the form is not attached to the server in any way. Here's the code:

```
<form action = "">
  <p>
    <button type = "button"
            onclick = "getAJAX()">
      Summon the vicious beast of Caerbannog
    </button>
  </p>
</form>
```

The button is attached to a JavaScript function called `getAJAX()`.

All you really need is some kind of structure that can trigger a JavaScript function.

AJAX isn't a complex technology, but it does draw on several other technologies. You might need to review some earlier JavaScript chapters if this material is unfamiliar to you. Although these examples don't require PHP, they do involve server-side responses like PHP does, so AJAX is usually studied by people already familiar with both JavaScript and PHP. I give a brief overview of PHP and how it is used with AJAX in Chapter 14.

Creating an XMLHttpRequest object

The key to AJAX is a special object called the `XMLHttpRequest` object. All the major browsers have it, and knowing how to use it in code is what makes AJAX work. It's pretty easy to create with the `new` keyword:

```
var request = new XMLHttpRequest();
```

Internet Explorer, in versions 5 and 6, had an entirely different way of invoking the `XMLHttpRequest` object — involving a technology called *ActiveX*. If you want to support these older browsers, use one of the libraries mentioned in Chapter 10. (I've decided not to worry about them in this introductory chapter.)

This line makes an instance of the `XMLHttpRequest` object. You'll use methods and properties of this object to control a request to the server (as shown in Table 9-1).

AJAX is really nothing more than HTTP, the protocol that your browser and server quietly use all the time to communicate with each other. You can think of an AJAX request like this: Imagine you have a basket with a balloon tied to the handle and a long string. As you walk around the city, you can release the basket under a particular window and let it rise up. The window (server) will put something in the basket, and you can then wind the string to bring the basket back down and retrieve the contents.

Table 1-1 Useful Members of the XMLHttpRequest Object

Member	Description	Basket analogy
open(protocol, URL, synchronization)	Opens up a connection to the indicated file on the server.	Stands under a particular window.
send(parameters)	Initiates the transaction with given parameters (or null).	Releases the basket but hangs on to the string.
status	Returns the HTTP status code returned by the server (200 is success).	Checks for error codes ("window closed," "balloon popped," "string broken," or "everything's great").
statusText	Text form of HTTP status.	Text form of status code, a text translation of the numeric error code returned by status.
responseText	Text of the transaction's response.	Gets the contents of the basket.
readyState	Describes current status of the transaction (4 is complete).	Is the basket empty, going up, coming down, or here and ready to get contents?
onReadyStateChange	Event handler. Attach a function to this parameter, and when the readyState changes, the function will be called automatically.	What should I do when the state of the basket changes? For example, should I do something when I get the basket back?

Don't worry about all the details in this table. I describe these things as you need them in the text. Also, some of these elements only pertain to asynchronous connections, so you won't always need them all.

Opening a connection to the server

The `XMLHttpRequest` object has several useful methods. One of the most important is the `open()` method. Here's what it looks like in action:

```
request.open("GET", "beast.txt", false);
```

The `open()` method opens up a connection to the server. As far as the server is concerned, this connection is identical to the connection made when the user clicks a link or submits a form. The `open()` method takes three parameters:

- **The `request` method:** The `request` method describes how the server should process the request. Typical values are GET and POST. The use of these values is described in Chapter 14.

- **A file or program name:** The second parameter is the name of a file or program on the server. This is usually a program or file in the same directory as the current page.

- **A synchronization trigger:** AJAX can be done in synchronous or asynchronous mode. (Yeah, I know, then it'd be AJAX or SJAX, but stay with me here.) The synchronous form is easier to understand, so I use it first. The next example (and all the others in this book) will use the asynchronous approach.

For this example, I use the GET mechanism to load a file called `beast.txt` from the server in synchronized mode.

Sending the request and parameters

Once you've opened up a request, you need to pass that request to the server. The `send()` method performs this task. It also provides you a mechanism for sending data to the server. This arrangement only makes sense if the request is going to a PHP program (or some other program on the server). Because I'm just requesting a regular text document, I send the value `null` to the server:

```
request.send(null);
```

This is a synchronous connection, so the program pauses here until the server sends the requested file. If the server never responds, the page will hang. (This is exactly why the normal approach is to use asynchronous connections.) Because this is just a test program, however, assume everything will work okay and motor on.

Returning to the basket analogy, the send() method releases the basket, which floats up to the window. In a synchronous connection, we're assuming the basket is filled and comes down automatically. The next step won't happen until the basket is back on earth. (But if something goes wrong, the next step might never happen, because the basket will never come back.)

Checking the status

The next line of code won't happen until the server passes some sort of response back. Any HTTP request is followed by a numeric code. Normally, your browser checks these codes automatically, and you don't see them. Occasionally, in the course of regular Web browsing, you run across an HTTP error code such as 404 (file not found) or 500 (internal server error). If the server was able to respond to the request, it will pass a status code of 200. (You never see a 200 status code in ordinary browsing, because that means the page request was successful, so you see the page.) The XMLHttpRequest object has a property called status that returns the HTTP status code. If status is 200, then everything went fine and you can proceed. If status is any other value, some type of error occurred.

Fun with HTTP response codes

Just like the post office stamping success/error messages on your envelope, the server sends back status messages with your request. You can see all the possible status codes on the World Wide Web Consortium's Web site at www.w3.org/Protocols/rfc2616/rfc2616-sec10.html, but the important ones to get you started are as follows:

✔ **200 = OK:** This is a success code. Everything went okay, and your response has been returned.

✔ **400 = Bad Request:** This is a client error code. It means that something went wrong on the user side. The request was poorly formed and couldn't be understood.

✔ **404 = Not Found:** This is a client error code. The page the user requested doesn't exist or couldn't be found.

✔ **408 = Request Timeout:** This is a client error code. The server gave up on waiting for the user's computer to finish making its request.

✔ **500 = Internal Server Error:** This is a server error code. It means that the server had an error and couldn't fill the request.

You'll want to make sure that the status of the request is successful before you run the code that's dependant upon the request. You can check for all the various status codes if you want, but for this simple example I'm just ensuring that status is 200:

```
if (request.status == 200){
  //we got a response
  alert(request.responseText);
} else {
  //something went wrong
  alert("Error- " + request.status + ": " + request.
       statusText);
} // end if
```

The request.status property will contain the server's response. If this value is 200, I want to do something with the results. In this case, I simply display the text in an alert box. If the request is anything but 200, I use the statusText property to determine what went wrong and pass that information to the user in an alert.

Using the status property is like looking at the basket after it returns: The container might have the requested data in it, or it might have some sort of note (along the lines of "Sorry, the window was closed. I couldn't fulfill your request."). There's not much point in processing the data if it didn't return successfully.

Of course, I could do a lot more with the data. If it's already formatted as HTML code, I can use the innerHTML DOM tricks described in Chapter 6 to display the code in any part of my page. If I'm dealing with some other type of formatted data (XML or JSON), I can manipulate it with JavaScript and do whatever I want with it. This technique is described in Chapter 14.

All Together Now: Making the Connection Asynchronous

The synchronous AJAX connection described in the previous section is easy to understand, but it has one major drawback: The client's page *completely stops processing* while waiting for a response from the server. This might not seem like a big problem at first glance, but it is. If aliens attack the Web server, it won't make the connection, and the rest of the page will never be activated. The user's browser will hang indefinitely. In most cases, the user will have to shut down the browser process with Ctl+Alt+Del (or the similar procedure on other OSs). Obviously it would be best to prevent this kind of error.

That's why most AJAX calls use the asynchronous technique. Here's the big difference: When you send an asynchronous request, the client keeps on processing the rest of the page. When the request is complete, an event handler processes the event. If the server goes down, the browser will not hang (although the page probably won't do what you want).

In other words, the readyState property is like looking at the basket's progress. The basket could be sitting there empty, because you haven't begun the process. It could be going up to the window, being filled, coming back down, or it could be down and ready to use. You're only concerned with the last state (ready), because that means the data is ready.

I didn't include a figure showing the asynchronous version, because to the user, it looks exactly the same as the synchronous connection. Be sure to put this code on your own server and check it out for yourself. (Or of course just look at it on my server.)

The asynchronous version looks exactly the same on the front end, but the code is structured a little differently:

```
<!DOCTYPE html PUBLIC
"-//W3C//DTD XHTML 1.0 Strict//EN"
"http://www.w3.org/TR/xhtml1/DTD/xhtml1-strict.dtd">
<html lang = "EN" xml:lang = "EN" dir = "ltr">
<head>
<meta http-equiv=»content-type» content=»text/xml;
          charset=utf-8» />

<title>asynch.html</title>
<script type = «text/javascript»>
//<![CDATA[

var request;  //make request a global variable

function getAJAX(){
  request = new XMLHttpRequest();
  request.open(«GET», «beast.txt»);
  request.onreadystatechange = checkData;
  request.send(null);
} // end function

function checkData(){
  if (request.readyState == 4) {
    // if state is finished
    if (request.status == 200) {
      // and if attempt was successful
      alert(request.responseText);
    } // end if
  } // end if
} // end checkData
```

```
//]]>

</script>

</head>

<body>
<h1>Asynchronous AJAX transmission</h1>
<form action = «»>
  <p>
    <button type = «button»
            onclick = «getAJAX()»>
      Summon the beast of Caerbannogh
    </button>
  </p>
</form>
</body>
</html>
```

Setting up the program

The general setup of this program is just like the earlier AJAX example. The HTML is a simple button which calls the getAJAX() function.

The JavaScript code now has two functions. The getAJAX() function sets up the request, but a separate function (checkData()) responds to the request. In an asynchronous AJAX model, it's typical to separate the request and the response in different functions.

Note that in the JavaScript code, I made the XMLHttpRequest object — the request object — into a global variable by declaring it outside any functions. I generally avoid making global variables, but it makes sense in this case because I have two different functions that require the request object. Look over Chapter 5 if you need a refresher on the advantages and disadvantages of global variables.

Building the getAJAX() function

The getAJAX() function sets up and executes the communication with the server.

```
function getAJAX(){
  request = new XMLHttpRequest();
  request.open("GET", "beast.txt");
  request.onreadystatechange = checkData;
  request.send(null);
} // end function
```

The code in this function is pretty straightforward. Here's what you do:

1. **Create the** request **object.**

   The request object is created exactly as it was in the first example.

2. **Call the request's** open() **method to open a connection.**

   Note that this time I left the synchronous parameter out, which creates the (default) asynchronous connection.

3. **Assign an event handler to catch responses.**

   You can use event handlers much like the ones in the DOM. In this particular case I'm telling the request object to call a function called checkData whenever the state of the request changes.

   You can't easily send a parameter to a function when you call it using this particular mechanism. That's why I made request a global variable.

4. **Send the request.**

   As before, the send() method begins the process. Because this is now an asynchronous connection, the rest of the page will continue to process. As soon as the request's state changes (hopefully because there's been a successful transfer), the checkData() function will be activated.

Reading the response

Of course, you now need a function to handle the response when it comes back from the server. This works by checking the ready state of the response. Any HTTP request has a ready state, which is a simple integer value describing what state the request is currently in. There are many ready states, but the only one we're concerned with is 4, because it means the request is finished and ready to process.

Ready, set, readyState!

The readyState property of the request object indicates the ready state of the request. It has five possible values:

✔ **0 = Uninitialized:** The request object has been created, but the open() method hasn't been called on.

✔ **1 = Loading:** The request object has been created, the open() method has been called, but the send() method hasn't been called.

✔ **2 = Loaded:** The request object has been created, the open() method has been called, the send() method has been called, but the response isn't yet available from the server.

✔ **3 = Interactive:** The request object has been created, the open() method has been called, the send() method has been called, the response has started trickling back from the server, but not everything has been received yet.

✔ **4 = Completed:** The request object has been created, the open() method has been called, the send() method has been called, the response has been fully received, and the request object is finished with all its request/response tasks.

Each time the readyState property of the request changes, the function you map to readyStateChanged is called. In a typical AJAX program, this will happen four times per transaction. There's no point in reading the data until the transaction is completed, which will happen when readyState is equal to 4.

The basic strategy for checking a response is to check the ready state in the aptly-named request.readyState property. If the ready state is 4, check the status code to ensure there's no error. If ready state is 4 and status is 200, you're in business, so you can process the form. Here's the code:

```
function checkData(){
  if (request.readyState == 4) {
    // if state is finished
    if (request.status == 200) {
      // and if attempt was successful
      alert(request.responseText);
    } // end if
  } // end if
} // end checkData
```

Once again, you can do anything you want with the text you receive. I'm just printing it out, but the data can be incorporated into the page or processed in any way you want.

Chapter 10

Improving JavaScript and AJAX with jQuery

In This Chapter

▶ Downloading and including the jQuery library

▶ Making an AJAX request with jQuery

▶ Using component selectors

▶ Adding events to components

▶ Creating a simple content management system with jQuery

*J*avaScript has amazing capabilities. It's useful on its own and when you add AJAX, it becomes incredibly powerful. However, JavaScript can be tedious. There's a lot to remember, and it can be a real pain to handle multiple platform issues. Some tasks (like AJAX) are a bit complex and require a lot of steps. Regardless of the task, there are always browser compatibility issues to deal with.

AJAX libraries have come to the rescue, and the jQuery library in particular is a powerful tool for simplifying AJAX. This chapter explains what JavaScript Libraries can do and introduces you to one of the most popular libraries in current use.

Introducing JavaScript Libraries

For these reasons, Web programmers began to compile commonly used functions into reusable libraries. These libraries became more powerful over time, and some of them have now become fundamental to Web development.

As these libraries became more powerful, the libraries not only added AJAX capabilities, but many library developers also add features to JavaScript/ DOM programming that were once available only in traditional programming languages. Many of these libraries allow for a new visual aesthetic as well as enhanced technical capabilities. In fact, most applications considered part of the Web 2.0 revolution are based in part on one of these libraries.

What is Web 2.0?

I'm almost reluctant to mention the term Web 2.0 here because it isn't really a very useful description. There are actually three main ways people describe Web 2.0 (if such a thing really exists).

Some talk about Web 2.0 as a design paradigm (lots of white space, simple color schemes, and rounded corners). I believe the visual trends will evolve to something else, and that other aspects of the Web 2.0 sensibility will have longer-lasting impact.

The technical aspects of Web 2.0 (heavy use of AJAX and libraries to make Web programming more like traditional programming) are more important than the visual aspects. These technologies make it possible to build Web applications in much the same way desktop applications are now created.

I personally think the most important emerging model of the Web is the change in the communication paradigm. Web 2.0 is no longer about a top-down broadcast model of communication, but more of a conversation among users of a site or system. Although the visual and technical aspects are important, the changing relationship between producers and users of information is perhaps even more profound.

The design and communication aspects are fascinating, but this book focuses on the technical aspects. When you can actually work in Web 2.0 technologies, you can decide for yourself how to express the technology visually and socially. I can't wait to see what you produce.

A number of very powerful JavaScript/AJAX libraries are available. All make basic JavaScript easier, and each has its own learning curve. No library will write code for you, but a good library can handle some of the drudgery and let you work instead on the creative aspects of your program. JavaScript libraries can let you work at a higher level than plain JavaScript, so you can write more elaborate pages in less time.

Several important JavaScript/AJAX libraries are available. Here are a few of the most prominent:

- ✔ **DOJO** (www.dojotoolkit.org/): A very powerful library that includes a series of user interface widgets (like those in Visual Basic and Java) as well as AJAX features.

- ✔ **MochiKit** (http://mochikit.com/): A nice lower-level set of JavaScript functions to improve JavaScript programming. It makes JavaScript act much more like the Python language, with an interactive interpreter.

- ✔ **Prototype** (www.prototypejs.org/): One of the first AJAX libraries to become popular. Includes great support for AJAX and extensions for user interface objects (through the scriptaculous extension).

✔ **YUI Yahoo! Interface Library** (`http://developer.yahoo.com/yui/`): This is the library used by Yahoo! for all its AJAX applications. It has released this impressive library as open source.

✔ **jQuery** (`http://jquery.com/`): jQuery has emerged as one of the more popular JavaScript and AJAX libraries. It's the library I emphasize in this book.

Getting to Know jQuery

This book focuses on the jQuery library. Although many outstanding AJAX/JavaScript libraries are available, jQuery has quickly become one of the most prominent. There are many reasons for the popularity of jQuery:

✔ **It's a powerful library.** The jQuery system can do all kinds of impressive things to make your JavaScript easier to write.

✔ **It's lightweight.** You'll need to include a reference to your library in every file that needs it. The entire jQuery library fits in 55K, which is smaller than many image files. It won't have a significant impact on download speed.

✔ **It supports a flexible selection mechanism.** jQuery greatly simplifies and expands the `document.getElementById` mechanism that's central to DOM manipulation.

✔ **It has great animation support.** You can use jQuery to make elements appear and fade, move and slide.

✔ **It makes AJAX queries trivial.** You'll be shocked at how easy AJAX is with jQuery.

✔ **It has an enhanced event mechanism.** JavaScript has very limited support for events. jQuery adds a very powerful tool for adding event handlers to nearly any element.

✔ **It provides cross-platform support.** The jQuery library tries to manage browser-compatibility issues for you, so you don't have to stress so much about exactly which browser is being used.

✔ **It supports user interface widgets.** jQuery comes with a powerful user interface library including tools HTML doesn't have, like drag-and-drop controls, sliders, and date pickers.

✔ **It's highly extensible.** jQuery has a plugin library that supports all kinds of optional features, including new widgets and tools like audio integration, image galleries, menus, and much more.

✔ **It introduces powerful new programming ideas.** jQuery is a great tool for learning about some really interesting ideas like functional programming and chainable objects. I explain these as you encounter them.

✔ **It's free and open source.** It's available under an open-source license, which means it costs nothing to use, and you can look it over and change it if you want.

✔ **It's reasonably typical.** If you choose to use a different AJAX library, you'll still be able to transfer the ideas you learned in jQuery.

Installing jQuery

The jQuery library is easy to install and use. Just go to `http://jquery.com` and download the current version (1.3.2 as of this writing). Store the resulting `.js` file (`jQuery-1.3.2.min.js`) in your working directory.

You might be able to choose from a number of versions of the file. I recommend the minimized version. To make this file as small as possible, every single unnecessary character (including spaces and carriage returns) has been removed. This file is very compact, but it's difficult to read. You can download the nonminimized version if you want to actually read the code, but it's generally better to include the minimized version in your programs.

That's basically all there is to it. Download the file and place it in the directory where you want to work.

To incorporate the library in your pages, simply link it as an external JavaScript file:

```
<script type = "text/javascript"
        src = "jquery-1.3.2.min.js"></script>
```

Be sure to include this script before you write or include other code that refers to jQuery.

Importing jQuery from Google

Easy as it is to download jQuery, there's another great way to add jQuery (and other AJAX library) support to your pages without downloading anything. Google has a publicly available version of several important libraries (including jQuery) that you can download from the Google servers. This method has a couple of interesting advantages:

✔ **You don't have to install any libraries.** All the library files stay on the Google servers.

✔ **The library is automatically updated.** You always have access to the latest version of the library without making any changes to your code.

✔ **The library might load faster.** The first time one of your pages reads the library from Google's servers, you have to wait for the full download, but then the library is stored in *cache* (a form of browser memory) so subsequent requests will be essentially immediate.

Here's how you do it:

```
<script type = "text/javacript"
        src="http://www.google.com/jsapi"></script>
<script type = "text/javacript">
  //<[CDATA[
  // Load jQuery
  google.load("jquery", "1");

  //your code here

  //]]>
</script>
```

Essentially, loading jQuery from Google is a two-step process:

1. **Load the Google API from Google.**

   Use the first `<script>` tag to refer to the Google AJAX API server. This gives you access to the `google.load()` function.

2. **Invoke** `google.load()` **to load jQuery.**

   The first parameter is the name of the library you want to load. The second parameter is the version number. If you leave this parameter blank, you get the latest version. If you specify a number, Google gives you the latest variation of that version. In my example, I want the latest variation of version 1, but not version 2. Although version 2 doesn't exist yet, I expect it to have major changes, and I don't want any surprises.

Note that you don't need to install any files locally to use the Google approach.

Using jQuery with Aptana

The Aptana editor is amazing. One of its most impressive features is the way it helps you build AJAX applications with several libraries. It has built-in support for jQuery, which is quite easy to use. Follow these steps to build a jQuery project within Aptana:

1. **Create a new default Web project.**

   Many developers ignore the project mechanism in Aptana and simply create individual files. The project tool allows you to group a series of files. The Web Project Wizard (invoked when you create a new Web project) allows automatic integration of an AJAX library.

2. **Select jQuery from the libraries wizard.**

   After you've entered a name for your project, you're given a list of AJAX libraries you can add to the project, as shown in Figure 10-1. Pick jQuery from this list.

3. **Do not create a hosted site.**

   The hosted site option allows you to simultaneously create an online version of your site within Aptana's server structure (the *cloud*). Although this is an excellent option for commercial sites, you need to pay for server access, and that isn't necessary when you're just starting out.

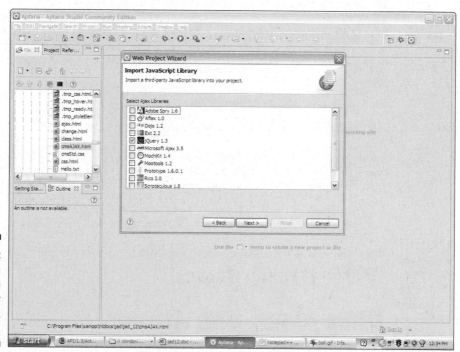

Figure 10-1:
Aptana
has built-in
support for
many AJAX
libraries.

4. **Look over your new project.**

   Aptana creates a directory structure for your project. It automatically includes access to the source files for jQuery.

5. **Add a script tag to your** `index.html` **document.**

   As you begin to write the `src` attribute, the autocomplete feature helps you include the jQuery files.

6. **jQuery functions are now supported in your editor.**

   As you write JavaScript code, Aptana gives you code completion hints for jQuery functions as if they were built into JavaScript. If you're running an up-to-date version of Aptana, it already has the latest version of jQuery and attaches it to your project.

7. **Note that now you're working in a project.**

   Aptana's project mechanism allows you to save an entire group of files (including the jQuery library together) so you can open them as one unit.

All these options for managing jQuery can be dizzying. Use whichever technique works best for you. I actually prefer using the local code, rather than the Google or Aptana solutions, because I find it easier, and this method works even if I'm offline. For smaller projects (like the demonstrations in this chapter), I don't like the overhead of the Aptana solution or the online requirement of Google. In this chapter, I simply refer to a local copy of the jQuery file.

Writing Your First jQuery App

As an introduction to jQuery, I show you how to build an application that you can already create in JavaScript/DOM. The following sections introduce you to some powerful features of jQuery. Figure 10-2 illustrates the `change.html` page at work, but the interesting stuff (as usual) is under the hood.

Figure 10-2:
The content
of this page
is modified
with jQuery.

> ## Basic jQuery demo
>
> I changed

Setting up the page

At first, the jQuery app doesn't look much different than any other HTML/
JavaScript code you've already written, but the JavaScript code is a bit different. Take a look at how jQuery simplifies this JavaScript code:

```
<!DOCTYPE html PUBLIC "-//W3C//DTD XHTML 1.0 Strict//EN"
"http://www.w3.org/TR/xhtml1/DTD/xhtml1-strict.dtd">
<html lang="EN" dir="ltr" xmlns="http://www.w3.org/1999/
        xhtml">
<head>
  <meta http-equiv=»content-type» content=»text/xml;
        charset=utf-8» />

  <title>change.html</title>
  <script type = «text/javascript»
        src = «jquery-1.3.2.min.js»></script>

  <script type = «text/javascript»>
    //<![CDATA[
    function changeMe(){
      $(«#output»).html(«I changed»);
    }

    //]]>
  </script>
</head>
<body onload = «changeMe()»>
        <h1>Basic jQuery demo</h1>
    <div id = «output»>
      Did this change?
    </div>
</body>
</html>
```

If you're already knowledgeable about jQuery, you might be horrified at my
use of `body onload` in this example. jQuery provides a wonderful alternative
to the `onload` mechanism, but I want to introduce only one big new idea at a
time. The next example illustrates the jQuery alternative to `body onload` and
explains why it is such an improvement.

The basic features of `change.html` are utterly unsurprising:

- **The HTML has a** `div` **named** `output`. This `div` initially says "Did this
  change?" The code should change the content to something else.

- **The HTML calls a function called** `changeme()` **when the body finishes
  loading.** This is a mechanism used frequently in DOM programming,
  although you see a new way to do this in the next section.

✔ **There is a reference to the jQuery library.** Any page that uses jQuery must load it using one of the mechanisms described earlier in this chapter.

✔ **The** `changeme()` **function looks really crazy.** When you run the program, you can tell what it does. The code gets a reference to the `output` `div` and changes its `innerHTML` property to reflect a new value (`"I changed"`). However, the syntax is really new. All that functionality got packed into one line of (funky looking) code.

Meet the jQuery node object

The secret behind jQuery's power is the underlying data model. jQuery has a unique way of looking at the DOM that's more powerful than the standard object model. Understanding the way this works is the key to powerful programming with jQuery.

The jQuery *node* is a special object that adds a lot of functionality to the ordinary DOM element. Any element on the Web page (any link, `div`, heading, or whatever) can be defined as a jQuery node. You can also make a list of jQuery nodes based on tag types, so you can have a jQuery object that stores a list of all the paragraphs on the page, or all the objects with a particular class name. The jQuery object has very useful methods like `html()`, which is used to change the `innerHTML` property of an element.

The jQuery node is based on the basic DOM node, so it can be created from any DOM element. However, it also adds significant new features. This is a good example of the object-oriented philosophy.

You can create a jQuery object in many ways, but the simplest is through the special `$()` function. You can place an identifier (very similar to CSS identifiers) inside the function to build a jQuery object based on an element. For example,

```
var jQoutput = $("#output");
```

creates a variable called `jQoutput`, which contains a jQuery object based on the `output` element. It's similar to

```
var DOMoutput = document.getElementById("output");
```

The jQuery approach is a little cleaner, and it doesn't get a reference to a DOM object (as the `getElementById` technique does), but it makes a new object called the jQuery object, which is an enhanced DOM object. Don't worry if this is a little hard to understand. It gets easier as you get used to it.

Because `jQoutput` is a jQuery object, it has some powerful methods. You can change the content of the object with the `html()` method. The following two lines are equivalent:

```
jQoutput.html("I've changed"); //jQuery version
DOMoutput.innerHTML = "I've changed"; //ordinary JS / DOM
```

jQuery doesn't require you to create variables for each object, so the code in the `changeMe()` function can look like this:

```
//build a variable and then modify it
var jQoutput = $("#output");
jQoutput.html("I've changed");
```

Or you can shorten it like this:

```
        $("#output").html("I changed");
```

This last version is how the program is actually written. It's very common to refer to an object with the `$()` mechanism and immediately perform a method on that object as I've done here.

Creating an Initialization Function

Many pages require an initialization function. This is a function that's run early to set up the rest of the page. The `body onload` mechanism is frequently used in DOM/JavaScript to make pages load as soon as the document has begun loading. I describe this technique in Chapter 8. Although `body onload` does this job well, the traditional technique has a couple of problems:

- **It requires making a change to the HTML.** Really the JavaScript code should be completely separated from HTML. You shouldn't have to change your HTML at all to make it work with JavaScript.

- **The timing still isn't quite right.** Code specified in `body unload` doesn't execute until after the entire page is displayed. It would be better if the code was registered after the DOM is loaded but before the page displays.

Using $(document).ready()

jQuery has a great alternative to `body onload` that overcomes its drawbacks. Take a look at the code for `ready.html` to see how it works:

```
<!DOCTYPE html PUBLIC "-//W3C//DTD XHTML 1.0 Strict//EN"
"http://www.w3.org/TR/xhtml1/DTD/xhtml1-strict.dtd">
<html lang="EN" dir="ltr" xmlns="http://www.w3.org/1999/
          xhtml">
<head>
  <meta http-equiv=»content-type» content=»text/xml;
          charset=utf-8» />

  <title>ready.html</title>
  <script type = «text/javascript»
          src = «jquery-1.3.2.min.js»></script>

  <script type = «text/javascript»>
    //<![CDATA[
    $(document).ready(changeMe);

    function changeMe(){
      $(«#output»).html(«I changed»);
    }

    //]]>
  </script>
</head>
<body>
    <h1>Using the document.ready mechanism</h1>
    <div id = «output»>
      Did this change?
    </div>
</body>
</html>
```

This code is much like the change.html, but it uses the jQuery technique for running initialization code:

✔ **The** <body> **tag no longer has an** onload **attribute.** This is a common feature of jQuery programming. The HTML no longer has direct links to the JavaScript because jQuery lets the JavaScript code attach itself to the Web page.

✔ **The initialization function is created with the** $(document).ready() **function.** This technique tells the browser to execute a function when the DOM has finished loading (so it has access to all elements of the form) but before the page is displayed (so any effects of the form appear instantaneous to the user).

✔ $(document) **makes a jQuery object from the whole document.** The entire document can be turned into a jQuery object by specifying document inside the $() function. Note that you don't use quotes in this case.

✔ **The function specified is automatically run.** In this particular case, I want to run the changeMe() function, so I place it in the parameter of the ready() method. Note that I'm referring to changeMe as a variable, so it has no quotes or parentheses. (Look at Chapter 8 for more discussion of referring to functions as variables.)

You might see several other places (particularly in event handling) where jQuery expects a function as a parameter. Such a function is frequently referred to as a *callback* function because it is called after some sort of event has occurred. You might also notice callback functions that respond to keyboard events, mouse motion, and the completion of an AJAX request.

Discovering alternatives to document.ready

Programmers sometimes use shortcuts instead of document.ready because it's so common to run initialization code. You can shorten

```
$(document).ready(changeMe);
```

to the following code:

```
$(changeMe);
```

If this code isn't defined inside a function and changeMe is a function defined on the page, jQuery automatically runs the function directly just like the document.ready approach.

It's also possible to create an anonymous function directly:

```
$(document).ready(function(){
  $("#output").html("I changed");
});
```

I think this method is cumbersome, but jQuery code frequently uses this technique.

Investigating the jQuery Object

The jQuery object is interesting because it's easy to create from a variety of DOM elements and because it adds wonderful new features to these elements.

Changing the style of an element

If you can dynamically change the CSS of an element, you can do quite a lot to it. jQuery makes this process quite easy. When you have a jQuery object, you can use the `css` method to add or change any CSS attributes of the object. Take a look at `styleElement.html` shown in Figure 10-3 for an example.

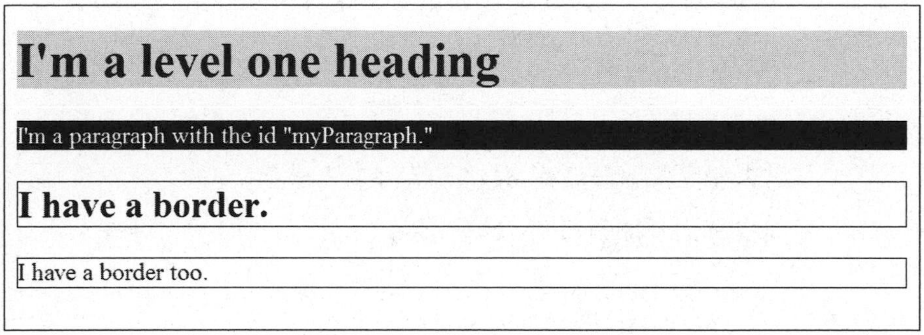

Figure 10-3:
All the styles here are applied dynamically by jQuery functions.

I'm a level one heading

I'm a paragraph with the id "myParagraph."

I have a border.

I have a border too.

The code displays a terseness common to jQuery code:

```
<!DOCTYPE html PUBLIC "-//W3C//DTD XHTML 1.0 Strict//EN"
"http://www.w3.org/TR/xhtml1/DTD/xhtml1-strict.dtd">
<html lang="EN" dir="ltr" xmlns="http://www.w3.org/1999/
          xhtml">
<head>
  <meta http-equiv=»content-type» content=»text/xml;
          charset=utf-8» />
  <script type = «text/javascript»
          src = «jquery-1.3.2.min.js»></script>

  <script type = «text/javascript»>
    //<![CDATA[
    $(init);

    function init(){
      $(«h1»).css(«backgroundColor», «yellow»);

      $(«#myParagraph»).css({«backgroundColor»:»black»,
                            «color»:»white»});

      $(«.bordered»).css(«border», «1px solid black»);
    }
    //]]>
  </script>
  <title>styleElements.html</title>
```

```
</head>
<body>
    <h1>I'm a level one heading</h1>
    <p id = «myParagraph»>
      I'm a paragraph with the id «myParagraph.»
    </p>

    <h2 class = «bordered»>
      I have a border.
    </h2>

    <p class = «bordered»>
      I have a border too.
    </p>
</body>
</html>
```

This program has a few interesting things going on in it. Take a look at the HTML.

- **It contains an** <h1> **tag.** I'm aware that's not too exciting, but I use it to show how to target elements by DOM type.

- **A paragraph has the ID** myParagraph. This paragraph is used to illustrate how to target an element by ID.

- **Two elements have the class** bordered. In ordinary DOM work, you can't easily apply code to all elements of a particular class, but jQuery makes it easy.

- **Several elements have custom CSS, but no CSS is defined.** The jQuery code changes all the CSS dynamically.

The init() function is identified as the function to be run when the document is ready. In this function, I use the powerful CSS method to change each element's CSS dynamically. I come back to the CSS in a moment, but first notice how the various elements are targeted.

Selecting jQuery objects

jQuery gives you several alternatives for creating jQuery objects from the DOM elements. In general, you use the same rules to select objects in jQuery as you do in CSS:

- **DOM elements are targeted as-is.** You can include any DOM element inside the $("") mechanism to target all similar elements. For example, use $("h1") to refer to all h1 objects, or $("p") to refer to all paragraphs.

- **Use the # identifier to target a particular ID.** This works exactly the same as CSS. If you have an element with the ID myThing, use this code: $("#myThing").

> ✓ **Use the . identifier to target members of a class.** Again, this is the same mechanism you use in CSS, so all elements with the class `bordered` attached to them can be modified with this code: `$(".bordered")`.
>
> ✓ **You can even use complex identifiers.** You can use complex CSS identifiers like `$("li img")`; this identifier targets only images inside a list item.

These selection methods (all borrowed from familiar CSS notation) add incredible flexibility to your code. You can now easily select elements in your JavaScript code according to the same rules you use to identify elements in CSS.

Modifying the style

After you've identified an object or a set of objects, you can apply jQuery methods. One very powerful and easy method is the `style()` method. The basic form of this method takes two parameters: a style rule and value. For example, to make the background color of all `h1` objects yellow, I used the following code:

```
$("h1").css("backgroundColor", "yellow");
```

If you apply a style rule to a collection of objects (like all `h1` objects or all objects with the `bordered` class), the same rule is instantly applied to all the objects.

A more powerful variation of the style rule allows you to apply several CSS styles at once. It takes a single object in JSON notation (JavaScript Object Notation described in Chapter 5) as its argument:

```
$("#myParagraph").css({"backgroundColor":"black",
                       "color":"white"});
```

This example uses a JSON object defined as a series of rule/value pairs. If you need a refresher on how JSON objects work, look at Chapter 5.

Adding Events to Objects

The jQuery library adds another extremely powerful capability to JavaScript. It allows you to easily attach events to any jQuery object. As an example, take a look at `hover.html`, shown in Figure 10-4.

When you move the mouse pointer over any list item, a border appears over the item. This effect would be difficult to achieve in ordinary DOM/JavaScript, but it's pretty easy to manage in jQuery.

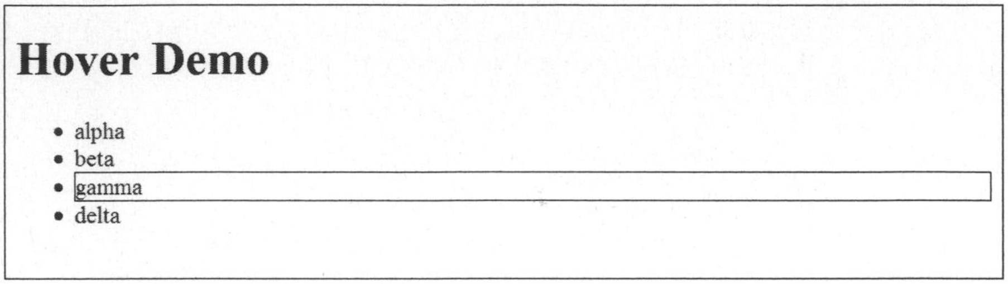

Figure 10-4:
A border
appears
around each
list item
when the
mouse is
over it.

> ### Hover Demo
>
> - alpha
> - beta
> - gamma
> - delta

Adding a hover event

Look at the code to see how it works:

```
<!DOCTYPE html PUBLIC "-//W3C//DTD XHTML 1.0 Strict//EN"
"http://www.w3.org/TR/xhtml1/DTD/xhtml1-strict.dtd">
<html lang="EN" dir="ltr" xmlns="http://www.w3.org/1999/
          xhtml">
<head>
  <meta http-equiv=»content-type» content=»text/xml;
          charset=utf-8» />

  <script type = «text/javascript»
          src = «jquery-1.3.2.min.js»></script>

  <script type = «text/javascript»>
    //<![CDATA[
    $(init);

    function init(){
      $(«li»).hover(border, noBorder);
    } // end init

    function border(){
      $(this).css(«border», «1px solid black»);
    }

    function noBorder(){
      $(this).css(«border», «0px none black»);
    }

    //]]>
  </script>

  <title>hover.html</title>
```

```
</head>
<body>
  <h1>Hover Demo</h1>
    <ul>
       <li>alpha</li>
       <li>beta</li>
       <li>gamma</li>
       <li>delta</li>
    </ul>
</body>
</html>
```

The HTML couldn't be simpler: It's an unordered list. The JavaScript isn't much more complex. It consists of three one-line functions.

- ✔ `init()`: This function is called when the document is ready. It makes jQuery objects out of all list items and attaches the `hover` event to them. `hover` accepts two parameters. The first is a function to be called when the mouse hovers over the object. The second parameter is a function to be called when the mouse leaves the object.

- ✔ `border()`: This function draws a border around the current element. The `$(this)` identifier is used to specify the current object. In this example, I use the `css` function to draw a border around the object.

- ✔ `noBorder()`: It's very similar to the `border()` function, but it removes a border from the current object.

In this example, I used three different functions. Many jQuery programmers prefer to use anonymous functions (sometimes called *lambda* functions) to enclose the entire functionality in one long line:

```
$("li").hover(
  function(){
    $(this).css("border", "1px solid black");
  },
  function(){
    $(this).css("border", "0px none black");
  }
);
```

Note that this is still technically a single line of code. Instead of referencing two functions that have already been created, I build the functions immediately where they're needed. Each function definition is a parameter to the `hover()` method.

---

jQuery events

jQuery supports a number of other events. Any jQuery node can read any of the following events:

- ✔ change: The content of the element changes.

- ✔ click: The user clicks the element.

- ✔ dblClick: The user double-clicks the element.

- ✔ focus: The user selects the element.

- ✔ keydown: The user presses a key while the element has the focus.

- ✔ hover: The mouse is over the element — a second function is called when the mouse leaves the element.

- ✔ mouseDown: A mouse button is pressed over the element.

- ✔ select: The user selects text in a text-style input.

If you're a computer scientist, you might argue that this isn't a perfect example of a lambda function, and you would be correct. The important thing is to notice that some ideas of functional programming (such as lambda functions) are creeping into mainstream AJAX programming, and that's an exciting development. If you just mutter "lambda" and then walk away, people will assume you're some kind of geeky computer scientist. What could be more fun than that?

Although I'm perfectly comfortable with anonymous functions, I often find the named-function approach easier to read, so I tend to use complete named functions more often.

Changing classes on the fly

jQuery supports another wonderful feature. You can define a CSS style and then add or remove that style from an element dynamically. Figure 10-5 shows a page with the ability to dynamically modify the border of any list item.

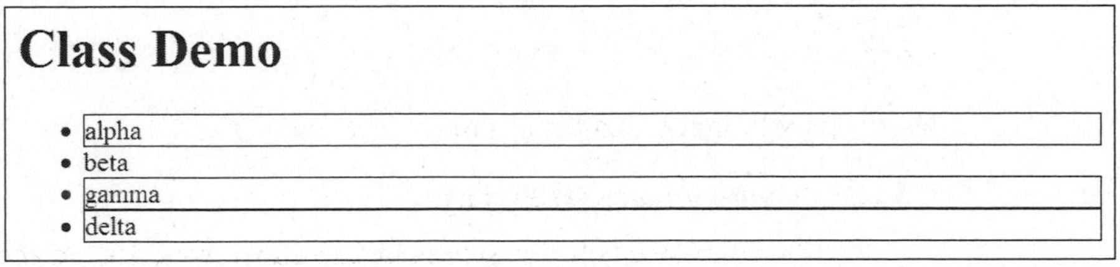

Figure 10-5:
Click a list item to toggle its border on and off.

Class Demo

- alpha
- beta
- gamma
- delta

The code for `class.html` shows how easy this kind of feature is to add:

```
<!DOCTYPE html PUBLIC "-//W3C//DTD XHTML 1.0 Strict//EN"
"http://www.w3.org/TR/xhtml1/DTD/xhtml1-strict.dtd">
<html lang="EN" dir="ltr" xmlns="http://www.w3.org/1999/
        xhtml">
<head>
  <meta http-equiv=»content-type» content=»text/xml;
          charset=utf-8» />
    <style type = «text/css»>
      .bordered {
        border: 1px solid black;
      }
    </style>
    <script type = «text/javascript»
            src = «jquery-1.3.2.min.js»></script>

    <script type = «text/javascript»>
      //<![CDATA[
      $(init);

      function init(){
        $(«li»).click(toggleBorder);
      } // end init

      function toggleBorder(){
        $(this).toggleClass(«bordered»);
      }
      //]]>
    </script>

  <title>class.html</title>
</head>
<body>
                                    <h1>Class Demo</h1>

    <ul>
      <li>alpha</li>
      <li>beta</li>
      <li>gamma</li>
      <li>delta</li>
    </ul>

</body>
</html>
```

Here's how to make this program:

1. **Begin with a basic HTML page.**

   All the interesting stuff happens in CSS and JavaScript, so the actual contents of the page aren't that critical.

2. **Create a class you want to add and remove.**

   I build a CSS class called `bordered`, which simply draws a border around the element. Of course, you can make a much more sophisticated CSS class with all kinds of formatting if you prefer.

3. **Link an `init()` method.**

   As you're beginning to see, most jQuery applications require some sort of initialization. I normally call the first function `init()`.

4. **Call the `toggleBorder()` function whenever the user clicks a list item.**

   The `init()` method simply sets up an event handler. Whenever a list item receives the `click` event (that is, the list item is clicked), the `toggleBorder()` function should be activated.

5. **The `toggleBorder()` function, well, toggles the border.**

   jQuery has several methods for manipulating the class of an element. `addClass()` assigns a class to the element, `removeClass()` removes a class definition from an element, and `toggleClass()` switches the class (by adding the class if it isn't currently attached or removing it otherwise).

Making an AJAX Request with jQuery

The primary purpose of an AJAX library like jQuery is to simplify AJAX requests. It's hard to believe how easy this can be with jQuery. Figure 10-6 shows `ajax.html`, a page with a basic AJAX query.

Figure 10-6:
The text file is requested with an AJAX call.

Including a text file with AJAX

The `ajax.html` program is very similar in function to the `asynch.html` program described in Chapter 9, but the code is much cleaner:

```
<!DOCTYPE html PUBLIC "-//W3C//DTD XHTML 1.0 Strict//EN"
"http://www.w3.org/TR/xhtml1/DTD/xhtml1-strict.dtd">
<html lang="EN" dir="ltr" xmlns="http://www.w3.org/1999/
          xhtml">
  <head>
    <meta http-equiv=»content-type» content=»text/xml;
          charset=utf-8» />
    <title>ajax.html</title>
    <script type = «text/javascript»
            src = «jquery-1.3.2.min.js»></script>

    <script type = «text/javascript»>
      //<![CDATA[
      $(document).ready(getAJAX);

      function getAJAX(){
        $(«#output»).load(«hello.txt»);
      }
      //]]>
    </script>

  </head>

  <body>
    <div id = «output»></div>
  </body>
</html>
```

The HTML is very clean (as you should expect from jQuery examples). It simply creates an empty div called output.

The JavaScript code isn't much more complex. A standard $(document). ready function calls the getAJAX() function as soon as the document is ready. The getAJAX() function simply creates a jQuery node based on the output div and loads the file hello.txt through a basic AJAX request.

This example does use AJAX, so if it isn't working, you might need to review how AJAX works. You should run a program using AJAX through a Web server, not just from a local file. Also, the file being read should be on the same server as the program making the AJAX request.

I cover more sophisticated AJAX techniques in Chapter 14. The load() mechanism is suitable for a basic situation where you want to load a plain text or HTML code snippet into your pages.

Building a poor man's CMS with AJAX

AJAX and jQuery can be a very useful way to build efficient Web sites even without server-side programming. Frequently a Web site is based on a series of smaller elements that can be swapped and reused. Such a technique is called a CMS (content management system). You can use AJAX to build a framework that allows easy reuse and modification of Web content.

As an example, take a look at cmsAJAX shown in Figure 10-7.

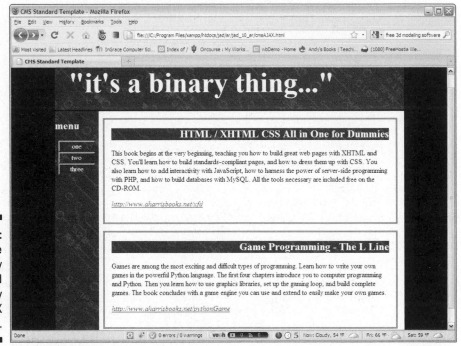

Figure 10-7:
This page is actually created dynamically with AJAX and jQuery.

Although there's nothing all that shocking about the page from the user's perspective, a look at the code shows some surprises:

```
<!DOCTYPE html PUBLIC "-//W3C//DTD XHTML 1.0 Strict//EN"
"http://www.w3.org/TR/xhtml1/DTD/xhtml1-strict.dtd">
<html lang="EN" dir="ltr" xmlns="http://www.w3.org/1999/
        xhtml">
  <head>
    <meta http-equiv=»content-type» content=»text/xml;
        charset=utf-8» />
```

```
    <title>CMS Standard Template</title>
    <link rel = «stylesheet»
         type = «text/css»
         href = «cmsStd.css» />
    <script type = «text/javascript»
            src = «jquery-1.3.2.min.js»></script>
    <script type = «text/javascript»>
      //<![CDATA[
      $(init);

      function init(){
        $(«#heading»).load(«head.html»);
        $(«#menu»).load(«menu.html»);
        $(«#content1»).load(«story1.html»);
        $(«#content2»).load(«story2.html»);
        $(«#footer»).load(«footer.html»);
      };
      //]]>
    </script>
</head>

<body>
  <div id = «all»>
    <!-- This div centers a fixed-width layout -->
    <div id = «heading»>
    </div><!-- end heading div -->

    <div id = «menu»>
    </div> <!-- end menu div -->

    <div class = «content»
         id = «content1»>
    </div> <!-- end content div -->

    <div class = «content»
         id = «content2»>
    </div> <!-- end content div -->

    <div id = «footer»>
    </div> <!-- end footer div -->

  </div> <!-- end all div -->
  </body>
</html>
```

The code has these interesting features:

✔ **The page has no content!** All the `div`s are empty. None of the text
  shown in Figure 10-7 is present in this document, but all is pulled from
  smaller files dynamically.

✔ **The page consists of empty, named** `divs`. Rather than any particular content, the page consists of placeholders with IDs.

✔ **It uses jQuery.** The jQuery library is used to vastly simplify loading data through AJAX calls.

✔ **All contents are in separate files.** The directory has very simple HTML files containing small parts of the page. For example, `story1.html` looks like this:

```
<h2>HTML / XHTML CSS All in One for Dummies</h2>


<p>
This book begins at the very beginning, teaching you how to build
great web pages with XHTML and CSS. You'll learn how to build
standards-compliant pages, and how to dress them up with CSS.
You also learn how to add interactivity with JavaScript, how to
harness the power of server-side programming with PHP, and how to build
databases with MySQL. All the tools necessary are included free on
the CD-ROM.
</p>


<p><em>
  <a href = "http://www.aharribooks.net/xfd">
  http://www.aharribooks.net/xfd</a>
</em></p>
```

✔ **The** `init()` **method runs on** `document.ready`. When the document is ready, the page runs the `init()` method.

✔ **The** `init()` **method uses AJAX calls to dynamically load content.** It's nothing more than a series of jQuery `load()` methods.

This approach might seem like a lot of work, but it has some very interesting characteristics. If you're building a large site with several pages, you usually want to design the visual appearance once and re-use the same general template over and over again. Also, you'll probably have some elements (such as the menu and heading) that will be consistent over several pages. You could simply create a default document and copy and paste it for each page, but this approach gets messy. What happens if you have created 100 pages according to a template and then need to add something to the menu or change the header? You would need to make the change on 100 different pages.

The advantage of the template-style approach is code reuse. Just like use of an external style allows you to multiply a style sheet across hundreds of documents, designing a template without content allows you to store code snippets in smaller files and reuse them. All 100 pages point to the same menu file, so if you want to change the menu, you change one file and everything changes with it.

Here's how you use this sort of approach:

1. **Create a single template for your entire site.**

   Build basic HTML and CSS to manage the overall look and feel for your entire site. Don't worry about content yet. Just build placeholders for all the components of your page. Be sure to give each element an ID and write the CSS to get things positioned as you wish.

2. **Add jQuery support.**

   Make a link to the jQuery library, and make a default `init()` method. Put code to handle populating those parts of the page that will always be consistent. (I use the template shown here exactly as it is.)

3. **Duplicate the template.**

   When you have a sense how the template will work, make a copy for each page of your site.

4. **Customize each page by changing the `init()` function.**

   The only part of the template that changes is the `init()` function. All your pages will be identical, except they will have customized `init()` functions that load different content.

5. **Load custom content into the `div`s with AJAX.**

   Use the `init()` function to load content into each `div`. Build more content as small files to create new pages.

This is a great way to manage content, but it isn't quite a full-blown content management system. Even AJAX can't quite allow you to *store* content on the Web. More complex content management systems use databases rather than files to handle content. You need some sort of server-side programming (like PHP) and usually a database (like mySQL) to handle this sort of work. I introduce these topics in Chapter 14.

Chapter 11

Animating jQuery

In This Chapter

▶ Setting up for animation

▶ Hiding and showing elements with jQuery

▶ Fading elements in and out

▶ Adding a callback function to a transition

▶ Understanding object chaining

▶ Modifying elements

▶ Using selection filters

*T*he jQuery library simplifies a lot of JavaScript coding. One of its biggest advantages is how it allows you to add features that would be difficult to achieve in ordinary JavaScript and DOM (document object model) programming. This chapter teaches you to shake and bake your programs by identifying specific objects; moving them around; and making them appear, slide, and fade.

Getting Prepared for Animation

To get your jQuery animation career started, take a look at `hideShow.html`, shown in Figure 11-1.

The `hideShow` program looks simple at first, but it does some very interesting things. All of the level-two headings are actually buttons, so when you click them, fun stuff happens:

✔ **The Show button displays a previously hidden element.** Figure 11-2 demonstrates the new content.

✔ **The Hide button hides the content.** The behavior of the `hide` button is pretty obvious. If the content is showing, clicking the button makes it disappear instantly.

✔ **The Toggle button swaps the visibility of the content.** If the content is currently visible, clicking the button hides it. If it is hidden, a click of the button makes it show up.

Hide and show
Show
Hide
Toggle
Slide Down
Slide Up
Fade In
Fade Out

Figure 11-1:
At first, the
page shows
nothing
much.

- ✔ **The Slide Down button makes the content transition in.** The slide down transition acts like a window shade being pulled down to make the content visible through a basic animation.

- ✔ **The Slide Up button transitions the content out.** This animation looks like a window shade being pulled up to hide the content.

- ✔ **The Fade In button allows the element to dissolve into visibility.** This animation looks much like a fade effect used in video. As in the sliding animations, you can control the speed of the animation.

  A special function is called when the fade in is complete. In this example, I call a function named present as soon as the fade in is complete. This is a callback function, which I explain in just a bit.

- ✔ **The Fade Out button fades the element to the background color.** This technique gradually modifies the opacity of the element so it gradually disappears.

Here are a couple of details for you to keep in mind:

- ✔ **You can adjust how quickly the transition animation plays.** For example, the hideShow program plays the slide down at a slow speed, and slide up faster. You can even specify exactly how long the transition takes in milliseconds (1/1000ths of a second).

- ✔ **Any transition can have a *callback* function attached.** A callback function is a function that will be triggered when the transition is complete.

Of course, the showHide example relies on animation, which isn't easy to see in a static book. Please be sure to look at this and all other example pages on my Web site: www.aharrisbooks.net. Better yet, install them on your own machine and play around with my code until they make sense to you.

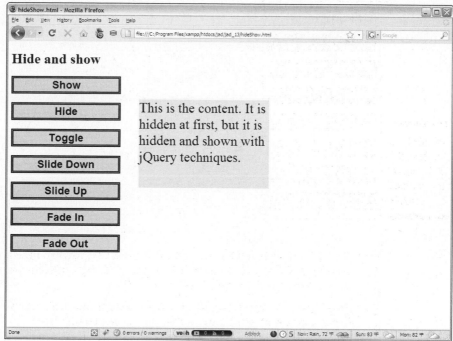

Figure 11-2:
The content
element is
now visible.

The animations shown in this example are useful when you want to selectively hide and display parts of your page. Being able to show and hide elements is useful in a number of situations. Menus are one obvious use. You might choose to store your menu structure as a series of nested lists, displaying parts of the menu only when the parent is activated. Another common use of this technology is to have small teaser sentences that expand to show more information when the user clicks or hovers the mouse pointer over them. This technique is commonly used on blog and news sites to let users preview a large number of topics, kind of like a text-based thumbnail image.

The jQuery library has built-in support for transitions that make these effects pretty easy to produce. Look over the entire `hideShow.html` program before digging in on the details.

```
<!DOCTYPE html PUBLIC "-//W3C//DTD XHTML 1.0 Strict//EN"
"http://www.w3.org/TR/xhtml1/DTD/xhtml1-strict.dtd">
<html lang=»EN» dir=»ltr» xmlns=»http://www.w3.org/1999/
          xhtml»>
<head>
  <meta http-equiv="content-type" content="text/xml;
          charset=utf-8" />
  <style type = "text/css">
  #content {
```

```
    width: 300px;
    height: 200px;
    font-size: 200%;
    background-color: yellow;
    position: absolute;
    left: 300px;
    top: 100px;
}
h2 {
    width: 10em;
    border: 5px double black;
    background-color: lightgray;
    text-align: center;
    font-family: sans-serif
}
</style>

<script type = "text/javascript"
        src = "jquery-1.3.2.min.js"></script>

<script type = "text/javascript">
    //<![CDATA[
    $(init);

    function init(){
      $("#content").hide();
      $("#show").click(showContent);
      $("#hide").click(hideContent);
      $("#toggle").click(toggleContent);
      $("#slideDown").click(slideDown);
      $("#slideUp").click(slideUp);
      $("#fadeIn").click(fadeIn);
      $("#fadeOut").click(fadeOut);
    } // end init

    function showContent(){
      $("#content").show();
    } // end showContent

    function hideContent(){
      $("#content").hide();
    } // end hideContent

    function toggleContent(){
      $("#content").toggle();
    } // end toggleContent

    function slideDown(){
      $("#content").slideDown("medium");
    } // end slideDown
```

```
      function slideUp(){
        $("#content").slideUp(500);
      } // end slideUp

      function fadeIn(){
        $("#content").fadeIn("slow", present);
      } // end fadeIn

      function fadeOut(){
        $("#content").fadeOut("fast");
      } // end fadeOut.

      function present(){
        alert("I'm here");
      } // end present
      //]]>
    </script>
    <title>hideShow.html</title>
  </head>
  <body>
    <h1>Hide and show</h1>
    <h2 id = "show">Show</h2>
    <h2 id = "hide">Hide</h2>
    <h2 id = "toggle">Toggle</h2>
    <h2 id = "slideDown">Slide Down</h2>
    <h2 id = "slideUp">Slide Up</h2>
    <h2 id = "fadeIn">Fade In</h2>
    <h2 id = "fadeOut">Fade Out</h2>

    <p id = "content">
      This is the content. It is hidden at first, but it is
          hidden and
      shown with jQuery techniques.
    </p>

  </body>
</html>
```

This example might look long and complicated when you view it all at once, but it isn't hard to understand when you break it into pieces. The following sections help you get comfortable with this example.

Writing the HTML and CSS foundation

The HTML used in this example is minimal, as is common in jQuery development. It consists of a single level-one heading, a series of level-two headings, and a paragraph. The level-two headings will be used as buttons in this example. I use a CSS style to make the <h2> tags look more like buttons (adding a border and background color). I added an id attribute to every button so I can add jQuery events later.

If I wanted the h2 elements to look and act like buttons, why didn't I just make them with button tags in the first place? That's a very good question. At one level, I probably should use the semantically clear button tag to make a button. However, in this example, I want to focus on the jQuery and keep the HTML as simple as possible. jQuery can help you make *any* element act like a button, so that's what I did. Users don't expect h2 elements to be clickable, so you need to do some styling (as I did) to help the users understand that they can click the element. For comparison purposes, the other two examples in this chapter use actual HTML buttons.

The other interesting part of the HTML is the content div. In this example, the actual content isn't really important, but I did add some CSS to make the content very easy to see when it pops up. The most critical part of the HTML from a programming perspective is the inclusion of the id attribute. This attribute makes it easy for a jQuery script to manipulate the component so that it hides and reappears in various ways. Note that the HTML and CSS does nothing to hide the content. It will be hidden (and revealed) entirely through jQuery code.

Initializing the page

The initialization sequence simply sets the stage and assigns a series of event handlers:

```
$(init);

function init(){
  $("#content").hide();
  $("#show").click(showContent);
  $("#hide").click(hideContent);
  $("#toggle").click(toggleContent);
  $("#slideDown").click(slideDown);
  $("#slideUp").click(slideUp);
  $("#fadeIn").click(fadeIn);
  $("#fadeOut").click(fadeOut);
} // end init
```

The pattern for working with jQuery should now be familiar:

1. **Set up an initialization function.**

   Use the $(document).ready() mechanism described in Chapter 12 or this cleaner shortcut to specify an initialization function.

2. **Hide the** content div.

   When the user first encounters the page, the content div should be hidden.

3. **Attach event handlers to each** `h2` **button.**

This program is a series of small functions. The `init()` function attaches each function to the corresponding button. Note how I carefully named the functions and buttons to make all the connections easy to understand.

Working with callback functions

As you look through the JavaScript and jQuery code in `hideShow.html`, you'll probably spot a pattern. The `init()` function adds event handlers to several of the elements on the page. These event handlers specify the names of various functions. The rest of the JavaScript code is simply the definitions of these functions.

This technique is heavily used in jQuery programming. When you define an event, you will often specify a function that should be called when that event is triggered. Such a function is often referred to as a *callback function*.

In this context, the function name is treated as a variable, so it doesn't need the parentheses you normally use when referring to functions.

Hiding and Showing the Content

All the effects on the page shown earlier in Figure 11-1 are based on hiding and showing the `content div`. The `hide()` and `show()` methods illustrate how jQuery animation works.

```
function showContent(){
  $("#content").show();
} // end showContent

function hideContent(){
  $("#content").hide();
} // end hideContent
```

Each of these functions works in the same basic manner:

1. **Identify the** `content div`.

Create a jQuery node based on the `content div`. If you need more information on creating jQuery node objects, please check Chapter 10.

2. **Hide or show the node.**

The jQuery object has built-in methods for hiding and showing.

The hide() and show() methods act instantly. If the element is currently visible, the show() method has no effect. Likewise, hide() has no effect on an element that's already hidden.

The following sections describe some fun tricks for revealing or concealing elements.

Toggling visibility

In addition to hide() and show(), the jQuery object supports a toggle() method. This method takes a look at the current status of the element and changes it. If the element is currently hidden, clicking the button makes it visible. If it's currently visible, clicking the button hides it. The toggle Content() function illustrates how to use this method:

```
function toggleContent(){
  $("#content").toggle();
} // end toggleContent
```

Sliding an element

jQuery supports a *window blind* effect that allows you to animate the appearance and disappearance of your element. The general approach is very similar to hide() and show(), but the effect has one additional twist:

```
function slideDown(){
  $("#content").slideDown("medium");
} // end slideDown

function slideUp(){
  $("#content").slideUp(500);
} // end slideUp
```

The slideDown() method makes an element appear like a window shade being pulled down. The slideUp() method makes an element disappear in a similar manner. These functions take a speed parameter that indicates how quickly the animation occurs. The speed can be a string value ("fast", "medium", or "slow") or a numeric value in milliseconds (measured in 1,000th of a second). The value 500 means 500 milliseconds, or half a second. If you leave out the speed parameter, the default value is "medium".

The show(), hide(), and toggle() methods also accept a speed parameter. In these functions, the object shrinks and grows at the indicated speed.

There is also a slideToggle() function available that toggles the visibility of the element, but using the sliding animation technique.

Fading an element in and out

Another type of animation is provided by the `fade` methods. These techniques adjust the opacity of the element. The code should look quite familiar by now:

```
function fadeIn(){
  $("#content").fadeIn("slow", present);
} // end fadeIn

function fadeOut(){
  $("#content").fadeOut("fast");
} // end fadeOut.

function present(){
  alert("I'm here");
} // end present
```

`fadeIn()` and `fadeout()` work just like the `hide()` and `slide()` techniques. The fading techniques adjust the opacity of the element and then remove it, rather than dynamically changing the size of the element as the slide and show techniques do.

I've added one more element to the `fadeIn()` function. If you supply the `fadeIn()` method (or indeed any of the animation methods described in this section) with a function name as a second parameter, that function is a callback function, meaning it is called upon completion of the animation. When you click the `fade in` button, the `content div` slowly fades in, and then when it is completely visible, the `present()` function gets called. This function doesn't do a lot in this example — it simply pops up an alert — but it could be used to handle some sort of instructions after the element is visible.

If the element is already visible, the callback method will be triggered immediately.

Changing an Element's Position with jQuery

The jQuery library also has interesting features for changing any of an element's characteristics, including its position. The `animate.html` page featured in Figure 11-3 illustrates a number of interesting animation techniques.

TIP

You know what I'm going to say, right? This program moves things around. You can't see that in a book. Be sure to look at the actual page. Trust me; it's a lot more fun than it looks in this screen shot.

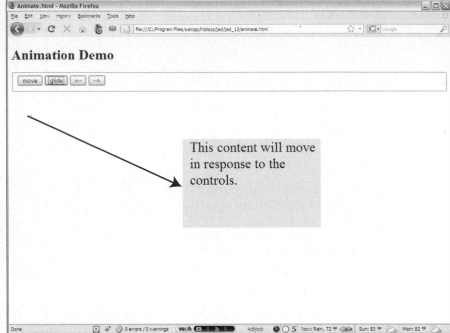

Figure 11-3:
Click the
buttons, and
the element
moves. (I
added the
arrow to
indicate
motion.)

This page (`animate.html`) illustrates how to move a jQuery element by modifying its CSS. (Check Bonus Chapter 2 on the Web site if you're unfamiliar with CSS.) It also illustrates an important jQuery technique called *object chaining* as well as a very useful animation method that allows you to create smooth motion over time. Look over the entire code first, and then in the following sections I break it into sections for more careful review:

```
<!DOCTYPE html PUBLIC "-//W3C//DTD XHTML 1.0 Strict//EN"
"http://www.w3.org/TR/xhtml1/DTD/xhtml1-strict.dtd">
<html lang="EN" dir="ltr" xmlns="http://www.w3.org/1999/
        xhtml">
<head>
  <meta http-equiv=»content-type» content=»text/xml;
        charset=utf-8» />

  <style type = «text/css»>
  #content {
    width: 300px;
    height: 200px;
    font-size: 200%;
    background-color: yellow;
    position: absolute;
    left: 300px;
    top: 100px;
    padding-left: .5em;
  }
```

```
    </style>

  <script type = «text/javascript»
          src = «jquery-1.3.2.min.js»></script>

  <script type = «text/javascript»>
    //<![CDATA[
    $(init);

    function init(){
      $(«#move»).click(move);
      $(«#glide»).click(glide);
      $(«#left»).click(left);
      $(«#right»).click(right);
    } // end init

    function move(){
      $(«#content»).css(«left», «50px»)
      .css(«top», «100px»);
    } // end move

    function glide(){
      //move to initial spot
      $(«#content»).css(«left», «50px»)
      .css(«top», «100px»);

      //slide to new spot
      $(«#content»).animate({
        «left»: «400px»,
        «top»: «200px»
      }, 2000);
    } // end glide

    function left(){
      $(«#content»).animate({«left»: «-=10px»}, 100);
    } // end left

    function right(){
      $(«#content»).animate({«left»: «+=10px»}, 100);
    } // end left
    //]]>
  </script>

  <title>Animate.html</title>
</head>
<body>
<h1>Animation Demo</h1>
<form action = «»>
  <fieldset>
    <button type = «button»
            id = «move»>
      move
```

```
      </button>
      <button type = «button»
             id = «glide»>
        glide
      </button>

      <button type = «button»
             id = «left»>
        &lt;--
      </button>

      <button type = «button»
             id = «right»>
        -->
      </button>

    </fieldset>
  </form>

  <p id = «content»>
    This content will move in response to the controls.
  </p>
  </body>
  </html>
```

Creating the HTML framework

The HTML always forms the foundation of a JavaScript program. The `animate.html` page is similar to the `hideShow` page (shown earlier in the chapter), but I decided to use a real form with buttons as the control panel. Buttons aren't difficult to use, but they're a little more tedious to code because they must be inside a form element as well as a block-level element, and they require more coding to produce than `h2` elements.

Note that I use `&lt;` in one of the button captions. (You can find it near the end of the `animate.html` listing.) This HTML attribute displays the less-than symbol. Had I used the actual symbol (<) the browser would have thought I was beginning a new HTML tag and would have been confused.

The buttons all have `id` attributes, but I didn't attach functions to them with the `onclick` attribute. When you're using jQuery, it makes sense to commit to a jQuery approach and use the jQuery event techniques.

The only other important HTML element is the `content` `div`. Once again, this element is simply a placeholder, but I added CSS styling to make it obvious when it moves around. It's important that you set this element to be absolutely positioned, because the position will be changed dynamically in the code.

Setting up the events

The initialization is all about setting up the event handlers for the various buttons. Begin with an `init()` function called when the document is ready. That function contains callback functions (such as move and glide) for the various events, directing traffic to the right functions when a user presses a button:

```
function init(){
  $("#move").click(move);
  $("#glide").click(glide);
  $("#left").click(left);
  $("#right").click(right);
} // end init
```

As usual, naming conventions make it easy to see what's going on.

Don't go chaining . . .

jQuery supports a really neat feature called *node chaining* that allows you to put several steps into one single line. This makes your code a lot easier to write, and it allows you to do several things to a particular element or group of elements at once. As an example, take another look at the `move()` function defined in `animate.html`.

The `move` function isn't really that radical. All it really does is use the `css()` method described in Chapter 10 to alter the position of the element. After all, position is just a CSS attribute, right? Well, it's a little more complex than that. The position of an element is actually stored in *two* attributes, `top` and `left`. Your first attempt at a `move` function would probably look like this:

```
function move(){
  $("#content").css("left", "50px");
  $("#content").css("top", "100px");
} // end move
```

Although this approach certainly works, it has a subtle problem. It moves the element in two separate steps. Although most browsers are fast enough to prevent this from being an issue, node chaining allows you to combine many jQuery steps into a single line.

Almost all jQuery methods return a jQuery object as a side effect. So, the line

```
$("#content").text("changed");
```

not only changes the text of the content node, but actually makes a new node. You can attach that node to a variable like this if you want:

```
var newNode = $("#content").text("changed");
```

However, what most jQuery programmers do is simply attach new functionality onto the end of the previously defined node, like this:

```
$("#content").text("changed").click(hiThere);
```

This new line takes the node created by $("#content") and changes its text value. It then takes this new node (the one with changed text) and adds a click event to it, calling the hiThere() function when the content element is clicked. In this way, you build an ever-more complex node by chaining nodes on top of each other.

These node chains can be hard to read because they can result in a lot of code on one physical line. JavaScript doesn't really care about carriage returns, though, because it uses the semicolon to determine the end of a logical line. You can change the complex chained line so it fits on several lines of the text editor like this:

```
$("#content")
.text("changed")
.click(hiThere);
```

Note that only the last line has a semicolon because what's shown is all one line of *logic* even though it occurs on three lines in the editor.

Building the move() function with chaining

Object chaining makes it easy to build the move function so that it moves the content's left and top properties simultaneously:

```
function move(){
  $("#content").css("left", "50px")
  .css("top", "100px");
} // end move
```

This function uses the css() method to change the left property to 50px. The resulting object is given a second css() method call to change the top property to 100px. The top and left elements are changed at the same time as far as the user is concerned.

Building time-based animation with animate ( )

Using the `css()` method is a great way to move an element around on the screen, but the motion is instantaneous. jQuery supports a powerful method called `animate()`, which allows you to change any DOM characteristics over a specified span of time. The `glide` button on `animate.html` smoothly moves the `content` div from (50, 100) to (400, 200) over two seconds.

```
function glide(){
  //move to initial spot
  $("#content").css("left", "50px")
  .css("top", "100px");

  //slide to new spot
  $("#content").animate({
    "left": "400px",
    "top": "200px"
  }, 2000);
} // end glide
```

The function begins by moving the element immediately to its initial spot with chained `css()` methods. It then uses the `animate()` method to control the animation. This method can have up to three parameters:

✔ **A JSON object describing attributes to animate:** The first parameter is an object in JSON notation describing name/value attribute pairs. In this example, I'm telling jQuery to change the `left` attribute from its current value to 400px and the `top` value to 200px. Any numeric value that you can change through the DOM can be included in this JSON object. Instead of a numerical value, you can use `"hide"`, `"show"`, or `"toggle"` to specify an action. Review Chapter 5 for more on JSON objects if you're unfamiliar with them.

✔ **A speed attribute:** The speed parameter is defined in the same way as the speed for fade and slide animations. There are three predefined speeds: `"slow"`, `"medium"`, and `"fast"`; speed can also be indicated in milliseconds (so 2000 means 2 seconds).

✔ **A callback function:** This optional parameter describes a function to be called when the animation is complete. I describe the use of callback functions earlier in this chapter in the section called "Fading an element in and out."

Move a little bit: Relative motion

You can use the animation mechanism to move an object relative to its current position. The arrow buttons and their associated functions perform this task:

```
function left(){
  $("#content").animate({"left": "-=10px"}, 100);
} // end left

function right(){
  $("#content").animate({"left": "+=10px"}, 100);
} // end left
```

These functions also use the `animate()` method, but there's a small difference in the position parameters. The `+=` and `-=` modifiers indicate that I want to add to or subtract from the value rather than indicating an absolute position. Of course, you can add as many parameters to the JSON object as you want, but these are a good start.

Note that since I'm moving a small amount (ten pixels) I want the motion to be relatively quick. Each motion lasts 100 milliseconds.

The jQuery `animation()` method supports one more option: *easing*. The term *easing* refers to the relative speed of the animation throughout its lifespan. If you watch the animations on the `animate.html` page carefully, you'll see that the motion begins slowly, builds up speed, and slows down again at the end. This provides a natural-feeling animation. By default, jQuery animations use what's called a `swing` easing style (slow on the ends, fast in the middle, like a child on a swing). If you want to have a more consistent speed, you can specify `"linear"` as the fourth parameter, and the animation will work at a constant speed. You can also install plugins for more advanced easing techniques.

Modifying Elements on the Fly

The jQuery library supports a third major way of modifying the page: the ability to add and remove contents dynamically. This is a powerful way to work with a page. The key to this feature is another of jQuery's most capable tools: its flexible selection engine. You've already seen how you can select jQuery nodes using the standard CSS-style selectors, but you can also use numerous attributes to modify nodes. The `changeContent.html` page demonstrates some of the power of these tools (see Figure 11-4).

Of course, the buttons allow the user to make changes to the page dynamically. Pressing the Add Text button adds more text to the content area, as you can see in Figure 11-5.

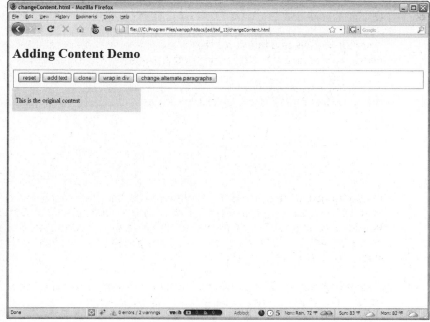

Figure 11-4:
The default
state of
change-
Content is a
little dull.

Click here to add more text to the Content area.

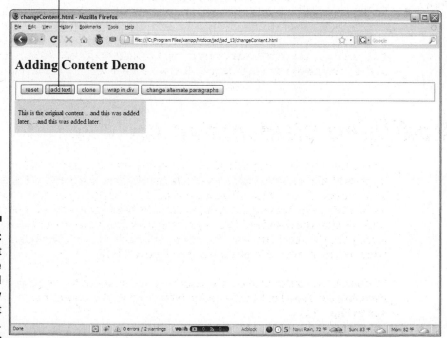

Figure 11-5:
More text
can be
appended
inside any
content
area.

The Clone button is interesting because it allows you to make a copy of an element and place it somewhere else in the document hierarchy. Pressing the Clone button a few times can give you a page like Figure 11-6.

It's possible to wrap an HTML element around any existing element. The Wrap in Div button puts a `div` (with a red border) around every cloned element. You can press this multiple times to add multiple wrappings to any element. Figure 11-7 shows what happens after I wrap a few times.

For readability, sometimes you want to be able to alternate styles of lists and tables. jQuery offers an easy way to select every other element in a group and give it a style. The Change Alternate Paragraphs button activates some code that turns all odd-numbered paragraphs into white text with a green background. Look at Figure 11-8 for a demonstration.

Finally, the Reset button demonstrates how you can reset all the changes you made with the other buttons.

Click the Clone button to copy content.

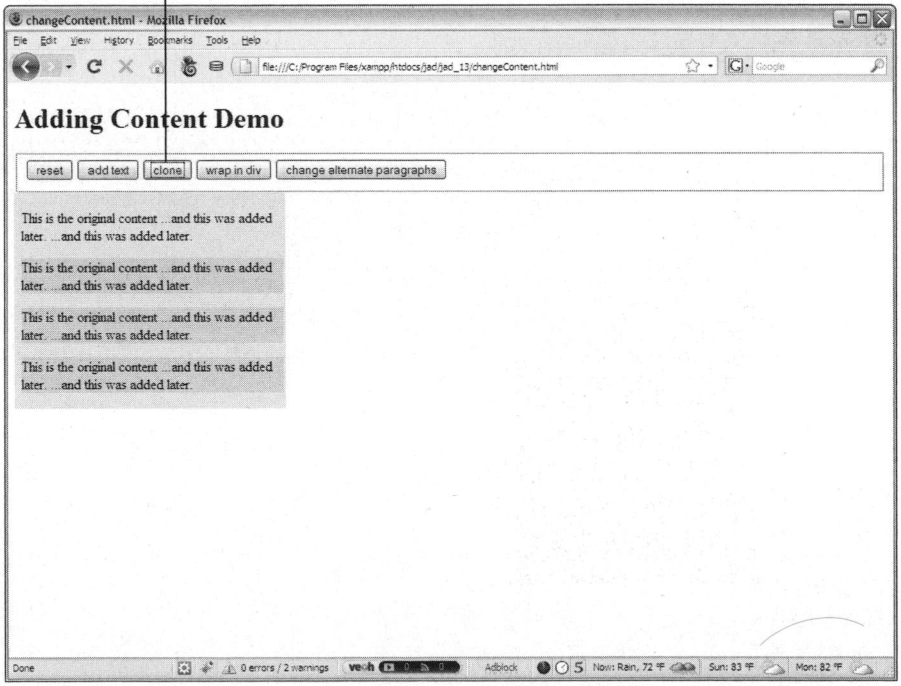

Figure 11-6:
I've made several clones of the original content.

Click to add a div.

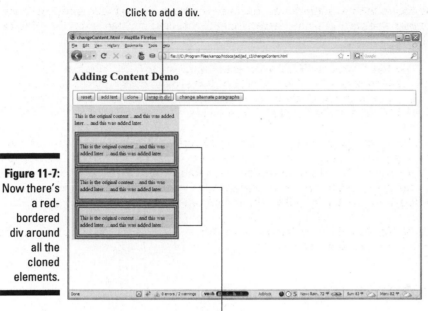

A div is added to each clone. (I clicked the button three times in this example.)

Click this button to alternate styles.

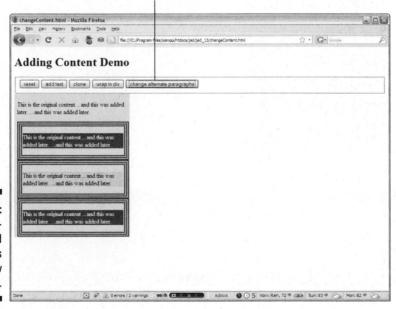

The code for changeContent.html seems complex, but it follows the same general patterns in jQuery programming that I show you earlier in this chapter. As always, look over the entire code first, and then I break it down.

```
<!DOCTYPE html PUBLIC "-//W3C//DTD XHTML 1.0 Strict//EN"
"http://www.w3.org/TR/xhtml1/DTD/xhtml1-strict.dtd">
<html lang="EN" dir="ltr" xmlns="http://www.w3.org/1999/
         xhtml">
<head>
  <meta http-equiv=»content-type» content=»text/xml;
         charset=utf-8» />

  <style type = «text/css»>
  #content {
    width: 300px;
    background-color: yellow;
    left: 300px;
    top: 100px;
    padding-left: .5em;

    border: 0px none black;
  }

  div {
    border: 2px solid red;
    padding: 3px;
  }
  </style>

  <script type = «text/javascript»
         src = «jquery-1.3.2.min.js»></script>

  <script type = «text/javascript»>
  //<![CDATA[
  $(init);

  function init(){
    $(«#reset»).click(reset);
    $(«#addText»).click(addText);
    $(«#wrap»).click(wrap);
    $(«#clone»).click(clone);
    $(«#oddGreen»).click(oddGreen);
  } // end init

  function reset(){
    //remove all but the original content
    $(«p:gt(0)»).remove();
    $(«div:not(#content)»).remove();
    //reset the text of the original content
```

```
        $(«#content»).html(«<p>This is the original
            content</p>»);
    } // end reset

    function addText(){
        $(«p:first»).append(« ...and this was added
            later.»);
    } // end addContent

    function wrap(){
        $(«p:gt(0)»).wrap(«<div></div>»);
    } // end wrap

    function clone(){
     $(«p:first»).clone()
     .insertAfter(«p:last»)
     .css(«backgroundColor», «lightblue»);
    } // end clone

    function oddGreen(){
        //turn alternate (odd numbered) paragraph elements
            green
        $(«p:odd»).css(«backgroundColor», «green»)
        .css(«color», «white»);
    } // end oddGreen
    //]]>
  </script>
  <title>changeContent.html</title>
</head>
<body>
  <h1>Adding Content Demo</h1>
  <form action = «»>
    <fieldset>
      <button type = «button»
              id = «reset»>
        reset
      </button>

      <button type = «button»
              id = «addText»>
        add text
      </button>

      <button type = «button»
              id = «clone»>
        clone
      </button>
```

```
     <button type = «button»
             id = «wrap»>
       wrap in div
     </button>

     <button type = «button»
             id = «oddGreen»>
       change alternate paragraphs
     </button>
   </fieldset>
 </form>

 <div id = «content»>
   <p>
     This is the original content
   </p>
 </div>
</body>
</html>
```

I admit, this program has a lot of code, but when you consider how much functionality this page has, it really isn't too bad. Look at it in smaller pieces, and it all make sense.

Building the basic page

As usual, begin by inspecting the HTML. The basic code for this page sets up the playground.

1. **Create a form with buttons.**

   This form becomes the control panel. Add a button for each function you want to add. Make sure each button has an ID, but you don't need to specify an `onclick` function, because the `init()` function will take care of that.

2. **Build a prototype** `content` div.

   Build a `div` called `content`, and add a paragraph to the `div`.

It's very important to be careful with your initial HTML structure. The manipulation and selection tricks that you experiment with in this chapter rely on a thorough understanding of the beginning page structure. Be sure you understand exactly how the page is set up so that you'll understand how to manipulate it. If your standard XHTML page (before any JavaScript/jQuery code is added) doesn't validate, it's unlikely your code will work as expected.

Initializing the code

The initialization section is pretty straightforward. Set up an `init()` function and use it to assign event handlers to all the buttons:

```
$(init);

function init(){
  $("#reset").click(reset);
  $("#addText").click(addText);
  $("#wrap").click(wrap);
  $("#clone").click(clone);
  $("#oddGreen").click(oddGreen);
} // end init
```

Adding text

Adding text to a component is pretty easy. The `append()` method attaches text to the end of a jQuery node. Table 11-1 shows a number of other methods for adding text to a node.

Table 11-1	Adding Content to jQuery Nodes
Method	*Description*
`append(text)`	Adds the text (or HTML) to the end of the selected element(s).
`prepend(text)`	Adds the content at the beginning of the selected element(s).
`insertAfter(text)`	Adds the text after the selected element (outside the element).
`insertBefore(text)`	Adds the text before the selected element (outside the element).

More methods are available, but these are the ones I find most useful. Be sure to check out the official documentation at `http://docs.jquery.com` to see the other options.

```
function addText(){
  $("p:first").append(" ...and this was added
      later.");
} // end addContent
```

The `append()` method adds the new text to the end of the text already inside the element, so it becomes part of the paragraph contained inside the `content div`. For example, if you have this element: `<div>one</div>` and you append `two` to the div, you'll get `<div>onetwo</div>`, not `<div>one</div>two`.

The more interesting part of this code is the selector. It could read like this:

```
$("p").append(" ...and this was added later.");
```

That would add the text to the end of the paragraph. The default text has only one paragraph, so that makes lots of sense. If there are more paragraphs (and there will be), the `p` selector will select them all, adding the text to all the paragraphs simultaneously. By specifying `p:first`, I'm using a special *filter* to determine exactly which paragraph should be affected. Many of the examples on this page use jQuery filters, so I describe them elsewhere in this section. For now, note that `p:first` means the first paragraph. Of course, there are also `p:last` and many more. Read on. . . .

Attack of the clones

You can clone (copy) anything you can identify as a jQuery node. This cloning makes a copy of the node without changing the original. The cloned node isn't immediately visible on the screen. You need to place it somewhere, usually with an `append()`, `prepend()`, `insertBefore()`, or `insertAfter()` method.

Take a look at the `clone()` function to see how it works:

```
function clone(){
  $("p:first").clone()
  .insertAfter("p:last")
  .css("backgroundColor", "lightblue");
} // end clone
```

1. **Select the first paragraph.**

   The first paragraph is the one I want to copy. (In the beginning, there's only one, but that will change soon.)

2. **Use the `clone()` method to make a copy.**

   Even though this step makes a copy, it still isn't visible. Use chaining to do some interesting things to this copy. (I explain chaining earlier in the chapter, in the section "Don't go chaining . . .")

3. **Add the new element to the page after the last paragraph.**

   The `p:last` identifier is the last paragraph, so `insertAfter ("p:last")` means put the new paragraph after the last paragraph available in the document.

4. Change the CSS.

Just for grins, chain the `css()` method onto the new element and change the background color to light blue. This just reinforces that you can continue adding commands to a node through chaining.

Note that the paragraphs are still inside the `content div`. Of course, I could have put them elsewhere with careful use of selectors, but that's where I want them.

Keeping track of changes to the page is difficult because a standard View Source command shows you the *original* source code, not the code that's been changed by your jQuery magic. jQuery changes the HTML of your page in memory, but doesn't change the text file that contains your page. If your page isn't doing what you expect, you need to look at the script-generated source code to see what's really going on. Firefox plugins are the key to headache-free debugging. The Web developer toolbar has a wonderful feature called View Generated Source (available under the View Source menu), which shows the page source as it currently exists in memory. If you prefer the Firebug extension, its inspect mode also inspects the page as it currently is displayed. Both tools are described in Chapter 1.

Note that the content of the first paragraph is cloned with its current content and style information copied to the new element. If you clone the paragraph and then add content to it and clone it again, the first clone has the default text, and the second clone contains the additional text. If you modify the CSS of an element and then clone it, the clone also inherits any of the style characteristics of the original node.

It's a wrap

Sometimes you want to embed an object inside another element (or two). For example, the `wrap` button on the `changeContent` page surrounds each cloned paragraph with a `<div></div>` pair. I've defined the `<div>`tag in my CSS to include a red border. Repeatedly clicking the Wrap button surrounds all cloned paragraphs with red borders. This would be a very tedious effect to achieve in ordinary DOM and JavaScript, but jQuery makes it pretty easy to do.

```
function wrap(){
    $("p:gt(0)").wrap("<div></div>");
} // end wrap
```

The `wrap` method is pretty easy to understand. If you feed it any container tag, it wraps that container around the selected node. You can also use multiple elements, so if you want to enclose a paragraph into a single item list, you can do something like this:

```
$("p").wrap("<ul><li></li></ul>");
```

The resulting code would surround each paragraph with an unordered list and list item.

Returning to the `wrap` function, I've decided not to wrap every paragraph with a `div`, just the ones that have been cloned. (Mainly I'm doing this so I can show you some other cool selection filters.) The selector `p:gt(0)` means "select all paragraphs with an index greater than zero." In other words, ignore the first paragraph but apply the following methods to all other paragraphs. There is also a less-than filter (`:lt`), which isolates elements before a certain index, and an equals filter (`:eq`), which isolates an element with a certain index.

Alternating styles

People commonly alternate background colors on long lists or tables of data, but this can be a tedious effect to achieve in ordinary CSS and JavaScript. Not surprisingly, jQuery selectors make this a pretty easy job:

```
function oddGreen(){
  //turn alternate (odd numbered) paragraph elements
      green
  $("p:odd").css("backgroundColor", "green")
  .css("color", "white");
} // end oddGreen
```

The `:odd` selector only chooses elements with an odd index and returns a jQuery node that can be further manipulated with chaining. Of course, you can use an `:even` selector for handling the even-numbered nodes. The rest of this code is simply CSS styling.

Resetting the page

If you can do all this modification to the page, you'll also need to be able to restore it to its pristine state. A quick jQuery function can easily do the trick:

```
function reset(){
  //remove all but the original content
  $("p:gt(0)").remove();
  $("div:not(#content)").remove();
  //reset the text of the original content
  $("#content").html("<p>This is the original
      content</p>");
} // end reset
```

This function reviews many of the jQuery and selection tricks shown in this chapter.

1. **Remove all but the first paragraph.**

   Any paragraphs with an index greater than zero is a clone, so it needs to go away. The `remove()` method removes all jQuery nodes associated with the current selector.

2. **Remove all `divs` but the original content.**

   I could have used the `:gt` selector again, but instead I use another interesting selector: `:not`. This selector means "remove every `div` that isn't the primary `content div`." Using this selector removes all `divs` added through the `wrap` function.

3. **Reset the original `content div` to its default text.**

   Set the default text back to its original status so the page is reset.

Truthfully, all I really need here is the last line of code. Changing the HTML of the `content div` replaces the current contents with whatever is included, so the first two lines aren't entirely necessary in this particular context. Still, it's very useful to know how to remove elements when you need to do so.

More fun with selectors and filters

The jQuery selectors and filters are really fun and powerful. Table 11-2 describes a few more filters and how you can use them.

Table 11-2	Common jQuery Filters
Filter	*Description*
`:header`	Any header tag (h1, h2, h3).
`:animated`	Any element that is currently being animated.
`:contains(text)`	Any element that contains the indicated text.
`:empty`	The element is empty.
`:parent`	This element contains some other element.
`:attribute=value`	The element has an attribute with the specified value.
`:Input`, `:text`, `:radio`, `:image`, `:button`, and so on	Matches on the specific element type (especially useful for form elements that are all variations of the input tag).

Note that this is a representative list. Be sure to check out the official documentation at `http://docs.jquery.com` for a more complete list of filters.

Chapter 12

Using the jQuery User Interface Toolkit

In This Chapter

▶ Exploring the jQuery user interface

▶ Installing the UI and templates

▶ Adding date pickers, dialog boxes, and icons

▶ Dragging and dropping

▶ Working with scrollbars

▶ Building a sorting mechanism

▶ Creating an accordion page

▶ Building a tab-based interface

*T*he jQuery library is an incredible tool for simplifying JavaScript programming. The library is so popular and powerful that developers began adding new features to make it even more useful. Among the most important of these is the jQuery UI (user interface) framework. This tool adds these welcome features to Web development:

✔ **New user interface elements:** As a modern user interface tool, HTML is missing some important tools. Most modern visual languages include built-in support for devices such as scrollbars, dedicated date pickers, and multiple tab tools. jQuery UI adds these features and more.

✔ **Advanced user interaction:** The jQuery widgets give users new and exciting ways to interact with your page. Using the UI toolkit, you can easily let users make selections by dragging and dropping elements and expanding and contracting parts of the page.

✔ **Flexible theme templates:** jQuery UI includes a template mechanism that controls the visual look and feel of your elements. You can choose from dozens of prebuilt themes or use a tool to build your own particular look. You can reuse this template library to manage the look of your other page elements, too (not just the ones defined by the library).

✔ **A complete icon library:** The jQuery UI has a library of icons for use in your Web development. It has arrows and buttons and plenty of other doodads that you can change to fit your template.

✔ **A clean, modern look:** You can easily build forward-looking visual designs with jQuery UI. It supports rounded corners and plenty of special visual effects.

✔ **The power of jQuery:** As an extension of jQuery, the jQuery UI adds to the incredible features of the jQuery language.

✔ **Open source values:** The jQuery UI (like jQuery itself) is an open-source project with quite an active community. You can modify its free library to suit your needs.

Looking Over the ThemeRoller

The jQuery UI Web site (http://jqueryui.com) is a helpful place to find the latest information about jQuery, and it also features the marvelous Theme Roller tool. Figure 12-1 shows the main Web page, which demonstrates many of the excellent jQuery features.

Before you use ThemeRoller to change themes, use it to become acquainted with the UI elements. Several useful tools are visible in the figure:

✔ **Accordion:** The upper-left segment of the page has three segments (Section 1, Section 2, and Section 3). By clicking a section heading, the user can expand that section and collapse others.

✔ **Slider:** Sliders (or scrollbars) are an essential user interface element that lets a user choose a numeric value by using an easy visual tool. You can adjust jQuery sliders in many ways to allow easy and error-free input.

✔ **Date picker:** Ensuring that users enter dates properly is difficult. The phenomenally useful date picker control automatically pops a calendar onto the page and lets the user manipulate the calendar to pick a date.

✔ **Progress bar:** Always design your code so that little delay occurs, but if a part of your program takes some time to complete, a progress bar is a useful reminder that something is happening.

✔ **Tabs:** The accordion technique is one way to hide and show parts of your page, and tabs are another popular technique. You can use this mechanism to build a powerful multi-tab document without having to do much work.

The datepicker is an automatic calendar.

Tabs allow you to organize a large amount of content.   The slider is a scroll bar.

Figure 12-1:
ThemeRoller
lets you look
over many
jQuery UI
elements
and modify
their look.

This section is an accordion.

The progress bar allows you to view an event's progress.

Scrolling down the page, you see even more interesting tools. Figure 12-2 shows some of these widgets in action.

These widgets demonstrate even more of the power of the jQuery UI library:

- ✔ **Dialog:** Pressing the Open Dialog button pops up what appears to be a dialog box. It acts much like the JavaScript alert, but it's much nicer looking and has features that make it much more advanced.

- ✔ **Formatting tools:** The jQuery UI includes special tools for setting apart certain parts of your page as warnings, as highlighted text, or with added shadows and transparency.

- ✔ **Icons:** jQuery UI ships with a large collection of icons you can use in your page. Hover the mouse over each icon on the ThemeRoller to see a description. You can easily use these icons to allow various user interactions.

Pop-up dialog

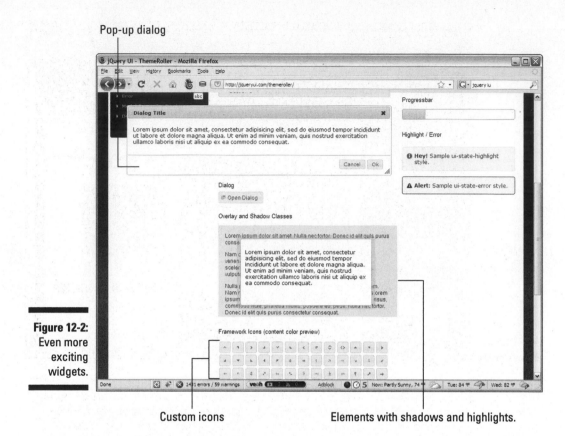

Figure 12-2:
Even more
exciting
widgets.

Custom icons   Elements with shadows and highlights.

Visiting the Theme Park

Impressive as all the jQuery UI widgets are, they're just a part of the story. jQuery supports the concept of *themes*, which are simply visual rule sets. A theme is essentially a complex CSS document (and some associated graphics files) designed to be used with the UI library. Go back to the top of the Theme Roller page and look at the left column. If you click the Gallery tab (yes, it's using a jQuery UI tab interface), you can see a list of prebuilt themes. Figure 12-3 shows the ThemeRoller page with an entirely different theme in place.

The built-in themes are impressive, but of course you can make your own. Though you're always free to edit the CSS manually, the whole point of the ThemeRoller application is to make this process easier.

Figure 12-3:
Now,
ThemeRoller
is using
the Le Frog
theme.

If you go back to the Roll Your Own tab, you see an accordion selection that you can use to pick various theme options. You can change fonts, choose rounded corners, select various color schemes, and much more. You can mess around with these options all you want and create your own visual style. You can then save that theme and use it in your own projects.

Wanna Drag? Dragging and Dropping Elements

It's time to build something. The first example I show you is a simple application that lets someone use the mouse to pick up a page element and move it. Although I tell you how to use JavaScript and the document object model (DOM) to do this in Chapter 8, you'll find that you can quite easily create the same effect by using jQuery UI. Figure 12-4 shows this page in action.

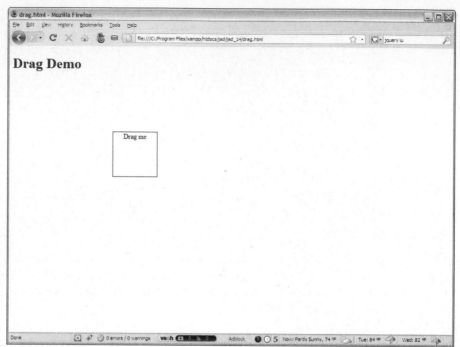

Figure 12-4:
The user
can simply
drag the box
anywhere
on the page.

This example is a good starting place for using the jQuery UI library because it's easy to get the project working. Often, the hardest part of writing jQuery UI applications is making the connections to the library. After you do that (and it's not *that* hard), the rest of the programming is ridiculously easy. Take a look at the following chunk of code to see what I'm talking about:

```
<!DOCTYPE html PUBLIC "-//W3C//DTD XHTML 1.0 Strict//EN"
"http://www.w3.org/TR/xhtml1/DTD/xhtml1-strict.dtd">
<html lang="EN" dir="ltr" xmlns="http://www.w3.org/1999/
          xhtml">
<head>
  <meta http-equiv=»content-type» content=»text/xml;
          charset=utf-8» />
  <style type = «text/css»>
  #dragMe {
    width: 100px;
    height: 100px;
    border: 1px solid blue;
    text-align: center;
  }
  </style>
  <script type = «text/javascript»
          src = «jquery-1.3.2.min.js»></script>
  <script type = «text/javascript»
```

```
          src = «jquery-ui-1.7.2.custom.min.js»></script>
  <script type = «text/javascript»>
    $(init);
    function init(){
      $(«#dragMe»).draggable();
    }
  </script>
  <title>drag.html</title>
</head>

<body>
  <h1>Drag Demo</h1>
  <div id = «dragMe»>
    Drag me
  </div>
</body>
</html>
```

The basic idea of this program is completely consistent with the jQuery concepts I describe in Chapter 13. The page uses simple HTML code. An initialization function creates a special jQuery node and gives it functionality. That's all there is to it.

Here are the basic steps:

1. **Create a basic HTML document.**

   You can use a standard document. I created one `div` with the ID dragMe, which is the `div` I want to make draggable. (You can, of course, apply dragging functionality to any element you can select with jQuery.)

2. **Add the standard jQuery library.**

   The first `<script>` tag imports the standard jQuery library. The UI library requires jQuery to be loaded first.

A ThemeRoller example

ThemeRoller gives you a good overview of the jQuery UI library and also serves as a great example of where the Web is going. It's not really a Web page as much as it's an application that happens to be written in Web technologies. Notice that the functionality of the page (changing styles dynamically) uses many jQuery and jQuery UI tricks: tabs, accordions, and dialog boxes, for example. This kind of programming, which is almost certainly the direction in which Web development is heading, might indeed be the primary form of application in the future. Certainly, it appears that applications using this style of user interface, and AJAX, for data communication and storage will be important for quite some time.

3. **Add a link to the jQuery UI library.**

   A second `<script>` tag imports the jQuery UI library. (See the section called "Downloading the Library" for details on how to obtain this library.)

4. **Create an initialization function.**

   Use the standard jQuery techniques to build an initialization function for your page. (As usual, I named mine `init()`.)

5. **Build a draggable node.**

   Use standard jQuery selection techniques to isolate the elements you want to make draggable. Use the `draggable()` method to make the element draggable.

6. **Test.**

   Believe it or not, that's all there is to it. As long as everything is set up properly, your element can be dragged! A user can drag it with the mouse and place it anywhere on the screen.

Downloading the Library

Writing jQuery UI code isn't difficult, but getting access to the parts of the library you need can be a bit confusing. The jQuery UI library is much larger than the standard jQuery package, so you might not want to include the entire package if you don't need it. Previous versions of jQuery UI let you download the entire package but stored each of the various elements in a separate JavaScript file. You would commonly have a half-dozen different `script` tags active just to put the various elements in place. Worse, there were some dependency issues, so you had to ensure that certain packages were installed before you could use other packages — all of which made a simple library quite complex to use.

Fortunately, the latest versions of the jQuery UI make this process quite a bit simpler. Whenever you begin to work on a project, you pick (or create) a visual theme, choose the widgets and tools you want, and download a custom form of the library that's tailored to your exact needs. Using this mechanism, you have much simpler code because you link only one JavaScript library for the UI no matter how many interface tools and gadgets you use (though you still need to link the standard jQuery library first).

Use this technique also to build in multiple themes so that you can easily switch the look of your program by changing the theme files.

Resizing on a Theme

This section demonstrates two important ideas in the jQuery UI package:

- **Resizable elements:** The user can drag an element's bottom or right border to change its size. Making an element resizable is similar to making it draggable.

- **Themes:** jQuery features a series of customized visual styles.

You can see in Figure 12-5 that the page has a definite visual style. The elements have distinctive fonts and backgrounds, and the headers are in a particular visual style. Though these styles aren't earth-shattering (after all, it's just CSS), the exciting news is that they're defined by the theme. You can easily select another theme (created by hand or by using ThemeRoller), and the visual look of all these elements will reflect the new theme. Themes provide a further level of abstraction to your Web site that makes changing the overall visual style much easier than modifying the CSS by hand.

The widget can be resized by dragging the edges or corner.

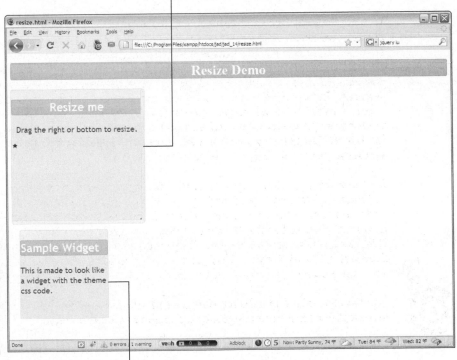

Figure 12-5:
A user can change the size of this lovely element.

An ordinary div styled to use the same widget format.

Figure 12-6 shows the page after the Resize Me element has changed sizes, and you can see that the rest of the page reformats itself to fit the newly resized element.

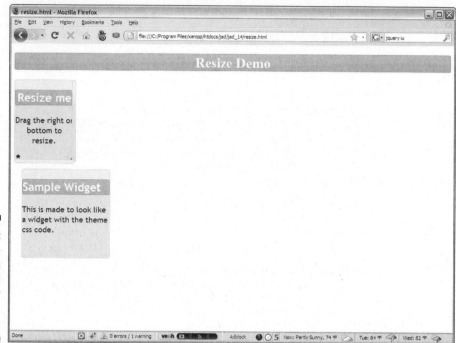

Figure 12-6:
When the element is resized, the remainder of the page adjusts.

The following chunk of code reveals that most of the interesting visual effects in Figure 12-6 are simple CSS coding, and the resizing is just more jQuery UI magic:

```
<!DOCTYPE html PUBLIC "-//W3C//DTD XHTML 1.0 Strict//EN"
"http://www.w3.org/TR/xhtml1/DTD/xhtml1-strict.dtd">
<html lang="EN" dir="ltr" xmlns="http://www.w3.org/1999/
        xhtml">
<head>
  <meta http-equiv=»content-type» content=»text/xml;
        charset=utf-8» />
  <link rel = «stylesheet»
        type = «text/css»
        href = «jquery-ui-1.7.2.custom.css» />

  <style type = «text/css»>
  h1 {
    text-align: center;
  }
```

```
#resizeMe {
  width: 300px;
  height: 300px;
  text-align: center;
}
#sample {
  width: 200px;
  height: 200px;
  margin: 1em;
}

</style>
<script type = «text/javascript»
        src = «jquery-1.3.2.min.js»></script>
<script type = «text/javascript»
        src = «jquery-ui-1.7.2.custom.min.js»></script>
<script type = «text/javascript»>
  //<![CDATA[
  $(init);
  function init(){
    $(«#resizeMe»).resizable();
    themify();
  } // end init

  function themify(){
    //add theme-based CSS to the elements
    $(«div»).addClass(«ui-widget»)
    .addClass(«ui-widget-content»)
    .addClass(«ui-corner-all»);
    $(«:header»).addClass(«ui-widget-header»)
    .addClass(«ui-corner-all»);
    $(«#resizeMe»)
    .append('<span class = «ui-icon ui-icon-star»></
        span>');
  }
  //]]>
</script>
<title>resize.html</title>
</head>

<body>
  <h1>Resize Demo</h1>
  <div id = «resizeMe»>
    <h2>Resize me</h2>
    <p>
      Drag the right or bottom to resize.
    </p>
  </div>

  <div id = «sample»>
    <h2>Sample Widget</h2>
    <p>
```

```
        This is made to look like a widget
        with the theme css code.
    </p>
  </div>

</body>
</html>
```

Examining the HTML and standard CSS

As usual, the HTML used in the code example in the preceding section is the foundation of the entire page. It's clean, and it shows the general structure of the page. The HTML consists of only three primary elements: a heading and two `div`s. Each `div` contains its own Level 2 heading and a paragraph. The `div`s are given IDs to make them easier to style.

I also included a basic CSS section in the example to handle the general layout of the page. Because I wanted the widgets to have specific initial sizes, I used ordinary CSS to create this effect.

Importing files

jQuery applications require the importation of JavaScript code libraries. In this (and most) jQuery UI applications, I import these three files:

- ✔ **The main jQuery library:** This essential jQuery base library is imported as described in Chapter 11, as an ordinary JavaScript file.

- ✔ **The jQuery UI library:** This file is also a standard JavaScript library. To obtain a custom version of this file, see the section "Downloading the Library," earlier in this chapter.

- ✔ **The theme CSS file:** When you create a theme with ThemeRoller, you're provided with a CSS file. This file is your theme. Because it's a CSS file rather than a chunk of JavaScript code, use the `link` tag to attach it to your page.

Not all jQuery UI examples require a theme, but most do. As you see in this example, themes provide some other excellent effects too, so it's worthwhile to include a theme CSS file whenever you want to use jQuery UI.

Making a resizable element

Surprisingly, the easiest part of the project is making the `resizable` element take on the resizable behavior, as shown in this example:

```
$(init);
function init(){
  $("#resizeMe").resizable();
  themify();
} // end init
```

It's a standard jQuery UI trick. Follow these steps:

1. **Begin with an initialization function.**

   Like all good jQuery code, this example begins with standard initialization.

2. **Make an element resizable.**

   Identify the `resizeMe` div as a jQuery node, and use the `resizable()` method to make it resizable. That's all there is to it.

3. **Call a second function to add theming to the elements.**

   Though the resizable method doesn't require the use of jQuery themes, the themes improve the look of the element.

Adding themes to your elements

The jQuery Theme tool helps you quite easily decorate your elements by using CSS. The outstanding feature of jQuery themes is that they're *semantic:* You specify the general purpose of the element and then let the theme apply the appropriate specific CSS. You can use the ThemeRoller application to easily create new themes or modify existing ones. In this way, you can create quite a sophisticated look and feel for your site and write a minimal amount of CSS on your own. Many jQuery interface elements (such as the Accordion and Tab tools, described elsewhere in this chapter) automatically use the current CSS theme. You can also apply the theme to any of your own elements, of course, to create a consistent look.

Themes are simply a set of predefined CSS classes. To apply a CSS theme to an element, you can just add a special class to the object. For example, you can make a paragraph look like the current definition of the `ui-widget` by adding this bit of code to it:

```
<div class = "ui-widget">
My div now looks like a widget
</div>
```

Of course, adding classes into the HTML violates one principle of semantic design, so you can more efficiently do the work in JavaScript by using jQuery:

```
function themify(){
  //add theme-based CSS to the elements
  $("div").addClass("ui-widget")
  .addClass("ui-widget-content")
  .addClass("ui-corner-all");
  $(":header").addClass("ui-widget-header")
  .addClass("ui-corner-all");
  $("#resizeMe")
  .append('<span class = "ui-icon ui-icon-star"></span>');
}
```

The `themify()` function adds all the themes to the elements on my page, using the CSS defined by the theme. I use jQuery tricks to simplify the process.

1. **Identify all** `div`**s by using jQuery.**

   To style all `div`s in your page as widgets, use jQuery to identify all `div` elements.

2. **Add the** `ui-widget` **class to all** `div`**s.**

   This class is defined in the theme. All jQuery themes have this class defined, but the specific characteristics (colors and font sizes, for example) vary by theme. In this way, you can swap out a theme to change its appearance and the code still works. The `ui-widget` class defines an element as a widget.

3. **Add** `ui-widget-content`**.**

   The `div`s need two classes attached, so I use chaining to specify that `div`s should also be members of the `ui-widget-content` class. This class indicates that the contents of the widget (and not just the class itself) should be styled.

4. **Specify rounded corners.**

   Rounded corners have become a standard feature of Web 2.0 visual design. This effect is extremely easy to achieve by using jQuery: Just add the `ui-corner-all` class to any element that you want to have rounded corners.

   Rounded corners use CSS3, which isn't yet supported by all browsers. Your page won't show rounded corners in most versions of Internet Explorer, but the page will still work fine otherwise.

5. **Make all headlines conform to the** `widget-header` **style.**

   The jQuery themes include an attractive headline style. You can easily make all heading tags (from <h1> to <h6>) follow this theme. Use the :header filter to identify all headings, and apply the `ui-widget-header` and `ui-corner-all` classes to these headers.

The jQuery UI package supports a number of interesting classes, as described in Table 12-1.

Table 12-1	Classes Supported by the jQuery UI Package	
Class	**Used On**	**What It Does**
`ui-widget`	Outer container of widget	Makes the element look like a widget
`ui-widget-header`	Heading element	Applies a distinctive heading appearance
`ui-widget-content`	Widget	Applies widget content style to an element and its children
`ui-state-default`	Clickable elements	Displays standard (unclicked) state
`ui-state-hover`	Clickable elements	Displays hover state
`ui-state-focus`	Clickable elements	Displays focus state when element has keyboard focus
`ui-state-active`	Clickable elements	Display active state when mouse is clicked on element
`ui-state-highlight`	Any widget or element	Specifies that element is highlighted
`ui-state-error`	Any widget or element	Specifies that an element contain an error message or a warning message
`ui-state-error text`	Text elements	Allows error highlighting without changing other elements (mainly used in form validation)
`ui-state-disabled`	Any widget or element	Demonstrates that widget is disabled

`ui-corner-all,`
 	
`ui-corner-tl (etc)`
	Any widget or element	Adds current corner size to element; corners specified by using tl, tr, bl, br, top, bottom, left, right

`ui-widget-shadow`	Any widget	Applies shadow effect to widget

Note there a few other classes are defined in UI themes, but the ones in this table are the most commonly used. Please see the current jQuery UI documentation for more details.

Adding an icon

Note the small star that appears inside the `resizeMe` element in Figure 12-6. This element is an example of a jQuery UI icon. All jQuery themes support a standard set of icons, which are small images (16 pixels square). The icon set includes standard icons for arrows as well as images commonly used in menus and toolbars (Save and Load or New File, for example). Some jQuery UI elements use icons automatically, but you can also add them directly.

To use an icon in your programs, follow these steps:

1. **Include a jQuery UI theme.**

   The icons are part of the theme package. Include the CSS style sheet that corresponds with the theme (as you did if you followed the instructions in Chapter 10).

2. **Ensure that the images are accessible.**

   When you download a theme package, it includes a directory of images. The images included in it are used to create custom backgrounds as well as icons. The CSS file expects a directory named `images` to be in the same directory as the CSS. This directory should contain several images that begin with `ui-icons`. These images contain all necessary icons. If the icon image files aren't available, the icons aren't displayed.

3. **Create a span where you want the icon to appear.**

   Place an empty span element wherever you want the icon to appear in the HTML. You can place the span directly in the HTML or add it by using jQuery. I prefer to add UI elements by using jQuery, to keep the HTML as pristine as possible.

4. **Attach the `ui-icon` class to the span.**

   This step tells jQuery to treat the span as an icon. The contents of the span are hidden and the span is resized to hold a 16-pixel-square icon image.

5. **Attach a second class to identify the specific icon.**

   Look at the ThemeRoller page to see the available icons. When you hover the mouse over an icon on this page, you see the class name associated with the icon.

You can add the code directly in your HTML:

```
<p id = "myPara">
  This is my text
  <span class = "ui-icon ui-icon-star"></span>
</p>
```

Or, you can use jQuery to add the appropriate code to your element:

```
$("#myPara").append('<span class = "ui-icon ui-icon-
          star"></span>');
```

Dragging, Dropping, and Calling Back

JQuery elements look good, but they also have interesting functionality. Most jQuery UI objects can respond to specialized events. As an example, look over the dragDrop.html page shown in Figure 12-7.

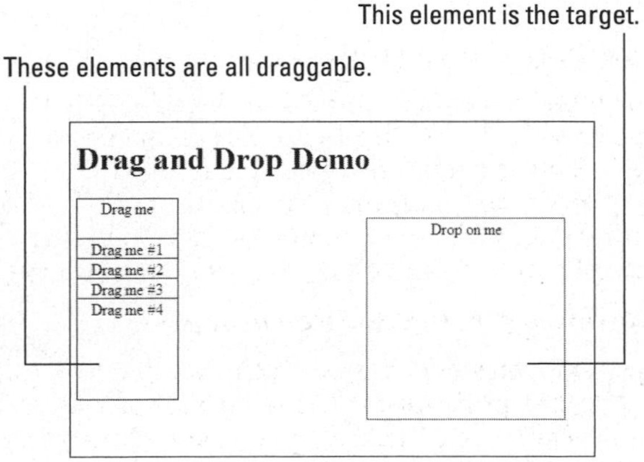

This element is the target.

These elements are all draggable.

Drag and Drop Demo

Drag me

Drag me #1
Drag me #2
Drag me #3
Drag me #4

Drop on me

Figure 12-7:
The page
has a group
of draggable
elements
and a target.

When you drop an element on the target, the color and content of the target change, as shown in Figure 12-8.

When a draggable element is dropped on the
target, the target takes on a new style.

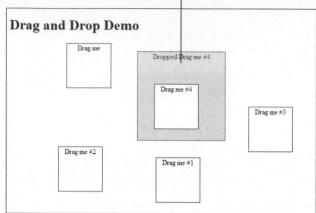

The program demonstrates how jQuery simplifies the task of working with a
number of elements.

Take a look at the entire program before you see its smaller segments:

```
<!DOCTYPE html PUBLIC "-//W3C//DTD XHTML 1.0 Strict//EN"
"http://www.w3.org/TR/xhtml1/DTD/xhtml1-strict.dtd">
<html lang="EN" dir="ltr" xmlns="http://www.w3.org/1999/
          xhtml">
<head>
  <meta http-equiv=»content-type» content=»text/xml;
          charset=utf-8» />
  <link rel = «stylesheet»
        type = «text/css»
        href = «jquery-ui-1.7.2.custom.css» />
  <style type = «text/css»>
  .dragMe {
    width: 100px;
    height: 100px;
    border: 1px solid blue;
    text-align: center;
    background-color: white;
    position: absolute;
    z-index: 100;
  }
  #target {
    width: 200px;
    height: 200px;
    border: 1px solid red;
    text-align: center;
    position: absolute;
```

```
    left: 300px;
    top: 100px;
    z-index: 0;
}
</style>
<script type = «text/javascript»
        src = «jquery-1.3.2.min.js»></script>
<script type = «text/javascript»
        src = «jquery-ui-1.7.2.custom.min.js»></script>
<script type = «text/javascript»>
//<![CDATA[
  $(init);

  function init(){
     // make some clones of dragMe
     cloneDragMe();

     //make all drag me elements draggable
     $(«.dragMe»).draggable();

     //set target as droppable
     $(«#target»).droppable();

     //bind events to target
     $(«#target»).bind(«drop», changeTarget);
     $(«#target»).bind(«dropout», resetTarget);

  } // end init

  function cloneDragMe(){
     for (i = 1; i <=4; i++){
        zValue = (101 + i) + «»;
        yPos = 100 + (i * 20) + «px»;

        $(«div:first»).clone()
        .insertAfter(«div:first»)
        .css(«top», yPos)
        .css(«zIndex», zValue)
        .append(« #» + i);
     } // end for loop
  } // end cloneDragMe

  function changeTarget(event, ui){
     $(«#target»).addClass(«ui-state-highlight»)
     .html(«Dropped «)
     .append(ui.draggable.text());
  } // end changeTarget

  function resetTarget(event, ui){
      $(«#target»).removeClass(«ui-state-highlight»)
      .html(«Drop on me»);
  } // end reset
```

```
  //]]>
  </script>
  <title>dragDrop.html</title>
</head>

<body>
  <h1>Drag and Drop Demo</h1>
  <div class = «dragMe»>
    Drag me
  </div>
  <div id = «target»>
    Drop on me
  </div>
</body>
</html>
```

Building the basic page

As is typical with jQuery, the HTML code on this page is misleadingly simple. It has, strikingly, only a single dragMe element, for example. It's simpler to build a single element in HTML and then use jQuery and JavaScript to make as many copies as you need than it would be to build all the elements by hand in straight HTML. The page also has a single target element. I added basic CSS (borders) to make the elements easy to see and set all the elements as absolutely positioned so that I can control their initial positions. Note that I attached an ID to the target (as there will be a single target on the page), and made dragMe a class (as I want the capability to have several draggable elements on the page).

Initializing the page

The initialization process is somewhat elaborate, but it still isn't too difficult to follow. The main addition is its capability to respond to some specialty events:

```
$(init);

function init(){
  // make some clones of dragMe
  cloneDragMe();

  //make all drag me elements draggable
  $(".dragMe").draggable();

  //set target as droppable
  $("#target").droppable();
```

```
//bind events to target
$("#target").bind("drop", changeTarget);
$("#target").bind("dropout", resetTarget);

} // end init
```

Follow these steps:

1. **Make copies of the** `dragme` **element.**

   This step isn't critical. (In fact, I added it after testing a single element.) However, if you want to have multiple copies of the draggable element, use a method to encapsulate the process.

2. **Make all** `dragme` **elements draggable.**

   Use the jQuery `draggable()` method on all elements with the `dragMe` class.

3. **Establish the target as a droppable element.**

   The `droppable()` method sets up an element so that it can receive events whenever a draggable element is dropped on it. Note that making something droppable doesn't have any particular effect on its own. The interesting part happens when you bind events to the element.

4. **Bind a drop event to the target.**

   Droppable elements can have events attached to them, just like any jQuery object can. However, the mechanism for attaching an event to a user interface object is a little different from the standard jQuery event mechanism, which involved a custom function for each event. Use the `bind` method to specify a function to be called whenever a particular event occurs. When the user drops a draggable element on the target element (the `drop` event), call the `changeTarget()` function.

5. **Bind a** `dropout` **event to the target.**

   You can bind another event, `dropout`, to occur whenever the user removes all draggable elements from the target. I told the sample program to call the `resetTarget()` function whenever this event is triggered.

You often see programmers using shortcuts for this process. Sometimes the functions are defined anonymously in the `bind` call, or sometimes the event functions are attached as a JSON object directly in the `droppable()` method assignment. Feel free to use these techniques if you're comfortable with them. I chose my technique based on its being the clearest model to understand.

Handling the drop

When the user drags a dragMe element and drops it on the target, the target's background color changes and the program reports the text of the element that was dragged. The code is easy to follow:

```
function changeTarget(event, ui){
  $("#target").addClass("ui-state-highlight")
  .html("Dropped ")
  .append(ui.draggable.text());
} // end changeTarget
```

To respond to a drop event, follow these steps:

1. **Create a function to correspond to the drop event.**

   The drop event is bound to the function changeTarget, so you need to create such a function.

2. **Include two parameters.**

   Bound event functions require two parameters. The first is an object that encapsulates the event (much like the one in regular DOM programming) and a second element, named ui, which encapsulates information about the user interface. You use the ui object to determine which draggable element was dropped on the target.

3. **Highlight the target.**

   You should signal that the target's state has changed. You can change the CSS directly (using jQuery) or use jQuery theming to apply a predefined highlight class. I chose to use the jQuery theme technique to simply add the ui-state-highlight class to the target object.

4. **Change the text to indicate the new status.**

   You normally want to do something to indicate what was dropped. If it's a shopping application, for example, add the element to an array so that you can remember what the user wants to purchase. In this example, I simply changed the text of the target to indicate that the element has been dropped.

5. **Use ui.draggable to gain access to the element that was dropped.**

   The ui object contains information about the user interface. The ui.draggable attribute is a link to the draggable element that triggered the current function. It's a jQuery element, so you can use whatever jQuery methods you want on it. In this case, I extract the text from the draggable element and append it to the end of the target's text.

Dropping out can be fun

Another function is used to handle the `dropout` condition, which occurs when draggable elements are no longer sitting on the target. I bound the `resetTarget` function to this event:

```
function resetTarget(event, ui){
    $("#target").removeClass("ui-state-highlight")
    .html("Drop on me");
} // end reset
```

1. **Remove the highlight class from the target.**

   The theme classes are easily removed. Remove the highlight class and the target reverts to its original appearance.

2. **Reset the HTML text.**

   Now that the target is empty, reset its HTML so that it prompts the user to drop a new element.

Cloning the elements

You can simply run the program as-is (with a single copy of the `dragMe` class), but drag-and-drop is more often used with a number of elements. For example, you might allow users to drag various icons from your catalog to a shopping cart. The basic `jQuery` library provides all the functionality necessary to make as many copies of an element as you want. Copying an element is a simple matter of using the jQuery `clone()` method. The more elaborate code is used to ensure that the various elements display properly:

```
function cloneDragMe(){
  for (i = 1; i <=4; i++){
    zValue = (101 + i) + "";
    yPos = 100 + (i * 20) + "px";

    $("div:first").clone()
    .insertAfter("div:first")
    .css("top", yPos)
    .css("zIndex", zValue)
    .append(" #" + i);
  } // end for loop
} // end cloneDragMe
```

To build multiple copies of the draggable element, follow these steps:

1. **Create a `for` loop.**

   Any time you're doing something repetitive, a `for` loop is a likely tool for the job. To make four clones numbered 1 through 4, as shown in the example, you name a variable `I`, which varies from 1 to 4.

2. **Create a `zValue` variable for the element.**

   The CSS `zIndex` property is used to indicate the overlapping of elements. Higher values appear to be closer to the user. In the example, I gave each element a `zOrder` of over 100, to ensure that each element appears over the target. (If you don't specify `zIndex`, dragged elements might be placed under the target and become invisible. The `zValue` variable is mapped to `zIndex`.)

3. **Determine the Y position of the element.**

   I want each successive copy of the `dragMe` element to be a bit lower than the previous one. Multiplying `i` by 20 ensures that each element is separated from the previous one by 20 pixels. Add 100 pixels to move the new stack of elements near the original.

4. **Make a clone of the first element.**

   Use the `clone()` method to make a clone of the first `div`. (Use the `:first` filter to specify which `div` you want to copy.)

5. **Remember to insert the newly cloned element.**

   The cloned element exists only in memory until it's added somehow to the page. I chose to add the element right after the first element.

6. **Set the top of the element with the `yPos` variable.**

   Use the `yPos` variable you calculated earlier in this function to set the vertical position of the newly minted element. Use the `css()` method to apply the `yPos` variable to the element's `left` CSS rule.

7. **Set `zIndex`.**

   As with the `y` position, the `zValue` variable you created is mapped to a CSS value. In this case, `zValue` is mapped to the `zIndex` property.

8. **Add the index to the element's text.**

   Use the `append()` method to add the value of `i` to the element's HTML. This way, you can tell which element is which.

Chapter 13

Improving Usability with jQuery

In This Chapter

▶ Creating an accordion page

▶ Building a tab-based interface

▶ Working with scrollbars

▶ Managing selectable items

▶ Building a sorting mechanism

▶ Using the dialog box tool

The jQuery UI adds some outstanding capabilities to your Web pages. Some of the most interesting tools are *widgets,* which are user interface elements not supplied in standard HTML. Some of these elements supplement HTML by providing easier input options. For example, getting users to enter dates in a predictable manner can be quite difficult. The `datePicker` widget's interface is easy for programmers to add and easy for users to use. Another important class of tools provided by the jQuery UI helps manage complex pages by hiding content until it is needed.

Multi-Element Designs

The issue of how to handle page complexity has been constant in Web development. As a page grows longer and more complex, navigating it becomes difficult. Early versions of HTML had few solutions to this problem. The use of frames was popular because it lets programmers place navigation information in one frame and content in another. Frames added usability problems, however, so they have fallen from favor. Although dynamic HTML and AJAX seem like perfect replacement technologies, they can be difficult to implement, especially in a reliable cross-browser manner.

The jQuery UI provides two incredible tools for the management of larger pages:

- **Accordion tool:** Creates a large page but display only smaller parts of it at a time.
- **Tabs tool:** Easily turns a large page into a page with a tab menu.

These tools are incredibly easy to use, and they add tremendously to your page development options. Both tools help automate and simplify the task of working with the DOM (document object model) and AJAX, which is necessary to build a large page with dynamic content.

Using the Accordion widget

Some of the most powerful jQuery tools are the easiest to use. The Accordion widget has become an extremely popular part of the jQuery UI toolset. Take a look at `accordion.html` in Figure 13-1 to see how it works.

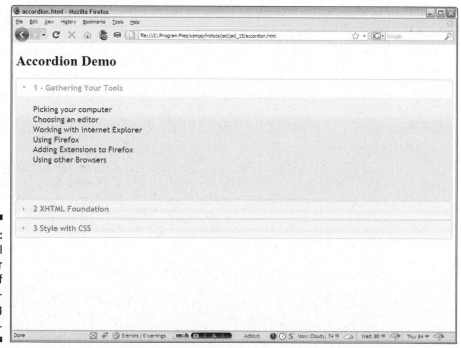

Figure 13-1:
The original chapter outline of a familiar-sounding book.

When you look at Figure 13-1, you see headings for the first three chapters of this book. The details for the first chapter are available, but the other chapters' details are hidden. If you click the heading for Chapter 2, you see the screen shown in Figure 13-2, where the Chapter 1 TOC is minimized and the Chapter 2 TOC is expanded.

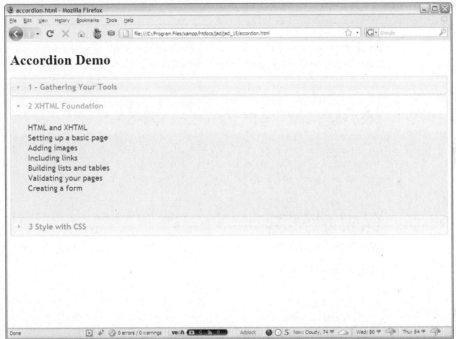

Figure 13-2:
The Chapter
1 TOC is
minimized;
the Chapter
2 TOC is
expanded.

This marvelous effect lets a user focus on a particular part of a larger context while seeing the overall outline. It's called an *accordion* because the various pieces expand and contract to let a user focus on a part of the page without losing track of its position in the whole. Collapsible content has become an important usability tool made popular by the system bar in the Mac OS and by other popular usability tools.

The accordion effect is strikingly easy to achieve with jQuery:

```
<!DOCTYPE html PUBLIC "-//W3C//DTD XHTML 1.0 Strict//EN"
"http://www.w3.org/TR/xhtml1/DTD/xhtml1-strict.dtd">
<html lang="EN" dir="ltr" xmlns="http://www.w3.org/1999/
        xhtml">
<head>
  <meta http-equiv=»content-type» content=»text/xml;
        charset=utf-8» />
  <link rel = «stylesheet»
        type = «text/css»
```

```
              href = «jquery-ui-1.7.2.custom.css» />

   <script type = «text/javascript»
          src = «jquery-1.3.2.min.js»></script>
   <script type = «text/javascript»
          src = «jquery-ui-1.7.2.custom.min.js»></script>
   <script type = «text/javascript»>
     //<![CDATA[

     $(init);

     function init(){
       $(«#accordion»).accordion();
     }
     //]]>
     </script>

   <title>accordion.html</title>
</head>
<body>
<h1>Accordion Demo</h1>

<div id = «accordion»>
   <h2><a href = «#»>1 - Gathering Your Tools</a></h2>
       <ul>
          <li>Picking your computer</li>
          <li>Choosing an editor</li>
          <li>Working with Internet Explorer</li>
          <li>Using Firefox</li>
          <li>Adding extensions to Firefox</li>
          <li>Using other Browsers</li>
       </ul>
   <h2><a href = «#»>2 Getting Started with JavaScript</
           a></h2>
       <ul>
          <li>Writing your first JavaScript program</li>
          <li>Introducing variables</li>
          <li>Using concatenation</li>
          <li>Understanding String objects</li>
          <li>Managing variable types</li>
       </ul>
     <h2><a href = «#»>3 Making Decisions with Conditions</
           a></h2>
       <ul>
          <li>Working with random numbers</li>
          <li>Using <em>if</em> to control flow</li>
          <li>Using the <em>else</em> clause</li>
          <li>Using <em>switch</em> for more complex
             branching</li>
          <li>Nesting <em>if</em> statements</li>
       </ul>
</div>
</body>
</html>
```

As you can see by looking over this chunk of code, it consists mainly of HTML. The accordion effect is easy to accomplish — follow these steps:

1. **Import all the usual suspects.**

   Import the jQuery and jQuery UI JavaScript files and a theme CSS file. (See Chapter 12 for a refresher.) Also, make sure that the CSS can access the images directory, with icons and backgrounds, because the CSS uses some of these images automatically.

2. **Build your HTML page in the normal way.**

   Build an HTML page, and pay attention to the sections you want to collapse. You should normally have a heading tag for each element, all at the same level (Level 2 headings, in my case).

3. **Create a** `div` **containing the entire collapsible content.**

   Put all collapsible content in a single `div` with an `id`. You'll turn this `div` into an accordion jQuery element.

4. **Add an anchor around each heading you want to specify as collapsible.**

   Place an empty anchor tag (`<a href = "#"></a>`) around each heading you want to use as a collapsible heading. The # sign indicates that the anchor will call the same page and is used as a placeholder by the jQuery UI engine. You can add the anchor directly in the HTML or by using jQuery code.

5. **Create a jQuery** `init()` **function.**

   Use the normal techniques (described in Chapter 10) to build a jQuery initializer.

6. **Apply the** `accordion()` **method to the** `div`.

   Use jQuery to identify the `div` containing collapsible content and apply `accordion()` to it:

```
function init(){
  $("#accordion").accordion();
}
```

The accordion tool automatically breaks the page into sections based on the header elements. Look into the jQuery UI documentation for details on other options. You can set some other element to indicate section breaks, allow for all elements to be collapsed at the same time, and other interesting effects.

Building a tabbed interface

Another important technique in Web development is the use of a tabbed interface. A user can then change the contents of a segment by selecting one of a series of tabs. Figure 13-3 shows an example.

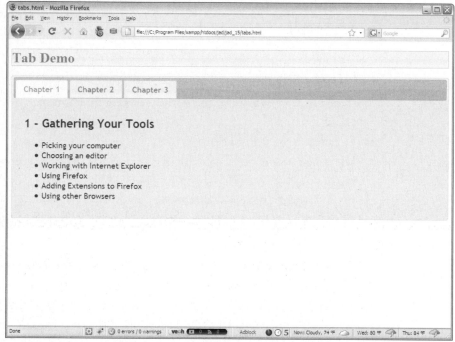

Figure 13-3: Another way to look at that hauntingly familiar table of contents.

In a tabbed interface, only one element is visible at a time, but all tabs are visible. The tabbed interface is a little more predictable than the accordion because the tabs (unlike the accordion's headings) remain in place. The tabs change colors to indicate which tab is highlighted, and a tab changes state to indicate that a user is hovering the mouse over it. Whenever you click another tab, the main content area of the widget is replaced with the corresponding content. Figure 13-4 shows you what happens when the user clicks the Chapter 3 tab.

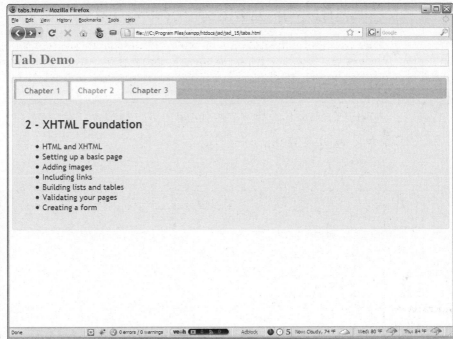

Figure 13-4:
Clicking a
tab changes
the main
content and
the appear-
ance of the
tabs.

Like the accordion, the tab effect is incredibly easy to achieve. Look over the
following chunk of code:

```
<!DOCTYPE html PUBLIC "-//W3C//DTD XHTML 1.0 Strict//EN"
"http://www.w3.org/TR/xhtml1/DTD/xhtml1-strict.dtd">
<html lang="EN" dir="ltr" xmlns="http://www.w3.org/1999/
        xhtml">
<head>
  <meta http-equiv=»content-type» content=»text/xml;
        charset=utf-8» />
  <link rel = «stylesheet»
        type = «text/css»
        href = «jquery-ui-1.7.2.custom.css» />

  <script type = «text/javascript»
        src = «jquery-1.3.2.min.js»></script>
  <script type = «text/javascript»
        src = «jquery-ui-1.7.2.custom.min.js»></script>
  <script type = «text/javascript»>
    //<![CDATA[

    $(init);

    function init(){
```

```
      $(«#tabs»).tabs();
    }
    //]]>
    </script>

  <title>tabs.html</title>
</head>
<body>
<h1 class = «ui-state-default»>Tab Demo</h1>

<div id = «tabs»>
  <ul>
    <li><a href = «#chap1»>Chapter 1</a></li>
    <li><a href = «#chap2»>Chapter 2</a></li>
    <li><a href = «#chap3»>Chapter 3</a></li>
  </ul>

  <div id = «chap1»>
    <h2>1 - Gathering Your Tools</h2>
      <ul>
        <li>Picking your computer</li>
        <li>Choosing an editor</li>
        <li>Working with Internet Explorer</li>
        <li>Using Firefox</li>
        <li>Adding extensions to Firefox</li>
        <li>Using other Browsers</li>
      </ul>
  </div>

  <div id = «chap2»>
  <h2>2 Getting Started with JavaScript</h2>
      <ul>
        <li>Writing your first JavaScript program</li>
        <li>Introducing variables</li>
        <li>Using concatenation</li>
        <li>Understanding String objects</li>
        <li>Managing variable types</li>
      </ul>
  </div>

  <div id = «chap3»>
    <h2>3 Making Decisions with Conditions</h2>
      <ul>
        <li>Working with random numbers</li>
        <li>Using <em>if</em> to control flow</li>
        <li>Using the <em>else</em> clause</li>
        <li>Using <em>switch</em> for more complex
          branching</li>
        <li>Nesting <em>if</em> statements</li>
      </ul>
  </div>
</div>
</body>
</html>
```

The mechanism for building a tab-based interface is quite similar to the one for accordions. Follow these steps:

1. **Add all appropriate files.**

   As with most jQuery UI effects, you need jQuery and jQueryUI and a theme CSS file. You also need to have access to the images directory for the theme's background graphics.

2. **Build HTML as normal.**

   If you're building a well-organized Web page anyway, you're already close to the organization you'll need for tabs.

3. **Build a** `div` **containing all tabbed data.**

   This element is the one you perform the jQuery "magic" on.

4. **Place main content areas in named** `div`**s.**

   Place each piece of content to be displayed as a page in a `div` with a descriptive `id`. Place each `div` in the tab `div`. (See the preceding code listing for organization if you're confused.)

5. **Add a list of local links to the content.**

   Build a menu of links and place it at the top of the tabbed `div`. Each link should be a local link to one of the `div`s. For example, my index looks like this:

   ```
   <ul>
     <li><a href = "#chap1">Chapter 1</a></li>
     <li><a href = "#chap2">Chapter 2</a></li>
     <li><a href = "#chap3">Chapter 3</a></li>
   </ul>
   ```

6. **Build an init function as usual.**

   Use the normal jQuery techniques.

7. **Call the** `tabs()` **method on the main** `div`**.**

   Incredibly, one line of jQuery code does all the work!

Using tabs with AJAX

You have an even easier way to work with the jQuery tab interface. Rather than place all your code in a single file, place the HTML code for each panel in a separate HTML file. You can then use a simplified form of the tab mechanism to automatically import the various code snippets by using AJAX calls. The following `AJAXtabs.html` code is an example:

```
<!DOCTYPE html PUBLIC "-//W3C//DTD XHTML 1.0 Strict//EN"
"http://www.w3.org/TR/xhtml1/DTD/xhtml1-strict.dtd">
<html lang="EN" dir="ltr" xmlns="http://www.w3.org/1999/
          xhtml">
<head>
  <meta http-equiv=»content-type» content=»text/xml;
          charset=utf-8» />
  <link rel = «stylesheet»
        type = «text/css»
        href = «jquery-ui-1.7.2.custom.css» />

  <script type = «text/javascript»
          src = «jquery-1.3.2.min.js»></script>
  <script type = «text/javascript»
          src = «jquery-ui-1.7.2.custom.min.js»></script>
  <script type = «text/javascript»>
    //<![CDATA[

    $(init);

    function init(){
      $(«#tabs»).tabs();
    }
    //]]>
    </script>

  <title>AJAXtabs.html</title>
</head>
<body>
  <h1>AJAX tabs</h1>
  <div id = «tabs»>
     <ul>
        <li><a href = «chap1.html»>Chapter 1</a></li>
        <li><a href = «chap2.html»>Chapter 2</a></li>
        <li><a href = «chap3.html»>Chapter 3</a></li>
     </ul>
  </div>
</body>
</html>
```

Note: I didn't provide a figure for the AJAXtabs.html page because it looks to the user exactly like tabs.html (refer to Figure 13-4).

This version of the code contains none of the actual content. Instead, jQuery builds the tab structure and then uses the links to make AJAX requests to load the content. As a default, it finds the content specified by the first tab (chap1.html) and loads it into the display area. This chunk of code shows you what chap1.html contains:

```
<h2>1 - Gathering Your Tools</h2>
  <ul>
    <li>Picking your computer</li>
    <li>Choosing an editor</li>
    <li>Working with Internet Explorer</li>
    <li>Using Firefox</li>
    <li>Adding extensions to Firefox</li>
    <li>Using other Browsers</li>
  </ul>
```

As you can see, `chap1.html` is simply a code snippet. It doesn't need the complete trappings of a Web page (such as a doctype or header) because it's meant to be pulled in as part of a larger page.

This technique is marvelous because it lets you build a modular system quite easily — you can build these code pages separately and include them in a larger page. You then have a good foundation for a content management system.

Improving Usability

Although the UI widgets are good looking and fun to use, another important aspect of these tools is how they can improve usability. Often, Web pages are used to get information from users. Certain kinds of information can be difficult for users to enter correctly. The jQuery UI elements include a number of tools to help you with this specific problem. The `UItools.html` page, shown in Figure 13-5, illustrates some of these techniques.

A great deal is happening on this page, but the tabbed interface truly cleans it up and lets users concentrate on one idea at a time. Using the tabbed interface can simplify your users' lives.

This page is a bit long because it has a number of sections. I demonstrate the code in chunks to make it easier to manage. Be sure to look on either of the Web site (`www.dummies.com/go/javascriptandajaxfd` or `www.aharrisbooks.net/jad`) for the complete code.

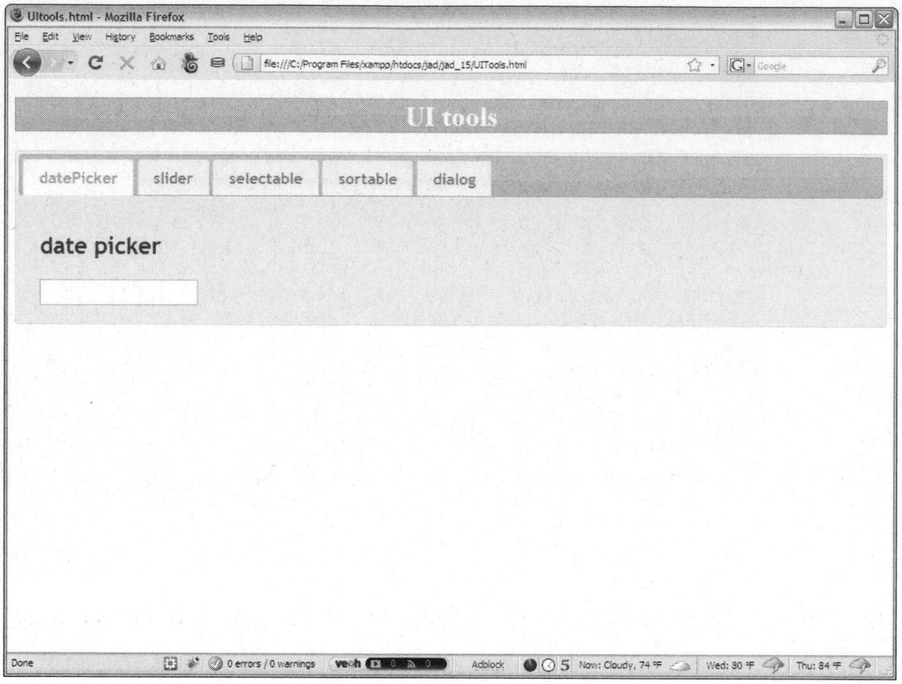

Figure 13-5:
The UITools
page uses
a tabbed
interface to
demonstrate
a few input
tools.

Here's the main HTML code so that you can see the general structure of the page:

```
<h1>UI tools</h1>
<div id = "tabs">
  <ul>
    <li><a href = "#datePickerTab">datePicker</a></li>
    <li><a href = "#sliderTab">slider</a></li>
    <li><a href = "#selectableTab">selectable</a></li>
    <li><a href = "#sortableTab">sortable</a></li>
    <li><a href = "#dialogTab">dialog</a></li>
  </ul>
```

A main `div`, named `tabs`, contains a list of links to the various `div`s that will contain the demonstrations. I describe each of these `div`s in the section that demonstrates it, later in this chapter. The page also imports `jQuery`, `jQueryUI`, and the theme CSS. The `init()` method contains most of the jQuery code:

```
$(init);

function init(){
  $("h1").addClass("ui-widget-header");

  $("#tabs").tabs();
  $("#datePicker").datepicker();

  $("#slider").slider()
  .bind("slide", reportSlider);

  $("#selectable").selectable();

  $("#sortable").sortable();

  $("#dialog").dialog();

  //initially close dialog
  $("#dialog").dialog("close");

} // end init
```

The details of the `init()` function are described in the following sections.

The dating game

Imagine that you're writing a program requiring a birth date or other date information. Getting date information from a user can be an especially messy problem because so many variations exist. Users might use numbers, month names, or abbreviations to indicate the month, for example. Some people use the format month/day/year, and others use day/month/year. Some people indicate the year by entering two characters, and other people use four. Worse, picking a date without a calendar in front of you is difficult.

The Date Picker dialog box is one of the coolest elements in the entire jQuery UI library. When you add `datepicker()` functionality to a text box, the text box becomes a date picker. When a user selects the date box, a calendar automatically pops up, like the one shown in Figure 13-6.

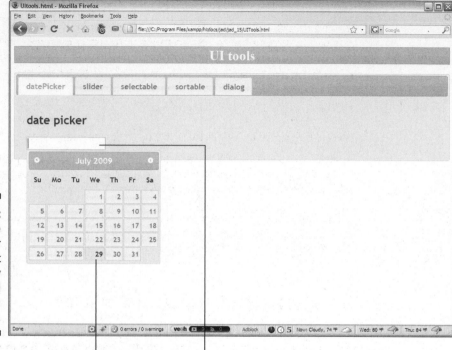

Figure 13-6:
The
datePicker
element
turns any
text field
into a
calendar.

The user clicks a date in the calendar...

...and the date appears in the text field.

After a user selects a date on the calendar, the date is placed in the text box in a standard format — there's no better way to get date input from the user. Building a date picker couldn't be easier. Follow these steps:

1. **Begin with a jQuery UI page.**

   You need jQuery and jQuery UI and a theme to use datePicker.

2. **Build a form with a text field.**

   Any standard text input element will work. Be sure to give the element an id so that you can refer to it in JavaScript:

   ```
   <div id = "datePickerTab">
     <h2>date picker</h2>
     <input type = "text"
            id = "datePicker" />
   </div>
   ```

3. **Isolate the text input element by using jQuery.**

   Build a standard jQuery node from the input element.

4. **Add** `datepicker()` **functionality.**

Use the `datePicker()` method to convert the text node into a date picker. The rest of the magic happens automatically. When the user selects the text area, it is automatically converted to the calendar. When the user has selected a date on the calendar, the element converts back to a text area with the appropriate date in place.

```
$("#datePicker").datepicker();
```

5. **Retrieve data from the form element in the normal way.**

When a user selects a date, it's placed in the text field automatically. As far as your program is concerned, the text field is still an ordinary text field. Retrieve the data as you do for a normal text field.

The date picker is a powerful tool with a large number of additional options. Look at the jQuery UI documentation to see how to use it to select date ranges, produce specific date formats, and do much more.

Picking numbers with the slider

Numeric input is another significant usability problem. When you want users to enter numeric information, ensuring that the data is truly a number, and that it's in the range you want, can be quite difficult. Traditional programmers often use *sliders* (sometimes called *scrollbars*) to simplify the acceptance of numeric input. Figure 13-7 shows a slider in action.

The slider is, like many jQuery UI objects, easy to set up. Here's the relevant chunk of HTML code:

```
<div id = "sliderTab">
  <h2>slider</h2>
  <div id = "slider"></div>
  <div id = "slideOutput">0</div>
</div>
```

The slider tab is a basic `div`. It contains two other `div`s. The `slider` `div` is empty. It's replaced by the slider element when the jQuery is activated. The other `div` in this section is used to output the current value of the slider.

Create the slider element in the `init()` function with some predictable jQuery code:

```
$("#slider").slider();
```

The `slider()` method turns any jQuery element into a slider, replacing the contents with a visual slider.

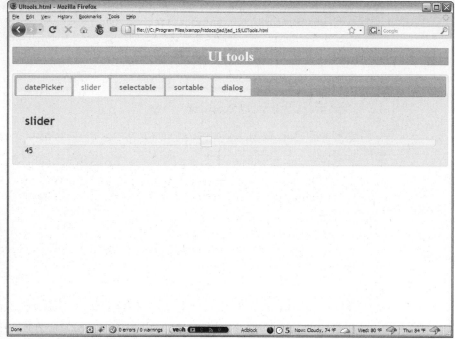

Figure 13-7:
Using a
slider to
choose a
number with
the mouse.

Note that you can add a JSON object as a parameter to set up the slider with various options. See `rgbSlider.html` on this book's Web site (www. dummies.com/go/javascriptandajaxfd or www.aharrisbooks.net/ jad) for an example of sliders with customization.

You can set up a callback method to be called whenever the slider is moved. In my example, I chained this callback code to the code that created the slider in the first place:

```
$("#slider").slider()
.bind("slide", reportSlider);
```

Use the `bind` method to bind the `reportSlider` function (described next) to the `slide` event.

The `reportSlider()` function reads the slider's value and reports it in an output `div`:

```
function reportSlider(){
  var sliderVal = $("#slider").slider("value");
  $("#slideOutput").html(sliderVal);
} // end reportSlider
```

To read the value of a slider, identify the jQuery node and invoke its `slider()` method again. This time, pass the single word *value* and you get the value of the slider. You can pass the resulting value to a variable, as I did, and then do anything you want with that variable.

Selectable elements

You may have a situation where you want users to choose from a list of elements. The `selectable` widget is a useful way to create this functionality from an ordinary list. Users can drag or Control-click items to select them. Special CSS classes are automatically applied to indicate that the item is selected or being considered for selection. Figure 13-8 illustrates the selection in process.

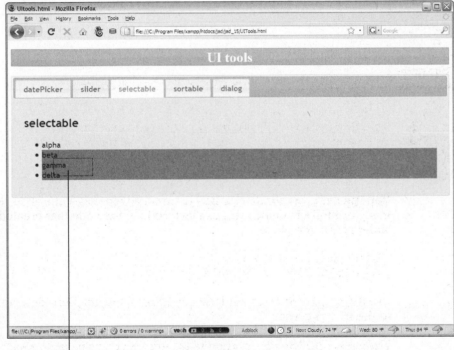

Figure 13-8:
You can easily choose selectable items with the mouse.

Dragging the mouse over these elements changes their style and marks them as selected.

To make a selectable element, follow these steps:

1. **Begin with an unordered list.**

2. **Build a standard unordered list in your HTML. Give the** `ul` **an** `id` **so that it can be identified as a jQuery node:**

```
<div id = "selectableTab">
  <h2>selectable</h2>
  <ul id = "selectable">
    <li>alpha</li>
    <li>beta</li>
    <li>gamma</li>
    <li>delta</li>
  </ul>
</div>
```

3. **Add CSS classes for selecting and selected states.**

   If you want to have a specific appearance when the items are being selected or have been selected, add CSS classes:

```
<style type = "text/css">
  h1 {
    text-align: center;
  }

  #selectable .ui-selecting {
    background-color: gray;
  }
  #selectable .ui-selected {
    background-color: black;
    color: white;
  }
</style>
```

4. **In the** `init()` **function, specify the list as a selectable node. Use the standard jQuery syntax:** `selectable()`:

```
$("#selectable").selectable();
```

   The `ui-selected` class is attached to all elements when they have been selected. Be sure to add some kind of CSS to this class or else you can't tell that items have been selected.

If you want to do something with all the items that have been selected, just create a jQuery group of elements with the `ui-selected` class:

```
var selectedItems = $(".ui-selected");
```

Building a sortable list

Sometimes, you want users to be able to change the order of a list, which is easily done by using the `sortable` widget. The top of Figure 13-9 shows the sortable list in its default configuration. The user can "grab" members of the list and change their order (see the bottom of Figure 13-9).

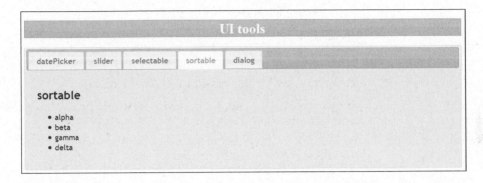

Figure 13-9:
Users can drag the elements of an ordinary list (top) into different orders (bottom).

Making a sortable list is easy. Follow these steps:

1. **Build a regular list.**

2. **Add an** id.

   Sortable elements are usually lists. The list is a regular list, but with an id:

   ```
   <div id = "sortableTab">
     <h2>sortable</h2>
     <ul id = "sortable">
       <li>alpha</li>
       <li>beta</li>
       <li>gamma</li>
       <li>delta</li>
     </ul>
   </div>
   ```

3. **Turn it into a sortable node by adding the following code to the** `init()` **method:**

```
$("#sortable").sortable();
```

Creating a custom dialog box

Although JavaScript supplies a few dialog boxes (the alert and prompt dialog boxes), they're quite ugly and relatively inflexible. The jQuery UI includes a technique for turning any `div` into a virtual dialog box. The dialog box follows the theme and can be resized and moved. Figure 13-10 shows a dialog box in action.

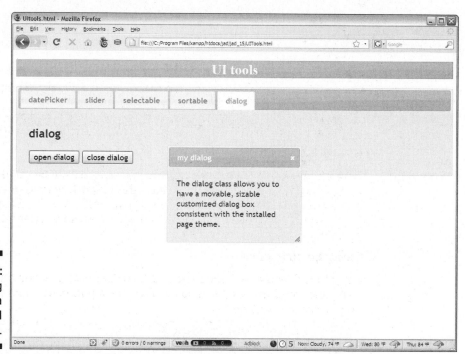

Figure 13-10:
This dialog box is a jQuery UI node.

Building the dialog box isn't difficult, but you need to be able to turn it on and off by using code. Follow these steps:

1. **Create the** `div` **you intend to use as a dialog box.**

   Create a `div` and give it an `id` so that you can turn it into a dialog box node. Add the `title` attribute, and the title shows up on the title bar of the dialog box:

   ```
   <div id = "dialog"
        title = "my dialog">
     <p>
        The dialog class allows you to have a movable,
           sizable
        customized dialog box consistent with the
           installed
        page theme.
     </p>
   </div>
   ```

2. **Turn the** `div` **into a dialog box.**

   Use the `dialog()` method to turn the `div` into a jQuery dialog box node in the `init()` function:

   ```
   $("#dialog").dialog();
   ```

3. **Hide the dialog box by default.**

   Usually, you don't want the dialog box visible until an event takes place. In this particular example, I don't want the dialog box to appear until the user clicks a button. I added some code that will close the dialog box in the `init()` function so that the dialog box doesn't appear until it's summoned.

4. **Close the dialog box.**

   Refer to the dialog box node and call the `dialog()` method on it again. This time, send the single value `"close"` as a parameter, and the dialog box immediately closes:

   ```
   //initially close dialog
   $("#dialog").dialog("close");
   ```

5. **Click the x to close the dialog box.**

   The dialog box has a small x icon that looks like the Close icon in most windowing systems. Users can close the dialog box by clicking this icon.

6. Write code to manage opening and closing the dialog box.

My Open and Close buttons call functions that control the behavior of the dialog box. For example, here's the function attached to the Open Dialog button:

```
function openDialog(){
  $("#dialog").dialog("open");
} // end openDialog
```

Chapter 14

Working with AJAX Data

In This Chapter

▶ Understanding the advantages of server-side programming

▶ Getting to know PHP

▶ Writing a form for standard PHP processing

▶ Building virtual forms with AJAX

▶ Submitting interactive AJAX requests

▶ Working with XML data

▶ Responding to JSON data

AJAX and jQuery are incredibly useful, but perhaps the most important use of AJAX is to serve as a conduit between the Web page and programs written on the server. In this chapter, you get an overview of how programming works on the Web server. First you look at traditional server-side programs, and then I explain how AJAX changes the equation. You find out the main forms of data sent from the server and how to interpret this data with jQuery and JavaScript.

Getting an Overview of Server-Side Programming

The JavaScript programming you do throughout this book primarily works on the Web browser — the *client*. However, all Web programming also has a relationship with the machine that hosts Web pages — the *server*. In the examples so far, the Web page is retrieved from the server, and then the JavaScript programs inside the page are executed by the client machine. This is a very powerful approach, but it does have limitations. Most importantly, client-side code cannot store data or access external programs for security reasons.

Fortunately, there's a solution. You can also write programs that reside on the Web server. They work a little differently than client-side programs. A server-side program runs on the Web server, and when it's done, it produces an ordinary Web page. The Web page is then sent to the client, where it's interpreted by the browser.

Server-side programs are processed *before* the data is transmitted to the browser, and client-side programs are processed *after* the transmission.

You can do things on the server that aren't allowed on the client, including storing data and accessing external programs. These are the two things that client-side programs can't do, so server-side programming is a perfect match for the client-side skills described in this book.

Introducing PHP

Several languages are used for server-side programming. The most popular of these are PHP, Java, and ASP.NET. For the examples in this book, I concentrate on PHP:

- ✔ **It's very popular.** PHP is used on thousands of Web sites and has a massive following among programmers.

- ✔ **It's quite powerful.** Although PHP isn't quite as powerful as some languages, it's robust enough to support some very large sites (like Facebook and Flickr).

- ✔ **It's entirely free.** PHP is an open-source language, which means it doesn't cost anything and can be freely modified. You also don't need to purchase any special editor to write PHP — the text editors you already use are perfectly fine.

- ✔ **It's readily available.** Pretty much every commercial server and even some free servers support PHP. You generally have to pay more for a custom server to handle Java or ASP.NET.

- ✔ **It's pretty easy.** Although PHP isn't exactly like JavaScript, it's quite similar. You'll be able to transfer much of your programming knowledge to PHP with only a few details to worry about.

Although you can practice JavaScript on a standalone computer, PHP only works through a Web server. If you want to experiment with PHP, you must have access to a Web server with PHP installed. There are two main ways to do this:

✔ **Get an online account.** If you have a hosting account for your Web pages, you probably already have support for PHP. You might need to check your control panel to see whether there are any restrictions or details you need to know. Many free accounts include PHP access, so you can try PHP without any cost to see if you like it. (The hosting service I use offers quite a good free service with PHP access. Check `http://freehostia.com`.)

✔ **Install your own Web server.** If you want to practice on your own computer, you can install your own Web server. The best way to do this is with a complete installation like XAMPP (`www.apachefriends.org/en/xampp.html`). The XAMPP package is a complete installation of all the tools you need including a Web server (Apache) programming languages (PHP and Perl) a database package (MySQL) and some other goodies, all configured to work together. XAMPP is available for all major operating systems, but if you're running Linux, you might already have everything you need.

Note that you can write PHP programs on any computer with the same text editor you use for other Web programming, but you can test PHP programs only when your program runs directly through a Web server. This is necessary because the Web server actually runs PHP before the user sees the page. If there is no Web server (or it is not configured properly), the PHP code will not execute.

Aptana (see Chapter 1) has a great PHP mode, but you'll have to download a free add-on to get this capability. Go to the My Aptana window (from the Window menu) and click the Plugins tab. You should see a link to download and install the PHP plugin. With the plugin installed, you'll have the same features (syntax highlighting, syntax completion, integrated help, and so on) with PHP that you already have for the other Web languages.

Writing a form for PHP processing

The best way to see how server-side programming (and PHP) works is to look at a simple example. Figure 14-1 illustrates a basic XHTML Web page with a form.

The page doesn't look too scary, but it does have an interesting twist. There is no JavaScript code in this form. When the user clicks the button, information is sent to the server, which finds a new program. This program (`greetUser.php`) examines the contents of the form and composes a new page in reply, which is shown in Figure 14-2.

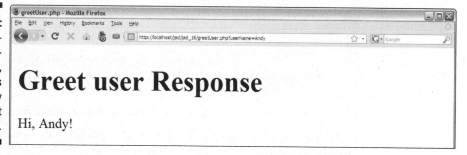

Figure 14-1:
This Web page has a form.

Figure 14-2:
In server-side programming, the result is an entirely different page.

This example points out a key difference between client-side and server-side processing: On the client (in JavaScript), your code resides on the Web page and modifies the same page. In server-side programming (like PHP), the request form and the response are entirely different pages. Typical PHP code involves building an entirely new page from scratch for the result.

Begin by looking at the XHTML source code:

```
<!DOCTYPE html PUBLIC "-//W3C//DTD XHTML 1.0 Strict//EN"
"http://www.w3.org/TR/xhtml1/DTD/xhtml1-strict.dtd">
<html lang=»EN» dir=»ltr» xmlns=»http://www.w3.org/1999/
        xhtml»>
        <head>
                        <meta http-equiv="content-type"
            content="text/xml; charset=utf-8" />
    <title>nameForm.html</title>
</head>

<body>
  <h1>Typical HTML Form</h1>
  <form action = "greetUser.php"
      method = "get">
    <fieldset>
```

```
        <input type = "text"
               name = "userName"
               value = "Andy" />
        <button type = "submit">
           submit
        </button>
      </fieldset>
   </form>
</body>
</html>
```

It's nothing too shocking, but if you're used to writing forms for JavaScript, you'll see there are a few differences when you write a form for server-side processing:

1. **No JavaScript is necessary.**

   It's possible to use client and server programming techniques together (in fact that is the point of AJAX), but it isn't necessary. For this first example, all code will be processed on the server.

2. **Designate a target program in the form's** action **attribute.**

   When you create a form for JavaScript use, the action attribute is empty, indicating that all processing will happen on the current page. For server-side processing, indicate the name of the program that will read the form data (in this case, greetUser.php) in the action attribute.

3. **Determine the transfer method.**

   There are two main ways to transmit form data to the receiving program. The get mechanism embeds data in the URL. This technique is useful for debugging (as the data is visible), but gets awkward for large forms. The post technique is preferred for larger forms, as it sends the data through a less visible mechanism.

4. **Add a** name **attribute to form fields.**

   In client-side programming, you typically use the id attribute to identify fields. Server-side programs prefer the name identifier. You can (and often will) use both. For this example, I've named the single text field userName.

5. **Include a** submit **button.**

   For client-side processing, you normally use a standard button. Server-side programming typically requires a submit button instead. When the user clicks the submit button, all the data in the form is automatically packaged and sent to the program indicated in the form's action attribute.

If you get an error message when you submit this program, make sure you're running it correctly. If the URL in your browser begins with `file://`, you're bypassing the server. This method is fine in client-side programming, but it doesn't work when you're messing with the server. You need to have an address that begins with `http://` in order for server-side programs to work correctly.

Responding to the request

When the user clicks the `submit` button of `nameForm.html`, the form information is bundled and passed to the `greetUser.php` program. If you look over the code for this program, you might find it surprisingly familiar:

```
<!DOCTYPE html PUBLIC "-//W3C//DTD XHTML 1.0 Strict//EN"
"http://www.w3.org/TR/xhtml1/DTD/xhtml1-strict.dtd">
<html lang="EN" dir="ltr" xmlns="http://www.w3.org/1999/
          xhtml">
          <head>
                            <meta http-equiv=»content-type»
          content=»text/xml; charset=utf-8» />
    <title>greetUser.php</title>
</head>

<body>
  <h1>Greet user Response</h1>
  <?php
  $userName = $_REQUEST[«userName»];
  print «<p>Hi, $userName!</p> «;
  ?>
</body>
</html>
```

For the most part, a PHP program looks a lot like an XHTML page, because mostly that's what it is. The general structure is just like XHTML. There are only a few key differences.

1. **The filename must end with** `.php`.

   This indicates to the server that the page isn't ordinary HTML but will need to be passed through the PHP interpreter before being sent to the user.

2. **The** `<?php` **marker indicates a switch to PHP syntax.**

   Most of this page is standard XHTML (and can include CSS and JavaScript, too). In the middle of the page, I indicate that a section of code should be processed by PHP. I signify this with the `<?php` symbol. (Occasionally you'll see other variations, but this almost always works.)

3. **Make a variable called** `$userName`.

PHP supports variables just like JavaScript, but PHP variable names always begin with the dollar sign ($). This turns out to be quite useful (as you'll see in a moment).

```
$userName = $_REQUEST["userName"];
```

4. **Grab the value of the** userName **field from the previous form.**

PHP has a structure called $_REQUEST, which is a package of all the data sent from the form. You can find the data in the field called userName by looking for $_REQUEST["userName"].

5. **Copy the form data into a PHP variable.**

Now I have a variable called $userName that contains the data from the userName field in the previous form. Repeat this process for each form variable you want to retrieve from the form.

6. **Print some new content.**

The print statement in PHP prints text to the current spot in the HTML. In essence, it allows you to customize parts of the page on the fly. In this case, I want to add a paragraph with a greeting. Note that you should still strive for valid XHTML in your print statements.

```
print "<p>Hi, $userName!</p> ";
```

7. **Interpolate variables.**

Notice how I added the $userName variable directly in the print statement. This technique is called *interpolation*. If PHP sees a term beginning with a dollar sign being printed, it knows it's looking at a variable and replaces the variable name with its value.

8. **End the PHP segment with** ?>**.**

This symbol indicates the end of PHP processing and takes you back to XHTML mode.

Obviously this is a very cursory overview of PHP. It's a complete language with a lot more potential than I'm showing in this basic example. If you want to know more, there are many books on PHP that can take you farther (including some I have written.) Take a look at www.php.net or my own site (www. aharrisbooks.net) for much more information on the PHP language. You can also visit www.wiley.com to find more great books packed with PHP info.

Sending Requests AJAX-Style

So far all the AJAX work in this book has involved importing a preformatted HTML file. That's a great use of AJAX, but the really exciting aspect of AJAX is how it tightens the relationship between the client and server. Figure 14-3 shows a page called AJAXtest.html, which uses a JavaScript function to call a PHP program and incorporates the results into the same page.

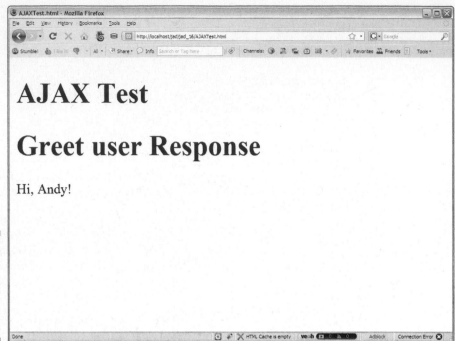

Figure 14-3:
This page
gets data
from PHP
with no
form!

Sending the data

The AJAX version of this program is interesting because it has no form, uses exactly the same PHP program as `nameForm.html`, and incorporates the results of the PHP program directly onto the same page. Begin by looking over the code:

```
<!DOCTYPE html PUBLIC "-//W3C//DTD XHTML 1.0 Strict//EN"
"http://www.w3.org/TR/xhtml1/DTD/xhtml1-strict.dtd">
<html lang="EN" dir="ltr" xmlns="http://www.w3.org/1999/
        xhtml">
<head>
  <meta http-equiv=»content-type» content=»text/xml;
        charset=utf-8» />

  <script type = «text/javascript»
        src = «jquery-1.3.2.min.js»></script>
```

```
<script type = «text/javascript»>
  //<![CDATA[

  $(init);

  function init(){
    $.get(«greetUser.php», { «userName»: «Andy» },
      processResult);
  }

  function processResult(data, textStatus){
    $(«#output»).html(data);
  }
  //]]>
  </script>

  <title>AJAXTest.html</title>
</head>
<body>
<h1>AJAX Test</h1>

<div id = «output»>
 This is the default output
</div>

</body>
</html>
```

This program uses a jQuery function to simulate a form. It generates its own virtual form and passes it directly to the PHP program. The PHP program then processes the form data and produces text results, which are available for JavaScript to handle directly. In essence, JavaScript and jQuery are directly managing the server request (rather than allowing the browser to do it automatically), so the programmer has more control over the process.

Here's how it works:

1. **Begin with an XHTML framework.**

   As always, XHTML forms the spine of any Web program. The XHTML here is quite simple: a heading and a `div` for output. Note that this example doesn't include a form.

2. **Include the jQuery library.**

   It's possible to do AJAX without jQuery, but there's not much reason to do that. The jQuery library makes life much easier and manages cross-browser issues to boot. You can also incorporate the jQuery UI and a theme if you choose, but they aren't absolutely necessary.

3. **Initialize as usual.**

   As soon as this program runs, it's going to get data from the server. (In the next example, I show you how to make this process more interactive.) Set up an init() function in the normal way to handle immediate execution once the page has loaded.

4. **Use the** .get() **function to set up an AJAX call.**

   jQuery has a number of interesting AJAX functions. The .ajax function is a very powerful tool for managing all kinds of AJAX requests, but jQuery also includes a number of utility functions that simplify particular kinds of requests. The .get() function used here sets up a request that looks to the server just like a form submitted with the get method. (Yep, there's also a post() function that acts like a post form.)

5. **Indicate the program to receive the request.**

   Typically your AJAX requests will specify a program, which should respond to the request. I'm using greetUser.php, the exact same program called by the simpler nameForm.html page.

6. **Pass form data as a JSON object.**

   Encapsulate all the data you want to send to the program as a JSON object. (Check Chapter 5 for a refresher on JSON.) Typically this is a series of name/value pairs. In this example, I'm simply indicating a field named userName with the value "Andy".

7. **Specify a callback function.**

   Normally you'll want to do something with the results of an AJAX call. Use a callback function to indicate which function should execute when the AJAX call is completed. In this example, I call the processResult function as soon as the server has finished returning the form data.

Responding to the results

The greetUser.php program on the server will be run by the AJAXTest.html page. As far as greetUser.php knows, the data came from an ordinary form. This means I can use exactly the same program to work with the AJAX request that I used for the previous example. I don't re-create the PHP code here because it hasn't changed.

Back in the HTML, I need a function to process the results of the AJAX request after it has returned from the server. The processResult() function has been designated as the callback function, so take another look at that function:

```
function processResult(data, textStatus){
  $("#output").html(data);
}
```

This function is pretty simple with jQuery:

1. **Accept two parameters.**

   AJAX callback functions accept two parameters. The first is a string containing whatever output was sent by the server (in this case, the greeting from `processResult.php`). The second parameter contains the text version of the HTTP status result. The status is useful for testing in case the AJAX request was unsuccessful.

2. **Identify an output area.**

   I just make a jQuery node from the `output` div.

3. **Pass the data to the output.**

   You'll sometimes do more elaborate work with AJAX results, but for now my results are plain HTML that I can just copy straight to the `div`.

Building a More Interactive Form

Although AJAX can replace the form mechanism, it's usually used in conjunction with ordinary forms to produce effects that would otherwise be difficult to achieve. For example, you might see a form that fills in some information for you by guessing at your data based on the first few characters of input. While it's pretty easy to get real-time interaction on the client, it's much more difficult to achieve this effect with server-side programs, because the server typically rebuilds the entire page at each pass. With AJAX, you can have the quick interaction of client-side programming along with the power of server-side programming. The `interactiveForm.html` demo, shown in Figure 14-4 shows a simple variation of this concept.

This example produces a complete round-trip to the server on each keystroke. That's a lot of overkill for this simple example (which could be achieved with ordinary JavaScript) but imagine how powerful it could be. On each trip to the server, the program can check my name against a list of hundreds of names, and it can provide a hint as soon as it has enough letters. A server-side program can perform data searches against huge databases. You've probably seen this effect on pages you've used. You need a little more knowledge of server-side programming and databases than I can provide in this book to achieve the entire effect, but you can clearly see from this example how the AJAX part works.

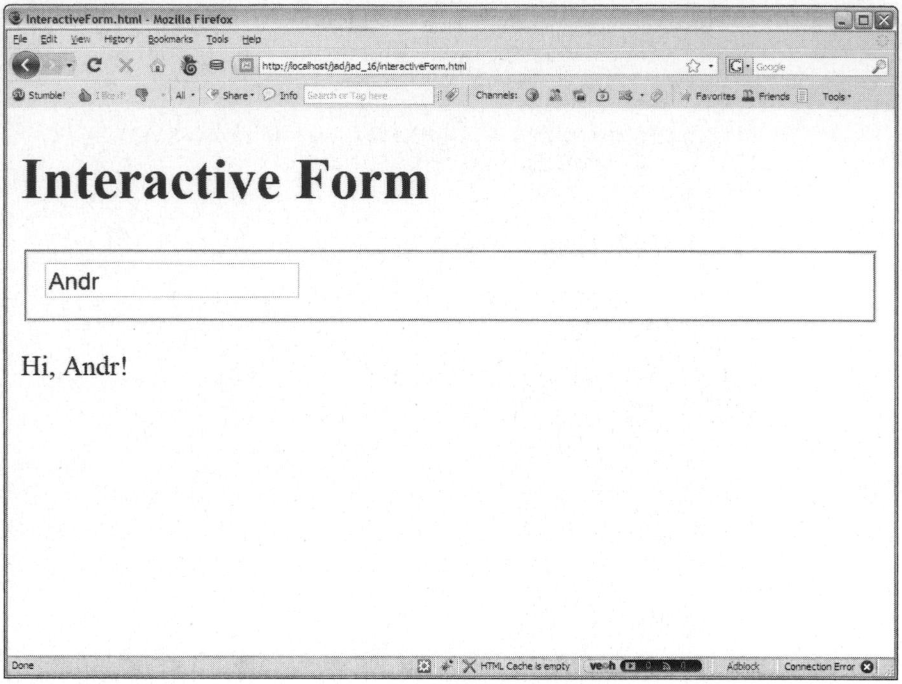

Figure 14-4:
This page
has a form.
As the user
types data
in, that data
is copied to
the output.

Creating an AJAX form

You can create a form for AJAX use much like any other form. Here's the full code for interactiveForm.html:

```
<!DOCTYPE html PUBLIC "-//W3C//DTD XHTML 1.0 Strict//EN"
"http://www.w3.org/TR/xhtml1/DTD/xhtml1-strict.dtd">
<html lang="EN" dir="ltr" xmlns="http://www.w3.org/1999/
        xhtml">
<head>
  <meta http-equiv=»content-type» content=»text/xml;
        charset=utf-8» />

  <script type = «text/javascript»
        src = «jquery-1.3.2.min.js»></script>

  <script type = «text/javascript»>
    //<![CDATA[

    function getGreeting(){
      var userName = $(«#userName»).val();
```

```
        $.get(«simpleGreet.php», { «userName»: userName },
            processResult);
    }

    function processResult(data, textStatus){
      $(«#output»).html(data);
    }
    //]]>
    </script>

  <title>InteractiveForm.html</title>
</head>
<body>
<h1>Interactive Form</h1>

  <form action = "">
    <fieldset>
      <input type = "text"
             id = "userName"
             value = "Andy"
             onkeyup = "getGreeting()" />
    </fieldset>
  </form>

<div id = "output">
 This is the default output
</div>

</body>
</html>
```

As you look over the XHTML code, you'll notice that the form is set up more for JavaScript than server-side processing:

1. **Include jQuery.**

   Have I mentioned how cool jQuery is?

2. **The form action can be null.**

   This time you're going to read the form in JavaScript and produce an AJAX request. The form action can (and should) be null, because you want JavaScript to submit the request, not the browser.

3. **You don't need to specify a transmission method in the form.**

   As far as the form is concerned, it's a client-side form, so you don't need to specify whether it is sent as a get or post request. (The AJAX call takes care of that.)

4. The input element has an `id` **attribute but no name.**

It can have a name, but it isn't necessary, because the server won't process it directly. You use the `id` attribute to get access to this element and then package your own JSON object to send to the PHP program through AJAX.

5. The event is called when the text field changes.

Often AJAX requests are meant to happen automatically, without requiring the user to press a submit button. To get this effect, you can use the `onkeyup` event handler. This event handler calls a function whenever the specified element has the focus and a key has been pressed and released.

Writing the JavaScript code

The JavaScript code is even simpler than normal. For one thing, this particular program doesn't require an `init()` because nothing needs to be initialized. Of course, it's likely that you'll have a more elaborate project that might involve initialization (with jQuery UI elements, for example), but I kept this example simple for clarity.

The `getGreeting()` function extracts data from the form and uses it to send an AJAX request:

```
function getGreeting(){
  var userName = $("#userName").val();
  $.get("simpleGreet.php", { "userName": userName },
    processResult);
}
```

The `getGreeting()` function encapsulates the process of sending a form.

1. Extract the value of the `userName` **field.**

Create a jQuery node from the `userName` field and use the `val()` method to extract its value.

2. Store the value in a variable.

Store the value in a variable also called `userName`.

3. Use the `get()` **method to set up an AJAX call.**

The jQuery `get()` method simulates sending a form through the `get` method. (Of course, there's also a `post()` method, if you prefer.)

4. **Indicate the program that will respond to the data.**

   For this example, I use a variation of the greetUser.php program called simpleGreet.php. Look at the next section to see how AJAX can simplify your PHP code.

5. **Send form fields as a JSON object.**

   The virtual form (which in this case is based on a real form) has one field called userName. I send it the value of the userName variable.

6. **Specify a callback function.**

   Most AJAX calls have a callback function that should be executed when the data transmission is complete. In this example, I'm using the processResult function.

Processing the result

The processing is quite easy in this case because I simply want to copy the results of the PHP program directly to the output div:

```
function processResult(data, textStatus){
  $("#output").html(data);
}
```

The data parameter contains the text data returned from the AJAX call. I simply grab that text and pass it to the output div.

Simplifying PHP for AJAX

One of the nice things about AJAX is how it simplifies your server-side programming. If you look back at greetUser.php, you'll see that it creates an entire XHTML page. Most PHP programs work that way, creating an entire page every time. However, because you're using AJAX, the PHP result doesn't have to be an entire Web page. The PHP can simply create a small snippet of HTML.

Take a look at simpleGreet.php and you'll see it's very stripped down:

```
<?php
$userName = $_REQUEST["userName"];
print "<p>Hi, $userName!</p> ";
?>
```

Although this program works just like `greetUser.php`, it's a lot simpler. All it needs to do is grab the user name and print it back out. The JavaScript function takes care of making the code go in the right place. Without AJAX, each PHP program has to re-create the entire page. When you're using AJAX, the HTML page stays on the client, and JavaScript makes smaller calls to the server. The PHP is simpler, and the code transmission is generally smaller and faster, because there's less repeated structural information.

Working with XML Data

Server-side work normally involves storage of data, as that's one thing that's easy to do on the server and difficult to do on the client. Data can be stored in many ways: plain text files, HTML, or XHTML, or in a specialized system called a *relational database* (a specialized program that allows you to store and query data efficiently). The database approach is most common because it's incredibly powerful and flexible. Normally programmers use a PHP program to request information from a Web page, and then use this information to prepare a request for the database in a special language called SQL (Structured Query Language). The data request is passed to the database management system, which returns some kind of result set to the PHP program. The PHP program then typically builds an HTML page and passes the page back to the browser.

Data management is beyond the scope of this book. See my Web site for more information about creating your own databases: `www.aharrisbooks.net`.

The process can be easier when you use AJAX because the PHP program doesn't have to create an entire Web page. All that really needs to be passed back to the JavaScript program are the results of the data query. Normally, you do this using a special data format so the JavaScript program can easily manage the data.

Review of XML

The XML format has become an important tool for encapsulating data for transfer between the client and the server. If you're using XHTML, you are already familiar with XML. XHTML is simply HTML following the stricter XML standard.

However, XML is much more than XHTML. It can actually be used to store any kind of data. For example, take a look at the following file (`pets.xml`):

```
<?xml version="1.0" encoding="utf-8"?>
<pets>
  <pet>
    <animal>cat</animal>
    <name>Lucy</name>
    <breed>American Shorthair</breed>
    <note>She raised me</note>
  </pet>
  <pet>
    <animal>cat</animal>
    <name>Homer</name>
    <breed>unknown</breed>
    <note>Named after a world-famous bassoonist</note>
  </pet>
  <pet>
    <animal>dog</animal>
    <name>Muchacha</name>
    <breed>mutt</breed>
    <note>One of the ugliest dogs I've ever met</note>
  </pet>
</pets>
```

If you look over `pets.xml`, you can see it looks a lot like HTML. HTML/
XHTML tags are very specific (only a few are legal) but XML tags can be anything as long as they follow a few simple (but familiar) rules:

1. **Begin with a doctype.**

   Formal XML declarations often have doctypes as complex as the XHTML
   doctype definition, but basic XML data usually uses a much simpler
   definition:

   ```
   <?xml version="1.0" encoding="utf-8"?>
   ```

   Any time you make your own XML format (as I'm doing in this example),
   you can use this generic doctype.

2. **Create a container for all elements.**

   The entire structure must have one container tag. I'm using `pets` as my
   container. If you don't have a single container, your programs will often
   have trouble reading the XML data.

3. **Build your basic data nodes.**

   In my simple example, each pet is contained inside a `pet` node. Each pet
   has the same data elements (but that isn't a requirement).

4. **Tags are case-sensitive.**

   Be consistent in your tag names. Use camel case and single words for
   each element.

5. **You can add attributes.**

You can add attributes to your XML elements just like the ones in XHTML. As in XHTML, attributes are name/value pairs separated by an equal sign (=), and the value must always be encased in quotes.

6. **Nest elements as in XHTML.**

Be careful to carefully nest elements inside each other like you do with XHTML.

You can get an XML file in a number of ways. Most databases can export data in XML format. More often, a PHP program reads data from a database and creates a long string of XML for output. For this simple introduction, I just wrote the XML file in a text editor and saved it as a file.

You can manipulate XML in the same way with JavaScript whether it comes directly from a file or is passed from a PHP program.

Manipulating XML with jQuery

XML data is actually familiar because you can use the tools you used to work with XHTML. Better, the jQuery functions normally used to extract elements from an XHTML page work on XML data with few changes. You can use all the standard jQuery selectors and tools to manage an XML file in the same way you use them to manage parts of an HTML page.

The readXML.html page featured in Figure 14-5 shows a JavaScript/jQuery program that reads the pets.xml file and does something interesting with the data. In this case, it extracts all the pet names and puts them in an unordered list. (See the following code.)

Figure 14-5:
The pet names came from the XML file.

```
<!DOCTYPE html PUBLIC "-//W3C//DTD XHTML 1.0 Strict//EN"
"http://www.w3.org/TR/xhtml1/DTD/xhtml1-strict.dtd">
<html lang="EN" dir="ltr" xmlns="http://www.w3.org/1999/
          xhtml">
<head>
  <meta http-equiv=»content-type» content=»text/xml;
          charset=utf-8» />

  <script type = «text/javascript»
          src = «jquery-1.3.2.min.js»></script>

  <script type = «text/javascript»>
    //<![CDATA[

    $(init);

    function init(){
      $.get(«pets.xml», processResult);
    } // end init

    function processResult(data, textStatus){
      //clear the output
      $(«#output»).html(«»);
      //find the pet nodes...
      $(data).find(«pet»).each(printPetName);
    } // end processResult

    function printPetName(){
      //isolate the name text of the current node
      thePet = $(this).find(«name»).text();

      //add list item elements around it
      thePet = «<li>» + thePet + «</li>»;

      //add item to the list
      $(«#output»).append(thePet);
    } // end printPetName
    //]]>
    </script>

  <title>readXML.html</title>
</head>
<body>
<h1>Reading XML</h1>

<ul id = «output»>
 <li>This is the default output</li>
</ul>

</body>
</html>
```

Creating the HTML

Like most jQuery programs, the readXML.html page begins with a basic HTML framework. This one is especially simple: a heading and a list. The list has an id attribute (so it can be recognized through jQuery easily) and a single element (which will be replaced by data from the XML file).

Retrieving the data

The init() function sets up an AJAX request:

```
$(init);

function init(){
  $.get("pets.xml", processResult);
} // end init
```

This function uses the get() function to request data:

1. **Use the jQuery get() mechanism to set up the request.**

   Because I'm just requesting a static file (as opposed to a PHP program), the get() function is the best AJAX tool to use for setting up the request.

2. **Specify the file or program.**

   Normally you call a PHP program to retrieve data, but for this example, I pull data straight from the pets.xml file. The get() mechanism can be used to retrieve plain text, HTML, or XML data. My program will be expecting XML data, so I should call an XML file or a program that produces XML output.

3. **Set up a callback function.**

   When the AJAX is complete, specify a function to call. My example calls the processResult function after the AJAX transmission is complete.

Processing the results

The processResult() function accepts two parameters: data and textStatus.

```
function processResult(data, textStatus){
  //clear the output
  $("#output").html("");
  //find the pet nodes...
  $(data).find("pet").each(printPetName);
} // end processResult
```

The `processResult()` function does a few simple tasks:

1. **Clear the** `output` **ul.**

   The `output` element is an unordered list (`ul`). Use its `html()` method to clear the default list item.

2. **Make a jQuery node from the data.**

   The data (passed as a parameter) can be turned into a jQuery node. Use `$(data)` for this process.

3. **Find each** `pet` **node.**

   Use the `find()` method to identify the `pet` nodes within the data.

4. **Specify a command to operate on each element.**

   Use the `each()` method to specify you want to apply a function separately to each of the `pet` elements. Essentially, this creates a loop that calls the function once per element. The each mechanism is an example of a concept called *functional programming*. (Drop *that* little gem at your next computer science function.)

5. **Run the** `printPetName` **function once for each element.**

   The `printPetName` is a callback function.

Printing out the pet name

The `printPetName` function will be called once for each `pet` element in the XML data. Within the function, the `$(this)` element refers to the current element as a jQuery node.

```
function printPetName(){
  //isolate the name text of the current node
  thePet = $(this).find("name").text();

  //add list item elements around it
  thePet = "<li>" + thePet + "</li>";

  //add item to the list
  $("#output").append(thePet);
} // end printPetName
```

1. **Retrieve the pet's name.**

   Use the `find()` method to find the name element of the current pet node.

2. **Pull the text from the node.**

   The name is still a jQuery object. To find the actual text, use the `text()` method.

3. **Turn the text into a list item.**

   I just used string concatenation to convert the plain text of the pet name into a list item.

4. **Append the pet name list item to the list.**

   The `append()` method is perfect for this task.

Of course, you can do more complex things with the data, but it's just a matter of using jQuery to extract the data you want and then turning it into HTML output.

Working with JSON Data

A new data format called JSON is becoming increasingly important. In fact, some are suggesting that JSON will replace XML as the standard data transmission format for AJAX.

XML has been considered the standard way of working with data in AJAX (in fact, the *X* in AJAX stands for XML.) Although XML is easy for humans (and computer programs) to read, it's a little verbose. All those ending tags can get a bit tedious and can add unnecessarily to the file size of the data block. Although XML isn't difficult to work with on the client, it does take some getting used to.

Understanding JSON

AJAX programmers are beginning to turn to JSON (JavaScript Object Notation) as a data transfer mechanism. JSON is nothing more than the JavaScript object notation described in Chapter 5 and used throughout this book. JSON has a number of very interesting advantages:

- **Data is sent in plain text.** Like XML, JSON data can be sent in a plain text format that's easy to transmit, read and interpret.

- **The data is already usable.** Client programs are usually written in JavaScript. Because the data is already in a JavaScript format, it's ready to use immediately, without the manipulation required by XML.

✔ **The data is a bit more compact than XML.** JavaScript notation doesn't have ending tags, so it's a bit smaller. It can also be written to save even more space (at the cost of some readability) if needed.

✔ **Lots of languages can use it.** Any language can send JSON data as a long string of text. You can then apply the JavaScript `eval()` function on the JSON data to turn it into a variable.

✔ **PHP now has native support for JSON.** PHP version 5.2 and later supports the `json_encode()` function, which automatically converts a PHP array (even a very complex one) into a JSON object.

✔ **jQuery has a** `getJSON()` **method.** This method works like the `get()` or `post()` methods, but it's optimized to receive a JSON value.

If a program uses the `eval()` function to turn a result string to a JSON object, there's a potential security hazard: Any code in the string is treated as JavaScript code, so bad guys could sneak some ugly code in there. Be sure you trust whoever is providing you the JSON data.

The `pet` data described in `pets.xml` looks like this when it's organized as a JSON variable:

```
{
  "Lucy": { "animal": "Cat",
            "breed": "American Shorthair",
            "note": "She raised me"},
  "Homer": { "animal": "Cat",
             "breed": "unknown",
             "note": "Named after a world-famous
          bassoonist"},
  "Muchacha": { "animal": "Dog",
             "breed": "mutt",
             "note": "One of the ugliest dogs I've ever
             met"}
}
```

Note that the data is a bit more compact in JSON format than it is in XML. Also, note that there's no need for an overarching variable type (like `pets` in the XML data) because the entire entity is one variable (most likely called `pets`). JSON takes advantages of JavaScript's flexibility when it comes to objects:

1. **An object is encased in braces ({}).**

   The main object is denoted by a pair of braces.

2. **The object consists of key/value pairs.**

   In my data, I used the animal name as the node key. Note that the key is a string value.

3. **The contents of a node can be another node.**

   Each animal contains another JSON object, which holds the data about that animal. You can nest JSON nodes (like XML nodes), so they have the potential for complex data structures.

4. **The entire element is one big variable.**

   JavaScript will see the entire element as one big JavaScript object that can be stored in a single variable. This makes it quite easy to work with JSON objects on the client.

Reading JSON data with jQuery

As you might expect, jQuery has some features for simplifying the (already easy) process of managing JSON data.

Figure 14-6 shows `readJSON.html`, a program that reads JSON data and returns the results in a nice format.

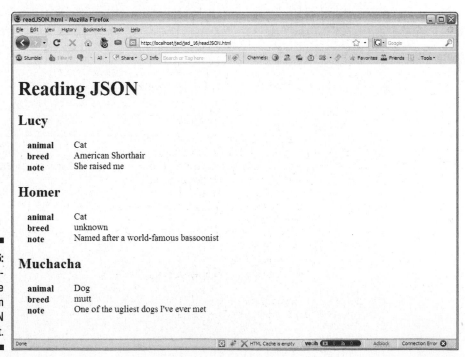

Figure 14-6: This program got the data from a JSON request.

Here's the complete code of `readJSON.html`:

```html
<!DOCTYPE html PUBLIC "-//W3C//DTD XHTML 1.0 Strict//EN"
"http://www.w3.org/TR/xhtml1/DTD/xhtml1-strict.dtd">
<html lang="EN" dir="ltr" xmlns="http://www.w3.org/1999/
          xhtml">
<head>
  <meta http-equiv=»content-type» content=»text/xml;
          charset=utf-8» />
  <style type = «text/css»>
    dt {
      font-weight: bold;
      float: left;
      width: 5em;
      margin-left: 1em;
      clear: left;
    }
  </style>
  <script type = «text/javascript»
          src = «jquery-1.3.2.min.js»></script>

  <script type = «text/javascript»>
    //<![CDATA[

    $(init);

    function init(){
      $.getJSON(«pets.json», processResult);
    } // end init

    function processResult(data){
      $(«#output»).text(«»);
      for(petName in data){
        var pet = data[petName];
        $(«#output»).append(«<h2>» + petName + «<h2>»);
        $(«#output»).append(«<dl>»);
        for (detail in pet){
          $(«#output»).append(«  <dt>» + detail +
            «</dt>»);
          $(«#output»).append(«  <dd>» + pet[detail] +
            «</dd>»);
        } // end for
        $(«#output»).append(«</dl>»);

      } // end for
    } // end processResults

    //]]>
    </script>

  <title>readJSON.html</title>
</head>
```

```
<body>
<h1>Reading JSON</h1>

<div id = «output»>
 This is the default output
</div>

</body>
</html>
```

Managing the framework

The foundation of this program is the standard XTML and CSS. Here are the details:

1. **Build a basic XHTML page.**

   Much of the work happens in JavaScript, so an h1 and an output div are all you really need.

2. **Put default text in the** output div.

   Put some kind of text in the output div. If the AJAX doesn't work, you see this text. If the AJAX does work, the contents of the output div are replaced by a definition list.

3. **Add CSS for a definition list.**

   I will print out each pet's information as a definition list, but I don't like the default formatting for <dl>. I add my own CSS to tighten up the appearance of the definitions. (I like the <dt> and <dd> on the same line of output.)

Retrieving the JSON data

The jQuery library has a special AJAX function for retrieving JSON data. The getJSON() function makes an AJAX call and expects JSON data in return.

```
$(init);

function init(){
  $.getJSON("pets.json", processResult);
} // end init
```

It isn't difficult to get JSON data with jQuery:

1. **Set up the standard** init() **function.**

   In this example, I'm pulling the JSON data in as soon as the page has finished loading.

2. **Use the** getJSON() **function.**

   This tool gets JSON data from the server.

3. **Pull data from** pets.json.

   Normally you make a request to a PHP program, which does some kind of database request and returns the results as a JSON object. For this simple example, I'm just grabbing data from a JSON file I wrote with a text editor.

4. **Specify a callback function.**

   Like most AJAX methods, getJSON() allows you to specify a callback function that is triggered when the data has finished transferring to the client.

Processing the results

The data returned by a JSON request is already in a valid JavaScript format, so all you need is some for loops to extract the data. Here's the process:

```
function processResult(data){
  $("#output").text("");
  for(petName in data){
    var pet = data[petName];
    $("#output").append("<h2>" + petName + "<h2>");
    $("#output").append("<dl>");
    for (detail in pet){
      $("#output").append("  <dt>" + detail +
        "</dt>");
      $("#output").append("  <dd>" + pet[detail] +
        "</dd>");
    } // end for
    $("#output").append("</dl>");

  } // end for
} // end processResults
```

1. **Create the callback function.**

   This function expects a data parameter (like most AJAX requests). In this case, the data object will contain a complete JSON object encapsulating all the data from the request.

2. **Clear the output.**

   I will replace the output with a series of definition lists.

   ```
   $("#output").text("");
   ```

3. **Step through each** `petName` **in the list.**

   This special form of `for` loop finds each element in a list. In this case, it gets each pet name found in the data element.

   ```
   for(petName in data){
   ```

4. **Extract the pet as a variable.**

   The special form of `for` loop doesn't actually retrieve the pets, but the key associated with each pet. Use that pet name to find a pet and make it into a variable using an array lookup.

   ```
   var pet = data[petName];
   ```

5. **Build a heading with the pet's name.**

   Surround the pet name with `<h2>` tags to make a heading and append this to the output.

   ```
   $("#output").append("<h2>" + petName + "<h2>");
   ```

6. **Create a definition list for each pet.**

   Begin the list with a `<dl>` tag. Of course, you can use whichever formatting you prefer, but I like the definition list for this kind of name/value data.

   ```
   $("#output").append("<dl>");
   ```

7. **Get the detail names from the pet.**

   The pet is itself a JSON object, so use another `for` loop to extract each of its detail names (animal, breed, and note).

   ```
   for (detail in pet){
   ```

8. **Set the detail name as the definition term.**

   Surround each detail name with a `<dt></dt>` pair.

   ```
   $("#output").append("  <dt>" + detail + "</dt>");
   ```

9. **Surround the definition value with** `<dd><dd>`**.**

   This step provides appropriate formatting to the definition value.

   ```
   $("#output").append("  <dd>" + pet[detail] + "</dd>");
   ```

10. **Close up the definition list.**

    After the inner `for` loop is complete, you're done describing one pet, so close up the definition list.

    ```
    $("#output").append("  <dd>" + pet[detail] + "</dd>");
    ```

As you can see, JSON is pretty easy to work with, so it's becoming much more common as a data transfer mechanism.

Part IV
The Part of Tens

The 5th Wave   By Rich Tennant

MIDTOWN

Where's the dang door?!

WebSite DESIGN Co.

C'mon in!

OUR AWARDS

In this part . . .

The Part of Tens feature is a staple of *For Dummies* books, but I've saved some of the best treats for the end.

Chapter 15 highlights a number of jQuery plugins. These tools add incredible features to JavaScript, like the ability to automatically translate your page to a foreign language, image galleries, graphing plugins, and much more.

Chapter 16 lists a number of other great places to get further information. Learn about other libraries, online communities, and great reference sites.

Chapter 15

Ten Amazing jQuery Plugins

T he jQuery library is amazing enough on its own, but it has yet another wonderful surprise up its sleeve: a marvelous plugin interface that makes new plugins or extensions to the library easy to add.

The plugins do many things, from changing the way your page looks to including audio and simplifying certain AJAX calls. This chapter contains a sampling of jQuery plugins I've found useful, but there are many more available at the jQuery main site (`http://plugins.jquery.com/`).

Using the Plugins

Each plugin is different, but the general approach to using them is the same:

1. **Visit the appropriate Web page.**

   Check the jQuery main site for a list of jQuery plugins (`http://plugins.jquery.com`). You can download each plugin from the jQuery site or get a link to the plugin's home page, where you'll generally find more complete help information.

2. **Download the plugin.**

   Most plugins are simply JavaScript files. Often other support material is available as well, including documentation, CSS files, and examples. Be sure to install the files you need in the working directory.

3. **Create a basic XHTML page.**

   Check the documentation to see what elements you need. Most jQuery plugins modify or replace some existing element in the Web page.

4. **Add an** `init()` **function.**

   Most jQuery functions (including plugins) require some sort of initialization function.

5. **Call the appropriate jQuery function.**

   Most plugins just add new functions to jQuery. For the most part, you'll apply these functions to jQuery nodes just as you would for a normal use of jQuery.

6. **Customize.**

   In this introduction, I tend to show the most basic form of each plugin for simplicity's sake. Be sure to check the documentation for each plugin to see how you can customize it; many plugins do far more than I have the space to show you in this chapter.

I've tended to include the simpler and more representative plugins in this chapter. I've omitted a number of especially useful plugins because they either require a special license (as the Google Maps plugin does) or require support for a database or PHP (as many of the cooler AJAX plugins do). Spend some time at `http://plugins.jquery.com/` to see the astonishing variety of plugins available.

ipwEditor

One very popular AJAX technique is to make a portion of the Web page editable. The ipwEditor plugin (`www.spacebug.com/IPWEditor_In-Place_WYSIWYG_Editor`) combines two different approaches to this issue, making it easy to turn ordinary pages into a simple content management system. First, take a look at the `editable` plugin (included with `ipwedit` or available on its own).

Adding a basic editor with editable

First, take a look at a very basic editor in Figure 15-1.

When you click the paragraph, it turns into an editable text area. The user can place her own text or HTML in the area and click the Done button to save the text. See Figure 15-2 for the editor in action.

The changes made are not permanent, but you could easily add an AJAX function to send the new data to a server-side script to make a permanent change to the page.

You obviously don't want to allow just anybody to make page changes. You'll probably want to have some sort of login system to ensure that only authorized people get access to the version of the page with editing enabled.

Click here to see the hidden feature.

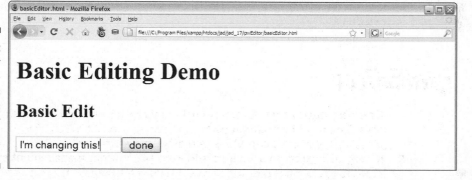

```
<!DOCTYPE html PUBLIC "-//W3C//DTD XHTML 1.0 Strict//EN"
"http://www.w3.org/TR/xhtml1/DTD/xhtml1-strict.dtd">
<html lang="EN" dir="ltr" xmlns="http://www.w3.org/1999/xhtml">
<head>
  <meta http-equiv=»content-type» content=»text/xml; charset=utf-8» />

  <script type = «text/javascript»
          src = «jquery-1.3.2.js»></script>
  <script type = «text/javascript»
          src = «jquery.editable.wysiwyg-1.3.3.1.js»></script>
  <script type = «text/javascript»>
    //<![CDATA[

    $(init);

    function init(){

      //create the simple editor
      $(«#basicEdit»).editable({submit: 'done'});
    }
```

```
    //]]>
    </script>

  <title>basicEditor.html</title>
</head>
<body>
<h1>Basic Editing Demo</h1>

<h2>Basic Edit</h2>
<div id = «basicEdit»>
Click me for a basic edit
</div>


</body>
</html>
```

Here's what you do to incorporate the simple editor:

1. **Include the** `jquery.editable` **or** `jquery.editable.wysiwyg` **script.**

   All the functionality you need for this example is provided in the `jquery.editable` plugin. However, the `jquery.editable.wysiwyg` plugin includes both this script and the more elaborate `wysiwyg` editor as well.

2. **Create an HTML area to edit.**

   In this example, I edit a `div` called `basicEdit`. In a production example, you might make each `div` or paragraph editable.

3. **Apply the** `editable` **function.**

   After the `editable` plugin is available, you can simply apply the `editable` function to all the jQuery elements you want to have editable behavior.

4. **Specify the button text.**

   The second parameter of the plugin is the text that will go on the supplied button.

5. **Save the data.**

   This particular example does nothing with the changed text, so it has limited functionality. In a production version of the program, you'll probably write some sort of AJAX code to package up all the new text and send it to a server-side program for processing and saving.

Incorporating more advanced editing with FCKedit

The ipwEditor includes the simple plugin (called the jquery editable plugin) and a second more sophisticated plugin. This second plugin allows a much more sophisticated editor to appear, with a word-processor-like user interface. If you've played around with content management systems, the chances are you've seen this interface, shown in Figure 15-3.

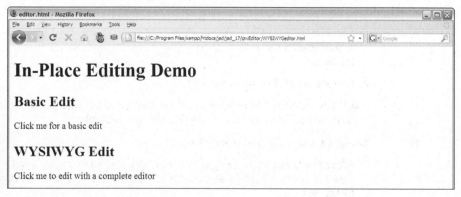

Figure 15-3: Now the page has two editable areas.

This example keeps the basic editor, but if you click the second paragraph, a much more elaborate editor appears, shown in Figure 15-4.

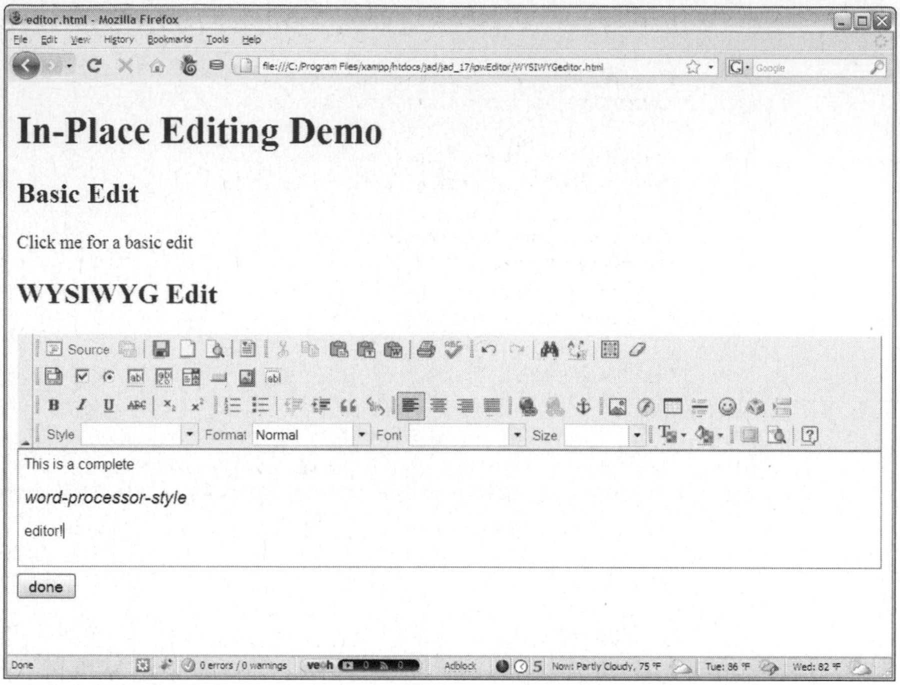

Figure 15-4:
This editor
looks a lot
like a word
processor.

The wysiwyg plugin adds the functionality of another very popular library called FCKedit (www.fckeditor.net/). This popular editor is used in many content management systems, and it's quite powerful and easy to modify. The FCKedit library is included with the ipwEditor plugin. The editable. wysiwyg plugin makes it easy to add FCKedit to your pages. Here's the code:

```
<!DOCTYPE html PUBLIC "-//W3C//DTD XHTML 1.0 Strict//EN"
"http://www.w3.org/TR/xhtml1/DTD/xhtml1-strict.dtd">
<html lang="EN" dir="ltr" xmlns="http://www.w3.org/1999/xhtml">
<head>
  <meta http-equiv=»content-type» content=»text/xml; charset=utf-8» />

  <script type = «text/javascript»
          src = «jquery-1.3.2.js»></script>
  <script type = «text/javascript»
          src = «jquery.editable.wysiwyg-1.3.3.1.js»></script>
  <script type=»text/javascript»
          src=»fckeditor/fckeditor.js»></script>
  <script type = «text/javascript»>
    //<![CDATA[

    $(init);

    function init(){
```

```
        //create an instance of fckeditor (only needed for wysiwyg version)

        var myFCKeditor = new FCKeditor('editor');
        myFCKeditor.BasePath = «./fckeditor/»;

        //create the simple editor
        $(«#basicEdit»).editable({submit: 'done'});

        //set up the wysiwyg version
        $(«#wysiwygEdit»).editable(
          {type: «wysiwyg»,
           editor: myFCKeditor,
           onSubmit: finished,
           submit: «done»
           });

    } // end init

    function finished(content){
      alert(content.current);
    } // end finished

    //]]>
    </script>

  <title>editor.html</title>
</head>
<body>
<h1>In-Place Editing Demo</h1>

<h2>Basic Edit</h2>
<div id = «basicEdit»>
Click me for a basic edit
</div>

<h2>WYSIWYG Edit</h2>
<div id = «wysiwygEdit»>
Click me to edit with a complete editor
</div>

</body>
</html>
```

This code is a bit more elaborate than the standard `editable` plugin, because it requires initialization of the (included) fckEdit library. Here's how it works:

1. **Be sure to have the fckeditor folder in your working directory**.

   This library is included with the `jquery.editable.wysiwyg` download.

2. **Build a Web page with editable areas**.

   Build your XHTML page as normal, considering which segments you want editable.

3. **Include the** `fckeditor` **script**.

   The `fckeditor` script is a `js` file available in the fckeditor folder. Include this script so your page will have access to the editor.

4. **Create an instance of the** `fckeditor` **class**.

   In your initialization function, create a single `fckeditor` variable. This will initialize `fckeditor`.

5. **Indicate the** `fckeditor` **base path**.

   This helps `fckeditor` find all its helper files in the subdirectory.

6. **Apply the** `editable` **function to any elements you want to make editable**.

   This process works exactly the same as the basic `editable` plugin.

7. **Set the type to** `wysiwyg`.

   The `wysiwyg` version of the `editable` plugin adds the capability to change your editor type.

8. **Apply the editor**.

   Set the editor parameter to the `fckeditor` variable you created in Step 4.

9. **Set the text of the Submit button**.

   As in the simpler `editable` area, a Submit button appears automatically. Set the text of this button with this parameter.

10. **Set a callback function if you want**.

    You can apply a callback function to editable objects; it indicates a function to send after submission is complete. Usually this function does some error-checking and then sends the new contents to a server-side script via AJAX. My version just displays the new contents.

The results of any edit are still HTML, which is ultimately plain text. You should be cautious with any changes you allow the user to make, because malicious users can cause you some major headaches.

jQuery Cookies

Cookies are a useful Web tool, even if they are somewhat misunderstood. A cookie is a simple text message that can be stored and received on the client by either the client or server programs. The type of data is severely limited, but this can still be a very useful tool:

- ✔ **Each cookie is a name / value pair:** You can think of a cookie as a variable you can save on the client.

- ✔ **Cookies are simply text data:** If you want another kind of data, convert it to text for storage.

- ✔ **Cookies are saved in a large text file:** Different browsers have different mechanisms, but in essence all the cookies saved by a particular user on a particular browser are saved in one text file.

- ✔ **Cookies have size limits:** It's not appropriate to store (for example) an entire database in a cookie. It's more common to keep login status so the system can make a request to a server-side database.

- ✔ **Cookies are mainly used to store state data:** The most common use of cookies is to keep track of a user's status with the application. Usually the server does all the heavy lifting.

Managing cookies is not difficult, but it's made even easier by a couple of tools. There's an amazing plugin called `jquery.cookies` (`http://code.google.com/p/cookies/`), which makes this job extremely painless.

Take a look at the code for `cookies.html`, which uses this plugin:

```
<!DOCTYPE html PUBLIC "-//W3C//DTD XHTML 1.0 Strict//EN"
"http://www.w3.org/TR/xhtml1/DTD/xhtml1-strict.dtd">
<html lang="EN" dir="ltr" xmlns="http://www.w3.org/1999/xhtml">
<head>
  <meta http-equiv=»content-type» content=»text/xml; charset=utf-8» />

  <script type = «text/javascript»
          src = «jquery-1.3.2.min.js»></script>
  <script type = «text/javascript»
          src = «jquery.cookies.2.1.0.js»></script>
  <script type = «text/javascript»>
    //<![CDATA[

    $(init);

    function init(){
      $.cookies.set(«myCookie», «Hi there!»);
      $(«#output»).html($.cookies.get(«myCookie»));
    }
    //]]>
    </script>

  <title>cookies.html</title>
</head>
<body>
```

```
<h1>jQuery cookies Demo</h1>

<div id = «output»>
default content
</div>

</body>
</html>
```

The process is painless:

1. **Include the** `jquery.cookies` **script.**

   As always, include jQuery and the script for this plugin.

2. **Use the** `$.cookies` **function to manage cookies.**

   This function encapsulates the content of the cookies library.

3. **Use** `$.cookies.set()` **to create a cookie and set its value.**

   If the cookie does not exist, it is created, and the specified value is added to the cookie.

4. **Use** `$.cookies.get()` **to retrieve the value of the cookie.**

   The `get()` function is an easy way to retrieve data from a cookie.

5. **Look over the documentation for more options.**

   The cookies library has more features — including the capability to check whether the browser is accepting cookies, to determine whether a cookie exists, to delete cookies, and more.

I didn't provide a screen shot for this program, because all the interesting stuff happens under the hood. Take a look at `cookies.html` on the Web page for the book to see it in action.

flot

Sometimes your Web pages need to display some kind of data. You can use any of various powerful graphing plugins for that purpose. One easy and powerful option is called `flot`, available at `http://code.google.com/p/flot/`. Figure 15-5 shows this tool in action.

To build a graph with `flot`, you'll need to have a data set available. I just made up a data set in this simple example, but often you'll pull data from a database or other application. Look over the code first:

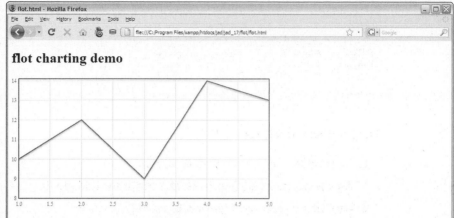

Figure 15-5:
This chart
was created
automati-
cally with
a jQuery
plugin.

```
<!DOCTYPE html PUBLIC "-//W3C//DTD XHTML 1.0 Strict//EN"
"http://www.w3.org/TR/xhtml1/DTD/xhtml1-strict.dtd">
<html lang="EN" dir="ltr" xmlns="http://www.w3.org/1999/xhtml">
<head>
  <meta http-equiv=»content-type» content=»text/xml; charset=utf-8» />
  <style type = «text/css»>
    #simpleChart{
      height: 300px;
      width: 600px;
    }
  </style>
  <script type = «text/javascript»
          src = «jquery-1.3.2.min.js»»</script>
  <script type = «text/javascript»
          src = "jquery.flot.js"></script>
  <script type = «text/javascript»>
    //<![CDATA[

    $(init);

    function init(){
      var myData = {
        data: [[1,10], [2,12], [3,9], [4, 14], [5, 13]],
        color: «red»
      };
      $.plot($(«#simpleChart»), [myData]);
    }
    //]]>
    </script>

  <title>flot.html</title>
</head>
```

```
<body>
<h1>flot charting demo</h1>

<div id = «simpleChart»></div>
</body>
</html>
```

Here's the general process:

1. **Import the libraries**.

   It won't surprise you that you need jQuery. You'll also need to bring in the `jquery.flot` script. Note that `flot` also includes some other scripts, which you'll need to make available (notably `excanvas`, which simulates the `<canvas>` tag on IE browsers).

2. **Build your page**.

   As usual, the page doesn't require a lot. Just add an empty `div` that will become your chart.

3. **Generate the data**.

   The data sets in `flot` are jQuery objects. Each object must have some data, but it can also have other attributes.

4. **Note that the data itself is a 2D array**.

   Each data point is an array of two integers, and the data set is an array of these objects.

5. **You can also specify the color and other attributes for the data.**

   See the `flot` documentation for many more attributes you can modify.

6. **Use the `$.plot()` function to draw the graph.**

   Note that the syntax is not exactly what you've used before. Use the jQuery `$.plot()` function to draw a plot on a particular jQuery node.

7. **Add as many data sets as you want.**

   My example has only one data set, but the `plot()` function expects an array of data ranges, so you can add more if you wish.

As you might guess, the `flot` plugin features many more incredible effects.

Tag Cloud

In recent years it has become popular to offer *data visualizations*, or ways to illustrate data. One such mechanism is the *tag cloud*. Essentially this tool places a number of words in semi-random positions. In a typical tag cloud, the position, size, and color of the words are used to represent the relative strength and relationship of the terms. See Figure 15-6 for a simple example of a tag cloud. Here the text was originally in an unordered list. The tag cloud changes the size and darkness of each element based on a ranking value.

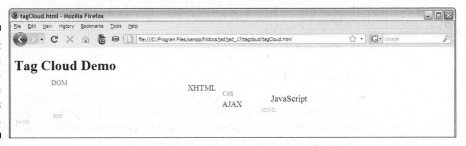

Figure 15-6:
This tag
cloud fea-
tures the
main topics
of this book.

The `jquery tagcloud` plugin (`http://code.google.com/p/jquery-tagcloud/`) makes it quite easy to build your own basic tag clouds. Here's the code:

```
<!DOCTYPE html PUBLIC "-//W3C//DTD XHTML 1.0 Strict//EN"
"http://www.w3.org/TR/xhtml1/DTD/xhtml11-strict.dtd">
<html lang=»EN» dir=»ltr» xmlns=»http://www.w3.org/1999/xhtml»>
<head>
  <meta http-equiv="content-type" content="text/xml; charset=utf-8" />
  <link rel = "stylesheet"
        type = "text/css"
        href = "jquery-ui-1.7.2.custom.css" />

  <script type = "text/javascript"
        src = "jquery-1.3.2.min.js"></script>
  <script type = "text/javascript"
        src = "jquery.tagcloud.min.js"></script>
  <script type = "text/javascript"
        src = "jquery.tinysort.min.js"></script>
  <script type = "text/javascript">
    //<![CDATA[

    $(init);

    function init(){
      $("#techList").tagcloud({height: 100,
                               width: 100})
      .css("width", "200px");
    }
    //]]>
    </script>

  <title>tagCloud.html</title>
```

```
head>
<body>
<h1>Tag Cloud Demo</h1>

<ul id = "techList">
  <li value = "4">HTML</li>
  <li value = "9">XHTML</li>
  <li value = "6">CSS</li>
  <li value = «10»>JavaScript</li>
  <li value = «7»>DOM</li>
  <li value = «9»>AJAX</li>
  <li value = «4»>PHP</li>
  <li value = «3»>MySQL</li>
</ul>

</body>
</html>
```

A tag cloud is a pretty fun element to build:

1. **Import the libraries.**

   You'll need the `jquery` and `jquery.tagcloud` scripts.

2. **Build a list**.

   The tagcloud library works on ordered lists and unordered lists.

3. **Add numeric values to list items if you wish**.

   If you want the elements to have different weights, add a `value` attribute to each. Those with small values will be very lightly colored and show up in a very small font size. Larger values will be darker colors and have larger fonts.

4. **Add the** `tagcloud()` **function to the** `ul` **with jQuery**.

   Use the standard mechanism to transform the jQuery node based on the `ul` into a tag cloud.

Note that the `value` attribute is not standard XHTML, so your page will no longer validate as strict XHTML. Most of the time, the value will be assigned through JavaScript code. (For example, count the number of times a word appears in a document and use that as the term's value.) Because primary validation happens before the code executes, you won't see any validation problems.

Tablesorter

AJAX programs often involve retrieving data, which is frequently displayed in an HTML table. The `tablesorter` plugin (`http://tablesorter.com/docs/`) allows the user to sort a table easily by clicking a heading. The top part of Figure 15-7 shows a standard HTML table. When the user clicks the "first name" header, the table is sorted by first names alphabetically, as shown in the bottom part of Figure 15-7.

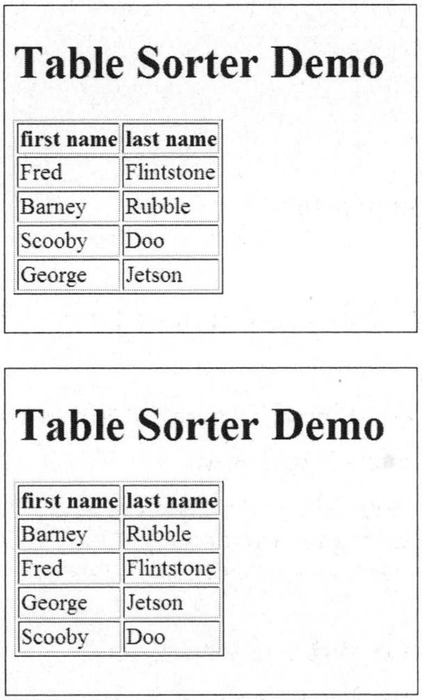

Table Sorter Demo

first name	last name
Fred	Flintstone
Barney	Rubble
Scooby	Doo
George	Jetson

Table Sorter Demo

first name	last name
Barney	Rubble
Fred	Flintstone
George	Jetson
Scooby	Doo

Figure 15-7:
Here is a basic table.

Click the "first name" header again to sort by first name in inverse order. The default behavior of the `tablesorter` plugin allows you to sort by any header field. Here's the code:

```
<!DOCTYPE html PUBLIC "-//W3C//DTD XHTML 1.0 Strict//EN"
"http://www.w3.org/TR/xhtml1/DTD/xhtml1-strict.dtd">
<html lang="EN" dir="ltr" xmlns="http://www.w3.org/1999/xhtml">
<head>
  <meta http-equiv=»content-type» content=»text/xml; charset=utf-8» />
  <link rel = «stylesheet»
        type = «text/css»
```

```
          href = «jquery-ui-1.7.2.custom.css» />

  <script type = «text/javascript»
          src = «jquery-1.3.2.min.js»></script>
  <script type = «text/javascript»
          src = «jquery.tablesorter.min.js»></script>
  <script type = «text/javascript»>
    //<![CDATA[

    $(init);

    function init(){
      $(«#myTable»).tablesorter();
    }
    //]]>
    </script>

  <title>tablesorter.html</title>
</head>
<body>
<h1>Table Sorter Demo</h1>

<table id = "myTable"
       border = "1">
  <thead>
    <tr>
      <th>last name</th>
      <th>first name</th>
    </tr>
  </thead>

  <tbody>
    <tr>
      <td>Fred</td>
      <td>Flintstone</td>
    </tr>

    <tr>
      <td>Barney</td>
      <td>Rubble</td>
    </tr>

    <tr>
      <td>Scooby</td>
      <td>Doo</td>
    </tr>

    <tr>
      <td>George</td>
      <td>Jetson</td>
```

```
    </tr>

  </tbody>
</table>



</body>
</html>
```

The process is standard jQuery magic:

1. **Import** `jquery` **and the** `jquery.tablesorter` **scripts.**

   The `tablesorter` plugin can also work with the jQuery UI for better-looking tables.

2. **Build a table**.

   The plugin requires that your table headings be surrounded by a `<thead></thead>` pair and the body be surrounded by `<tbody></tbody>`. Otherwise you can build your table however you like.

3. **Add** `tablesorter()` **to the table's jQuery node**.

   In the `init()` function, just specify the table as a `tablesorter` node, and you're ready to go.

The `tablesorter` plugin has dozens of options that make it a real powerhouse. Check the official documentation at `http://tablesorter.com/docs/`.

Note that a form of `tablesorter` was previously included in the jQuery UI, but now it's a separate plugin.

Jquery-translate

The jQuery `translate` plugin (`http://code.google.com/p/jquery-translate/`) is an incredibly useful tool for language translation. Take a look at the basic page shown in the top half of Figure 15-8. When the user clicks the paragraph, watch what happens (see the bottom half of Figure 15-8).

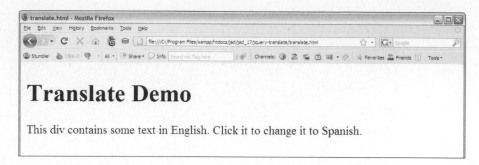

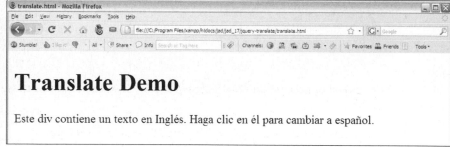

Figure 15-8:
The user can change this paragraph from English to Spanish!

The `translate` plugin connects to the Google language API and automatically translates the text of its node to one of several languages. The code that does the trick looks like this:

```
<!DOCTYPE html PUBLIC "-//W3C//DTD XHTML 1.0 Strict//EN"
"http://www.w3.org/TR/xhtml1/DTD/xhtml1-strict.dtd">
<html lang="EN" dir="ltr" xmlns="http://www.w3.org/1999/xhtml">
<head>
  <meta http-equiv=»content-type» content=»text/xml; charset=utf-8» />

  <script type = «text/javascript»
        src = «jquery-1.3.2.min.js»></script>
  <script type = «text/javascript»
        src = «jquery.translate-1.3.9.min.js»></script>
  <script type = «text/javascript»>
  //<![CDATA[

  $(init);

  function init(){
    $(«#contents»).bind(«click», translate);
  } // end init

  function translate(){
    $(«#contents»).translate(«Spanish»);
```

```
      } // end translate

    //]]>
    </script>

  <title>translate.html</title>
</head>
<body>
<h1>Translate Demo</h1>

<div id = «contents»>
This div contains some text in English. Click it to change it to
Spanish.
</div>

</body>
</html>
```

Considering how powerful this trick can be, it's almost embarrassingly easy to do:

1. **Include the** `jquery` **and** `jquery.translate` **scripts**.

   As usual, this program uses jQuery and an additional plugin to perform its magic.

2. **Create content to translate**.

   The translate API can only handle a limited number of characters at a time, so don't try to translate the entire page in one pass. Instead, send smaller chunks (such as a `div` or paragraph). In this example, I'm translating only one `div`.

3. **Bind the** `click` **event to your elements**.

   In this example, I want my `div` to begin in English and switch to Spanish when the user clicks it. I bind the `click` event to a function called `translate()`.

4. **The** `translate()` **function calls the** `language` **API, sending the contents**.

   You can determine the original language as well as the translated language. Dozens of languages are available. The contents of the `div` are replaced with translated text.

Machine-generated translation only goes so far. Often the general intent of the message will be discernable, but the translation will not be nearly as reliable as a human translation. The API has a particularly difficult time with colloquialism and technical language.

This plugin has many useful parameters. Check the documentation at `http://code.google.com/p/jquery-translate/` and experiment!

Droppy

Drop-down menus have become an important usability tool in Web sites. There are hundreds of jQuery plugins to handle this feature. I like `droppy` (`http://onehackoranother.com/projects/jquery/droppy/`) because it's very easy to use.

Figure 15-9 shows a simple version of `droppy` in action.

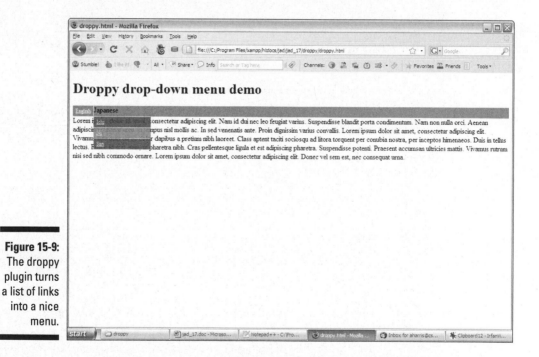

Figure 15-9:
The droppy plugin turns a list of links into a nice menu.

Most navigation systems are ultimately nested lists of links. The `droppy` plugin simply takes an unordered list with a bunch of links (nested as deeply as you want) and turns it into a nicely formatted drop-down menu. Take a look at the code:

```
<!DOCTYPE html PUBLIC "-//W3C//DTD XHTML 1.0 Strict//EN"
"http://www.w3.org/TR/xhtml1/DTD/xhtml1-strict.dtd">
<html lang="EN" dir="ltr" xmlns="http://www.w3.org/1999/xhtml">
<head>
  <meta http-equiv=»content-type» content=»text/xml; charset=utf-8» />
  <link rel = «stylesheet»
        type = «text/css»
        href = «droppy.css» />

  <script type = «text/javascript»
          src = «jquery-1.3.2.min.js»></script>
  <script type = «text/javascript»
          src = «jquery.droppy.js»></script>
  <script type = «text/javascript»>
    //<![CDATA[

    $(init);

    function init(){
      $(«#nav»).droppy();
    }
    //]]>
    </script>

  <title>droppy.html</title>
</head>
<body>
<h1>Droppy drop-down menu demo</h1>

<ul id = «nav»>
  <li><a href = «#»>English</a>
    <ul>
      <li><a href = «#»>One</a></li>
      <li><a href = «#»>Two</a></li>
      <li><a href = «#»>Three</a></li>
    </ul>
  </li>
  <li>Japanese
    <ul>
      <li><a href = "#">Ichi</a></li>
      <li><a href = "#">Ni</a></li>
      <li><a href = «#»>San</a></li>
    </ul>
  </li>
</ul>

<div>
  - lorem ipsum filler text deleted for space -
</div>

</body>
</html>
```

The general process should be familiar to you by now, but here it is anyway:

1. **Include the necessary scripts**.

   This plugin requires `jquery.js` and `jquery.droppy.js`. It also requires an (included) CSS file called `droppy.css`.

2. **Create an unordered list for navigation**.

   In your HTML code, place the unordered list where you want the menu to be (typically this will be at the top of your page; `droppy` creates horizontal menus.)

3. **Make each top-level element an anchor**.

   The `droppy` plugin uses the anchor `<a></a>` tags for formatting, so make sure the top-level elements (in my example, the language names) are embedded in anchors. It doesn't matter where the anchor goes, so set the anchor to link back to the page with the # character.

4. **Make each interior element a link as well**.

   Typically the interior elements will be links to other places in your system (or external pages). In my example, I made them empty links, but the important thing is that they contain link elements.

5. **Be sure your lists validate**.

   If you're sloppy with your nested lists, the plugin will have a hard time figuring out what you're trying to accomplish, and will probably fail.

6. **Build another level of menus if you like**.

   You can build the navigation structure as deep as you want.

7. **Modify the CSS for customization**.

   You can change the `droppy.css` file to make the menus fit your needs more closely. The most common changes are colors and fonts, to fit the overall look of the site where the menu will be installed.

galleria

Image galleries are another very popular plugin topic. There are many image galleries available to play with. I'm demonstrating `galleria` (`http://devkick.com/lab/galleria/`) because it's popular, powerful, and doesn't require any server-side scripting. Figure 15-10 shows this beautiful tool in action.

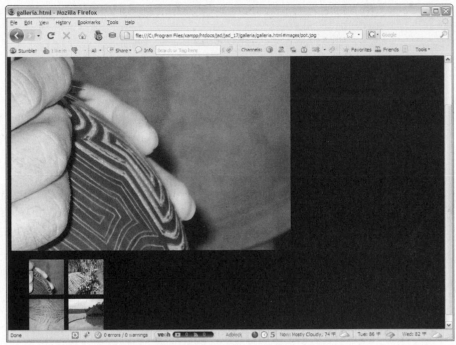

Figure 15-10:
The galleria
plugin auto-
matically
turns a list
of images
into a
gallery.

The default image gallery has some great features:

✓ **Images are pre-loaded.** Each image is loaded into memory when the page initializes, so there will be no delay when the user switches between images.

✓ **The** galleria **tool automatically creates thumbnail images**. The smaller index (thumbnail) images are automatically created and added to the page.

✓ **Clicking a thumbnail expands it into the viewing area**. The larger viewing area contains a larger version of the current image.

✓ **Click the viewing area to view the next image**. The default behavior lets you easily cycle through images with mouse clicks.

✓ **The output is based on CSS.** Use the included CSS file to manage the display of your page, including how and where the thumbnails go, how large the display image is, and more.

✓ **It has many options**. The galleria plugin is very customizable. It features many advanced options. Check the documentation for more.

My favorite part of the `galleria` plugin is how easy it is to use. Take a look at the code:

```
<!DOCTYPE html PUBLIC "-//W3C//DTD XHTML 1.0 Strict//EN"
"http://www.w3.org/TR/xhtml1/DTD/xhtml1-strict.dtd">
<html lang="EN" dir="ltr" xmlns="http://www.w3.org/1999/xhtml">
<head>
  <meta http-equiv=»content-type» content=»text/xml; charset=utf-8» />
  <style type = «text/css»>
  body {
    color: white;
    background-color: black;
  }
  </style>

  <link rel = «stylesheet»
        type = «text/css»
        href = «galleria.css» />

  <script type = «text/javascript»
          src = «jquery-1.3.2.min.js»></script>
  <script type = «text/javascript»
          src = «jquery.galleria.js»></script>
  <script type = «text/javascript»>
    //<![CDATA[

    $(init);

    function init(){
      $(«ul.gallery»).galleria();
    }
    //]]>
    </script>

  <title>galleria.html</title>
</head>
<body>
<h1>Galleria Image Viewer Demo</h1>

<ul class = «gallery»>
  <li><img src = "images/pot.jpg" /></li>
  <li><img src = "images/tree.jpg" /></li>
  <li><img src = "images/hands.jpg" /></li>
  <li><img src = "images/lake.jpg" /></li>
</li>

</body>
</html>
```

Using `galleria` is much like any other jQuery plugin. Add the appropriate scripts, write some basic HTML, and add a magical jQuery node:

1. **Import the scripts**.

   You'll need `jquery` as always, as well as `jquery.galleria` and the `galleria.css` CSS stylesheet.

2. **Create a list of images**.

   Make each list item an image.

3. **Add the** `galleria()` **node to the list**.

   That's really all you need to do!

4. **Play with the options**.

   Look over the documentation for some great options, including the ability to use custom thumbnails, specify your own output container, and run callback functions when the user selects an image or thumbnail.

Jmp3

The Web has become a phenomenal multimedia experience, but some important tools are missing. HTML 5 promises (at long last) an audio tag that will allow you to add audio directly to Web pages. Integrating audio (and other multimedia elements) into Web pages has been very complex so far. Most pages use some sort of plugin technology (such as Flash or various media players). The `jmp3` plugin (`www.sean-o.com/jquery/jmp3/`) is a wonderful compromise. It uses a very small Flash component (pre-built — you don't need to know anything about Flash) to load an audio file you specify and place that file in your page.

Figure 15-11 illustrates a page with an mp3 file embedded in it.

The mp3 files are actually played by a small Flash program, which you can configure in a number of ways — setting the colors and width, and determining whether the player includes a Download button. Take a look at the code to see how it works:

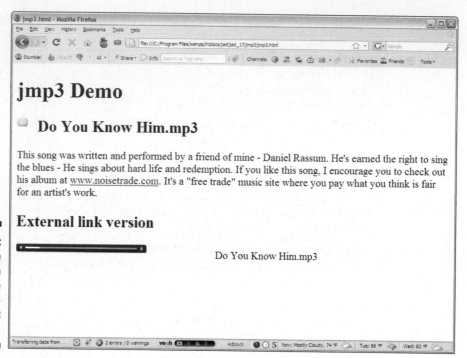

Figure 15-11:
This page
has an
attractive
and func-
tional MP3
player.

```
<!DOCTYPE html PUBLIC "-//W3C//DTD XHTML 1.0 Strict//EN"
"http://www.w3.org/TR/xhtml1/DTD/xhtml1-strict.dtd">
<html lang="EN" dir="ltr" xmlns="http://www.w3.org/1999/xhtml">
<head>
  <meta http-equiv=»content-type» content=»text/xml; charset=utf-8» />

  <script type = «text/javascript»
          src = «jquery-1.3.2.min.js»»></script>
  <script type = «text/javascript»
          src = «jquery.jmp3.js»»></script>
  <script type = «text/javascript»»
    //<![CDATA[

    $(init);

    function init(){
      $(«#song»).jmp3();
      $(«#external»).jmp3({
        filepath: «http://www.aharrisbooks.net/jad/»,
        backcolor: «000066»,
        forecolor: «ffffff»,
        showdownload: «true»,
        width: 300
```

```
      });
    } // end init
    //]]>
    </script>

  <title>jmp3.html</title>
</head>
<body>
<h1>jmp3 Demo</h1>

<div>
  <h2 id = «song»>Do You Know Him.mp3</h2>
  <p>
    This song was written and performed by a friend of mine - Daniel Rassum.
    He's earned the right to sing the blues - He sings about hard life and
    redemption.  If you like this song, I encourage you to check out his
    album at <a href = «http://www.noisetrade.com/blog/index.php?p=316»>www.
            noisetrade.com</a>.
    It's a «free trade» music site where you pay what you think is fair for an
            artist's work.
  </p>
  <h2>External link version</h2>
  <p id = «external»>Do You Know Him.mp3</hp>

</div>


</body>
</html>
```

Using `jmp3` follows a familiar pattern:

1. **Include the necessary files**.

   `jmp3` uses `jquery` and `jquery.jmp3`. It also requires the (included) `singlemp3player.swf` file be available in the working directory. It's easiest if the mp3 files are also in the current directory, but not absolutely necessary.

2. **Create elements containing the file name**.

   The plugin uses the text of the element to determine the song file. The node can contain nothing except the filename of the mp3 file. Be sure to use appropriate capitalization.

3. **Apply the** `jmp3()` **method to appropriate elements**.

   Apply the `jmp3()` method to `jquery` nodes that contain the mp3 file. (It's perfectly feasible to apply this method to an entire class, as the filename is determined by the contents of the element rather than a `jquery` parameter.)

4. **Add any parameters you prefer**.

   You can add parameters by attaching a JSON object to the `jmp3()` call.

5. **Change colors**.

   You can specify foreground and background colors (but note the non-standard color syntax: `forecolor` instead of `color`, and no # symbol on color numbers).

6. **Set the width**.

   You can also determine the width of the Flash element. Non-default widths will also include a small scrubber so the user can find a particular part of the song.

7. **Specify a file path**.

   The `filepath` parameter allows you to link to a file on a remote server. Be sure you have the permission of the file owner to do this. When the user plays the file, the Flash player will begin a progressive download of the file and begin playing as soon as a sufficient fraction of the file is available.

8. **Allow downloads**.

   The `showdownload` feature allows you to add a small widget to the Flash player. If the user clicks this button, she is given the option to save the mp3 file.

   As always, ensure you have the rights to distribute the file before using this option.

Chapter 16

Ten Great Resources

*J*avaScript and AJAX are phenomenal tools, but one of the most interesting (and frustrating) aspects of Web development is how fast it's changing — and how much there is to learn. Here's a list of ten interesting resources for further exploration. Some are reference sites; some are other libraries and frameworks you may want to investigate. All are resources I think you might enjoy.

Have fun!

jQuery PHP library

`http://jquery.hohli.com/`

Very frequently you'll write AJAX code with a server-side language, often PHP. This library adds a `jquery` object to PHP. You can use jQuery-style syntax within PHP, and the library automatically writes the jQuery code and sends it to your browser.

JSAN — JavaScript Archive Network

`www.openjsan.org/index.html`

This repository for JavaScript code offers a library that simplifies importing multiple scripts. If you want to try something in JavaScript, check here to see whether somebody's already done it. If you come up with a clever new trick, post it here for the community to share.

W3Schools tutorials and examples

www.w3schools.com/default.asp

W3Schools has become a go-to site for tutorials. There are a lot of tutorials about a lot of topics. The quality varies, but most are quite good. Note that some of the tutorials are out of date. Standards have changed over the years, and it's hard to tell which tutorials are following standards from several years ago, and which are using the current best practices. Still, this is a site worth bookmarking, and if you can't find what you're looking for in this book, you might find it there.

Google AJAX APIs

http://code.google.com/apis/ajax/

Google has been extremely committed to the AJAX and open-source movement. The company has released a number of incredible APIs that allow developers access to powerful Google tools. Investigate how to connect to Google Maps, Google searching, visualization tools, and even Google Earth!

Aflax

www.aflax.org/

This really promising Flash/JavaScript project brings the functionality of Flash into the JavaScript environment.

MochiKit

http://mochikit.com/

A complete JavaScript library heavily influenced by Python. Support for functional programming, simplified syntax, and an interactive interpreter. If you're a Python programmer, you'll love MochiKit. If not, you might still look it over to see what the buzz is all about.

Dojo

www.dojotoolkit.org/

A powerful alternative to jQuery, Dojo has a very strong user interface library. Dojo widgets (*dijits*) are the Dojo answer to user-interface objects. The many very powerful dijits in Dojo include tools for date and time input, data tables (which automatically retrieve data from an AJAX request and then populate an HTML table), and menu systems.

Ext JS

http://extjs.com/products/extjs/

If you outgrow the capabilities of jQuery (hard to believe, but it happens), extJS will likely serve your needs. This extremely powerful JavaScript/AJAX toolkit is a bit more complex than jQuery, but it does just about everything.

YUI

http://developer.yahoo.com/yui/

As Yahoo has built cutting-edge AJAX applications, it has also released its own development library for programmers. The Yahoo User Interface (YUI) is an incredibly powerful application tool with DOM support, event management, and a huge number of components.

DZone

www.dzone.com/links/index.html

My favorite feature of this very nice developers' news site is its reference cards. The site has a huge library of quick-reference cards on just about any development topic you might consider. Each card is available as a free, downloadable PDF. (I actually wrote the XHTML reference card.)

Index

• Symbols and Numerics •

@ (ampersand), 171
* (asterisk), 179
\ (backward slash), 148, 178
^ (beginning of string character), 174, 176–177
: (colon), 66–67
// (comment character), 36
{ } (curly brace), 179
$ (end of string character), 174, 176–177
== (equal operator), 60–61
/ (forward slash), 148, 176
$() function, 247–249
> (greater than operator), 60
>= (greater than or equal to operator), 60
{ (left brace), 59
< (less than operator), 60
<= (less than or equal to operator), 60
/* */ (multi-line comment character), 36
!= (not equal operator), 60
. (period), 174, 177
+ (plus sign), 50–51, 179
} (right brace), 59
; (semicolon), 37
[ ] (square bracket), 110
200 HTTP response code, 233
400 HTTP response code, 233
404 HTTP response code, 233
408 HTTP response code, 233
500 HTTP response code, 233

• A •

<a> tag, B1–12
absolute positioning, B2–31, B2–32, B2–33, B2–34
accordion effect, 319–321
Accordion tool, 294, 318–321
accordion.html program, 318–320
account, PHP, 341
action attribute, 343
action button, B1–27
active state, 307
ActiveX technology, 230
addClass() method, 258
addInput program, 52
additive color, B2–13
Adobe graphics editor, 17
AJAX
    about this book, 4–5
    asynchronous transaction, 225–228, 234–235
    basic description of, 15
    client-server communication, 224
    CMS (content management system), 260–263
    connection, 227–229
    overview, 224.225
    technological advancement, 1–2
    uses for, 226
    what it is, 224
    what it's not, 223
ajax.html program, 258–259
AJAXtabs.html program, 325–327

alert dialog box, 37
alert() method, 36, 52, 96
Alfax Web site, 398
alignment, text, B2–19
alphabetical comparison, 60
ampersand (@), 171
Animate button, 12
animate() method, 206–207, 218, 279
:animated filter, 291
animation
    compound image, 209–213
    fading technique, 272
    image-swapping, 203–209
    natural-feeling, 280
    positioning technique, 273–277
    relative motion, 280
    sliding animation technique, 272
    speed parameter, 272, 279
    swing easing style, 280
    time-based, 279
append() method, 287–288
Aptana editor
    basic description of, 23
    code completion, 32
    Debug perspective, 89–93
    directory structure, 245
    error warning, 33, 79–80
    example of, 24
    help file, 33
    integrated help option, 33
    jQuery library with, 243–245
    syntax highlighting, 32
    Web Project Wizard, 244
archive, 397
argument, function, 103–104
Ari SpriteLib Web site, 211

array
  accessing data in, 110
  defined, 97, 109
  length, 112
  with `for` loop, 111–113
  pre-loaded value in, 111
  storing list of data in,
    109–110
  two-dimensional, 114–118
assignment operator, 61
asterisk (*), 179
`asynch.html` program,
  258
Asynchronous JavaScript
  And XML. *See* AJAX
asynchronous transaction,
  225–228, 234–235
`:attribute=value` filter,
  291
automatic movement,
  200–202

● *B* ●

\b (word boundary
  character), 174, 178
background color, 134, 137
background image, B2–21,
  B2–22, B2–23
`backgroundColor`
  variable, 134
`background-image`
  property, 211–212
`backgroundPosition`
  attribute, 214
backward `for` loop, 73–74
backward slash (\), 148,
  178
bad request HTTP response
  code, 233
`basicAjax.html`
  program, 227–229
beginning of string
  character (^), 174,
  176–177
`big()` method, 44

binary format, 49–50
binary notation, 63
`bind` call, 313, 332
`block` element, B2–27
Bluefish editor, 20
`body onload` value, 248
`<body>` tag, 184, 249, B1–6
bold font, B2–18
bookmarklet, 84
border, B2–20
`border()` function, 255
bounce movement, 190
`break` statement, 66–67
breakpoint, 87–88
browser
  Chrome, 26
  cross-browser
    compatibility, 228
  Firefox, 25–29, 33, 82
  Internet Explorer 6, 25
  Internet Explorer 7 and
    8, 26
  Legacy, 25
  Opera, 26
  Safari, 26
  selection consideration,
    33
  specialty, 26
  standardization, 24–25
browser war, 25
button
  JavaScript and, 10
  radio, 167–168, 170
button event, 137–139
`:button` filter, 291
`button` tag, 270

● *C* ●

cache, 243
callback function, 127, 250,
  266, 271
carriage return, 112
Cascading Style Sheet. *See*
  CSS

case-sensitivity
  tag, 355
  XHTML, B1–3
`CDATA` marker, 36
chaining
  node, 277–278
  object, 274, 278
Change Alternate
  Paragraphs button, 282
`change` event, 256
`changeColor()` function,
  140–141, 159
`changeContent.html`
  program, 284–286
`changeTarget()` function,
  313
character
  punctuation, 178
  in regular expression, 176
  special, 177–178
character class, 177
character data, 36
character set, B1–8
Cheat Sheet, 6
check box
  basic description of, 164
  building page for, 165–166
  how to build, B1–25
  responding to, 166–167
`checkBounds()` function,
  188–189
`checkData()` function, 236
`checked` property, 166
Chrome browser, 26
class
  defined, 122
  jQuery UI supported, 307
  methods, 258
  name, 122
  as new data type, 123
  paragraph in, B2–9
`class` attribute, B2–10
`class.html` program,
  256–257
clean code, B1–1
`click` event, 256

client-server
    communication, 224,
    234, 237–238
client-side program,
    339–340
Clone button, 282
clone() function, 288–289,
    315–316
cloud, 244
CMS (content management
    system), 260–263
code
  accordion effect, 319–320
  accordion.html
    program, 319–320
  addInput program, 52
  ajax.html program, 259
  AJAXtabs.html
    program, 325–327
  array, 109–110
  asynchronous
    transaction, 235–236
  automatic movement,
    200–201
  backward for loop, 73
  basicAjax.html
    program, 228
  beginning block of, 59
  changeContent.html
    program, 284–286
  check box, 165–166
  class.html program,
    257
  clean, B1–1
  compound image, 211–214
  content management
    system, 261
  cookies.html program,
    377–378
  DOM, 139–140
  drag and drop, 298–299
  dragDrop.html
    program, 310–312
  drop-down list, 158–159
  droppy plugin, 389
  embedding, 35–36
  endless loop, 78

followMouse.html
    program, 197–198
form, B1–18, B1–19
function, 99, 101–103
galleria plugin, 392
getAJAX() function,
    236–237
Hello, World! program, 34
hideShow program,
    267–269
hover.html program,
    254–255
if else statement, 63
images, adding, B1–9
image-swapping
    animation, 204–208
interactiveForm.html
    program, 350–351
ipwEditor plugin, 371–372
jmp3 plugin, 394–395
JSON format, 124
keyboard page, 192
length property, 44
method example, 45
move() function, 278
move.html program, 183
multi-selection list box,
    161
nested if statement, 68
number, adding together,
    48
object, 118–119
"one expression with lots
    of values" situation,
    64–65
order() function,
    166–167
radio button, 168–170
random number
    generation, 56–57
readXML.html program,
    356–357
request.readyState
    property, 238
reset() method, 290
resizing element, 302–304
run.js program, 216–217

setInterval() function,
    204–205
sprite movement, 187
styleElement.html
    program, 251–252
tabbed interface, 323–324
table structure, B1–16
tablesorter plugin,
    383–385
tag cloud plugin, 381–382
translate plugin, 386–387
valid, B1–2
while loop, 75–76
XHTML framework,
    143–144
code completion, 23, 32
codetch editor, 21–22
collapsible content,
    319–321
colon (:), 66–67
color
  additive, B2–13
  background, 134, 137
  border, B2–20
  changeColor() function,
    140–141, 159
  document, 134, 136
  font, 44
  foreground, 137
  hex, B2–13, B2–14, B2–15
  named, B2–4
  setColor() function, 139
  subtractive, B2–13
  variable, 41
combination movement,
    190
comment
  HTML, B1–6
  multi-line, 36
  nested if statement
    and, 70
comment character (//), 36
comparison operator,
    60–61
completed value, 238
complex relationship, JSON
    format, 127

compound image
  basic description of,
    209–210
  demo, 210
  global variable, 212–213
  HTML and CSS setup,
    211–212
  image preparation, 211
  initialization, 213
  rows and columns, 211
  size, 211
  sprite animation, 213–214
computer
  selection consideration,
    15–16
  what you need, 2
concatenation, 40–42
condition
  Boolean function, 60
  Boolean variable, 60
  `break` statement, 66–67
  comparison operator,
    60–61
  flow control, 58–61
  `for` loop, 72
  `if else` statement, 61–64
  multiple, 64
  "one expression with lots
    of values" situation,
    64–65
  random number
    generation, 55–57
  `switch` statement, 65–67
constant, 186
constructor, 121
`constructor` property, 44
container tag, 355
`:contains` filter, 291
content management
    system (CMS), 260–263
continue movement, 190
conversion function, 51–52
cookie
  `cookies.html` program,
    377–378
  defined, 376

name/value pair, 377
  size, 377
corner, rounded, 306
Count button, 11
critical path, 202
cross-browser
    compatibility, 228
CSS (Cascading Style Sheet)
  basic description of, 15
  clean code, B2–3
  introduction to, B2–1
  level, B2–10
  overview, B2–2
  refresher on, 12
`css()` method, 277–278
CSS theme, 305
CSS View and Edit option
    (Firebug), 28
curly brace ({ }), 179
customized dialog box,
    336–338

• *D* •

\d (single numerical digit
    character), 174, 178
data model, jQuery library,
    247
`data` parameter, 358, 365
data type
  array and object, 50
  basic description of, 38
  Boolean, 50
  floating-point number, 50
  integer, 50
  new class as, 123
  string, 50
data visualization, 380–381
database
  MySQL, 341
  relational, 354
date format, 329–330
Date Picker tool, 294,
    329–331
`datepicker()` function,
    329, 331

`dblClick` event, 256
debugger
  `alert()` method, 96
  Aptana Debug
    perspective, 89–93
  basic description of, 86
  breakpoint, 87–88
  features, 87
  Firebug, 94–96
  pause mode, 87
  running the, 88
  support, 18
  testing, 87
definition list, 364
delta-x parameter, 187
delta-y parameter, 187
design, multi-element,
    317–318
dialog box
  alert, 37
  customized, 336–338
  modal, 36
  `prompt` statement, 39
`dialog()` method, 337
dijit (Dojo widget), 399
disabled widget, 307
Div button, 282
`div` element, 147
`divOutput` variable, 148
doctype, 355, B1–3
document
  color, 134, 136
  multiple document
    support, 18
  writing to the, 146–148
`document` object, 132
Document Object Model.
    See DOM
`document.ready`
    parameter, 250
DOJO library, 240
Dojo widget (dijit), 399
DOM (Document Object
    Model)
  basic description of, 131
  code, 139–140

`document` variable, 132
in Firefox, 132–133
`history` variable, 132
`location` variable, 132
primary objects of, 132
property, 132–133
`status` variable, 132
`window` object, 134
domain registration, 16
dot notation, 124, 127
drag and drop
building the page, 312
`dragDrop.html`
program, 309–312
draggable element copy,
315–316
`dropout` element, 315
example, 297–300
initialization, 312–313
page demo, 13
responding to event, 314
`dragDrop.html` program,
309–312
`draggable()` method, 300,
313
`dragme` element, 313
drop-down list
code, 158–159
extracting data from,
157–159
how to build, B1–23
reading the, 159–160
`dropout` element, 315
`droppable()` method, 313
droppy plugin, 388–390
`dx` property, 187
`dy` property, 187

• E •

e parameter, 195
`each()` method, 359
easing, 280
editor
Aptana, 23–24, 32–33, 244
Bluefish, 20

codetch, 21–22
emacs, 19
graphics, 17
jEdit, 21–22
notepad++, 20
programmer's, 18
vi, 19
visual, 17
WYSIWYG, 17
`else` statement, 62–63
emacs editor, 19
embedding code, 35–36
empty element, 291
`:empty` filter, 291
end of string character ($),
174, 176–177
end tag, B1–4
endless loop, 78–79
equal operator (==), 60–61
error. *See also* debugger
Aptana error notification,
79–80
debugging support, 18
Firebug error-handing,
82–83
Firefox error-handling, 82
highlighting, 307
HTTP error code, 233
IE error indication, 81–82
logic, 84–86
error detection, 23
error warning, 33
`eval()` method, 52, 361
event
adding to object, 252–256
button, 137–139
`change`, 256
`click`, 256
`dblClick`, 256
defined, 42
`focus`, 256
`hover`, 256
jQuery, 256
`keydown`, 256
`mouseDown`, 256
`select`, 256
event object, 195

event-driven programming,
142–143
event-handling, 193–194
expert, JavaScript, 15
extJS Web site, 399

• F •

Fade In button, 266
Fade Out button, 266
`fadeIn()` method, 272
`fadeOut()` method, 272
`fast` speed parameter, 279
FCKedit library, 373–376
`<fieldset>` tag
`filepath` parameter, 396
filter, jQuery library, 291
`find()` method, 359–360
Firebug feature
AJAX Monitoring option,
29
CSS View and Edit feature,
28
debugger, 94–96
error-handling, 82–83
Firebug lite option, 29, 84
formatted printing syntax,
86
Inspect Window feature,
28
JavaScript Debugging
option, 28–29
Live code view, 29
logic error-handing, 84–85
source code, viewing,
154–155
Firefox browser
advantage of, 26–27
basic description of, 25
DOM in, 132–133
error-handling, 82
Firebug extension, 28–29
HTML Validator
extension, 27–28
JavaScript console
feature, 33

Firefox browser *(continued)*
  View Source page, 27
  Web Developer Toolbar, 27
500 HTTP response code, 233
Flash Game Programming For Dummies (Harris), 219
Flash program, 393
Flash/Javascript project, 398
`float` attribute, B2–28
floating position, B2–24, B2–25, B2–26
floating-point number, 50, 52
flot plugin, 378–380
flow control, 58–61
`focus` event, 256
focus state, 307
font
  color, 44
  size, B1–5
  style, B2–18
`fontColor()` method, 44
`for` loop
  array with, 111–113
  backward version of, 73–74
  basic description of, 71
  condition, 72
  counting by five example, 74–75
  initialization, 72
  `lap++` operator, 73
  modification, 72
foreground color, 137
form
  code, B1–18, B1–19
  frameset, B1–3
  HTML, 230
  interactive, 349–353
  for layout, B1–2
  margin, B2–29
  PHP language, 341–344

request response, 344–345
strict, B1–3
tag, B1–21
transmission method, 351
form element, 146–148, 152
`<form>` tag, B1–21
formatted HTML, 226
formatted printing syntax, 86
formatting tool,
  ThemeRoller tool, 295
forward slash (/), 148, 176
400 HTTP response code, 233
404 HTTP response code, 233
408 HTTP response code, 233
`frame` variable, 206, 217
frameset form, B1–3
function. *See also* method
  `$()`, 247–249
  argument, 103–104
  Boolean, 60
  `border`, 255
  breaking code into, 97–99
  callback, 127, 250, 266, 271
  `changeColor()`, 140–141
  `changeTarget()`, 313
  `checkBounds()`, 188–189
  `checkData()`, 236
  `clone()`, 288–289, 315–316
  code example, 99, 101–103
  conversion, 51–52
  `datepicker()`, 329, 331
  defined, 97
  `getAJAX()`, 230, 236, 259
  `getGreeting()`, 352–353
  `init()`, 255
  initialization, 248–250
  JQuery, 245
  `json_encode()`, 361
  `keyListener()`, 194
  lambda, 255–256
  `loadImages()`, 209

`Math.random()`, 55–56
`move()`, 277–278
`moveSprite()`, 195–196
name, 122
named-function approach, 256
`noBorder()`, 255
`order()`, 166–167
parameter, 104
passing data into and out of, 100–105
`plot()`, 380
`present()`, 272
`processResult()`, 348–349, 358–359
`reportSlider()`, 332
`resetTarget()`, 313
returned value of, 101–102
scope, 105–108
`setColor()`, 139
`setInterval()`, 201
`showChoices()`, 162
structure of, 98–99
`themify()`, 306
`toggleBorder()`, 258
`translate()`, 387
`updateImage()`, 218
`updatePosition()`, 218–219
function call, 201
functional programming, 359

● *G* ●

galleria plugin, 390–393
Gallery tab (ThemeRoller tool), 296
Game Programming: The L Line (Harris), 219
generated source, 153–155
generated-code technique, 153–154
`get` attribute, 343, 352
`getAJAX()` function, 230, 236–237, 259

`getElementById()` method, 144–145
`getGreeting()` function, 352–353
`getJSON()` method, 361, 364–365
Gimp graphics editor, 17
global variable
  basic description of, 106
  compound image, 212–213
  image-swapping animation, 206
  movement example, 185–186
Google Ajax API, 398
Google Earth, 398
Google Maps, 398
graphics editor, 17
greater than operator (>), 60
greater than or equal to operator (>=), 60
greeting, 40–42, 352–353

• *H* •

`<h2>` tag, 269–270
Harris, Andy
  Flash Game Programming For Dummies, 219
  Game Programming: The L Line, 219
  HTML, XHTML, and CSS All-in-One Desk Reference For Dummies, 2, 34, B1–5
  Web site, 4–6
`<head>` tag, B1–5
`:header` filter, 291
header tag, 291
heading, 269–270, 307, B1–6
Hello, World! program, 34–35
help file (Aptana editor), 33
hex color, B2–13, B2–14, B2–15
hidden field, 148–150

Hide button, 265
`hide()` method, 271–272
`hideShow` program
  code, 267–269
  Fade In button, 266
  Fade Out button, 266
  Hide button, 265
  Show button, 265
  Slide Down button, 266
  Slide Up button, 266
  Toggle button, 265
highlighted element, 307
highlighting
  error, 307
  syntax, 18, 23
`history` object, 132
`<h1>` tag, 252
hosting service, 16
`hover` event, 256
hover state, 307
`hover.html` program, 253–255
`href` attribute, B1–12
HTML (Hypertext Markup Language)
  basic description of, 9, 15
  basic page example, B1–4
  comment, B1–6
  form, 230
  formatted, 226
  `innerHTML` property, 146, 148
  structure, B1–2
  XHTML versus, B1–2
`html()` method, 247, 359
HTML Tidy program, 27–28
HTML Validation program, 27–28
HTML, XHTML, and CSS All-in-One Desk Reference For Dummies (Harris), 2, 34, B1–5
HTTP error code, 233
`<h2>` tag, 269–270
Hypertext Markup Language. *See* HTML

• *I* •

icon
  about this book, 5
  adding to page, 308–309
icon library, jQuery UI, 294–295
ID, 252
`id` element, 150
IE (Internet Explorer), 81–82
`if else` statement, 61–63
`if` statement, 59, 67–70
image
  adding, B1–10
  background, B2–21, B2–22, B2–23
  `background-image` property, 211–212
  compound, 209–213
  pre-loaded, 391
image gallery, 390–393
image-swapping animation
  `animate()` method, 206–207
  building the page, 204–205
  file format, 204
  `frame` variable, 206
  global variable, 206
  preloading, 207–209
  preparation considerations, 203–204
  `setInterval()` function, 204
  small image, 204
  `spriteImage` variable, 206
  transparency, 204
`<img>` tag, B1–10
`imgList` variable, 217
indentation
  line after `if` statement, 59
  nested `if` statement and, 69
  support, 18
`indexOf()` method, 44, 46

inheritance, 122
init() method
  compound image, 213
  jQuery object, 255
  keyboard movement, 193
  movement, 186–187
initialization
  compound image, 213
  drag and drop, 312–313
  for loop, 72
  mouse controlled
    movement, 199
  moving image-swap
    animation, 218
initialization function,
  248–250
innerHTML property, 146,
  148
:input filter, 291
insertAfter() method,
  287
insertBefore() method,
  287
Inspect Window feature
  (Firebug), 28
installation, jQuery library,
  242
integer
  converting floating-point
    number to, 52
  converting text to, 51
integer data type, 50
interactive form, 349–353
interactive value, 238
interactiveForm.html
  program, 350–351
internal server found HTTP
  response code, 233
international keyboard, 197
Internet Explorer 6
  browser, 25
Internet Explorer 7
  browser, 26
Internet Explorer 8
  browser, 26

Internet Explorer (IE),
  81–82
interpolation, 345
ipwEditor plug-in
  editable plugin, 370–372
  editable text area, 370
  FCKedit library, 373–376

• J •

Java language, 15, 32
JavaScript
  about this book, 3, 5
  advantage of, 32
  basic description of, 15
  development of, 31
  expert, 15
  reason for using, 10–12
  technological
    advancement, 1–2
JavaScript Archive Network
  (JSAN) Web site, 397
JavaScript console feature,
  33
JavaScript Object Notation.
  See JSON
jEdit editor, 21–22
jmp() method, 395
jmp3 plugin, 393–396
jQoutput variable,
  247–248
jQuery library
  advantages of, 241–242
  animate() method, 279
  animation support, 241
  basic description of, 241
  callback function, 250
  cookie, 376–378
  cross-platform support,
    241
  data model, 247
  download, 242, 300
  droppy plugin, 388–390
  enhanced event
    mechanism, 241
  event, 256

  filter, 291
  flexible selection
    mechanism, 241,
    280–281
  flot plugin, 378–380
  function, 245
  galleria plugin, 390–392
  hideShow program,
    265–269
  importing from Google,
    242–243
  initialization function,
    248–250
  installation, 242
  introductory application,
    245–248
  ipwEditor plugin, 370–376
  jmp3 plugin, 393–396
  node, 247–248
  node chaining, 277–278
  object, 250–253
  PHP library, 397
  plugins, how to use,
    369–370
  positioning technique,
    273–277
  project, building with
    Aptana, 243–245
  selecting object in,
    252–253
  tablesorter plugin,
    383–385
  tag cloud, 380–382
  translate plugin, 385–388
  user interface widget
    support, 241
  window blind effect, 272
jQuery UI (user interface)
  Accordion tool, 318–321
  advanced user
    interaction, 293
  classes supported by, 307
  Date Picker tool, 329–331
  features, 293–294
  formatting tool, 295
  icon library, 294

importing file into, 304
new user interface
    element, 293
open source value, 294
power of, 294
resizable element, 301
selectors and filters, 291
Tabs tool, 318
ThemeRoller tool, 294–297
Web site, 294
JSAN (JavaScript Archive
    Network) Web site, 397
JSON (JavaScript Object
    Notation)
advantage of, 127, 360–361
basic description of, 124
callback function, 127
complex structure
    example, 125–126
data retrieval, 364–365
plain text data, 360
readJSON.html
    program, 362–364
results processing,
    365–366
storing data in, 124–125
support, 127
json_encode() function,
    361

• K •

keyboard movement,
    191–195
keyboard page, 191–193
keyboard script, 193
keyboard.html page, 192
keyboard.js script file,
    192
keycode, 196–197
keyCode property, 195
keydown event, 256
keyListener() function,
    194
keystroke response, 194–196
key/value pair, 361

• L •

<label> tag, B1–21
lambda function, 255–256
language, B1–7
lap++ operator, 73
Leet (L337) gamer, 67
left brace ({), 59
left property, 187
left-arrow key, 196
Legacy browser, 25
<legend> tag, B1–21
length
    array, 112
    string, 43–44
length property, 43–44
less than operator (<), 60
less than or equal to
    operator (<=), 60
library
    directory structure, 245
    DOJO, 240
    FCKedit, 373–376
    jQuery, 241
    MochiKit, 240
    Prototype, 240
    reference, 241
    reusable, 239
    update, 243
    YUI Yahoo! Interface, 241
license, plugin, 370
linear parameter, 280
link, B1–11, B1–12, B1–13
link tag, 304
list
    alternating style of, 282
    building, B1–13, B1–14,
        B1–15
    definition, 364
    drop-down, B1–23
    sortable, 335–336
literal, 41
Live code view (Firebug), 29
load() method, 259
loaded value, 238

loadImages() function,
    209
loading value, 238
local variable, 106
location object, 132
logic error, 84–86
loop
    bad-natured, 77–79
    endless, 78–79
    for, 71–75
    reluctant, 77–78
    while, 75–77
lowercase, 44, 46

• M •

macro, 18
main() function, 117
margin, B2–29
match
    pattern, 179–180
    specifying number of, 179
match() method, 174, 176
Math.ceil() method, 52,
    56–57
Math.floor() method, 52
Math.random() function,
    55–56
Math.round() method, 52
MAX_X variable, 217
medium speed parameter,
    279
memory, pattern match,
    179–180
menu, 267
meta tag, B1–8
method. *See also* function
    addClass(), 258
    adding to objet, 120–121
    alert(), 36, 52, 96
    animate(), 206–207, 218,
        279
    append(), 287–288
    big(), 44
    class, 258
    code example, 45

method *(continued)*
  css(), 277–278
  defined, 42
  dialog(), 337
  draggable(), 300, 313
  droppable(), 313
  each(), 359
  eval(), 52, 361
  fadeIn(), 272
  fadeOut(), 272
  find(), 359–360
  fontColor(), 44
  getElementById(), 144–145
  getJSON(), 361, 364–365
  hide(), 271–272
  html(), 247, 359
  indexOf(), 44, 46
  init(), 184, 186–187
  insertAfter(), 287
  insertBefore(), 287
  jmp(), 395
  load(), 259
  match(), 174, 176
  Math.ceil(), 52, 56–57
  Math.floor(), 52
  Math.round(), 52
  object, 118
  onload(), 216, 249
  onReadyState
    Change(), 230
  open(), 230, 232
  parameter, 45
  parseFloat(), 52
  parseInt(), 51, 145
  prepend(), 287
  processForm(), 152
  readyState(), 230, 235, 238
  removeClass(), 258
  replace(), 44, 174
  reset(), 290–291
  resizable(), 305
  responseText(), 230
  search(), 44
  send(), 230

show(), 271–272
slice(), 44
slideDown(), 272
slider(), 331–332
slideToggle(), 272
slideUp(), 272
status(), 230, 233–234
statusText(), 230
string, 44–46
substring(), 44, 46
tabs(), 325
text(), 360
text manipulation, 44–46
toggle(), 272
toggleClass(), 258
toLowerCase(), 44, 46
toString(), 52
toUpperCase(), 44, 46
val(), 352
wrap(), 289
Microsoft Word word
  processor, 16
MochiKit library
  basic description of, 240
  overview, 398
  Web site, 240, 398
modal dialog box, 36
mouse controlled
  movement
  followMouse.html
    program, 197–198
  HTML setup, 199
  initialization, 199
  mouse listener, 199–200
mouseDown event, 256
move() function, 277–278
movement
  automatic, 200–202
  bounce, 190
  bouncing ball example, 182
  boundaries, checking for, 189–190
  combination, 190
  compound image, 209–213
  continue, 190

drag and drop, 297–300
global variable, 185–186
image-swapping
  animation, 203–209
init() method, 186–187
keyboard, 191–195
mouse controlled, 197–200
move.html program
  example, 183
moving code to external
  file, 185
moving image-swap
  animation, 214–218
relative, 280
sprite, 187–189
stop, 190
timer-based, 200–202
moveSprite() function, 195–196
mp3 file, 393–394
multi-element design, 317–318
multi-line comment
  character (/* */), 36
multi-line text box, B1–22
multiple condition, 64
multi-selection list box, 160–162
MySQL database, 341

• *N* •

\n (newline character), 112, 177
name
  class, 122
  cookie, 377
  function, 122
  variable, 38
name attribute, 169
named paragraph, B2–9
nested if statement
  basic description of, 67
  code, 68
  comment use, 70
  how to use, 69

indentation and, 69
testing, 70
newline character (\n),
  112, 177
noBorder() function, 255
node chaining, 277–278
node, jQuery library,
  247–248
not equal operator (!=), 60
not found HTTP response
  code, 233
notebook keyboard, 197
notepad++ editor, 20
Notepad tool, 16–17
number
  adding together, 47–48
  binary format, 49–50
  floating-point, 50
  integer, 50
  rounding downward, 52
  rounding upward, 52
  special characters for, 178
numeric comparison
  operator, 60
numeric index, 124
numeric input, 331–333

• O •

object. *See also* JSON
  adding event to, 252–256
  adding methods to,
    120–121
  basic code example,
    118–119
  basic description of, 42–43
  class, 122
  constructor, 121
  document, 132
  event, 42, 195
  history, 132
  inheritance, 122
  jQuery library, 250–253
  location, 132
  method, 42, 118
  property, 42, 118

prototyping, 122
re-usable, 121
select, 159, 162
status, 132
window, 134
XMLHTTPRequest,
  230–232
object chaining, 274, 278
object-oriented
    programming (OOP),
    42–43
offset variable, 214
offsetList variable, 212
onclick parameter, 141
onkeyup event handler,
  352
online hosting service, 16
onload() method, 216, 249
onReadyStateChange()
  method, 230
OOP (object-oriented
    programming), 42–43
open() method
  description of, 230
  file/program name, 232
  request() method, 232
  synchronization trigger,
    232
Opera browser, 26
operation system, 2
operator
  comparison, 60
  overloaded, 51
  regular expression,
    174–175
  repetition, 178–179
order() function, 166–167
organization, about this
    book, 3–4
output data
  div element, 147
  divOutput variable, 148
  jQoutput variable,
    247–248
overloaded operator, 51

• P •

padding attribute, B2–30
paragraph
  adding text to end of, 288
  in class, B2–9
  named, B2–9
  odd-numbered, 282
  ordinary, B2–8
parameter
  function, 104
  method, 45
:parent filter, 291
parseFloat() method,
  52, 145
parseInt() method, 51,
  145
password field, 148–150,
  B1–22
pattern match, 179–180
pause mode, debugger, 87
Pederick, Christ (Web
    Developer Toolbar), 27
period (.), 174, 177
Photoshop graphics editor,
  17
PHP language
  account, 341
  availability, 340
  basic description of, 15
  ease of use, 340
  free use of, 340
  overview, 340–341
  popularity of, 340
  request response, 344–345
  writing form for, 341–344
PHP library (jQuery
    library), 397
plain text data, 360
plot() function, 380
plugin
  droppy, 388–390
  flot, 378–380
  galleria, 390–392
  how to use, 369–370

plugin *(continued)*
ipwEditor, 370–376
jmp3, 393–396
license, 370
tablesorter, 383–385
tag cloud, 380–382
translate, 385–388
wysiwyg, 374
plus sign (+), 50–51, 179
post attribute, 343, 352
pre-loaded image, 391
prepend() method, 287
present() function, 272
printing, 359–360
processForm() method, 152
processResult() function, 348–349, 358–359
program. *See* code
progress bar, ThemeRoller tool, 294
project file, 18
prompt statement, 39
property
defined, 42
DOM, 132–133
object, 118
Prototype library, 240
prototype property, 44
prototyping, 122
punctuation character, 178
pwd element, 150

quote, 141

radio button
adding, B1–26
basic description of, 167–168
code, 168–170
group, 169
name attribute, 169
:radio filter, 291
random number generation
application used by, 55
code, 56–57
floating point value, 56
Math.ceil() function, 56–57
Math.random() function, 55–56
random seed, 56
readJSON.html program, 363–364
readKeys parameter, 197
readXML.html program, 356–357
readyState() method, 230, 235, 238
red circle error indicator, 80
red squiggly line error indicator, 80
reference, 145, 241
registration, domain, 16
regular expression
basic description of, 170–171
characters in, 176
operator, 174–175
textbox element, 175
validation, 171–173
Reiner's Tilesets Web site, 203
relational database, 354
relative motion, 280
removeClass() method, 258
repetition operator, 178–179
repetitive task. *See* loop
replace() method, 44, 174
reportSlider() function, 332
request() method, 232
request response, 344–345, 348–349
request, sending, 345–347
request timeout HTTP response code, 233
request.readyState property, 238
request.status property, 234
Reset button, 282
reset() method, 290–291
resetTarget() function, 313
resetting the page, 290–291
resizable() method, 305
Resize menu (Web Developer Toolbar), 27
resizing, on theme, 301–302
response, to request, 39, 344–345
responseText() method, 230
result, 353
right brace (}), 59
Roll Your Own tab (ThemeRoller tool), 297
rounded corner, 306
rounding downward, 52
rounding upward, 52
ruler, 27
run.js program, 216–217

Safari browser, 26
scope, 105–108
<script> tag, 35
scrollbar, 331
search() method, 44
seed, random, 56
select event, 256
select object, 159, 162
selectable element, 333–334

selection mechanism,
 jQuery library, 280–281
semantic theme, 305
semicolon (;), 37
send() method
 basket analogy, 233
 description of, 230
 sending request and
  parameter, 232–233
sentry variable, 72, 77
server
 client-server
  communication, 232,
  234
 cloud structure, 244
 opening connection to,
  232
server-side program,
 339–340
setColor() function, 139
setInterval() function,
 201, 204
shadow, 307
Show button, 265
Show Code button, 13
show() method, 271–272
showChoices() function,
 162
showdownload feature, 396
single numerical digit
 character (\d), 174, 178
site. See Web site
size
 compound image, 211
 cookie, 377
 font, B1–5
slice() method, 44
Slide Down button, 266
Slide Up button, 266
slideDown() method, 272
slider() method, 331–332
slider, ThemeRoller tool,
 294
slideToggle() method,
 272
slideUp() method, 272

sliding animation
 technique, 272
slow speed parameter, 279
sortable list, 335–336
source code, viewing, 154
spaces in concatenated
 phrase, 41–42
special character, 177–178
specialty browser, 26
speed, animation, 272, 279
sprite movement, 187–189
sprite variable, 217
spriteImage variable,
 206, 217
square bracket ([ ]), 110
src attribute, 245
statement
 break, 66–67
 else, 62–63
 if, 59, 67–68
 if else, 61–64
 switch, 65–67
static document, 13
status() method
 description of, 230
 HTTP error code, 233
 request.status
  property, 234
status object, 132
statusText() method,
 230
stop movement, 190
strict form, B1–3
string
 defined, 42
 length, 43–44
 method, 44–46
 substring, 46
 text manipulation method,
  44–46
string data, 42
string data type, 50
style
 alternating, 290
 border, B2–20
 element, 251–252

font, B2–18
 of list, 282
 of table, 282
style attribute, 214
style sheet, B2–17
styleElement.html
 program, 251–252
submit attribute, 343
substring() method, 44,
 46
subtractive color, B2–13
sum variable, 48
support
 debugging, 18
 indentation, 18
 JSON format, 127
 multiple document, 18
 syntax, 18
swing easing style, 280
switch statement, 65–67
synchronization trigger, 232
syntax error. See error
syntax highlighting, 18, 23
syntax support, 18

• T •

tab cloud plugin, 380–381
tabbed interface, 322–325
table
 alternating style of, 282
 building, B1–13, B1–14,
  B1–15
 for layout, B1–2
 structure, B1–17
table of contents (TOC),
 319
tablesorter plugin, 383–385
tabs() method, 325
Tabs tool (jQuery UI), 318
tag
 <a>, B1–12
 <body>, 184, 249
 button, 270
 case-sensitivity, 355
 container, 355

tag *(continued)*
  end, B1–4
  `<fieldset>`, B1–21
  `<form>`, B1–21
  `<h1>`, 252
  `<h2>`, 269–270
  `<head>`, B1–5
  header, 291
  `<label>`, B1–21
  `<legend>`, b1–21
  `link`, 304
  meta, B1–8
  `<script>`, 35
  single-element, 146
  `<title>`, B1–6
`target` element, 312
technological
  advancement, 1
template, 262–263
testing
  debugger, 87
  nested `if` statement, 70
text
  adding new, 287–288
  alignment, B2–19
  bold, B2–18
  converting to floating-
    point value, 52
  converting to integer, 51
  font color, 44
  font size, B1–5
  indicated, 291
  multi-line text box, B1–22
  plain text data, 360
  underlined, B2–19
  wrapped, 289–290
text area, 148–149, 151
text editor, 17
text field
  hidden field, 148–150
  password field, 148–150
  text area, 148, 151, 1479
text input, B1–21
`text()` method, 360
`text-alignment`
    attribute, B2–30

`textarea` element, 151
`textbox` element, 175
TextEdit text editor, 17
`textStatus` parameter,
    358
theme
  adding to element,
    305–306
  built-in, 296–297
  CSS, 305
  resizing on a, 301–302
  rounded corner, 306
  semantic, 305
ThemeRoller tool
  Accordion tool, 294
  date picker tool, 294
  Gallery tab, 296
  progress bar, 294
  Roll Your Own tab, 297
  Sliders, 294
  tabs, 294
`themify()` function, 306
thumbnail view, 391
Tidy program (HTML), 27
time interval, 201
time-based animation, 279
timer-based movement,
    200–202
`title` attribute, 337
`<title>` tag, B1–6
TOC (table of contents),
    319
Toggle button, 265
`toggle()` method, 272
Toggle Style button, 12
Toggle Visibility button, 11
`toggleBorder()` function,
    258
`toggleClass()` method,
    258
toggling visibility, 272
`toLowerCase()` method,
    44, 46
toolbar, Web Developer, 27
`top` property, 187
`toString()` method, 52

`toUpperCase()` method,
    44, 46
`translate()` function, 387
translate plugin, 385–388
transparency, 204
tutorial, 398
200 HTTP response code,
    233
two-dimensional array
  defined, 114
  distance calculator
    example, 114–116
  `main()` function, 117
  setting up, 115–116
`txtArea` element, 151
`txtName` variable, 145
`type` attribute, 35

• U •

`ui-corner-all` class, 307
`ui-corner-tl` class, 307
`ui-icon` class, 308
`ui-state-active` class,
    307
`ui-state-default` class,
    307
`ui-state-disabled`
    class, 307
`ui-state-error` class,
    307
`ui-state-error text`
    class, 307
`ui-state-focus` class,
    307
`ui-state-highlight`
    class, 307
`ui-state-hover` class,
    307
`ui-widget` class, 307
`ui-widget-content`
    class, 307
`ui-widget-header` class,
    307
`ui-widget-shadow` class,
    307

unclicked state, 307
underlined text, B2–19
uninitialized value, 238
update, library, 243
`updateImage()` function, 218
`updatePosition()` function, 218–219
uppercase, 44, 46
usability improvement, 327–329
user information, 39
`userName` variable, 352–353

• V •

`val()` method, 352
valid code, B1–2
validation, 27–28, B1–28
validation tool (Web Developer Toolbar), 27
`value` property, 166
`var` statement, 38
variable
  assigning value to, 48
  basic description of, 37
  Boolean, 60
  characteristic, 38
  color, 41
  combining with text example, 40
  constant, 186
  conversion function, 51–52
  creating for data storage, 38
  data type, 38
  global, 106
  initial value, 38
  literal comparison, 41
  local, 106
  name, 38
  name re-use, 108
  `prompt` statement, 39
  sentry, 72, 77
  `sum`, 48
variable scope, 106–108

vi editor, 19
`view source` command, 153
View Source page (Firefox), 27
visibility, 272
visual editor, 17

• W •

Web browser. *See* browser
Web Developer Toolbar
  Edit CSS option, 27
  outline table design, 27
  Resize menu, 27
  ruler options, 27
  source code view, 154
  validation tool, 27
Web Project Wizard, 244
Web site
  Aflax, 398
  Ari SpriteLib, 211
  DOJO, 240
  DZone, 399
  extJS, 399
  Harris, Andy, 4–6
  jQuery UI, 294
  JSAN (JavaScript Archive Network), 398
  MochiKit, 240, 398
  Prototype, 240
  Reiner's Tilesets, 203
  YUI (Yahoo User Interface), 399
Web 2.0 technology, 240
what you see is what you get (WYSIWYG) editor, 17
`while` loop, 75–77
widget
  content style, 307
  disabled, 307
  making element look like, 307
width, border, B2–20
window blind effect, 272

`window` object, 134
word boundary character (\b), 174, 178
word processor, 16
Wrap button, 282
`wrap()` method, 289
wrapping, 189
W3C (World Wide Web Consortium), 25
W3Schools tutorial, 398
wysiwyg plug-in, 374
WYSIWYG (what you see is what you get) editor, 17

• X •

x variable, 186
XAMPP package, 341
XHTML
  basic description of, 15
  basic page creation, B1–7
  case-sensitivity
  HTML versus, B1–2
  refresher on, 12
XHTML framework, 143–144
XML data
  doctype, 355
  file example, 354–356
  `readXML.html` program, 356–357
`XMLHTTPRequest` object
  `onReadyStateChange()` method, 230
  `open()` method, 230, 232
  overview, 230
  `readyState()` method, 230
  `responseText()` method, 230
  `send()` method, 230, 232–233
  `status()` method, 230, 233–234
  `statusText()` method, 230

• Y •

y variable, 186
yPos variable, 316
YUI Yahoo! Interface
    Library, 241
YUI (Yahoo User Interface)
    Web site, 399

• Z •

zero or more element, 179
zIndex property, 316
Zone Web site, 399
zOrder property, 316
zValue property, 316